College fo

College for Convicts

The Case for Higher Education in American Prisons

CHRISTOPHER ZOUKIS

Foreword by ALEX FRIEDMANN

McFarland & Company, Inc., Publishers

Jefferson, North Carolina

Library of Congress Cataloguing-in-Publication Data

Zoukis, Christopher.
    College for convicts : the case for higher education
in American prisons / Christopher Zoukis ; foreword
by Alex Friedmann.
        p.   cm.
    Includes bibliographical references and index.

    ISBN 978-0-7864-9533-7 (softcover : acid free paper) ∞
    ISBN 978-1-4766-1799-2 (ebook)

    1. Prisoners—Education (Higher)—United States.   2. Education,
Higher—Aims and objectives—United States.   3. Recidivism—Prevention.   I. Title.
    HV8883.3.U5Z68 2014
    365'.666—dc23   2014038278

British Library cataloguing data are available

Cover: © 2014 iStock/Thinkstock

Printed in the United States of America

*McFarland & Company, Inc., Publishers
    Box 611, Jefferson, North Carolina 28640
    www.mcfarlandpub.com*

To the late Charles E. Colson, whose steadfast dedication to the cause of rehabilitation and reintegration inspires me and others to be more and do more.

Table of Contents

Acknowledgments   ix

Foreword by Alex Friedmann   1

Introduction   3

1. Why Do We Care?   7
2. A Historical Perspective on Prison Education   39
3. Prison Education Today: A Reality Check   46
4. Barriers to Betterment: Roadblocks in the Cell Block   66
5. Oases in the Desert   82
6. Options for Distance Learning   134
7. Too Late, Too Old?   140
8. No Guts, No Gain   151
9. What the World Knows   165
10. Thinking Inside the Box to Make It Happen   182

Appendices

    I. Federal Bureau of Prisons Program Statements   201

    II. Prisoner Publications and Pen-pal Clubs   215

    III. Funding for Correctional Education   233

    IV. Free and Discounted Books for Prisoners   235

    V. Federal Financial Aid for Incarcerated Individuals FAQ   246

    VI. Numbers Tell a Story   248

VII. Prison Education in Europe 250

VIII. Reentry Facts 252

Chapter Notes 255
Bibliography 275
Index 285

Acknowledgments

First and foremost, I'd like to thank my mom and dad for their impassioned support during these challenging years. It is they who have stood by me while I've engaged in the calling of prison education advocacy. They have supported me both emotionally and financially. This text could not have been completed if it wasn't for their essential support.

I owe a huge debt of gratitude to my editors, Barbara Carole and Randy Radic. Both were instrumental in researching, editing, and preparing this work for publication. Life simply wouldn't be what it is without them, and if it weren't for them, the cause of prison education advocacy wouldn't be where it is today. I regularly find strength in Barbara's convictions about the absolute need to educate America's prisoners, and there would be no PrisonEducation.com, Prison-LawBlog.com, or ChristopherZoukis.com were it not for Randy. Some like to throw around the phrase that someone is their "rock." Well, Barbara and Randy are more than just my "rocks"; they are a large part of my sense of identity. And I cannot thank them enough for that. Without them, I wouldn't be who I am today.

Another big thank you to Laine Cunningham for her copyediting, critique, and tremendous marketing assistance. Sometimes it is hard to see the forest for the trees. Laine greatly assisted in helping me to realize what I needed to highlight and share with the world in an effort to bring people to the cause of educating America's incarcerated class. Converting thinkers into readers is half the battle. The other half is converting readers into activists. Laine at Writer's Resource helped with both.

My thanks to Sangye Rinchen and Lewis Patt, Jr., who critiqued this work and helped me finalize it. May both of them continue to find my faults and help me to grow through them for years to come. I couldn't ask for a better support team and friends to boot.

A tremendous thank you goes out to Laura Winzeler and Phoebe Harrell, who have done a spectacular job in helping me to stay connected to the outside world. Please forgive the ridiculously broad research inquiries.

Thanks to the teams at Great Leap Studios, Gal-Friday Publicity and SquareSpace for their terrific assistance with everything related to book promotion and online technology. I couldn't do it without all of you at my side.

Last, but certainly not least, my writing endeavors wouldn't be possible without the competent legal work of Alan Ellis and Todd Bussert, who led the team of attorneys defending me and my writing when I was locked in solitary confinement for fabricated disciplinary charges related to my prison education advocacy. They fought hard for me and made it possible for me to write and advocate again.

Foreword
by Alex Friedmann

College for Convicts states the obvious—that educating prisoners reduces recidivism, thus leading to less crime and victimization, while increasing the ability of ex-offenders to enter the workforce with all of the economic benefits that entails. But this is an obvious truth that many policy makers and members of the public do not want to hear. Christopher Zoukis lays out the well-documented connections between prison education programs and rehabilitation and discusses the reasons why post-secondary education is an important tool in a corrections system where around 95 percent of prisoners will one day be released.

Do we want prisoners to return to our communities with no more than a GED, few job skills, and even fewer employment prospects—a recipe for a relapse to crime? Or do we want them to obtain educational achievements that provide a road map for success once they're released, thereby reducing recidivism rates and the human and fiscal costs of our bloated corrections system? The answer is as clear as Zoukis's examination of this important issue, in which he analyzes the pros of higher education for cons and lists examples of such programs in prison systems nationwide, as well as distance learning and reentry resources.

For those who are tired of a punitive corrections system that has done the same thing for decades at enormous cost with few socially beneficial results, this book provides an alternative way to look at prisons: as schools rather than warehouses. Recommended reading for both those on the inside and those on the outside.

Alex Friedmann is the associate director of the Human Rights Defense Center and managing editor of the HRDC's monthly publication, Prison Legal News.

Introduction

Hundreds of articles and studies about prison education, and many papers presented at academic and professional conferences, almost all come to the same conclusions:

- Prison education reduces crime,
- Prison education reduces recidivism, and
- Prison education will make an enormously positive impact on our national economy.

This is an idea that stirs up a lot of controversy because most people are more concerned with educating their own children than with educating prisoners. And the idea of providing post-secondary education in prisons is a hard sell because most of the public is unaware of how it can impact our economy and the safety of our communities.

Let's understand from the start: the concept of educating prisoners is *not* a "bleeding-heart, humanitarian, feel-good-for-the-imprisoned" kind of cause. On the contrary, it is an issue with a huge impact upon the economic stability of our country, the protection of our communities, and a higher quality of life for law-abiding citizens.

Consider this: the U.S. accounts for only 5 percent of the world's population, but it holds 25 percent of the world's prisoners.[1] With our prison population now at 2.3 million, we, as a nation, incarcerate far more people per capita than any other country in the world—almost double the next closest nation. Our state and federal prison population has increased almost ten-fold since 1970 and this explosive growth not only creates an untenable financial burden for state and national budgets but also creates an impossible situation for our judiciary overburdened by high recidivism rates.[2] In some states, like California, prisons are so overcrowded that the U.S. Supreme Court ruled that their prison populations must be reduced by tens of thousands because their systems were "incompatible with the concept of human dignity."[3]

The growth rate of federal prisons is even worse than that of state prisons. While state prison populations dropped in 2009 and 2010, federal prisons are bursting at the seams, and federal prison budgets are increasing by 10 percent a year to accommodate the ever-growing prison population.[4] Lawmakers are calling for the creation of a second federal "supermax" similar to "the notorious Florence ADX in Colorado—a place where solitary confinement has been raised to a torturous art, and prisoners seldom, if ever, see another human being. Conditions at this 'Alcatraz of the Rockies' are so harsh that the European Court of Human Rights initially refused to extradite terrorism suspects to the United States lest they end up in ADX."[5]

All the studies and all the research in the field of criminology affirm that prison education is the least expensive and most effective solution to overcrowding and strain on the budget caused by recidivism. Nevertheless, despite overwhelming evidence, policy makers and the general public still do not support funding post-secondary higher education in prisons. Year after year, even the most basic correctional educational programs are further reduced. Computers are not allowed. The result? Increased prisoner unrest and violence and more money spent for security.

Today, higher education for prisoners is almost nonexistent. And as we shall see, our failure to invest in opportunities for correctional college education weakens the very fabric of our society. With proper implementation, the impact of prison education can be enormous—not just on prisoners, but on our entire society and our nation's prosperity. Let us hope that greater understanding will result in wise legislative action for our common good.

"In response to the American public's growing fear of crime and the call for more punitive measures ... many legislators and policy makers have promoted building more prisons, enacting harsher sentencing legislation, and eliminating various programs inside prisons and jails. But more than half these prisoners are in on drug charges and another 10 percent on immigration violations, so that more than 72 percent of our incarcerated population are offenders with no history of violence.[6] With re-arrest rates averaging around 67 to 80 percent, it is clear that incarceration alone is not working."[7]

In the opinion of Chief Justice William Ray Price of the Supreme Court of Missouri, "We may have been tough on crime, but we have not been smart on crime." He noted further, "For years we have waged a 'war on drugs,' enacted 'three strikes and you're out' sentencing laws, and thrown away the key to be tough on crime. What we did not do was check to see how much it costs, or whether we were winning or losing. In fact, it has cost us billions of dollars and we have just as much crime now as we did when we started."[8]

Despite all the studies that confirm the significant benefits to be reaped from it, the idea of providing post-secondary education in prisons is a hard sell. The public appears to have a visceral, but understandable, reaction against the idea of higher education for prisoners. Why, people ask, should Americans pay to provide a college education for prisoners when so many law-abiding, tax-paying citizens struggle to send themselves or their children to school? It doesn't seem fair. Honest people have to pay to receive an education; why should prisoners get it for free?

And besides, say some of the opponents to correctional education, if we provide a learning environment for prisoners, perhaps prison will seem less terrible and serve as a less effective deterrent to crime.[9] However, the deterrent argument fails, because people do not decide whether or not to commit a crime based on the program opportunities available if they are sent to prison.

Others believe that people who commit a crime have chosen to limit their opportunities and freedoms, including access to valuable privileges like education. Therefore, handing it free to people who break the law feels wrong, feels like a slap in the face of justice.

These are legitimate concerns, but there are strong, legitimate solutions.

Despite the fact that I am a prisoner myself, I do not dispute the concept of getting tough on crime. I do not advocate creating a cushy environment for prisoners. And I certainly do not propose taking privileges from deserving, hard-working people to pamper prisoners. That is not what educating prisoners is about.

So why, then, should we care about educating prisoners—educating people who didn't care about the victims they hurt, the communities they impoverished, and the society they endangered?

We care, very simply, because they get out.[10] Almost everyone who is locked up now is going to be set free one day. If we treat prisoners like animals the whole time they are locked up, that's what we'll get when they're back on the streets: wild, dangerous animals.[11] But if we educate these people, give them positive reinforcement, and introduce the idea that they will have something to offer society when they return to their communities, that's what we will get when they are free: people who have something to offer society.

1

Why Do We Care?

The Prohibitive Price We Pay

The national deficit has reached a critical point. Everyone agrees we have to spend less and cut budgets. So if we said there was a way to save approximately $60 billion every year without cutting existing programs, a way to save $60 billion while at the same time improving public safety and the welfare of society, would anyone listen?

That's right. Providing post-secondary and academic education to only 10 to 30 percent of our prison population can translate to *more than $60 billion a year added to state and national coffers.*

Every year. And maybe a lot more.

Taxpayers Pay the Price

According to the highly publicized Pew Research Center report of 2011, the first to provide state-level data from almost all the nation's correctional systems, "spending on corrections quadrupled during the past two decades, making it the second fastest-growing area of state budgets, trailing only Medicaid."[1]

Taxpayers shoulder a massive burden, with $70 billion of their tax dollars going each year to our state and federal prison system of more than 2.3 million prisoners. This outlandish number appears to be driven by recidivism, not arrests for new crimes and first-time offenders. Most of the 725,000 prisoners released into society every year return to prison—far more than the number of newcomers.

What a shame most of that $70 billion is not being used to enhance our nation's educational institutions.[2]

Annual state spending alone for prison facilities is now estimated at about *$52 to $62 billion,*[3] the bulk of which is spent building new facilities; operating and maintaining more prisons; providing food and health care for the prisoners; and administration and staff salaries and benefits. We must then add to that amount the emotional price and the financial cost of increasing crime upon individual citizens and the national psyche.[4]

But despite the increase in prison spending, the system does not reduce criminal behavior. It has failed. The Pew report concludes: "That is an unhappy reality, not just for offenders, but for the citizens of American communities."[5]

Legislators must recognize what prison authorities and correctional educators have known for decades: correctional education will save money. As one example: prison education has saved $95 million per year in the state of Texas alone. Texas correctional authorities have recognized that there is no other crime-prevention method nearly as cost-effective.[6] As another example: if the single state of California reduced its rate of recidivism by only 10 percent, it would save $233 million in a single year.[7] In fact, even a slight 2 percent reduction in recidivism has been shown to result in significant cost savings for the state.[8] Los Angeles County Sheriff Lee Baca, who serves on the board of the California Department of Corrections and Rehabilitation, knows it is true. In a state that is "strapped with budget woes," he said, "it's up to us to [educate prisoners] without asking the taxpayers for billions of dollars with which to do it.... This can be done in a way that's cost-effective." He goes on to say that given what crime and incarceration cost the taxpayers, "I'm astounded that the public isn't clamoring for efficient educational opportunities in prisons."[9] Another study, from the University of California–Los Angeles, found that the same amount of money invested in education prevents twice the number of crimes as the money invested in incarceration.[10]

In one other state, Florida, a mere 4 percent reduction in recidivism for a two-year period saved $65 million in costs to victims and the criminal justice system.[11]

Two states, Washington and Virginia, were concerned with the need for building additional prison facilities if crime and recidivism were to continue at their current rates, so they conducted studies on how to lower the inmate population to save tax dollars and reduce crime. The studies found that a modest investment in prison education was the solution and, in Virginia, made recommendations that low-income inmates be permitted to receive state grants for post-secondary education and job-training programs.[12]

In Washington State, the exploding growth of the prison population caught the attention of the state legislature. Recognizing the high cost of prison construction ($250 million per prison) and operation ($450 million per year), the Washington State Institute for Public Policy[13] was able to show that correctional education, including post-secondary education, would lower the prison population, and that for every $1 spent on correctional education, the state would save $12. Based on these findings, Washington's DOC received an additional

$2.9 million for vocational programs, $2.1 million for basic skills, and $117,000 for parenting courses in 2007. Additional money was made available for resume-writing services and workforce readiness training.[14] This is a laudable step in the right direction, but it highlights the absence of any funding for advanced academic education leading to a college degree.

Increasing access to college programs in prisons can save taxpayers millions of dollars that are now spent on making prisons more secure and harsh. In-prison programs also create a safer prison environment for both prisoners and prison officials, which would further reduce costs for health care, employee insurance, and lawsuits. In-prison education, from basic literacy through to college courses, is by far the most promising investment the United States can offer its citizens.[15]

Christopher Pauls wrote in his 2011 thesis studying prisoner education, "Society should recognize that the cost of college is really very insignificant when you compare the cost of the damage done by crime."[16] "It's one of the wisest ways we spend taxpayer money," agreed Michigan Department of Corrections spokesman John Cordell. "Better educated individuals make better choices."[17]

If we can only educate 10 to 30 percent of the incarcerated and reduce recidivism by as little as 6 percent, in-prison educational programs would pay for themselves.[18] In addition, we could reverse the trend of building more of those very costly correctional facilities. And that is just the beginning of the fiscal benefits we'd see.

Beyond saving $32.1 billion in prison construction and operating costs, we would release into society hundreds of thousands of people who, when finding stable employment, will become taxpayers and consumers who bolster our state and national economies. These released prisoners would also support their families and get them off our state welfare systems, thereby generating further savings.

Considering the effectiveness of prison education in generating revenue and eliminating significant expenses from our budgets, it should be an important component of policy strategies.[19] Since this is true, why are we not looking to cut costs here, instead of for Social Security and Medicare?

Recidivism: A Plague on Society

We will be talking a great deal about the rates of recidivism (the numbers of prisoners who are released from prison and later return to crime and re-imprisonment). That is because there is a direct, compelling link between recidivism and community safety. We know that 70 to 85 percent of ex-prisoners return to crime after their release from prison and go back to prison within three to five years.[20] If we can reduce those rates of recidivism, we can increase the safety and well-being of our communities. And, as we shall see a little further on, the more we can reduce recidivism, the more we reduce the exploding cost to the nation of our prison systems.

Therefore, the re-integration of released prisoners into our society in a productive and law-abiding way is the responsibility of both the offenders themselves and the community in which they will be living.[21]

As compared to the general population, the great majority of prisoners come from disadvantaged backgrounds, are members of minority groups, have low skill levels, and have held low-paying jobs, if any at all. Typically they are poorly educated, and many are illiterate.

Families of the incarcerated are typically immersed in poverty, illiteracy, and crime. Ex-offenders return to criminal activity because they lack the educational and social skills necessary to function on a job or within society.[22] Research indicates that "prison life and culture can lead inmates to adopt values and norms that reduce their ability to succeed in the community and labor market."[23] In other words, time spent in prison may actually "decrease one's ability to cope in traditional society, as the values needed to succeed in prison often directly conflict with societal norms."[24]

Within the prisons, overcrowded conditions intensify violence and hostility. And every year, almost all of those angry prisoners are sent back into society. Most of them are young, between 20 and 40. Do they come out to enhance our communities, or do they come out prepared to commit even more crimes that threaten our citizens?

The answer is evident in the fact that 85 percent of those released back into society are re-arrested within five years. Most of those arrested are returned to prison. The important question is: why? Why do these young people fall back into a life of crime, endangering our streets and frightening the public?

As it is today, many of the 2.3 million people we keep behind bars have reading and math skills below the sixth-grade level. Many, unable to read or write at all and completely lacking the most basic work or living skills, likely have negative views of themselves and damaging attitudes toward the world and everyone in it. Released back into society, after their minds and spirits have been distorted by the abuse they knew before they were convicted and further warped by the violence they experienced in prison,[25] people like this are bombs waiting to explode.

And they will be released. According to Bureau of Justice Statistics,[26] 95 to 97 percent of prisoners will be released back into our communities, most at a poverty-income and low-skills level. Best estimates for recidivism rates say up to 94 percent of released prisoners will be re-arrested, and from 67.8 percent up to 81 percent will wind up behind bars again. In short, almost all of them will revert to crime, the only way they know to survive, and return to prison within five years.

That is no surprise. It has been said that insanity is doing the same thing over and over and expecting a different result. Releasing a prisoner back onto the street with the same skills that got him or her arrested in the first place while expecting a different result is insanity. People do what they know. Even if they want to, ex-offenders like this have no idea how to make a positive contribution to their communities.

Imagine living in a society where people were rarely victimized, and where most of the formerly imprisoned were legally employed. Is this an impossible vision? Perhaps. It is foolish to believe that higher education can transform or rehabilitate all prisoners. But there are many who do wish to be rehabilitated and who do have the ability to reform. "If we fail to support them ... and deny them the tools they did not receive outside of prison, then we are simply setting them up to re-offend when they are released,"[27] says H.J. McCarty in his 2006 article *Educating Felons.*

A large body of research, literally hundreds of studies over the last two decades, documents the correlation between participation in prison education programs—particularly post-secondary educational programs—and a significant reduction in rates of recidivism.[28] This translates to a significant reduction in the fiscal burden of prison systems.[29] The most common findings are:

1. Inmates who participate in educational programs have lower recidivism rates, better post-release employment patterns, and better institutional disciplinary records,[30] as compared to nonparticipants,[31] and
2. Prison-based programming (education, vocational training, prison industries, and employment services) is effective in reducing recidivism by one third if education is targeted at inmates with the lowest levels of education.[32]

"Of the various kinds of rehabilitative programs offered to prisoners, only education has been shown to unequivocally correlate with a strong reduction in recidivism,"[33] reports *Prison Legal News.* Post-secondary correctional education enhances job opportunities for released prisoners, and those who have jobs are 50 percent less likely to recidivate. Jails and prisons are crowded with people who are there only because they could not find work. "The idea of securing a decent job ... with no computer skills is fanciful at best. Every course of study ... should begin by teaching basic computer skills."[34]

Educated ex-prisoners who earn a stable income do not typically return to a life of crime. Instead, ex-prisoners with good jobs are more likely to act responsibly toward their families and become contributors to society instead of destructive forces. Quite simply: employment opportunity translates into reduced crime and recidivism, improved safety within society, and, as we will show later, an enormously positive impact upon the nation's economy.

"[There is] overwhelming evidence linking prison-based education programs to dramatically reduced recidivism rates and crime prevention ... such programs [are] among the most effective of all crime prevention programs nationwide ... far more effective than boot camps and shock incarceration,"[35] concludes the Open Society Institute.

The Federal Bureau of Prisons officially agrees. "There is an inverse relationship between recidivism rates and education. The more education received, the less likely an individual is to be re-arrested or re-imprisoned."[36]

Correctional education is a solution well-documented by the "Three-State Recidivism Study," numerous studies in the *Journal of Correctional Education*,[37] and countless others. All of them show that simply attending school behind bars has a significant impact on reducing the return to a life of crime and prison.

The need to reduce recidivism is significant and urgent. Some 2003 research studies of the Earl Carl Institute for Legal and Social Policy, Inc., as well as more current updates, strongly recommend that we take some of the huge sums of money we currently spend on imprisoning people and redirect them toward educating the incarcerated instead. The research reported that would be a prudent use of funds, because it will keep released prisoners from repeating criminal offenses that lead to them back to prison.[38] The official position of the Earl Carl Institute is that *the single most effective solution to reducing recidivism is education in the prison system.* Other measures, such as drug treatment and rehabilitation, are also important in achieving this goal, but the effect of education is by far the most compelling.[39]

Using the Texas prison system as an example, the Earl Carl Institute points out that more than 50 percent of people in prison are non-violent offenders. "One of the tragedies of the Texas penal system is that while many inmates enter as petty offenders, they become 'hardened' by the penal system.... If we were to expand secondary and college level academic programs and institute advanced education and training programs in prison, it would go a long way to helping solve this problem."[40]

It would be unrealistic to think we can rehabilitate 100 percent of all the people who commit crimes, but if we were successful with even a modest 10 to 30 percent, the impact it would have on our world would be enormous.

Even more effective than programs at the basic educational levels, an analysis of data shows, is *post-secondary* education offered in prison. This has proven to reduce recidivism with "substantive and statistical significance."[41] And by far the greatest reduction in recidivism comes with *college* education while incarcerated. Those who have received college-level education separate in statistics from all other groups.[42]

Every study in the field confirms that the higher the educational level achieved, the lower the rate of recidivism.[43] The data shows a direct correlation: for every additional year of education, the recidivism rate is significantly reduced,[44] so that the rates of recidivism are inversely proportional to the level of education attained by the offender.[45]

Among inmates who have completed some high school courses, recidivism rates drop to about 54.6 percent. Those who complete high school, or the GED, have an even lower rate. Vocational training brings recidivism further down to approximately 30 percent. For prisoners who attain an associate's degree: 13.7 percent recidivism; For prisoners who attain a bachelor's degree: only 5.6 percent recidivism; and For prisoners who attain a master's degree: 0 percent recidivism.[46] *Zero!*

One can always find a slight variation in statistics relating to recidivism, partially because of differences in survey methods. Recidivism can be measured by repeated arrests, convictions, or incarcerations. In addition, it can be measured by repeated offenses in differing time periods.[47] Nevertheless, the majority of studies have produced similar results with regard to the impact of education upon recidivism.

There are many challenges in tracking these numbers, including:

1. The numbers reported are not current, and they keep getting higher over time;
2. existing research does not take into account the number of released prisoners who returned to prison in other states;
3. existing research does not include relapses that have occurred in the year(s) following the end of the study;
4 existing research does not encompass relapses that have taken place in courts other than where the original case was tried; and
5. existing research does not include prisoners released from state prisons who are later jailed for a federal crime.

So, while reporting is neither systematic nor complete, and understanding that the real numbers are most likely higher than reported, the findings available on all the research and studies are consistent: they all agree that recidivism rates are very high and that correctional education will lower them significantly. They agree that the higher the level of education achieved, the lower the rates of recidivism. And they agree *unanimously* that for prisoners who attain education at the graduate level of academia, recidivism is virtually eliminated. The rate is zero.

This is confirmed by a U.S. Department of Justice report[48] that says the average recidivism rate for the U.S. prison population is 67 to 80 percent. According to this report, whose findings are consistent with so many others, "Prison-based education is the single most effective tool for lowering recidivism." Clearly then, more advanced education, even more than the basic teaching offered in most prison systems, is most effective in reducing recidivism.[49]

A high-school diploma, or the GED equivalent, is typically as far as prisoners can go today in most prisons across the country. It is certainly better than nothing and will reduce recidivism by about 20 to 25 percent, but a GED will not qualify anyone for more than an entry-level position. The farther we can go beyond that, the higher the level of education we can bring into prisons, including serious vocational training and academic college courses with the opportunity to earn degrees, the greater the chances an ex-prisoner has for an economically stable life. We know that the primary cause of recidivism is proven to be *unemployment,* the inability to find a decent, steady job. Therefore, the greater the number of ex-prisoners working in good jobs and supporting their families, the greater the chance we have, as a society, for reducing crime and costly recidivism.

Most people who commit violent crimes do not have adequate reading, writing, or computing skills.[50] That is an important consideration, because, as studies bear out (and simple common sense makes obvious) there is a strong correlation between education and income levels—between education and the ability to get a solid job. In fact, three years after release, a follow-up study showed that recidivism increased in direct correlation with the level of poverty of the parolee.[51] There is only one cure for poverty, and that is gainful employment. Since 89 percent of those who return are unemployed, we know that jobs will keep people from returning to prison. But while obtaining steady employment upon release is critical, it is also extremely difficult, especially with the stigma connected to a criminal record. That stigma often proves detrimental, mentally, financially, and socially, to many ex-prisoners during the reentry process and commonly follows them throughout the remainder of their lives.[52]

Laws that punitively restrict employment because of an individual's criminal history should be reviewed. In today's economic downturn, the industries that have traditionally been open to ex-convicts (i.e., construction and building) are not employing people now. The nonprofit organizations designed to assist ex-prisoners with reentry have also been badly hit.

Education is the deciding factor between returning to criminal activity and finding good employment.[53] Employment is the key to solving the incarceration explosion we have created.[54] Those with career skills find jobs more easily despite their criminal record. College graduates earn more, 60 percent more on average, than high school graduates.[55] These higher earners contribute increased tax revenue to the country, greater productivity, and an improved quality of life for their offspring without having to rely on welfare or financial support from the government.[56]

The strong connection between employment and lower recidivism rates has been documented in literally hundreds of studies.[57] Moreover, employment provides structure, routine, positive networks, and self-esteem to help the former prisoner become a productive citizen.[58]

Put a person back on the streets with the same skills they had when they first went to prison, and they will use those same skills to survive, because that is all they have. We can't expect people to succeed without providing them with the tools they need to compete.

Prisoners fortunate enough to have received a post-secondary education while in prison—especially college-educated ex-prisoners who return to the streets with a new set of skills, new knowledge, and a new way of thinking—are almost always successful at obtaining employment that supports a decent standard of living, and they remain employed over the long term.

"Even moderately successful [educational] programs may ... result in tremendous financial gains for released prisoners,"[59] but the higher the level of education a prisoner attains, as research in the field universally affirms, the lower the probability of a return to prison.

The Virginia Department of Correctional Education commissioned a study of college programs as part of the state's Incarcerated Youth Offender program and found that college participants had significantly lower recidivism rates than non-participants; they earned 13 percent more, post-release, than other ex-offenders; and the wage increase was even higher for prisoners who had earned an associate's degree.

Students who enrolled in academic and vocational courses more frequently enrolled in colleges post-release than all other ex-offenders. Interestingly, these prisoners had a higher grade-point average than non-incarcerated students enrolled in the same courses on campus.[60] Similar findings are reported in *Corrections Today* (Oct. 2006), which stated, "The overwhelming consensus among public officials [is] that post-secondary education in our prisons is the single most successful and cost-effective method of preventing crime,"[61] and the FBOP Office of Research and Evaluation, which found unequivocally that inmates who actively participate in education programs have significantly lower likelihoods of recidivating.[62]

Here at FCI Petersburg, where I am imprisoned, there are numerous courses prisoners can take. The problem, however, is that none of these programs, with the exception of the GED Program, allows prisoners to earn any credentials. All that is offered when completing courses is a BOP (Bureau of Prisons) certificate. This certificate is just a piece of paper with ink on it; it counts for nothing, other than to give one a sense of accomplishment. It cannot transfer to any college for credit or garner any recognition in the outside world. In fact, showing such a certificate to an employer can create a negative impression, because it only highlights one's prison history.

While these courses do help to add new living skills to the prisoner's tool kit, unfortunately they do not help him compete in the job market. For prisoners to be able to get jobs upon release, they need an opportunity to learn a real skill, something that can help create a resume. Released prisoners have to be able to compete with the rest of the world. If they can't, they will just keep on doing what they know how to do in order to make it on the outside.

We release about 725,000 prisoners every year into our communities. How will they live? Unless they can get a job to support themselves and their families, many end up looking for quick and easy ways to make money. Usually that means stealing and dealing drugs.

The failure of our prison systems to provide rehabilitative education creates an increase in repeat offenders. In other words, a failure to provide educational programs amounts to a failure in the state's ability to protect the public.[63]

Conversely, where there is college in prisons, there is less violence behind bars and more hope of converting released prisoners into productive, tax-paying citizens. Those who begin graduate or undergraduate courses while in prison usually seek ways to continue studying after their release to earn the coveted degree. Some have become professors at universities. Some run youth services programs or work for major corporations or are ministers. They work, raise families, pay taxes, and contribute, as consumers, to the gross national product.

Yet in the U.S., we continue to keep prisoners away from the one thing that can truly change their lives, their thinking, and their actions to reduce crime in our society: education.[64]

College programs inside prison walls ensure the public's safety. Stephen Steurer, Executive Director of the Correctional Education Association, tells us that a lower crime rate cuts down not only the rate of return to prison, but it cuts down on violence. It produces positive-thinking, tax-paying, law-abiding citizens.[65]

More than simply developing skills and knowledge, higher education can effect a total transformation in an individual. Education changes how people think and teaches them to react to situations in a more positive, constructive way than they have known before.[66] It affects moral thinking and promotes pro-social attitudes,[67] altering the prisoner's values and beliefs and conveying "a positive civic externality by teaching students not only to be productive, but to be law-abiding and loyal to their country."[68] Education, not imprisonment, is the key to developing responsibility and character building. It is a life lesson that hard work really does pay off.

"Education," said Nelson Mandela, the former prisoner-turned-president of South Africa, "is the most powerful weapon that we can use to change the world." Not just here and now, but more importantly, for a long-term impact on society. Because when one single person breaks through the cycle of poverty and crime, and when that person experiences the sense of self-worth that an education brings, that person creates a ripple effect on people around him or her.

It is indisputable that education changes people. And that's what prisons should do. Policies focused on increasing the length of prison sentences do not prevent crime. They merely reduce learning opportunities[69] and, by overcrowding the prisons, make inmates that much more violent. This in turn makes the transition from prison to society that much more difficult. If education will change the way people think and live, prisoners who have benefited from these programs and who are released from prison will no longer threaten community safety and drain our economic resources.

At the end of the day, while post-secondary correctional education may benefit the prisoner, it benefits even more the society to which that prisoner returns. With education and proper reentry preparation, prisoners can return to their communities with a better understanding of, and willingness to follow, society's laws. They can come back with a new purpose in life, motivated to find meaningful employment and care for their families.

One may wonder if the kind of motivated individual who pursues a higher education would be likely to lapse back into criminal behavior anyway. Studies tracking control groups on that specific issue verify that it is education itself which makes the difference, not the personal characteristics of the prisoners who seek out education.[70]

In his book *Preventing Violence,* psychiatrist James Gilligan, who directed prison mental health services for many years, reports on his study of prisoners who served time for violent crimes. Tracking them for a period of 25 years and monitoring the effectiveness of various programs on recidivism rates, he determined that advanced education, college, was the *only* program with a 100 percent success rate. In his study, not a single prisoner who had earned a college degree returned to prison for a new crime.[71]

The results are utterly compelling. *Recidivism is radically reduced and almost completely eliminated when prisons have college-level education programs.*[72] Not a single study has ever disputed this well-documented truth. The Institute for Higher Education Policy (IHEP) confirms it. "Higher education for prisoners, often the subject of public controversy, remains a crucial strategy to reduce recidivism and slow the growth of the nation's incarcerated population."[73]

People who oppose making an investment in educating prisoners simply do not understand the tremendous difference it can make in creating safer communities. Too often viewed as a privilege, education is not understood as a major deterrent to crime[74] and as an investment in people who represent rich, untapped human potential.[75] Having discovered some personal dignity, educated prisoners, when released, will likely play a positive role as members of society, rather than posing a danger.

This is not a Pollyanna position. We know one cannot mandate education for all prisoners. Just as in society as a whole, higher education is not for everyone, and many within the prison population are not good candidates for advanced education. "Inmates with mental health problems, violent propensities, or extreme substance abuse problems" will not benefit from educational opportunities.[76] However, there are others—many others—who have demonstrated the intelligence and motivation to be successful students and productive, law-abiding citizens.[77] The ones who desire education enough to undergo discipline and hardship and sacrifice to get it, those who pursue and persist to accomplish the work and achieve the grades, should be given access to it.

As those who persist succeed, we will likely see more and more of those around them inspired to follow suit. And as more and more of them succeed, we as a society might begin to see prisoners not as the dregs of society, but as a disadvantaged group with tremendous potential that can be tapped with our help.

Chief Justice Warren Burger saw it clearly. He said, "We must accept the reality that to confine offenders behind walls without trying to change them is an expensive folly with short-term benefits."[78]

The Next Generation

There are almost 2 million children of prisoners, at an average age of eight years, in our country. Two million small citizens, many of whom have had difficult lives even before their parent's incarceration, now suffer trauma, anxiety, guilt, shame, fear, sadness, withdrawal, and low self-esteem. How are they are faring?

Not much is known, except that imprisoned parents often mean that children go to foster care and become at high risk for crime, so the problem is perpetuated from one generation to the next. Many perform poorly in school and tend toward drugs, alcohol, and aggression.[79] Contact with their incarcerated parent(s) is difficult and rare. Distance and visitation restrictions tend to discourage, not encourage, parent-child relationships. We do know that very little if anything is being done for them in our schools, communities, or prison systems. These children are not recognized as a group by any state agency or department.

If we continue to neglect the education and rehabilitation and parenting skills of their parents, we can be sure most of these children will follow in their parents' footsteps and will one day replace their parents in prisons. The system creates a new generation destined for the fate of its parents.[80]

The picture changes radically, however, if we invest in learning for their incarcerated parents. Because many of them will be the first in their families (or even in their communities) to have earned a college degree, they will become role models who encourage their children to pursue, despite all odds, a higher education. Tanya said,

> My daughter is proud of me and it gives her incentive to want to go [to college] ... she asked me if she had to go to college if she didn't want to. My response was no, she didn't have to if she didn't want. Then I sent her my grades with a little note that said, "Not bad for a 30 year old Mom, huh?" When I spoke with her after that she said, if her mother could do it so could she.[81]

Educated ex-prisoners who have experienced the personal transformation that comes with an education can model positive behaviors and aspire to a different kind of future for their families and children.[82] They are almost always determined that their children be educated, too. "Educated inmates are more likely to get and retain a job, raise healthy, educated children and engage positively in civic activities ... they are less likely to commit additional crimes."[83]

Said Commissioner Brian Fischer of the NY State Department of Correctional Services, "Correctional education provides far more than reduced recidivism, far more than huge economic savings for society. It provides a transformation in the individual which no other program can. And those who experience that transformation extend that education to their own children. In that way, correctional education provides safety and security to our communities not just now, but for generations to come."[84]

The inevitable result of a modest investment to educate prisoners? We would reduce the likelihood that the children of criminals will break the law and reduce the now growing population of prisoners in our nation. Our criminal population would decrease more and more with every generation.

Research clearly indicates that the best predictor of a child's educational success is the educational attainment of his or her parents. Children of educated individuals do much better in school and have higher educational aspirations than others. Interviews with early adolescent children revealed their pride in their parents' pursuit of college. For some, their incarcerated parents are role models for perseverance, hard work, and a vision of possibility. For others, the pride in their prisoner-parent's accomplishments was tinged with understanding that academic success may not have been possible had their parent not gone to prison.

If, indeed, prison becomes a place for intellectual, emotional, and social growth which, for these people, would not have been experienced on the outside, wouldn't prisoners and all of society as a whole be better off?

Evidence Ignored

Aside from any humanitarian concerns, we advocate advanced education in prisons because "the overwhelming consensus among researchers and public officials [is] that post-secondary education is the most successful and cost-effective method of preventing crime" and violence.[85] Combining opportunities for higher education with support services upon release from prison will provide enormous safety and fiscal benefits to our communities—not just now, but increasingly so in generations to come. While for some it seems unfair to extend such privileges to the "unworthy," they will hopefully come to understand that the benefits to honest, taxpaying citizens are so many that they far outweigh such objections. The fact that education behind bars has proven to be the single most effective tool for reducing recidivism and crime is almost completely ignored.

Or worse than ignored. Despite clear evidence of how educational programs in prisons are extraordinarily effective in reducing crime, such programs have been, and continue to be, *eliminated*.[86] American prisons do not give access to either academic or vocational opportunities. But the elimination of prison education programs has not reduced public fear, nor has it protected our society from victimization and violence. Eradicating prison education simply has not made society safer.[87]

"The policy of state and federal criminal justice systems, within the past two decades, has been to imprison more offenders for longer periods of time.... This strategy has failed in two significant aspects: it has failed to prepare offenders for reintegration back into society and it has failed to reduce recidivism."[88]

"*To be really tough on crime, we must educate prisoners.*" So said Stephen Steurer, Executive Director of the Correctional Education Association.[89] "All of us want to be safe and secure," Steurer acknowledges. "Public policy on crime and punishment should be determined by the most effective crime prevention and reduction technique available through proven research."[90]

The Center on Crime, Communities and Culture also confirms that education lowers recidivism *more effectively than any other correctional rehabilitation programs* [emphasis added][91] and concludes that because education in prison aids in rehabilitation, it should be expanded.[92]

Learning leads to employment, better wages, increased tax revenue, reduced reliance on welfare, increased civic engagement, and public safety in communities at risk for violence and victimization.[93]

Despite the proven success of post-secondary correctional education in reducing recidivism and transforming criminals into productive citizens, however, education is notably absent from state and national policy agendas.[94] Our current policy of locking up criminals and providing no educational rehabilitation is dangerous.[95] It is literally a national security risk.

Professional and academic researchers all agree: "There is consistency across the board in study after study that correctional education works. The results for success in obtaining employment and staying out of prison is incontrovertible, making education the number one way to save money and reduce crime.[96] And yet, this is the first area where we make budget cuts when the economy is pressed.

Hundreds of studies dating back to 1939 confirm the benefits of prison education. "...These data show that the risk of recidivism reduces with education. We go one step further in showing that recidivism reduces incrementally as the level of education is increased..."[97] But despite the unanimous findings of hundreds of studies, policy makers have made no inroads for increasing funding for prison education.

It is understandable that we see prisoners through angry eyes because they have victimized people. It is normal to want them incarcerated and punished. At the same time, we have to think about what we want that criminal to be when he or she gets out: do we want them to continue to victimize people? Or to stop it altogether?[98]

In-Prison Educational Programs Pay for Themselves and More

Numerous cost/benefit analyses have shown it is far more fiscally efficient to provide higher education for prisoners than to pay the wildly escalating costs of unemployability and re-imprisonment resulting from a lack of education.[99] Studies show consistently the extraordinary costs—fiscal, social and personal— paid by all Americans as a result of *not* educating prisoners.[100] According to the Correctional Education Association, every dollar spent on education for prisoners returns more than two dollars in reduced prison costs to taxpayers by reducing recidivism from current 60 to 80 percent levels down to less than 15 percent.[101]

For every $5,000 invested in prison education, we get a $20,000 return by reducing incarcerations and the use of social services, according to a report from the Washington State Institute of Public Policy.[102] That's a 400 percent return on investment. "But prison officials are not asking for more money; they are [only] asking for the flexibility to invest some of the agency's current education budget in higher education."[103]

The Pew Center study calculates that if only the 41 states that provided data for their 2004 survey could reduce recidivism rates by just 10 percent, they could save more than $635 million in averted prison costs in one year alone.[104] Based on percentage, therefore, if all 50 states reduced recidivism by only 10 percent, we could have saved $774.4 million in 2004. And that doesn't include the savings that can be realized by the Federal Bureau of Prisons. Today the savings would be exponentially higher.

Post-release employment made possible by education while still incarcerated results in reduced criminal justice costs, increased tax revenue, reduced welfare burdens on taxpayers, and more. And the most effective programs for ensuring employment for released prisoners are the post-secondary correctional education programs, those that go beyond the high-school diploma.[105]

"Selling [the idea of] vocational or trade-training for offenders is much easier than [selling] the liberal arts academic degree track. However, the benefits of such academic programming are well documented."[106] With only $1,400 per year, we can provide a college education to a prisoner. Comparatively, it costs $25,000 to $55,000 (depending on the state) to incarcerate each prisoner for a year.[107]

Ten times more to incarcerate than to educate!

Given how significantly recidivism is lowered by education, it doesn't take much to do the math. A small investment can save states many millions each year.

A study by the Texas Department of Criminal Justice shows that for prisoners who earned only an associate's (two-year) degree, the reduction in the rate of recidivism saved Texans far more than what it cost them to educate those prisoners before their release.[108] A study of the Criminal Justice Policy Council found that by establishing a prison school district, the state would realize "a projected savings of $6.6 million dollars for every one percent reduction in recidivism.... Furthermore, these cost savings do not include the money saved from the direct cost of crimes on the citizens of Texas, nor do they include the physical or the emotional cost to the victims imposed by these repeat offenders."[109]

A report by the Correctional Association of New York says, "A $1 million investment in incarceration will prevent around 350 crimes, while that same investment in education will prevent more than 600 crimes.[110] Correctional education is almost twice as cost-effective as incarceration."[111]

Government analysts in the state of Maryland calculated that in-prison educational programs saved taxpayers $24 million each year, more than double what the state spends to create the education programs.[112]

In Nevada, a Pew Center study found that a decline of only 1.6 percent in the incarcerated population saved the state $38 million in one year and realized an additional savings of $1.2 billion in prison construction costs. That's for a mere 1.6 percent reduction in recidivism, in only one state, in just one year!

To cite still another example, higher education programs in Illinois would have saved up to $47.3 million in 2002 alone. Those same Illinois prisoners, if working, would have contributed $10.5 million per year to the state's economy. In other words, the state will incur fewer expenses and take in more revenue when citizens are returned to productive lives.[113]

What does not enter into the calculations is that prisoners who participate in educational programs typically earn good time credits and leave their prison facilities earlier. That creates a further savings in prison costs. For example: Inmates receiving associate's or bachelor's degrees at Indiana prisons in 2001 "saved the state nearly $12.5 million in good time credits."[114]

If we educate only 10 percent of our incarcerated population, we can potentially add a savings of $30.1 billion per year to our national economy. That would be added to the money we would accrue when those 70,000 ex-convicts are working, paying taxes, functioning as consumers, supporting their families, and making a positive contribution to our economy. And this does not include the incalculable reduction in the financial and emotional cost of crime to our individual citizens.[115]

"Given the relatively low cost to educate an individual prisoner-college student—and the manifold benefits and returns—it's hard to fathom why there isn't a national, fully funded prison education program in every facility."[116]

The cost of keeping a prisoner in prison for one year exceeds the cost of educating a prisoner for one year by a *ten-to-one ratio*. That's right: incarcerating a person for one year costs *ten times* what it costs to educate [and keep out of prison] that same person for a year.[117] Based on a very conservative calculation of only a 7 to 9 percent reduction in recidivism, $1,182 spent on vocational training saves $6,806 in future costs for crime. Every $962 spend on academic education saves $5,306.[118] And that does not include the cost of building and maintaining high-tech prison facilities. A 1,000 percent return on investment. Would any business-minded person turn that down?

But let's step back from the numbers to take a broader view. Educated workers provide greater productivity for our nation than unskilled illiterates. Productivity stimulates business and the larger economy. Thus, when one single prisoner-student is released and remains successful in society, he or she can earn money from a job and start contributing to the national coffers by paying taxes to local, state, and federal governments. He or she will spend money as a consumer and bolster our economy and create jobs for others. Further—and this is an often forgotten factor—when a prisoner can support his or her family, taxpayers no longer have to support them with welfare and public assistance. The result, according to one study, is that a modest investment in prisoner education (roughly $962) creates "approximately $2 million in economic stimulus and $375,000 in tax revenues—for just one state, for each year of a single graduate's working lifetime."[119] Therefore, if we only educated 10 percent of our prison population—a conservative 10 percent—those numbers will have a serious impact upon our economy.

"The cost of educating offenders is marginal, insignificant, as compared to the costs incurred by lengthy or repetitive incarceration" or the cost of damages created by crime.[120] With a very limited investment, perhaps by adding only 10 percent to current prison budgets, states can achieve two goals simultaneously: they can prevent crime and reduce recidivism. Educating prisoners can thereby save the states billions of dollars now spent for building, maintaining, and operating prisons. They can enjoy an influx of funds from these educated and employed individuals who will be paying taxes and contributing as consumers to the general economy. In addition, society will save the costs of crime to individual citizens[121] and the costs of operating an overburdened criminal justice system.[122]

One more factor should be added to the fiscal equation: educated ex-prisoners almost always make sure their children become educated. What that means is a continually reducing crime rate, generation after generation. At that point, the benefits are almost *incalculable.*

No one, to my knowledge, has ever actually calculated the total package. We should. Because the cuts our government has made in funding prison education betray not just the prison population; they betray the public good.

To provide post-secondary education to prisoners is not advocating that we be "soft on crime." It is simply the most effective and least expensive method of getting some control over crime and reducing the crippling tax burden that crime imposes on law-abiding citizens.

Education, by increasing cognitive skills, creates changes in behavior. Prisoner-students live a crime-free life (a) because they want to, and (b) because they have the tools to obtain meaningful employment and are able to do so.

The numerical evidence notwithstanding, we have continued to spend far more for prisons than for higher education over the last 20 years. Why?

According to State Senator John Whitmire of Houston, TX, "It's always been safer politically to build the next prison, rather than stop and see whether that's really the smartest thing to do. But we're at a point where I don't think we can afford to do that any more."[123]

Wouldn't it be nice to know our tax dollars are being spent on truly productive activities like public schools, infrastructure, environment, and health care? Our failure to invest in opportunities for correctional college education not only diminishes economic opportunity for low-income prisoner-students, it weakens the very fabric of society. The fiscal and social costs to our nation, in the end, are inestimable.[124]

In a tight economic climate, it is more critical than ever to fund visionary and cost-effective projects. Cutting budgets to save money today may well cost us much more tomorrow. And nowhere is this truer than funding post-secondary correctional education. Having studied the issue, the research think tank Rand Corporation concluded, "Crime prevention is more cost-effective than building prisons. And of all crime prevention methods, education is the most cost-effective."[125]

One source of revenue for prison education, says Sheriff Lee Baca of Los Angeles County, is money from the fees paid to the county by businesses that operate vending machines, pay phones, and other prisoner services. There is enough there to educate every inmate.[126]

Turning a Deaf Ear

Sadly, no matter how much correctional education has proven to save taxpayers and support our national economy, *policy makers and the general public still do not support funding post-secondary higher education in prisons.*

And to put a faster spin on the cycle, year after year, as prison populations and budgets soar, states are slashing correctional education budgets. "Do those reductions make sense, either from a crime-control perspective or from a ... budget perspective?"[127] Clearly not. "The generous funding for prisons makes a grim kind of sense in the context of a budget that slashes education, health care and social services. A country that can't spare the funds to properly educate its children or care for its sick, poor, or unemployed is destined to remain an incarceration nation."[128]

Our continually decreasing investment in correctional education programs does not keep up with the exploding population of prisoners.[129] Quite the opposite: as the prison population explodes, funding for prison education declines.

Our current trend of taking public dollars away from educational institutions to put them into prison construction, and then withdrawing funds from education within prisons, is producing disastrous consequences all Americans will have to live with.

Arguments against increasing education within prisons typically focus on the lack of available funding. This is short-sighted thinking. The investment we'd have to make in education is very small when compared to the savings and revenue increases we could achieve by reducing recidivism. If we were to systematically expand correctional educational programs and install college courses in prisons, we could be saving billions of dollars. Many billions.

It's been studied. It's been shown. It's been ignored.

Our Educational System Pays the Price

The $62 billion it takes each year to imprison all these people is money we drain away from education. If we could reduce our prison populations, we'd have the funds we need to maintain educational institutions, programs, schools, scholarships, and especially the state and community colleges. We would be able to maintain educational standards that would allow us to compete with the most highly educated nations in the world.

There is almost a dollar-for-dollar tradeoff between spending for corrections and spending for education. When the State of New York increased its corrections budget by 76 percent (because of longer prison terms and the need for increased prison construction), it reduced university funding by 28 percent. Each time we build a new prison, a post-secondary institution loses funding; for every new prison guard hired, scholarships are reduced; and for every security camera mounted inside a prison, textbooks may become unavailable to some students.[130]

Bottom line: The more prisons we build, the fewer educational institutions we have.[131]

In many states, the prison budget exceeds the budget for higher education. From 1982 to 2000, California had built 23 new prisons at an approximate average cost of $44.72 million per year. It needs another $66.27 million each year to house the state's 141,000 prisoners. That's almost $111 million a year for just one of 50 states: California alone.

Illinois is also typical of most other states in that it diverts resources away from K-12 public schools and higher educational institutions for building and operating prisons.[132]

We have been spending far more for prison institutions than for higher education in the last 20 years. In fact, prison budgets have grown at six times the rate of our nation's educational budget. There is a direct correlation between communities with high incarceration rates and low-performing schools.[133] If we invested more in education, we would need less for prisons!

The U.S. lags behind other nations in educating children, but leads the world in incarcerating prisoners.[134] Where is the logic in this? It costs ten times less to prevent crime than it does to put lawbreakers behind bars.[135] What does this say about our priorities?

"Spending more on prisons than universities is no way to proceed into the future."[136] The reduction in government spending for education places the burden on students and parents and reduces opportunities for those from low-income families.

Beyond the enormous social and fiscal benefits of correctional post-secondary education, these programs benefit our college systems, as well. That is because 68 percent of educational programs offered in prisons are provided by local two-year community colleges.[137] Their practical curricula and focus on providing education to everyone in their communities, including non-traditional and underserved students, make the two-year community colleges perfect partners for the prison system. They are well-suited to the endeavor of educating prisoners.

Prison education is not only good for the prisoners and for society as a whole; it is also good for the schools. It allows them to increase their enrollment revenue, which is important, because the funding they receive is based on the number of students enrolled. And students who don't require new buildings or increased full-time faculty, like prisoners, are even more advantageous.[138]

Community colleges, with their open-access admission policies, are natural providers for prisons offering education to their inmates because of their affordability, convenient locations, status as accredited, and willingness to partner.[139] Some offer courses at all levels, including literacy and GED; others offer only post-secondary vocational and academic courses.

When asked if it is difficult to get professors to teach in prison, Max Kenner, originator of the Bard College Prison Initiative, said that every professor who has ever taught in a prison program has wanted to do it again. Teachers found that prisoners are hungry to learn, and they study hard. Without the benefit of computers or the internet, much of their studying is at night in their cells, amidst a constant din of noise. Still, if the homework isn't challenging enough, they ask for more.[140] What professor is not willing to teach students with a passion to learn?

Community colleges that are willing to serve prisoner-students in their communities, and who are able to do it via correspondence (because prisoners generally have no access to online courses,) would benefit from significant economic opportunities. The funds they would receive from prisoner-students can go a long way to helping develop and expand their program offerings.

Most universities actively attempt to create a more diverse student population, and they recruit from minority groups. Prisons located nearby can supply a large number of minority men and women seeking an opportunity to rebuild their lives with education.[141] An excellent example of this is the Lassen Community College in Northern California, which serves two state prisons and a federal prison close to its campus. This program has literally saved the school, which had been on the brink of failure but is now flourishing. (For more information, contact: Lassen Community College, 478–200 Highway 139, P.O. Box 3000, Susanville, California 96130. Tel: (530) 257–6181 or www.lassencollege. edu.)

An Effective Tool for Prison Management

Educational programs provide an effective tool for the prison administration and staff in managing a prison facility. Facilities that offer higher education within the prison have proven to run more smoothly and with less violence than correctional institutions without educational programs.[142]

Obviously, the primary focus of a prison facility has to be security. Therefore, prison administrators must be convinced that education programs will not threaten institutional security, but that on the contrary, such programs will actually promote security. These administrators should be assured by the numerous studies whose findings consistently show that where inmates are engaged in studies, they tend to be better behaved, less likely to provoke violence, and more likely to have a positive effect on the general prison population. Educated inmates have shown themselves to be a stabilizing influence in an otherwise chaotic environment, enhancing the safety and security of all who live and work in the correctional facility.

It has been demonstrated universally that changes in inmate behavior brought about by post-secondary correctional education create improved conditions in prison facilities. There are fewer disciplinary problems, better relationships among inmates and the correctional staff, and the emergence of positive peer role models.[143]

When inmates are allowed to enroll in computer and other educational courses, disciplinary problems decrease dramatically. "Computer access, even restricted access, can be a powerful 'carrot' in the management of students in correctional settings."[144] Says Dr. Jon Marc Taylor, "I have personally seen ... the power of a university extension program to divert a riot."[145] The educated prisoners understood how a riot would result in lost lives and worsened conditions and were able to communicate this to the riot leaders, convincing them to calm their followers. On a smaller scale, this kind of intervention is also common in daily prison life. The way inmates who participate in prison education programs interact with one another is very different from the way other inmates interact. Therefore, prisons offering these programs experience less fighting and fewer conduct issues. Inmate behavior becomes more positive and the prison environment safer.[146]

In a study of Texas inmates participating in Lee College programs, 147 prisoners who were enrolled in vocational programs had only 13 rule infractions as compared to 115 infractions in the three months preceding their involvement in the program.[147] These same participants in the vocational training programs were more successful after release in finding employment and staying out of prison.

Inmates enrolled in college courses had even fewer violations than those in lower-level educational programs. With each additional year of education, the number of violations or instances of misconduct further decreased. Not surprisingly, the same prison programs that result in decreased misconduct are also associated with the largest reductions in recidivism.[148]

Some scholars have attributed the drop in disciplinary problems to a rise in self-esteem and appreciation for a new-found ability to achieve.[149] In short, "Prison activities programs, of which education is a large part, are among the best management tools in corrections, because they keep inmates busy in a positive way" and create a safer environment for prison officers.[150] They "make ... control of prison populations much easier."[151] At San Quentin, where a college-education program is offered, the result is evident: San Quentin has fewer racial and gang problems than other prisons.[152]

While no studies have yet specifically correlated an increase in prison violence with the marked decrease in prison education funding, anecdotal evidence suggests that might be the case. It cannot be ignored that several decades after the Attica uprising, prison violence continues to plague our correctional system, so that the increasing spiral of violence remains to the point where housing-unit and other officers in federal prisons are authorized to carry oleoresin capsicum (pepper spray) weapons, as laid out in the Federal Bureau of Prisons Operations Memorandum 003–2012 (June 2012).

Prison education not only reduces recidivism but also develops improved communication between the prison staff and the prisoners, and it develops positive peer role models for other prisoners, according to Stephen Steurer, executive director of the Correctional Education Association. Correctional educational programs, he contends, break down racial barriers and produce prisoners who are better behaved, more cooperative, and better adjusted while incarcerated.[153] Another study concludes, "The positive influence of correctional education, especially at the post-secondary level, [is] an effective and necessary management tool in prisons today."[154]

"Education," affirms noted correctional psychiatrist James Gilligan, "is a quantifiable form of violence prevention"[155] that creates a more humane, more positive prison environment for both prisoners and for prison staff.

Miles D. Harer, from the Federal Bureau of Prisons Office of Research and Evaluation, confirms the concept. "Prison education programs are [one of] what I call normalizing prison programs ... that serve to increase prison safety and decrease recidivism. Normalizing programs and operations achieve these goals ... by reducing prisonization and by nurturing prosocial norms."[156] Harer's report then identifies "five pains" of imprisonment:

- isolation from the larger community,
- lack of material possessions,
- blocked access to heterosexual relationships,
- reduced personal autonomy, and
- reduced personal security.

According to Harer, "these deprivations foster what is ... referred to as 'prisonization,' that is, alienation from the prison staff and management and from the larger society."[157] Additionally, he says, criminologists argue that many inmates bring to prison a commitment to criminal subcultures and criminal norms.

To combat this, Harer says normalizing programs and operations can take various forms, and he lists many of them, including educational courses. "Prison education programs," he states, "are one critically important component in this new normalization paradigm.... Education programs serve to occupy the inmate's time productively, thus limiting the negative influence of prisonization, and further serve to socialize/resocialize inmates toward acceptance of prosocial norms.... We find strong evidence that education programs reduce recidivism, possibly through normalization."[158]

Discussions about mental development, positive influences, and deterrence effects are not merely academic. Living in prison, I have personally witnessed prisoner-students who previously would not have thought twice about breaking the rules, but who now refrain from doing so because of the potential consequences. "Inmates for whom participation in educational programs may be at risk are more likely to walk away from confrontations.... In a prison system fundamentally structured by violence, the importance of this reduction in violence cannot be underestimated. In addition, these reductions in discipline problems lead directly to lower personnel costs for the facility."[159]

Prisoners enrolled in educational programs are easier for the prison administrators and staff to manage. Rarely do prisoner-students stir up trouble or start fights, including those participating in academic courses, vocational training, music, art, or creative writing, but especially those who are pursuing college courses. In short, studies show repeatedly (as does empirical experience) that educational programs reduce violence within prison walls.[160] Arguments among inmate-students are more likely to be of a more intellectual nature; they've been overheard debating the merits of Rousseau versus Machiavelli, for example, or ancient ideas of ethics, morality, and philosophy. These prisoners are focused on their studies and on new ideas they have to think about. They enjoy the rewards of certifications, grades, credits, learned skills, and improved decision-making abilities. It is a process that develops social values and a sense of responsibility.[161]

For the average prisoner who does not participate in an educational program, "trouble" may simply entail losing commissary or visitation privileges for a set amount of time. But for the prisoner-student, getting into trouble can result in removal from an educational course or failing a class. The latter can occur when the infraction is severe enough that the prisoner-student is placed in the hole, where he can't complete his assignments or take a proctored exam. So, for the prisoner-student who places a high value on his or her educational program, that is sufficient deterrence to stay out of trouble. This, in turn, makes the prison a safer place and benefits the administration. (To inject a note of reality, however, a prisoner's commitment to stay out of trouble is no guarantee that he or she can. I have personally been wrongfully placed in "the hole" [solitary confinement] and was forced to abandon my college courses when absolutely no wrongdoing had occurred. The prison authorities later admitted that no violation of any rules had taken place, but only after I had lost almost half a year of studying while in solitary.)

In a 1993 study by the Senate Judiciary Committee that interviewed prison wardens, 93 percent said they "strongly supported educational and vocational programming in adult correctional facilities."[162] They and the vast majority of corrections officials believe that educational programs not only benefit inmates, but also the facility's administration and staff. These officials have urged reinstating college programs because of their "multiple positive effects."[163] Consistent with their experience, "studies show that higher education improves cognitive function [and helps] to diminish the antisocial attitudes and behaviors associated with criminal activity. Many prisoners have credited education with ... their ability to disengage from a 'prison mentality,' maintain positive goals, and develop ... the ability to shape and steer one's life in a meaningful way."[164]

Education behind bars is no threat to institutional security. On the contrary, "by enhancing cognitive abilities and moral reasoning, education can help change individuals who have become acculturated to the negative values of [the] prison subculture" so that their thinking, attitudes and behaviors turn toward a more positive direction.[165]

Bottom line: with reduced misconduct among prisoners, prison authorities encounter fewer disciplinary problems, rules violations, violence, or security issues because inmates recognize that misbehavior can jeopardize their course work. In addition to creating a safer environment and potentially impacting the entire prison culture,[166] prisoner-students may be more compliant with parole expectations upon release due to an improved sense of social responsibility.

Positive for Prisoners

It goes without saying that prisoners themselves reap rewards from educational programs. Most prisoners know they will be released one day. If they want that to be a one-way trip, to leave the prison world and never return, they will have to survive—more than survive, *succeed*—when they re-enter society. For most, given their record, it won't be easy to find a good, steady job without, at the very least, either solid vocational training or an advanced degree.

Studies consistently determine that the primary reason recently released prisoners find themselves back in prison is unemployment. And a released prisoner's ability to secure steady employment increases the higher his or her educational level. Prisoner-students who are able to complete a college education or get an advanced degree have the greatest opportunities when they are released.[167] They can qualify for the better jobs, higher salaries, and a good standard of living. Workers with a bachelor's degree, for instance, earn, on average, 93 percent more than workers with only a high-school diploma.[168] And the good news is that 75 percent of college-educated former prisoners are able to overcome the stigma of their criminal record and find stable employment.

Education is a prisoner's hope for getting out and staying out. It's his or her ticket to a second chance at life, and prisoners know it. Their primary reason for wanting to enroll in classes is their belief it will help to secure employment when they are "out."

While it is obviously true that higher education is not a top priority for everyone and may not even be appropriate for some, the highest number (94 percent of the individuals surveyed) said they did want an education. In fact, they placed the need for education above other life-essential services such as financial assistance (86 percent), a driver's license (83 percent), job training (82 percent), and employment (80 percent). This remarkably strong showing of a desire for education is a personal statement of motivation to seek a better life.[169] And their orientation to that new way of life must begin long before they finish serving their sentences.[170]

These findings are corroborated by the *Police Journal*, which said, "More should be spent on expanding and strengthening basic education and GED programs for inmates"[171] because prisoners themselves want more educational programs; they consider education and learning important for achieving their goals and for attaining the job skills necessary for various career options.

Many living within prison walls have suffered from broken families, inadequate schools, failure at early educational experiences, racial discrimination, and physical or sexual abuse. An opportunity to get an education "may be the first glimmer of hope that they can escape the cycles of poverty and violence that have dominated their lives."[172]

Inmates typically learn about educational opportunities from other inmates. Business courses are considered especially helpful, as well as health and wellness and courses in communications, computer skills, and writing. Most don't expect to complete a degree while in prison, but plan to continue their education after release. Some, however, do earn a degree and are working on a second degree while incarcerated.[173]

Prisoners who participate in educational programs see their future differently. They develop a more positive outlook and are supported in this by association with other inmates who are also pursuing education. Prior to taking courses, they had imagined themselves returning to prison, but schoolwork helps them see themselves as being able to do more than menial labor and they become interested in pursuing their education and career goals when released. Those who enroll are more motivated, mature, and goal-driven than others, and many, concerned that employers may not be willing to hire them, expressed a desire to own a business upon release.[174] Seeing themselves as a student overshadows seeing themselves as a prisoner "doing time." They feel a different identity, something other than that of a criminal. They are "repositioned as college students, rather than inmates..."[175]

One prisoner in North Carolina, given the opportunity to take college courses through the Youth Offender Program, or YOP (renamed the Incarcerated Individual Program, which is now defunct due to a cessation of all funding in 2012), said that ending up in prison provided an opportunity to reposition himself in the world.[176] Other participants in the program felt it kept them busy and out of trouble and that getting serious about their education was a life-changing decision. Many had to first complete their GED in prison. The prison courses, a very different experience from their previous schooling, were an overwhelmingly positive experience. Said one participant, "You know these classes, I love them! I don't want to miss these classes ... I see that it is helping me."[177] Prisoner-students were enthusiastic not just for the credits they earned, but for a real interest in the knowledge they were gaining. For many it was a confidence-building revelation that they could "do school," and they felt it was important to continue on with their education after release. Some said reading and doing assignments relieved stress. Others talked about the camaraderie between people taking classes who help one another. There is an excitement about completing coursework and making presentations of what they've learned. "Yes, [I'm excited] because I think mine is the best! I want to go first ... so ... whoever's after me will have to make sure they're on their A game, 'cause I ain't gonna be playin' no games when I give mine!"[178] The YOP gave prisoners hope and aspirations for continuing their education and creating a positive future after their release.

One prisoner-student expressed fascination with his studies about government and politics and the Constitution. Another said he could do things that weren't possible before his incarceration, like "actually try to learn something ... get a degree ... and apply it to the world. That's really beyond blessing right there." And from a third, the idea that "there are people out there who don't think of you as just a number and that are willing to help ... it kind of makes you feel good to know. It kind of gives you a little hope..."[179]

Prisoner-students and their family members feel proud of their accomplishments. Many serve as role models, encouraging relatives and children to get on with their schooling, too.[180] Said one enrolled prisoner, "I wanna be able to have an intelligent conversation with a stranger without feeling dumb and useless. I want to make my mother proud of me ... I want to help my little sister with her homework and teach her how to be an adult."[181]

Prison schooling, said one prisoner with obvious emotion, was the "only thing positive I've ever done in my life on my own."[182]

There is nothing sadder than to see so many young lives and minds wasting in the prison limbo, eyes glazed and dulled by perpetual TV watching, passing days, weeks, months, and years in a passive, do-nothing state that rots the mind and spirit. For many, the only positive and stimulating experience in their entire lives is when they participate in correctional educational programs, whether vocational, basic literacy, high-school equivalency, peer-to-peer sessions, or college courses.

"Correctional educational programs are one of the few experiences and places within any prison where the basic reality of prison life can, even temporarily, be overcome. The classroom becomes ... a 'refuge,' a sanctuary from the realities of the prison where the 'geniality' between teachers and students can prevail ... the existence of a sort of 'campus camaraderie' among college level inmate-students."[183] They create an environment where prisoners feel safer and more cooperative, the one and only place where one can share, tell one's story and hear the stories of others.[184] In the experience of Roz, a college graduate serving 50 to life,

> ... when I started going to school ... it was a whole new world. Being able to exchange ideas and learn new ways of life, and learn about the classics and learn about methodology—opened this whole new world for me. I was overwhelmed at first, but I wanted to learn more. I wanted to get more ... understanding the world better; understanding ... my crime and why I was here ... I just wanted to read everything ... I wanted to explore ... I started surrounding myself with people of like minds. Because when I first came here I ... had a chip on my shoulder that I wanted somebody to knock off ... I stayed in trouble. I was disrespectful. I had no self-respect, no respect for others. And it took a while for me to change gradually and ... when I started going to college that was like the key point for me of rehabilitation, of changing myself. And nobody did it for me, I did it for myself ... I have an education and this education is going to carry me someplace. And even if I don't get a better job, I'll be a better person because of it. And that's, that's what it's all about.[185]

Prisoner-students also say that they highly value relationships with teachers who work one-on-one with them and inspire them to continue their education for a better life.[186] None of them want to be career felons.

If we reinstated college programs within prisons, we would be sending an important message to prisoners that society believes they are salvageable, that they have potential, that they are not human refuse.[187] The idea that someone can see them in this light is for most a first-time, mind-expanding, and motivating experience.

"Data show that inmates at the lowest levels of educational achievement benefit most from participation."[188] These prisoners learn that they are more intelligent than they had ever thought, and they take pride in being the first in their family to graduate. The graduation ceremony is very meaningful to them and serves to inspire other inmates.

Learning exposes prisoners to the idea that they can succeed through hard work and dedication. For those on the "outside," that may be a self-evident concept. But for many within the walls of prison, it is something they realize for the first time in their lives. Working at class assignments gives prisoners a purpose in life and a focus. Success with completion of a course or earning a good grade can produce an understanding of the consequences of one's actions and a desire to take responsibility for them. Success in course work builds their self-esteem and helps them envision a different kind of life than that of crime. Changes of this nature are essential if the individual is to "make it" when released into the world.[189]

Studying helps to keep prisoners busy and, therefore, makes time pass more easily. It provides mental stimulation and an opportunity to relate to others as someone other than just a criminal. Some enroll in college courses out of loneliness, because it opens lines of communication to people with whom they previously had little reason to talk with. In one study, most of the prisoners said they enrolled in college to escape the negativity of the prison environment and do something of worth, something of which their families could be proud of despite their criminal behavior.[190]

It is powerfully liberating to develop an ability to reason logically and analytically. Given the harshness of prison life, the daily brutality that strips one's self-control and connectedness, writing and education reacquaint the prisoner with a most basic freedom: that of expression. Writing becomes a tool for preserving one's sanity, for healing, and for giving voice to those who are silenced. It allows autonomy in a world where none exists. Senses numbed in prison awaken and release creativity that is both therapeutic and rehabilitative.[191] Men and women writing from prison have demonstrated an astonishing potential that can develop into real talent within a structured learning environment.[192]

Dr. Jon Marc Taylor has said that time and again he personally witnessed the transformation of people society had labeled as worthless and beyond redemption. By offering a cultural foundation, critical thinking, and communication skills, higher education has the power to change attitudes and perceptions and behaviors; it can achieve a personal revolution in the criminal character.[193]

Education is a primary means of recovering one's dignity in prison,[194] of developing an improved self-image, communication skills, and a willingness to engage in thoughtful conversations. It leads to logical thinking and higher ambitions. Also, inmates become more supportive of one another, finding friendships with others who pursue the same goals; they develop more responsibility in facility jobs and encourage other inmates to pursue education. "When you have people that care about you and want you succeeding, you are able to care for someone else. You motivate. When you are motivated, you help motivate the next man."[195]

Transcending imprisonment with fresh discovery is freedom, an inner freedom that even prison cannot take away.[196] The body may be trapped, but the mind is liberated, opened to new visions and new worlds. Studies help counter a stultifying daily existence and provide an escape from the boredom, the monotony, the do-nothing that turns a brain into Silly Putty.

While prisoner-students do gain practical skills they will use upon release,[197] prison education is not just about acquiring knowledge, skills, facts, concepts or theories; it is about learning *how to think*. How to express oneself clearly and in a healthy manner. How to develop stable personal and business relationships. Exposure to the liberal arts is about acquiring new values, becoming more conscientious, responsible, and more developed morally.[198] Ultimately, it's about constructing a new life and staying out of prison forever. It's about the transformation of a person.

Can we realistically consider education for all the incarcerated? No; of course some are unable to manage it. "You can't do much about deranged predator types. You can give them all the education in the world, but if they're predators, they're predators. But those beyond rehabilitation are very few in number, not even 1 percent of the [incarcerated] population," according to Los Angeles Sheriff Lee Baca. Baca has seen that "90 percent are hungry for new knowledge.... They flat-out are a very good student population."[199] The vast majority of criminals can be turned from crime and live a constructive, law-abiding life.[200]

The bottom line is this: providing educational and college programs in prisons costs a small fraction of what it costs to re-incarcerate perpetrators of crime. It reduces criminal behavior and recidivism rates and increases safety in society. It reduces violence within prisons and makes the management of correctional facilities easier, and it reduces the tax burden of citizens everywhere. Most important: prison education helps to transform and rehabilitate wasted lives with a new sense of social responsibility, turning criminals into productive, tax-paying citizens.

For any prisoner who aspires to be successful in today's economy when released, who wants a job that is interesting and satisfying, who cares about supporting and raising a family and serving as a positive role model, there is only one way: education.

Education for Those Who Are Incarcerated for Life?

And what about prisoners who have no hope of ever being released? Is there any point to putting themselves through the grueling hard work?

One graduate student from the University of California–Berkeley teaches male prisoners who will be locked up permanently or for a very long time. Nevertheless, he says, they desire meaningful interactions and an intellectual and academic challenge because it helps to combat the deadening effect of prison. They want to be productive. In the Boston University prison-education program, for example, some of them work as on-site administrators[201] and facilitate the education of others.

"But to think they are developing resumes or preparing for upward mobility and social climbing is delusional."[202] So is it worth the effort?

Indeed it is. Some of the reasons are obvious: to build a sense of self-worth, to escape the stress and tension of a violent environment, and so forth. But there is another reason, more profound and more compelling than any other: education is the path to restitution.

Too often, prisoners feel their lives count for nothing, that their years have been a destructive waste. Education can help them make amends and make a meaningful contribution to society, even within prison walls.

If prisoners with lifelong sentences are educated they, in turn, can teach others who are eager to learn, who want a way out of their going-nowhere lifestyle.

Most prisoners cannot afford to enroll in traditional courses. But educated "lifers" can teach them. Tutor them. Help them to pass exams. They can become part of a process to transform fellow prisoners, and when those prisoners leave the prison world, they would be prepared to pursue further education. For both the teacher and the student, studying is a way to embark on the adventure of new discoveries, to experience a productive life, and to rediscover an enthusiasm for living, even while confined.

2

A Historical Perspective on Prison Education

Throughout our history of prisons, there has always been a tension between the need for security and the necessity for rehabilitation to change the behavior of prisoners. In other words, there is a controversy between punishment and reform.[1] When rehabilitation was in favor, education prospered; when punishment was favored, education diminished.

The earliest American prison was created by the Quakers in 1791 with the goals of (1) ensuring public safety, (2) reforming prisoners, and (3) "humanity toward those unhappy members of society."[2] Quakers believed in restoration rather than punishment. As part of that restoration, they added a school to the prison in 1798. Prisoners were kept totally isolated, treated well, and given a rudimentary education, primarily a religious one, because a spiritual connection was thought to be effective in rehabilitation.

A different approach came into being in the early 1890s in New York, where prisons established mass-production industries and had the prisoners working all day in monotonous tasks. These prison keepers did not believe in education for prisoners; they felt it took time away from their labor.[3] Toward the end of the 19th century, however, it was thought criminals were victims of their environments and should be allowed to rehabilitate. In the 1930s, academic and vocational education spread throughout the prisons and began to play a more important role; this is when the first post-secondary education programs began with education that was job-specific.[4] Vocational education was viewed as the best route because it would eliminate inmate idleness and provides prisoners with marketable skills to assist with post-release employment.[5]

This approach continued into the early 20th century, with vocational courses by correspondence offered in selected prisons, such as Sing Sing. With the advent of the Great Depression, however, the public's interest in prison education declined and prisons reverted to the policy of prison labor.[6]

Higher education entered the nation's penal institutions in 1953, but prior to 1965, in-prison educational programs were almost nonexistent and no prisons had programs that granted degrees.[7] A milestone event took place in 1965 when Congress passed Title IV of the Higher Education Act, enabling qualified prisoners to receive Pell Grants for college-level studies. That is when the number of college programs in prisons proliferated and were offered in almost all states.[8]

A greater awareness of the need for education behind bars was sparked on September 9, 1971, by the rebellion at Attica. In "the bloodiest prison massacre the country had ever seen,"[9] inmates at Attica State Prison in New York rioted against their squalid living conditions and took their guards hostage. "We are MEN!" the Attica inmates protested. "We are not beasts."[10] They demanded adequate food, water, shelter, and medical treatment. They demanded minimum wages for their work (they were earning 30 cents a day) and access to education and true rehabilitative programs, an allotment of more than one toilet paper roll per month, religious freedom, an end to censoring newspapers, magazines, and letters, and to be allowed to be politically active.[11] They also asked that the prisons recruit black and Hispanic officers because racism and segregation were rampant. One prisoner, arrested for selling marijuana, would not allow his children to visit him because, he said, "If they want to see an animal, they could go to a zoo."[12] The rioting prisoners invited doctors and journalists to come in and see how dehumanizing their living conditions were and show the world what was happening.

In response, Governor Rockefeller "unleashed a lethal aerial assault, dropping tear gas from helicopters and ordering in the National Guard, which fired 2,200 bullets in nine minutes, killing 29 prisoners and 10 of the prison guards."[13]

Despite being squashed by government police, the prisoners' cry for reform was heard.[14] The uprising at Attica and the continued organizing of prisoners afterward was the beginning of national prison reform.[15] At a time when popular belief was that nothing could regenerate prisoners or turn them from their criminal ways, the revolt swayed public opinion toward the concept of prisons providing rehabilitation, not just punishment, and made prison officials aware that prisoners were intent on finding a way to obtain education. That was when federal and state financing was directed toward prison-based college programs.

Unfortunately, many of those reforms would be rolled back in decades that followed. Pell Grants and educational programs were slashed. People were locked up for nonviolent drug crimes and parole violations. Sentences became longer, prisons were overcrowded, and health care has been poor.

Long before the outbreak, educated prisoners had been teaching fellow prisoners, often imparting radical political ideas. Prisoner-educators helping prisoner-students was nothing new now, or even back then. It has a long history. But the rebels at Attica wanted more formal education programs.

As a result, government-sponsored high-school and college education programs became a focal point. In the wake of Attica, a prisoner liaison committee was created to handle grievances between prisoners and guards, and a pre-release center was established to connect prisoners with community contacts and help them complete their studies or find jobs when they were released. Together with prison administrators, community leaders, and Marist College (a Catholic school in Poughkeepsie, NY), the prisoner-scholars from Attica set up a four-year bachelor's degree program funded by Pell Grants.[16]

One prisoner, a ninth-grade dropout, remembers the Attica prisoner-scholars convincing him he could succeed in courses like economics and urban planning. The professors coming in to conduct classes, he recalls, were amazed at how articulate the prisoners were and at how, even without formal education, they had developed an ability for critical thinking. Mostly, he says, the teachers were struck by how hungry the prisoner-students were for knowledge, how they devoured the books and asked questions continually until the sessions ended.[17]

By 1973 there were 182 educational programs in prisons; by 1976, 237 programs; and by 1982, 350 educational programs flourished in prisons throughout the country.[18] The Pell Grants supported studies for associate's, bachelor's, and master's degrees in prisons, of which 60 percent were in maximum- and medium-security prisons. They taught math, reading, and vocations such as horticulture, food service, auto mechanics, and others to 27,000 prisoners, or 9 percent of the prison population at the time.[19] Two-year community colleges and technical/vocational schools sponsored 75 percent of the courses, and most classes were held live, inside the prisons; only 13.5 percent were provided via correspondence. As a result, rehabilitation through educational programs was an inherent part of our prison systems.

Repeal of the Pell Grants: The Collapse of Prison Education

The history of post-secondary education in prisons in America is marked by a cataclysmic event: the end of Pell Grants for prisoners. Prison education had expanded successfully until the trend was reversed in the early 1990s, at the peak of the "tough on crime" frenzy in American politics. Politicians responded, often proclaiming untrue statements, to the outcry. They enacted the Violent Crime Control and Law Enforcement Act of 1994 and the Higher Education

Reauthorization Act in 1994. As one of the provisions of the 1994 Crime Act, Congress withdrew federal support by making prisoners—all prisoners, whether incarcerated in state or federal prisons—ineligible for Pell grants or student loans.[20] In many states, including New York, prisoners were even barred from taking college extension courses. Not only did college education programs suffer, many secondary programs (high school or the equivalent) suffered as well.

No more Pell Grants for prisoners. The primary source of funding for higher education in prisons was gone. For the prison population, repeal of Pell Grant eligibility had devastating consequences.[21] Within weeks, nearly all of the 350 educational programs had collapsed.[22] In New York alone only four of the 70 previously existing programs remained.[23] They closed down nationwide, ending the presence of the most affordable and effective crime-prevention program in the history of American criminal justice.

There was protest from the people closest to the issue who saw firsthand what it meant. When Congress abolished all federally financed college education in prisons and eliminated Pell Grants to prisoners, there was resistance from educators, from the Department of Education, and from prison authorities alike. The denial of Pell Grants to prisoners was hotly protested by the National Association for the Advancement of Colored People (NAACP), the New York State Correctional Association, the Coalition for Criminal Justice, the Urban League, the Correctional Education Association and many, many other prominent organizations.[24] To no avail.

Academic education in prisons ended abruptly, diminishing to the point where none (except a few privately funded ones) exist today. Funding once set aside for prison education went instead to constructing new facilities and medical care for an aging, sicker, long-term population.[25] Now, with access to academic education forbidden to prisoner-students who cannot otherwise afford higher learning, prisoners spend more and more time locked in cells with little to do. What a hotbed of violence and paranoia we have created. What a profoundly foolish move.

"As late as the early nineties, several colleges and universities, as well as a smattering of community colleges, offered academic programs in prisons leading to associate and bachelor's degrees," said John Britton in Harvard's *Nieman Watchdog*. Some even offered access to a master's degree. But "legislators have deliberately reduced education opportunities for the prison populations and for released prisoners."[26] Notwithstanding statistical evidence that graduates of those programs seldom returned to a life of crime, educational opportunities in prisons have disappeared.

Said Xavier McElrath-Bey, imprisoned as an accomplice to murder as a teen, "There's a therapeutic component to education. It gives a sense of belonging. Inmates receiving an education start to realize they can be agents of social change. The first time I gave a presentation in front of my fellow student inmates, I felt great. It made me want to go out and get my master's when I came out." His transformation was profound. McElrath-Bey subsequently went to work as a field researcher for Northwestern University.[27] Today, however, such success stories are not possible. It was the Pell Grant program that allowed him access to a college education.

Too many people did not understand the larger picture. They did not understand how correctional education supports the economic and social fabric of our country, or how education reduces crime when it converts former criminals into skilled and professional workers. Instead, a small but vocal group of people complained about Pell Grants providing even a small amount of federal funding (only 1/10 of 1 percent) to allow prisoners to take college courses; they even criticized colleges and universities that were willing to participate in these programs.[28]

Despite the success of educational programs in rehabilitating and transforming offenders, the general public had the impression that prison life was too "soft." They believed (erroneously) that Pell grants went to prisoners at the expense of law-abiding students. Even political leaders who should have known better assumed that money for prison education was being taken away from monies available to law-abiding students.

They were wrong. Every traditional applicant who qualified received Pell Grant money, regardless of the number of applicants.[29] Not a single traditional student had ever been denied a Pell Grant because of prisoner participation in the program.[30] In fact, when prisoners were later barred from receiving Pell Grant aid, there were no additional grants awarded to traditional students. "Funding that had previously gone to prisoner-students, [had it been] equally divided among the millions of [traditional Pell] grant recipients, [would have] amounted to an insignificant extra five dollars per semester."[31] To be accurate, note that it was not the prisoners themselves who received money from Pell Grants; it was the educational institutions that received it to cover the expense of providing the education.

Politicians should have known that only 1/10 of 1 percent of Pell money was used to support prison education programs. But that small percentage went a long way. Nevertheless, the idea of providing post-secondary education in prison had become unpopular.[32] And cuts in funding, as those which blocked prisoners from eligibility for Pell Grants, are primarily politically motivated. "We've seen a lot of 'get tough' initiatives that make very little sense but that sound good to the voters."[33]

All government and academic studies have shown that the impact of the

Pell Grants was enormously positive, and all of them unanimously recommend that Pell Grants be restored to qualified prisoner-students. Even a very small fraction of Pell funding had proved to radically slash the rates of recidivism and reduce crime.

According to a report from the Center on Crime, Communities & Culture, "The reinstatement of federal financial assistance in the form of Pell Grants to inmates is crucial."[34] At a time when funding for public universities is being cut back, and the tuition burden faced by our students is increasing, it will be very, very difficult to persuade Congress to restore Pell funding. But the time is right for a national re-examination of that ban. First, because the amount of money in question is modest and the programs are cost-effective, and second, because it would create significant reductions in recidivism. This small investment of dollars would save enormous amounts of money for states and localities.[35]

If the public and our political representatives didn't care from a humanitarian point of view, they should have thought about what it meant from a fiscal point of view and from a community-safety point of view. Post-secondary education costs a small fraction of what we now pay for released prisoners returning to crime in our communities and, eventually, back to prison.

In 2009, the NAACP called upon the courts to make education a condition of probation and parole in appropriate cases and urged Congress to restore Pell Grant eligibility to prisoners. Restoration of Pell Grants to prisoners is also strongly supported by the Earl Carl Institute, The Correctional Education Association, and almost every other organization engaged in research on the socioeconomic benefits of providing higher education to prisoners.[36]

It is a tragic irony. The 1994 bill signed by President Clinton swept Pell Grants out of prisons because citizens who feared crime were calling for it. Instead, the "get tough on crime" mentality shot itself in the foot, so to speak, when it swept out the single most effective means of crime reduction.[37]

Pell Grants will be available to most prisoners after they serve their term in confinement. But why should intelligent and motivated inmates not use their time in prison to develop their minds? If educational activity at the college level in prison is associated with lower recidivism rates, then the use of Pell Grants by prisoners who are pursuing undergraduate degrees is an investment that will pay huge dividends. Inmates who become productive citizens add to the economic growth and prosperity of the country, and they save billions of government dollars each year that we taxpayers have to spend on prisons because so many of them are re-incarcerated.[38]

A glimmer of hope on the horizon: In December 2012, Rutgers University held a conference at which they called for reinstating Pell Grants nationwide to prisoners and for reversing the law that bars access to the most effective rehabilitation and recidivism-reducing program that exists.[39] "I think that education in our prisons is the key to preventing recidivism," said John J. Farmer, former New Jersey Attorney General and currently a dean and law professor at the Rutgers School of Law. He said the restoration of Pell Grants to prisoners is one of the most important aspects of law enforcement, particularly because funding is the key barrier to enrolling incarcerated students in college courses."[40] Others who advocate for reversing the ban to prisoners are currently petitioning Congress and the U.S. Department of Education.[41]

Vivian Nixon, director of the College and Community Fellowship and co-founder of Education from the Inside Out (EIO), announced that they hope to pass a bill to turn back the repeal of Pell Grants for prisoners. Her organization functions on the belief that economic conditions, prison overcrowding, and the need to reduce crime and recidivism demand education for prisoners. She is supported by such individuals and organizations as Warren Buffett, George Soros, and the Gates and Ford foundations, to name a few, who are providing funds to get the word out and to ask Congress to reverse the law that most people don't even know exists. "But changing federal legislation is a slow, painful process," Ms. Nixon cautioned. "If prisoners can earn an associate's degree behind bars, they can pursue a bachelor's or even a master's, once released. That's what will ultimately keep people away from crime. Isn't it worth it?"[42]

With 725,000 prisoners released back into society every year, Dr. Jon Marc Taylor urges, it is time to restore the Pell Grants to the prison population.[43] Even if some people believe we shouldn't give benefits to prisoners, we need to do it because we care about the rest of us. Only education can "halt the disastrous trend toward building more fortresses of fear which will become in the 21st century this generation's monuments to failure."[44]

Restoring Pell and TAP grants (The New York State Tuition Assistance Program: "TAP") for this purpose, and allowing people convicted of drug crimes to be eligible for federal financial aid after they have paid their debt and are released from prison would go a long way. As Mayor Ed Koch was heard to ask, "When is the punishment over?"[45]

3

Prison Education Today:
A Reality Check

Federal mandates exist to increase the educational and vocational skills of prisoners in order to reduce recidivism:

1. Title II of the Workforce Investment Act of 1998 requires that 10 percent of state funding be spent on correctional education for offenders, including basic education, special education, English literacy, and secondary school credit programs,[1] and

2. The Carl D. Perkins Career and Technical Education Act of 2006 requires that 1 percent of state funds be used to provide academic and vocational skills. Technology being so basic in today's economy, people must have computer skills, in addition to literacy and vocational training, to work.[2]

The U.S. Department of Education has an Office of Correctional Education, but there is not enough funding to support its initiatives and very little consistency from one state to another.[3] The privately supported initiatives are good, but few and far between (see Chapter 5).

Federal Bureau of Prisons' Official Policy on Correctional Education

The official policy of virtually all federal prisons (98 percent) is to offer basic education, secondary education, and post-secondary vocational training. This is reflected in the Federal Bureau of Prisons Program Statement on Education (see Appendix I), but note that the educational programs of the Federal Bureau of Prisons do not include advanced academic or university-level courses.

46

Regarding academic college courses, the Program Statement says the pursuit of a college education is entirely the responsibility of the prisoner. The prisoner must find all the necessary information on his or her own and must incur all associated costs.

It is clear that the FBOP will take no responsibility for providing advanced education, although the FBOP's program statement (see Appendix I) claims to support the efforts of prisoners who seek an advanced education. However, my empirical experience and personal observations indicate it does not reflect the reality prisoners encounter in numerous facilities.

Most state prisons claim to provide some sort of educational programs as well.[4] But we have little documentation about the quality of these programs, how—or if—prisoner participation is encouraged, or whether there is a correlation between educational needs and educational offerings. However, in prison facilities that offer classes, instructors tell us that inmates show a real enthusiasm for learning. They observe behavioral changes in prisoners and see them develop a sense of responsibility for their lives.

Higher education, of course, cannot be mandatory. Not all prisoners are up to it and not all prisoners desire it. It has to be reserved for those who are willing to put in the hard work advanced education requires. However, if advanced schooling were available for prisoners who desire it, the research is consistent in finding this is the most effective path to rehabilitation.

Locked Away from Learning

In prisons, security is paramount. Extraordinary amounts of money are spent on controlling prisoners, not on rehabilitating them. The thinking is that prison is prison; it is not a school. It is not even a vocational school.

We incarcerate law breakers, according to the Virginia State Department of Corrections, "(1) to protect society, (2) to punish the prisoner, and (3) to rehabilitate the prisoner."[5] We do protect the public by locking prisoners away and keeping them inside as long as possible to incapacitate them. And we do punish the offenders, because prison can be a living hell. But rehabilitation has been largely ignored. America's prisons are about retribution, not rehabilitation. They are human warehouses in which the post–Attica Age of Enlightenment has ended. At least for now.

Of course, we must protect the people from those who would harm them; we have no argument there. But we would give our communities far greater protection if we rehabilitated prisoners so that when they return to society, as most of them do, they will no longer pose a threat.

Prison budgets have skyrocketed, according to Stephen Steurer, Executive Director of the Correctional Education Association, because our prison population is expanding exponentially. However, the funds allocated for prison education have drastically decreased.[6] It makes no sense, but there it is: Decreased!

As a result, there are hardly even token state- or federal-sponsored vocational or advanced academic programs in prisons today. The few educational programs that do exist focus on bare basics, not on vocational training or academics.

In California, for just one example, a state struggling with a $60 billion budget deficit, prison officials slashed funding for prison education by $250 million. The cuts, as reported in *Prison Legal News,* impacted California's rehabilitative programs by laying off 850 teachers and vocational instructors, including prison staff who run substance abuse and anger management programs.[7] Prior to the cuts, almost one third of California's prisoners participated in educational or vocational programs. About 7 percent took substance abuse classes. But the biggest cuts have been in the area of post-secondary education.

What did the savings of $250 million gain for California? In the long run, the costs of increased prison violence and recidivism will undoubtedly exceed the short-term savings. Educators, a former San Francisco District Attorney,[8] and a report issued by The Council for Advancement of Adult Literacy[9] protested that cutting prison educational programs was unwise. Prison officials were warned that if parolees and other released prisoners do not have the skills needed to obtain and keep a job, they will find themselves back in the circumstances that created their criminal behavior in the first place, with all the resulting endangerment to public safety and the economy. We must, they argued, maintain the policies, funding, and programming needed to help released prisoners find meaningful jobs and transition into post-secondary education. "Because inmates return to an increasingly technological society, access to technology is needed, along with knowledge of how to locate information. Computer literacy is essential."[10]

"Most offenders will be out in a few years and become our neighbors. Is it not better to have an educated [and law-abiding] neighbor who contributes to the community?"[11]

What little of the slashed funding remains available for educational programs is, of necessity, spent on Adult Basic Education (ABE) and GED classes. There is not much left for anything else. In facilities where education is offered, most prisons provide two kinds of classes:

1. classes in literacy and English as a second language, and
2. classes in which inmates who have not completed high school can earn a GED, the recognized equivalent to a high-school diploma.

That's it. No academics. However, literacy, basic living, and GED courses do not necessarily develop skills of critical thinking or of effective oral and written communication. They don't shape moral reasoning or even an ability to work in teams. They don't teach respect for diversity. Our prisons' educational offerings do not go very far to address the cognitive issues associated with criminal and antisocial behavior.[12]

But here is an interesting question: while adult basic education is offered in most federal and state prisons, and federal policy encourages prisoners to participate in these basic classes, a startling statistic tells us that *less than 2 percent of prisoners actually receive or complete these courses.*[13]

The relevant question is not whether these programs are offered, but simply, why have only two percent of the incarcerated participated?[14] Correctional educators observe that prisoners are generally enthusiastic about learning.[15] They are eager to be occupied and engaged in educational efforts that lift them out of an otherwise idle, bored, and frustrated existence.

Studies have been consistent in finding that those who participate in correctional education programs have substantially lower rates of re-arrest, reconviction, and reincarceration than people who leave prison without educational intervention. And yet, despite the overwhelming evidence, economic and political pressures have succeeded in creating a reduction in educational programs and staffing—just the opposite of what is needed.

Even in a state like New Mexico, where the recidivism rate is lower than the national average, the year 2009 saw a 25 percent reduction in jobs within the Education Bureau of the Department of Corrections. This meant that 25 percent of the state's prisoners—that is, 1,900 out of 6,462—who had hoped to be in classes were no longer able. According to Gail Oliver, retired deputy corrections secretary for prisoner reentry, "That many job vacancies in the Education Bureau defeat our efforts to lower the recidivism rate." Her experience had shown that "education is the number-one way of preventing people from going back to prison."[16]

Within the federal prison system, every facility has an Education Department, and many state prisons do, too. Prisoners who seek to go beyond the penal system to independently pursue an education via correspondence courses usually must seek assistance from the Education Department. What they usually discover, however, is that the Education Department does not maintain lists of schools or courses available to prisoners. The prisoners must somehow find (without the aid of computers or the internet) the information they need.

At FCI Petersburg, where I am imprisoned, the Education Department houses a leisure library for the inmate population and a number of law library texts, along with typewriters, TVs with DVD players, and classrooms for the GED courses. The Education Department, staffed by guards and some teachers, is primarily there to oversee the administration of the GED classes. They are not there to assist anyone with pursuing a more advanced education.

When we use the term "post-secondary correctional education," it does not refer to basic education or literacy or life skills education or programs to earn a GED. We use it only for vocational or academic courses *beyond* the high-school diploma.

In most states, prisons focus their limited educational budget on basic education, not college-level education for inmates, but education, and the higher the level the better, is what is needed to survive in our society.[17] While the majority of inmates are poor and undereducated, there are still a significant number of college-eligible inmates who have no access to higher education.[18]

Regarding post-secondary educational classes, in 2003–2004, there were *less than 5 percent* of the total prison population nationwide enrolled—approximately 85,000 prisoners, according to a report from the Institute for Higher Education Policy.[19] And of that 5 percent of prisoners involved in post-secondary education,[20] almost all of them, about 89 percent,[21] were incarcerated in only 15 prison systems.[22] The majority of these prisoner-students were enrolled in the shorter, less expensive vocational and certificate programs, rather than academic college or university degrees.

Not having access to Pell Grants, prisoners who desire a college or university education should consider themselves lucky if they can enroll in vocational, rather than academic courses. Completing a vocational credential while in prison may be helpful, but it will hardly prepare prisoners for release. We will discuss this further in a later chapter.

Post-secondary educational prison courses prove ineffective when there is insufficient money to pay qualified teachers or install adequate libraries and computer labs. Some states have even denied measures to grant prisoners access to college-level classes. "It is highly disconcerting that several recent education policies have made it *more difficult*—not less difficult—to use prison time to enroll in post-secondary education and to access college after leaving prison."[23]

For female prisoners, opportunities to pursue education beyond a high-school diploma or GED are fewer still. Out of the 98 state prisons housing women, only 20 percent offer any kind of college-level educational programming and, for the most part, these are privately funded, experimental programs (see Chapter 5). Women wanting to matriculate in an on-site degree-granting program can do so in only a few specific facilities within six states: Kentucky, Massachusetts, Minnesota, New York, North Carolina, and Texas.[24] (Note: figures reported for enrollment in post-secondary correctional education programs do not include prisoners who are independently pursuing correspondence courses that they pay for out of their own pockets.[25])

In the rare prison facility where college-level courses are available, most of the instruction is provided by public two-year community colleges. But prison systems impose a number of eligibility requirements before allowing prisoners to enroll. Prisons consider the inmate's age and placement test scores, length of sentence, reason for imprisonment, length of time until release, and infractions committed while in prison. (In the opinion of the author, the reason for imprisonment should not be a factor in consideration. Only academic qualifications; the prisoner's drive, focus, and motivation to work; and the desire for transformation should determine eligibility.) In any case, by limiting the participants in their post-secondary education programs, prisons can help ensure that those enrolled are able to complete their certificate or degree programs.[26]

Even when prisoners possess the minimal requirements—a high-school diploma or GED—many are not prepared academically, and they require remedial classes (which some of the colleges provide). This is not surprising, since prisoners often come from areas where schools are below par.[27] Nevertheless, many have shown a willingness to do the necessary remedial work, motivated by the idea of acquiring a post-secondary education.[28]

At the end of the day, however, it still remains true that "inmates are not earning college degrees, not even at the associate level, in any significant numbers."[29] And of the small handful who do take academic courses, very few can complete their degrees while in prison. The benefits of advanced education that increase with higher degrees are still out of reach, with rare exceptions, for those who seek to transform their lives while still incarcerated.[30]

Learning at the Lowest Level

Offerings from the education department, with some classes instructed by prisoners and others by staff, typically include:

1. *Literacy* classes for those who cannot read and write. While "many rehabilitative efforts have proved disappointing in their lasting efforts, literacy programs are a key exception."[31] The National Institute for Literacy tells us that most prisoner-students have had less than six years of education before entering prison. Some had worked in restaurants or in construction; others had no work experience at all. Almost 70 percent of prisoners cannot write a letter, explain an error on a credit card bill, or understand a bus schedule. Most have reading skills below an eighth-grade level.[32] Here at FCI Petersburg (Medium) where I am imprisoned, I've been

asked on numerous occasions to help fellow prisoners with writing and sending letters pertaining to personal and legal matters. Earlier, in the county jail, I helped translate letters into Spanish for prisoners who could not read or write English, including letters that came from their own attorneys.

2. *ESL (English as a Second Language)* for individuals who are not proficient in English. Literacy and ESL are both required by the Comprehensive Crime Control Act of 1990 for prisoners who don't have a high-school diploma or the equivalent.

3. *ABE (Adult Basic Education)* or, as it is called in some prisons, ACE (Adult Continuing Education) is elementary arithmetic, reading, and writing up to the eighth-grade level. These classes are conducted by prisoners themselves, not by trained teachers.

As described in *Field Notes* (Winter 2002), "The room is bright. Student art and projects cover the walls. Sets of colorful books fill the bookshelves.... Students are sitting around four tables, and each group is engaged in intense discussion facilitated by a group leader."[33] This is an ABE class for the incarcerated funded by the Massachusetts Department of Education (MDOE). MDOE is committed to a belief in the value of correctional education for society as a whole, because prisoners who partake in educational programs while incarcerated are far less likely to become repeat offenders.

Note that most of these classes are not mandatory. They provide a certificate of completion when completed, but they do not translate into any college credit or serve any other practical purpose. No matter: they teach important living skills, and they are helpful.

At my facility, ACE classes include Money Management, Basic Legal Research, Spanish, Commercial Driver's License (CDL), Small Engine Repair, Real Estate, Business Planning, and Financial Planning. The majority of these classes have been shortened from their original 12-week format to an eight-week format. They have been made easier, but less informative, in order to move a greater number of students through.

In 2011, the FCI Petersburg Education Department underwent a number of significant changes, one of which was a major shift in the number and quality of ACE courses offered. Another change was a newly created inmate position of "ACE Coordinator" to help facilitate the ACE courses and function as a prisoner liaison to the Education Department. As one of the Education Coordinator's first official actions, he invited all prisoners interested in teaching to come to an informal session. The response was surprising. Twelve potential instructors, both English- and Spanish-speaking, volunteered. I personally proposed to teach a course on writing and publishing which was approved and subsequently well attended. Unfortunately for the inmates at FCI Petersburg, the Education Department coordinator in charge of ACE was promoted and transferred. Her replacement destroyed everything she had established. In 2012, course offerings were slashed, dedicated instructors were dismissed, program hours were cut, and the inmate instructors who had contributed so much to the program were dismissed.

4. *Life skills* programs to help deal with decision-making, obtaining a job, bill paying, family relationships, anger management, victim empathy, parenting, and other behavioral skills that will help a released prisoner live more successfully in society. In these classes, as well, the "teachers" are not certified instructors. Typically they are prison guards with no training or particular calling for education. Even more often, the classes are informally taught by the more educated prisoners.

5. *Addiction recovery*: From the psychology department we get classes to help those who are dealing with addiction and "Smart Recovery," which is about evaluating and changing our thinking patterns. Both of these classes are run by prisoners.

   Other classes coming from the psychology department are conducted either by prisoners or by prison staff. They include drug education, criminal thinking, the habits of highly effective people, a young men's group, and groups for sexual offenders. Ranging from 24 to 40 hours (with the exception of the sexual offender groups, which are broken into three phases of six months or more for each), these courses take time to complete. All these courses provide certificates of completion, and they are very useful in addressing a specific problem or need.

6. *Religious classes and worship*: All prisoners in our facility have access to a variety of worship services, just about every day of the week for most of the major religions. For Protestants and Catholics, there are church services on several mornings and evenings, as well as a prayer group and a discipleship class. The Chapel does not, of course, offer certificates (except for baptism).

7. *GED, or high school equivalency*: For prisoners who have not earned

a high-school diploma, prisons provide the opportunity to earn a GED (General Educational Development), which is recognized as an equivalent to completion of the 12th grade. Studies found that prisoners who had a diploma from a high school did better than those who earned the GED equivalent in prison with regard to academic achievement, educational aspirations, progress toward a degree, and personal development.[34]

Admittedly, getting a GED is not the same learning experience as having attended and graduated from a real high school, but it does make it possible to continue on with an academic, post-secondary education.

All prisons within the Federal Bureau of Prisons require prisoners to either earn their GED or spend a minimum of 240 hours in class, whichever comes first (see Appendix I). Failure to complete the minimum requirements can result in denial of good time credits. Pursuant to the Violent Crime Control and Law Enforcement Act of 1994 and the Prison Litigation Reform Act of 1996, prisoners who withdraw prior to the required number of hours in class are to be denied 7 of the 54 days of earned time off for good behavior available annually to federal inmates.

Prisoners attend these classes every weekday, just like in school. At my facility, about 8 to 9 percent of prisoners are currently enrolled, with a long waiting list of others eager to get into the program. If prisoners have the necessary knowledge, they can bypass the course and ask to take the tests required to complete the GED.

For any prisoner who wants to build something positive in his or her future, the GED high school equivalent is extremely important. It is required by all vocational schools and colleges for admission; it is also required by many employers before they will hire an applicant. The year 2014 brings a significant change in the GED program. A new, more rigorous test has been adopted by most states for earning a GED, and the test will no longer be delivered with pen and paper, but with a computer. Prison educators now have to teach in different ways to prepare for the test so that students demonstrate a deeper level of knowledge in the four subject areas (language arts. math, science, and social studies) and can show-higher level thinking skills. The new test will not only enable one to earn a GED, but will also measure readiness for career and college. A critical difference is that students have to take the test using a computer. The lack of computer literacy among inmates is a major barrier to implementing the new test, but "these changes also importantly will help push the growing role of computer technology in correctional education to the forefront."[35] It will require new equipment and the installation of new software and computer labs in prison facilities. Teachers will have to learn new instructional strategies for preparing students and create a new curriculum that includes the teaching of computer skills. This new way of delivering GED testing can pave the way to using technology to expand educational programs within prisons. In fact, it may drive funding for a technology infrastructure to the forefront.[36]

But even though GED programs exist in most prisons, many prisoners are not participating. In fact, the level of participation in educational programs has actually *decreased,* with the largest declines found in vocational training and adult secondary education.[37] Currently, only 6 percent of the incarcerated population is enrolled in all correctional education (basic, vocational or academic), with a much smaller percentage enrolled in post-secondary correctional education.[38] Enrollments vary enormously from one state to another because almost all prisoners enrolled in classes are located in only thirteen states. As an example, South Dakota reported only 50 prisoner-students enrolled in educational courses, while North Carolina boasts 16,500.

There are various reasons for the small enrollment percentages. They have declined partly because of the rapid growth in prisons, the frequent transferring of offenders from one facility to another, decreased federal funding for higher education programs, and greater interest in short-term substance abuse treatment and anger management programs.[39] Prison systems with the largest enrollments tend to focus on shorter vocational programs and they utilize state funding. But very few produce academic degrees in any significant numbers.[40] Prisons might consider offering incentives to increase enrollment, such as good time credit, payment, free books and school supplies, and assistance with college enrollment after release.[41]

"Participation in correctional education has diminished since [the banning of Pell Grants to prisoners in] 1994 for all types of education programs, including vocational training and those leading to a high-school credential. It is unclear, however, if participation rates have dropped because of long waiting lists for education programs, because of inmates having to spend their free hours working for bare necessities, or because of states cutting services in the face of budget constraints."[42] In 2002, a small percentage of inmates participated in the programming.[43] It has not increased significantly today.

Minimal, If Any, Vocational Training

"Vocational training programs ... are considered by many correctional experts to have the most potential for positive results. [Some] prisons work with local businesses to offer vocational training through work release programs where inmates learn a variety of job skills by participating in on-the-job training situations. These training programs involve varying degrees of counseling and support, as well as close monitoring of the prisoners. They may include role models and mentoring programs to ... help prepare [inmates] for successful reintegration into society."[44]

This description of prison vocational training programs presented at the Florida International University College of Education Annual Research Conference sounds good. However, in various prisons where I have been incarcerated over the past years, I have not seen any evidence of it. I have not found any vocational training available to develop skills that would make prisoners employable. The work assigned to prisoners is typically too menial to serve as "training" for any occupation. Some prisoners work in the kitchen or in the laundry or spend their years picking up trash, sweeping, mopping, and waxing floors. Some days, they are told to walk around the prison or sit against a wall until they are instructed to return to their housing units. For this, they get paid from approximately $5.25 to around $7.40 per month. Assignments like these do not provide vocational training that can lead to a real job upon release.

If we are serious about preparing prisoners for employability, correctional administrators must redesign vocational training programs and make them relevant to the current employment climate. And if they can get the redesigned programs certified by appropriate agencies, they can help obtain occupational licenses for prisoners upon their release.[45] Instead, the authorities seem to consider work for convicts as a privilege, not a right. In the outside world, you must work or starve. "In prison," say Convict Criminology founders Ross and Richards, "you work to keep from dying of boredom."[46]

Access to Academics?

With very few exceptions (see Chapter 5), college education is almost nonexistent in American prisons today. And yet, we learn from the Correctional Education Association, there is a steadily growing number of inmates who would qualify for and benefit from such programs. Sixty percent of state prisoners and 73 percent of federal prisoners are eligible for post-secondary correctional education because they possess a secondary credential (either a high-school diploma or a GED), as documented by the National Assessment of Adult Literacy.[47] However, only about 11 percent of those eligible actually have access to post-secondary education. And of the 11 percent that participate, more than 90 percent enroll in *vocational*—not academic—programs.[48]

We do not see many academic programs offering English, sociology, economics, psychology, political science, literature, philosophy, history, or environmental science. The very few enrolled in college classes were working on a two-year associate's degree. Most of these programs are delivered on-site, with some utilizing video or satellite instruction; very few use internet technology because of security requirements.[49] Therefore, they tell us, access to post-secondary programs is more difficult than ever.

Prisoners themselves identify education as the most pressing need for their employment prospects and success at reentry.[50] The majority of them are eager to learn, prove themselves in a challenging situation, and "become a better person."[51] Studies show that an inmate's desire for and interest in education is more influential on a positive outcome than their background or available resources.[52]

The only access most prisoners have to post-secondary education is through distance-learning programs which they must find, enroll in, and pay for on their own. However, since most prisoners have no access to computers or to the internet, the only way they can take courses and earn degrees is through correspondence (via snail-mail, not e-mail). Therefore, most distance-learning programs are not accessible to prisoners, because almost all of them are taught online. What makes it even harder is that each year, as more and more educational institutions expand their online offerings, fewer and fewer offer courses by correspondence. Just within the past two years, more than 20 schools have stopped offering paper-based courses in favor of online offerings.

Even if they have succeeded in doing all the ground work, prisoners still need the assistance of the prison's "Education Coordinator" to proceed. From what I have observed in several penal institutions, many of these staffers do not appear eager, or even willing, to help prisoners pursue an education. While there are some, admittedly, who do care, they are all too few. Where I am in prison, we used to call our Education Coordinator the "gatekeeper to higher education." He made sure no one got through!

All that said, there are prisoners who persist in finding and enrolling in independent correspondence study programs, and many have done so with resounding success.

In some facilities, prisoners who have had a good education or good business experience have informally organized courses. Classes such as these, taught by prisoner-volunteers, are unofficial if they are not of the ABE or ACE variety, and they are not supported by prison authorities. But educated prisoners sometimes share their knowledge with others who are interested: teaching how to start a small business, how to write a business plan, or how to apply for a loan. Some tutor in foreign languages. And in some prisons where attorneys are incarcerated, they can, if they are willing, help their fellow inmates with motions, appeals, and other legal procedures. (In the Federal Bureau of Prisons, inmates are permitted to assist one another with legal papers, provided there is no fee or item of value exchanged, according to *Program Statement 1315.08: Inmate Legal Activities.*)

If a prisoner is incarcerated where this kind of informal teaching is taking place, he or she is fortunate. But the learning cannot be translated into college credits. Formal, credit-based college courses are still generally unavailable unless prisoners pursue them independently and pay for them from their own resources.

Despite all the evidence that education is good for public safety, good for our economy, good for prison systems and administrators, good for colleges, and good for prisoners, still, for prisoners wanting to pursue a more advanced education, opportunities are very few.

Access to post-secondary vocational and academic education behind bars is a rare exception to the general rule—both here and in the Canadian prison system. High-school and university courses and courses in trade skills that existed in the late 1980s mostly disappeared in the 1990s, so that by 2010 Canadian prisons have fully eradicated all meaningful employment training and release preparation."[53] Collins claims the "CSC has never complied with legislated mandates to have programming available for prisoners prior to ... reaching parole eligibility dates."[54]

Prisons have become overcrowded holding cells that release prisoners without the tools, education, or skills needed to get a job or become contributing members of the communities to which they will be returned. The system all but guarantees these people will once again break the law and return to prison.

Returning to the World: Sink or Swim

Incarceration is a horrific experience. One would imagine an inmate who was finally released would do anything to get out and stay out of prison. It is difficult to understand why, of the approximately 725,000 prisoners released into society every year,[55] most of them will be re-arrested and returned to prison.[56] The inordinately high rate of recidivism is disturbing. And destructive.

Returning to and adjusting to freedom is difficult. Free society is complex, demanding, and full of obligations. Prison life is simpler. Most released prisoners have no money with them, not even street clothes, unless someone has mailed a package to them. They walk out to the streets with only the clothes on their backs. If there is no one to come get them, they have to walk or hitch hike home—if, in fact, they have a home to go to. Theoretically, federal prisoners are entitled to a "release gratuity" of up to $500 according to the *Bureau of Prisons Program Statement 5873.06: "Release Gratuities, Transportation, and Clothing*; however, few, if any, prisoners are provided with more than a bus ticket upon release and money for a snack during travel to their destination. They have only their release papers to prove their identity, and such documents do not endear them to prospective employers. Without a driver's license or Social Security card, many prisoners can't work. Clearly, they are not always welcomed back to the outside world with open arms.

Released prisoners are not prepared to navigate the complex maze of agencies, departments, and credits they encounter to obtain employment or continue their education. In-prison workshops are needed to prepare them for this.[57] As an attempt to reintegrate prisoners back into society, most federal inmates are sent to "halfway houses," typically about six months prior to the end of their sentences. The amount of time depends on a variety of factors. During this time, if a prisoner violates the halfway house rules, he or she is returned to prison. Unfortunately, these halfway houses tend to be more like homeless shelters and a less severe form of prison than a bridge to anything else.

Prisoners don't have either the money or the know-how to rent an apartment or live on their own. They don't know how to seek a job. But even for those who might have job-hunting skills, most businesses will not hire them. Finding a job is their most pressing need and the toughest to fulfill.

Statistically, a large percentage of people arrested are unemployed at the time of their arrest. There is a significant correlation between unemployment, inability to earn a living, and crime. Therefore, if we release prisoners back into society without preparing them to be successfully employed, we must take responsibility for the high rate of recidivism that will inevitably result.[58]

We know that ex-prisoners are often excluded from job opportunities—most particularly if they are not educated. Even those who do find jobs are often paid up to 30 percent less and have lower positions and fewer benefits than their counterparts who have not been incarcerated.[59]

"Employment prospects for ex-prisoners are further diminished because many of them have already developed behavior patterns that make holding a job difficult. Their bonds to conventional society are weakened after years of engaging in a criminal lifestyle, and then years in a prison culture, so that reestablishing these bonds becomes problematic."[60]

Many prisoners have lost contact with family, home, work, and social networks. Having adjusted to a prison regimen, they have lost hope and stimulation, and some have become passive and dependent. Many suffer from clinical depression. They are demoralized at best, or traumatized from prison conditions and violence at worst. They may be in poor health. Some have lost the ability to make decisions, form a plan, and withstand obstacles to achieve it. And, after excessive deprivation and harsh treatment, others are angry; they have become hostile to authority.

"... [I]f the institutions are boring, oppressive and lack programs preparing inmates for release, they come out angry, vindictive, frustrated, snarling like animals released from long confinement in a cage.... Cruel lockups, isolations, injustices, and harassment deliberately inflicted on prisoners unable to fight back make non-violent inmates violent, and those already dangerous more dangerous."[61]

Even the most intelligent and educated prisoners have a hard time. Ex-inmates, regardless of their educational levels, encounter numerous barriers to successful reintegration:

- Inadequate preparation for the job market due to prison security restrictions or low program funding and outdated equipment,
- low self-esteem and behavioral disorders, and
- reluctance of the business world to hire ex-inmates.

The obstacles associated with successfully re-entering society are even worse for 68 percent of parolees who are hardly literate and have had no schooling beyond the sixth grade. They are overwhelmingly undereducated compared with the general population, have lower literacy levels, fewer high-school diplomas, and almost no post-secondary education.

Women who are released from prison may encounter additional difficulties regaining custody of their children, dealing with aging relatives who need care, negotiating transportation difficulties, and overcoming poor health.

How long will the ex-inmate attempt reintegration before he or she gives up and returns to illegal behaviors to survive?[62]

Almost all prisoners, about 95 percent, are eventually released. "What happens when they are, however, is of little interest to the legislators who passed mandatory sentencing laws, abolished parole boards, and eliminated funding for prisoner education."[63]

According to Sheriff Lee Baca of Los Angeles, who manages the largest county jail system in the United States, we may protect society while criminals are in prison, but "you're not doing much when they get out.... They have to be better prepared ... to think differently about the free world and their choices."[64] Baca believes it's even more about changing the prisoners' mindset than teaching them specific knowledge.

The greatest barriers to successful reintegration into society for the released prisoner are drug and alcohol use, an inability to secure a job or pay for housing, and lack of family or social support.[65] At one time, parole boards evaluated a prisoner's preparation for release: whether there was a place to live, a job, or family support. Today, in this era of no-parole, "truth in sentencing" laws, they are released with no regard to the level of support available.[66]

The greatest risk of recidivism occurs within the first three to five months post-release. This is the most difficult time, as inmates try to reconnect with former relationships, both positive and negative, as they struggle to find work and housing and attempt to establish functional social networks. Recidivism can be further reduced by providing strong post-release support services, such as continued educational opportunities, introductions to employers who are willing to hire felons, assistance with housing and transportation, and substance abuse treatment as needed during those first very vulnerable post-release months.[67]

Sen. Patrick Leahy (D-VT) summed it up succinctly. He said, "I believe strongly in securing tough and appropriate prison sentences for people who break our laws. But we must also work to prevent crime and improve the reentry process to reverse the dangerous cycle of recidivism and violence."[68]

"Individuals need reentry planning and case management to help them navigate the reentry process and ensure that all the pieces are in place to facilitate their employment and continuing education."[69] "... prisoners should begin to prepare for their return home—even if it is years in coming—as soon as they are incarcerated. Prisons must provide the tools for a drug-free and crime-free life, [which would include] transitional job training and career planning the day the offender arrives at the prison."[70]

According to the Federal Bureau of Prisons website, their reentry preparation program begins with making available literacy classes, English as a second language, parenting instruction, wellness education for a healthier lifestyle and habits, library services, and leisure activities. Federal prisons offer a GED program for prisoners who have not graduated from high school, and they might provide rudimentary vocational training through on-the-job work assignments and post-secondary vocational education, in the few prisons where it is available.

Release preparation, the site continues, intensifies at least 18 months prior to release, and while some prisoners acquire work experience and skills through the Federal Prison Industries program or vocational training—which appears to be one and the same as the UNICOR program (*described in a later chapter*)—most do not. Sorting hangers, recycling trash, and similar chores, as are assigned in my prison, do not constitute vocational training. But even prisoners who have learned some skills do not know how to look for a job. This is an area where real training would be valuable.

The Federal Bureau of Prisons places some released prisoners in halfway houses intended to help them adjust to life on the outside and claims to help ex-prisoners find jobs and training opportunities after their release. Their website also says, "Some inmates will be eligible for a release gratuity, clothing, or money for transportation to their release destination." It does not specify which prisoners, or how many, or how much such gratuities amount to. What I have personally observed, watching fellow prisoners leave, is that most of them go with nothing more than a bus ticket.

Also available, according to the FBOP website, is additional pre-release employment assistance from The Inmate Transition Branch. This Branch is allegedly designed to help prisoners prepare folders that include a resume, education certificates, diplomas, transcripts, and other needed documents for a successful job interview. In some institutions (which ones, and how many, are not specified), the Inmate Transition Branch may present their skills to community employers when prisoners are about to be released and help prisoners practice interviewing skills. However, if such a department exists at my place of incarceration, it is well hidden from view.

Between what the website claims to offer for preparation for reentry into society and what prisoners claim to experience, there is a chasm of shadows.

Finding themselves impoverished, hungry, begging on street corners, and sleeping on streets, ex-prisoners get into trouble again. "Returning prisoners face challenges on many fronts ... [so that] education and training may not be their first priority as they struggle to meet their basic needs and reconnect with their families."[71] Those who do pursue education or employment may have difficulty with issues as basic as finding transportation to class or to their work.

Released prisoners reporting to a parole or probation officer may have to pay monthly fees to defray the costs of supervision and drug testing. Too frequently, parole and probation officers are unable to provide any real service. Underpaid, overworked, and dealing with sometimes angry or violent ex-prisoners, the attitude of these officers may be more adversarial than supportive. While there are many hard-working, committed professionals in this field, circumstances in which they work leave many unable to be of significant assistance to their clients.

A series of studies conducted by the Texas Criminal Justice Policy Council all confirm that by strengthening the intellectual, cognitive, and life skills of prisoners, prison education helps them overcome the barriers to positive community reintegration.[72] But even released prisoners who were fortunate enough to have received in-prison reentry preparation or training in study skills and life skills still need help. "We might get the prisoner training, education, and skills that qualify him or her for a good job in the community, but if they don't know how to look for a job, our investment is futile.... Some who are very skilled end up with a minimum-wage menial job because they don't know how to search for better work. Once they leave prison, the staff is cut off from them."[73] Many still don't know how to access funding, prepare a resume, or conduct an interview; they need basic computer skills and counseling. If they have taken post-secondary education courses while incarcerated, most would have done so via correspondence courses. That does not prepare them for live classroom education in a college or university.

The most critical factor in a re-entering individual's ability to succeed is funding. They enter the community with a very low-paying job or no job at all, with no savings or assets and poor credit histories. Many ex-prisoners have no credit history at all, because none of the major reporting agencies retain records on events occurring more than a decade ago. No credit history is considered as negatively as a bad credit history by many lenders. Frequently a large debt awaits their return, accrued from owed child support payments and/or criminal justice expenses. Many qualify for financial aid, but have no idea where or how to get it. The challenges a newly released prisoner faces are numerous.

Bottom line: Released inmates are hitting the street worse off than when they entered prison, without access to employment or training or education. "If we are serious about preventing and reducing crime," we must develop a greater focus on post-release support services.[74]

More than anything, we need to identify and implement effective strategies to prepare these people for reintegration into society in a way that allows them to become productive citizens. We need it not just for them, but for their families, for the safety and well-being of their communities, and for the prosperity of our nation. Reintegration of ex-prisoners should be an urgent priority for national, state, and local leaders.

A successful return to society, and the ability to remain out there, depends on a combination of factors:

1. sound correctional reentry planning and training programs,
2. a full-range correctional education program, including high school, vocational, and credit-based, degree-oriented college programs that ensure that course credits and certificates obtained during incarceration are recognized by the academic and employment communities to which these prisoners return outside of prison; and
3. help with applications to college, financial aid, and links to opportunities in the community—i.e., employment connections.[75]

Vocational training programs should be designed with reentry in mind. They must provide up-to-date skills and technologies and certifications that help released prisoners obtain stable employment and sustainable wages. They must be relevant to the job market and must take into account legal issues that bar felons from working in certain industries. It would certainly increase the effectiveness of an educational program to inform prisoners, when they begin their studies, of what jobs or careers they would be barred from so they don't waste time studying for these trades or professions.

One element of successful rehabilitation is seldom mentioned, but policy makers in Finland realize its importance, and that is family. Family support is key to an individual's ability to reintegrate. In the U.S., policies that restrict visitation, locate prisoners far from home, and charge exorbitant fees for phone calls weaken family ties.[76]

Few states provide focused reentry planning.[77] One exception may be North Carolina, which some say offers a model for success. In North Carolina, they have developed a business-and-industry advisory committee to provide input to the state on how to design basic and vocational education programs for incarcerated students.[78] This kind of interaction with community leaders and lawmakers can help to change the status quo.

One study[79] proposes a useful suggestion: Jobs could be reserved for released prisoners doing building maintenance, park services, street repair, etc. Obtaining paid employment immediately upon release to pay for food and shelter would help put ex-prisoners in a position to plan for vocational training or advanced education. It would turn them away from "the underground street economy" and provide a way to stay out of prison.

States could provide tax incentives to employers who hire ex-prisoners and the federal government can offer fidelity bonds to insure businesses that hire ex-offenders against potential employee dishonesty and theft.

Programs like these could be administered through the parole office. But to be successful, information about the programs must be disseminated effectively to all employers who might benefit. We currently spend tens of millions of dollars each year on homeless shelters and social services. With reformed prisoners gainfully employed, we could apply a good portion of that money to paying for productive post-release programs. Because turning ex-prisoners into productive, tax-paying citizens is far, far more economically advantageous than seeing them return to prison and having to pay for that.[80]

There still remains the question: Will the stigma of a prison record overpower the status of an education in the released prisoner's ability to find a good job? Prisoners could be taught how to deal positively with the issue as it comes up in interviews.

Jobs reduce recidivism. Especially jobs with a respectable level of compensation that permit a former prisoner to support a family and pay back debts. That is the key factor in transforming offenders into positive, law-abiding citizens.

Some prisons place prisoners in short-term reentry programs just before release. This is better than nothing, but not very effective. What we need are well organized, long-term programs.[81]

Current reentry programs have failed. Resources for supervising parolees are inadequate for their growing numbers, and many released prisoners are charged with technical violations that land them back in prison. "It is not at all clear that ... locking up parole violators enhances public safety. What we can say is that this approach is expensive."[82] "In order to break this cycle, we need to rethink the entire incarceration process, as well as procedures for release and recall."[83]

The harsh recession from 2008 to 2011 forced significant budget cuts, and corrections departments had to look for ways to effectively reduce recidivism. As a result, there is growing recognition of the need for comprehensive reentry services, and that they must begin at the start of incarceration.[84]

In 2007, Colorado adopted the Crime Prevention and Recidivism Reduction Package, reforms from which the state projected a cost savings of more than $380 million in five years.[85] Louisiana's inmates are evaluated when they enter the system for educational, health, and mental health needs, and they undergo three to six months of pre-release programs.[86] Maryland and Michigan are also expanding reentry initiatives to support greater rates of success upon release. They also found they could identify certain groups of prisoners who can be released safely after serving shorter terms.[87]

Historically, it has always been education that made assimilation, prosperity, and a high quality of life possible for immigrant populations. It can do the same for the incarcerated population. The safety, security, and prosperity of our nation require the successful reentry of released prisoners. Successful reentry for hundreds of thousands of ex-prisoners leaving prisons to live in our communities requires sound preparation that leads to jobs. And good jobs require postsecondary education. How difficult can that be for our policy makers to understand?

4

Barriers to Betterment: Roadblocks in the Cell Block

Prisoners engaged in educational activities report a lack of support or cooperation from correctional officers, some of whom are resentful and some of whom were reported to be baiting inmates into arguments and undermining students' efforts.[1] Some correctional staff have openly admitted to resenting the idea of prisoners receiving education when they, themselves, do not.[2]

Even though GED programs are offered in most prisons, many inmates cannot participate. If they don't have financial support from their families—and most do not—they have to choose between going to school and working to earn basic necessities like soap, toothpaste, etc. It was suggested that if correctional institutions provided the same incentives for pursuing an education as they do for prison labor, more prisoners would choose to pursue their education. "Why reward washing pots and pans," one prisoner asks, "instead of rewarding someone bettering themselves with a college education?"[3]

A number of factors limit the effectiveness of prison education programs in changing the skill levels and attitudes of inmates. Extreme crowding in prisons (many at 180 percent of capacity) and the need to maintain a secure environment at all times are two factors that most affect prison education programs. Even when courses are offered in prisons (usually at a very basic level), they may not be accessible. Some are full and have long wait times,[4] and many are not offered every semester. Science courses are especially limited because of laboratory restrictions, and students lack computer and keyboarding skills.[5] Also, prisons typically do not have adequate libraries, and there is no access to search engines, the Library of Congress, or other research sources.

There are other barriers as well:

1. A facility's commitment to education is dependent on the availability of private funding sources and the preferences of individual wardens;
2. an estimated 50 to 80 percent of inmates have learning disabilities, but few prison educators have been trained to recognize and accommodate learning disabilities;
3. the prison education programs may emphasize participation, but they do not support completion;
4. teaching strategies in adult basic education and high-school equivalency classrooms have not been adapted to the specific learning needs of an adult prison population;
5. the curriculum does not include instruction in social skills, self-control, conflict resolution, empathy, and cooperation; and
6. there is insufficient staff development for teachers.[6]

For the few prisoners who are fortunate enough to have the means for distance learning, there is no interaction with, or feedback from, an instructor, and that can make it hard to stay motivated. One cannot ask questions or get answers from DVDs and textbooks, and there are long delays in receiving feedback through the mail.[7]

Isolation is another factor. Many prisons make contact with family and supportive friends difficult because they are located far away in rural areas. Phone calls are expensive, and visiting requirements are "draconian." It creates an alienated, isolated underclass of people who cannot be easily reintegrated into society.[8]

All this could be overcome if online education were permitted, but this, too, requires the development of secure internet portals, as well as the resources for computers and video instruction.[9] However, the cost of these would be a small fraction of the cost of in-class live instruction.

In a period of economic and budgetary constraints, another innovative solution proposed was that rather than having inmates watching nonsensical TV programs all day, the prisons can substitute educational media, programs that teach socialization, life skills, health issues and preparation for employment. This can be done utilizing servers in the prison connected to the cable TV system and getting input from prison educators on appropriate programs and materials.[10]

Budgets Slashed in the Recession

As of 2012, all federal funding for post-secondary education in prisons has been eliminated. That's the long and the short of it.

While the federal penal code and criminal statutes in most states put forth the mission of prisoner rehabilitation, in reality the rapid growth of the prison population, together with current economic conditions, have forced significant reductions in budgets, which resulted in shutting down prison educational programs. "Prisoners may ... be the only group of U.S. citizens systematically barred from ... access to higher education."[11] Prisoners normally don't have the money to take courses on their own.[12] If the states or federal government do not provide education to inmates, they don't get any.

Previously there had been the Adult Education and Family Literacy Act of 1998, the Carl D. Perkins Career and Technical Education Improvement Act of 2006, and the only federal funding dedicated to post-secondary correctional education, the Incarcerated Youth Offender (IYO) grant, later renamed the Incarcerated Individuals Program.[13] All are gone now.

Whenever prison budget cuts become necessary, educational programs are the first to go. As a result, excellent funding sources and programs have been shut down entirely. Why? Because prison administrators see them as non-essential, or because other services, like medical care and sanitation are legally required and, therefore, get priority.[14] Lack of funding, space, and resources means limited class materials, poor equipment for vocational programs, obsolete technology, and untrained instructors. Therefore, if any prison education programs exist, they have to be operated and staffed by nonprofit organizations, volunteers, or the prisoners themselves.

The Incarcerated Individual Program (IIP)—Where the money comes from to provide advanced education to prisoners varies a great deal from one state prison system to another (see Appendix III for a more detailed discussion of funding sources). Until 2012, the most common source of funds for prison education (more than half) came from the IYO grants program, the name of which, in 2008, was changed to the Incarcerated Individual Program (IIP). Through this program, the U.S. Department of Education offered $1,500 to prisoners under the age of 25 and within five years of release. Later legislation expanded eligibility to prisoners under the age of 35 within seven years of release and increased the grants to $3,330. In North Carolina, the program was directed by the DOC's Education Services, with academic courses taught on-site in the prisons by numerous cooperating colleges and universities. It grew, expanded, and proved to be very effective in achieving student progress and a low recidivism rate. Said one student, "I need these classes to survive so I don't end up back in here." Or as others described it, the program was "turnin' coals into diamonds."[15]

"... [E]ducation directors in participating correctional facilities became avid supporters" of the program when they saw that it changed inmates' attitudes about education, it had a positive effect on post-release employment, and it served as a "catalyst for productive citizenry."[16]

In addition to providing college courses normally taken in the first two years at a four-year institution, IIP focused on strategies for problem solving, critical thinking and reasoning, negotiating conflict, and consequences to unproductive behavior. They also taught how to create resumes and cover letters, practiced job interview techniques, and helped students produce a plan for future education. Through its network of inter-organizational relationships, IIP had plans to double its curricula so prisoner-students could actually earn their degrees while still incarcerated.[17]

Alas, in 2012, funding for IIP was completely cut off. All programs dependent on IIP funding no longer exist. Alternative sources are hard to find in an economically tumultuous time. "This is a great setback for post-secondary correctional education and an issue that CEA is taking very seriously," said Stephen Steurer, Executive Director of the Correctional Education Association. "We are in constant contact with federal officials and legislators and involved in the efforts that are underway to reinstate funding in the next federal budget."

The Transforming Lives Network—Another extraordinary program that fell by recent budget cuts was the Transforming Lives Network, an accredited distance-learning service provided by the Correctional Education Association in partnership with the Wisconsin Department of Corrections and the Milwaukee Area Technical College. For a nominal fee of $1,195 per year, a prison facility could enroll an unlimited number of students or staff members in educational courses—more than 600 hours for staff development courses, and 1,500 hours of courses for prisoners which included academics and GED preparation, language arts, writing, math, social studies, science, ESL, and for-credit college courses through the College of the Air program. In addition, they offered courses in life skills and character development, finances, reentry transition, parenting, and many others.[18]

In 2005–2006 they had enrolled more than 300,000 prisoner-students! Yet, this program, as so many others, no longer exists because funding was withdrawn.[19]

Other states have fared no better. Until 2010, states' corrections budgets had steadily increased, but in the year 2010, at least half of all state prisons significantly reduced their budgets and eliminated educational programs, as well as cut prison staff that provided education,[20] even though funding requirements for prison education are small within the overall corrections budget.[21] With these forced reductions in 26 states, educational programs were the hardest hit.

According to the IHEP study of 2011, state financial support is vital to the success of post-secondary correctional education.[22] Unfortunately, however, the sources of funding for in-prison education that previously existed have mostly disappeared in our current climate of economic austerity.

Even in states where there are partnerships with community colleges, prisoner-students still have to pay tuition, books and other costs—an almost impossible burden for most.

An extreme example is in the state of Oregon, where, in 1980, an inmate could learn a vocation or study all the way up to a Ph.D. Today the state penitentiary has not a single teacher on its staff.[23]

North Carolina pays its community colleges according to student headcount. Prisoners included in that count earn the same dollars for the schools as traditional students.

Kansas had made huge improvements in community supervision practices and was a leader in reducing recidivism rates, but budget cuts now jeopardize this progress.[24]

Texas, a state that has consistently demonstrated commitment to prison education through the innovative creation of the Windham School District, has seen an unfortunate cut in its educational budgets by a whopping 25 percent, with a corresponding decrease in the number of prisoners who now have access to education. One of our country's model programs, alas, is severely reduced. This is a surprising development, considering that Texas has an innovative prison repayment program in place whereby prisons repay the State of Texas the cost of their education after their release. It means school closings, a lay-off of 271 staff members, and a serious reduction in school supplies. Windham's contracts with seven colleges that provided both academic and vocational training were not renewed.[25]

Indiana's current budget eliminated $9 million for college programs for prisoners. This state is now focusing almost entirely on vocational courses, those which lead to work skills. In so doing, the DOC canceled contracts with six colleges, eliminating all their liberal arts curriculums. Previously, 1,760 prisoners were enrolled in college courses, one of the highest enrollments in the country. "This is a tragic loss for prisoners, in favor of a more narrow vocational education."[26]

In Washington State, cuts in a grant from the Department of Education eliminated the college degree program at Connell prison and slashed half the program at the Walla Walla penitentiary, despite the recognition that educational classes are "one of the best ways to reduce recidivism."[27] The *Seattle Times* (March 4, 2013) called for lifting the ban on using state funds for higher education in prison and for reallocating the DOC's education funds to include higher education. It cited a report from the Washington State Institute of Public Policy that found that for every dollar invested in prison education, $4 is saved from costly incarcerations and use of social services. "Further savings come from crimes avoided, including property losses, medical costs, lost earnings and costs associated with a reduced quality of life."[28] The dividends paid in public safety are hard to quantify, but they are likely enormous.

California's prison education program is now a disaster. Despite having the highest recidivism rate in the entire country, the state of California experienced a $250 million budget cut in prison education programs. Legislators liquidated programs, slashed class hours, and fired two-thirds of the state's 1,200 prison teachers. To take their place, prisons trained long-term offenders as one-on-one peer tutors.[29]

In 2000, California legislation proposed to strengthen education within California prisons, and enrollment in college courses had increased among juvenile prisoners. However, budget cuts of recent years slashed—actually decimated—California's educational programs. Today, "California prisons are more anti-education than any prison system I've ever seen," said Tom Gehring, the director of the Center for the Study of Correctional Education at California State University–San Bernardino.[30]

At one time, Coastline College in Fountain Valley provided free correspondence programs and an associate's degree for prisoner-students. The state reimbursed the college for tuition, so that prisoners paid only for books and materials. In June, 2010, however, this program, sadly, came to an end. This is a prime example of short-term vision and lack of strategic planning. In the long run, it will have a devastating impact, not just on California's fiscal solidity, but on the well being of the entire state.

"Such short-term savings will undoubtedly result in long-term expenses, as education has been proven to reduce recidivism."[31] We must invest in innovative, evidence-based options that cut corrections costs while maintaining or improving public safety.[32]

Kansas, Michigan, New Jersey, and New York are making good strides in downsizing prisons. They have not, however, applied any of the savings to their education budgets.[33]

Despite hundreds of studies that show education to be the most effective method of cutting crime,[34] the trend in recent years has been to eliminate education within prisons. Even basic literacy programs (never mind higher academic programs) do not keep pace with rising prison populations.[35]

Community Education Centers, Inc.—Nineteen of the 26 states whose corrections budgets have been slashed are trying to cut costs by placing more offenders under community supervision, as an alternative to incarceration. Partnering with government and non-profit agencies to reduce recidivism, Community Education Centers, Inc. delivers therapeutic services in a healthy, drug-free, and safe environment to change addictive and criminal behaviors. They provide in-prison therapies that focus on drug rehabilitation, anger management, job readiness, vocational development, site-specific release preparation, relapse prevention, life skills, and risk assessment.

Once released, ex-prisoners can participate in CEC's Residential Reentry Services for substance abuse treatment, individual and group counseling, life skills, education (mostly ABE and GED and some post-secondary education), and vocational training programs.

However, community supervision alone has not been effective in preventing parolees or probationers from recidivating and, therefore, may not lower the incarcerated population or save state funds in the long run. Correctional education opportunities are difficult to obtain when individuals are under community supervision. Also, students in community-based correctional education programs generally have lower literacy and workforce skills than people in the general population.[36]

For most released prisoners and their parole or probation officers, the ultimate goal is for the student to find employment.[37] Programs must focus on helping offenders gain the skills they need to be productive members of society, striving to "not only change the lives of individuals, but also reduce recidivism and increase employment." These programs must be able to show results, documenting and collecting data that will demonstrate to policy makers and taxpayers that this is a good investment.[38]

A successful community supervision plan must include education and workforce training, treatment for substance abuse, assistance with housing, family reunification, mental health services and medical care, as well as assistance with finding employment that pays a living wage.[39] In addition to data and partnerships, hiring good instructors is key to success. Teachers who project a caring and nonjudgmental attitude can energize students who initially lack motivation.

Community-based educational programs must also have post-release case management and supervision. Such services, however, are rarely available to those with criminal records, either while incarcerated or after release from prison.[40]

Frequently these programs are provided by public school systems, community colleges, criminal justice agencies, and nonprofits working cooperatively with representatives of the criminal justice system, including parole and probation officers, residential facilities, and courts.[41]

Community supervision, however, has its challenges, including motivation on the part of released prisoners, as well as for their parole and probation officers. Many offenders struggle with substance abuse, discouragement, unemployment, inadequate housing, transportation, or medical care. If community-based correctional education programs do not address these factors, they cannot succeed.[42]

Some programs require offenders without a high-school diploma to attend school every day. Although ex-prisoners generally do not like to be required to attend school, the mandate at least gets them in the front door, and then it is up to the instructor to motivate them to learn. Some programs are housed within a correctional agency, an environment that gives the students more reason to comply.[43]

Another common challenge facing those running community-based correctional education programs is a lack of coordination and information-sharing from the correctional institution where the individual had been incarcerated. Although correctional institutions offer some educational programs, these programs are typically not aligned with those offered in the community, and the educational data collected by prisons generally do not align with data used by community-based correctional education programs. This disconnect within the correctional system only adds to an already difficult transition process for offenders.[44]

A more cost-efficient alternative to incarceration that will improve public safety and decrease recidivism rates may be achieved by coordinating community supervision with community-based correctional education and other support services.[45] To find out more, contact:

> Community Education Centers
> 35 Fairfield Place
> West Caldwell, New Jersey 07006
> Phone: (973) 226–2900
> http://www.cecintl.com
> Email: info@cecintl.com

In addition to drastic reductions in prison budgets, which have hit the prison education programs the hardest, and the lack of money on the part of prisoners, other barriers also prevent inmates from furthering their education.

Inadequate Basic Education

Teaching adult inmates is unlike teaching in any other environment. As compared to the general population, prisoners are under-educated and are more likely to come from a culture of poverty. They possess fewer skills for handling everyday tasks and have little or no experience in a trade or career.[46] As a result, prisoner-students often carry skewed, troublesome experiences of life and the world.

In the classroom, there will be many who have previously failed in the public education system, individuals with a wide range of cognitive abilities, a prevalence of learning disabilities, emotional and behavioral disorders, and mental illness, often undiagnosed and untreated. A significant number have limited English language skills,[47] and many of them require a lot of remedial help in English and math before they can attempt to participate in more advanced educational classes.

One teacher of a special education class (also known as a "learning lab") found that most of her prisoner-students had less than a fifth- or sixth-grade proficiency in reading and math. Another instructor observed that half the prison population where she taught was medicated. Even inmates who really wanted to learn could not absorb the information because of the effect of the medication on their thinking. Occasionally students from mental health units came into classrooms and created disruptions and had to be escorted out.[48]

In New Mexico, corrections officials reported that 10 percent scored at or below the third-grade level, 32 percent tested at or below sixth-grade levels in reading and math, only 50 percent had a high-school diploma, and fewer than 20 prisoners out of the state's almost 6,500 (.003 percent) had some college-level education.[49]

It boils down to the fact that many prisoner-students are not sufficiently prepared. Even those with a GED may be ill-prepared for college courses. They need more advanced study skills and writing ability. Math and science offerings are very limited, and there is no tutoring, nor research materials available to them.[50]

Health Issues, Physical and Mental

Instructors and teachers have to be unusually devoted to their work in order to penetrate the harsh realities of their prisoner-students' understanding. They must get past the clouded thinking of drug addiction and alcoholism, developmental disabilities, alienation, and despair that characterize some of the population, while trying to infuse new knowledge that will change destructive behaviors.[51]

There is a need for better methods of evaluating the eligibility and preparation of prisoners who are interested, because prisons also contain a growing population of individuals who are ready and able to succeed at college, people whose lives can be transformed by higher education. Prisoners like these are good candidates for college-level studies; they are the ones who will make a real difference in post-release success rates.

Teachers Need Tenacity

Because prisoners cannot leave the prison facility to attend classes, when courses require professional instructors the instructors must go into the prisons to reach them. But qualified educators in prison education programs are rare to nonexistent. ABE and GED courses are often taught by prison employees or inmates, not professional instructors. Credit from these courses may not be acceptable at other institutions, or by employers,[52] although standard requirements must be met for earning a GED.

To develop advanced college-level programs in prisons, the most proven way is for prisons to partner with external institutions: local colleges and universities who are willing to send in teachers.[53] However, because most prisons are built in geographically isolated areas, getting qualified teachers to come to the prison for on-site instruction can be difficult.

Without on-site instruction, the only other option is to teach through distance-learning technology. But this technology is not possible in prisons, because tools a normal school will take for granted are not allowed. Prisoners are barred from access to the internet, and prison libraries typically do not carry the needed materials. Even such items as rulers are sometimes considered contraband.

For teachers who are willing to teach on-site behind bars, prison security requirements impose significant constraints. Instructors and volunteers cannot enter or leave the facility easily. Clearance to come and go is difficult and, once inside, professors often must endure extensive security procedures before reaching the classroom and again on the way out. And there is no flexibility for instructors to run even a few minutes over class time to speak individually with students because "controlled movement" in prisons allows only 10 minutes for inmates to reach their next destination once a "move" is announced. Moreover, classes can be arbitrarily cancelled[54] and work assignments and hours can be changed without notice, so the students' attendance is not reliable.

These "facilities are first and foremost institutions of control and security, not classrooms or schools."[55] Prison culture and academia are diametrically opposed. "Prisons are closed institutions in which control is the primary concern and questioning authority is not tolerated ... colleges and universities are theoretically open places that encourage questioning."[56]

In addition to commuting the distance and subjecting themselves to security procedures, teachers have to adapt the courses and assignments they use on campus in order to accommodate restrictions imposed upon their prisoner-students.

Gathering prisoners with varying security classifications in one place can be tricky. Furthermore, teachers must accept frequent interruptions to students' participation in classes and students being absent for reasons beyond their control. Prisoners may be prevented from attending class because of an infraction, an upcoming parole hearing, or a visit from their attorneys. Even greater barriers keep prisoners out of classes, including short stays, frequent transfers, and disciplinary or other restrictions.[57]

If, at a time when classes are scheduled, the prison initiates a "lockdown," then prisoners must return immediately to their cells and remain. Lockdowns are a common occurrence in some prisons, sometimes lasting for weeks or months. In other prisons, they may occur only when an inmate is not where he or she is supposed to be.

It takes a lot of dedication and perseverance on the part of instructors to overcome the obstacles presented by a prison environment. They need special training and orientation to the peculiarities of prison teaching where security, not learning, has to be the priority. Many do not feel it is worth it, until they see how many prisoners are truly starved for education; that can really turn it around. Prisoner-students look to their teachers as the only people who have not given up on them, who believe in them and in their abilities. In many cases, these instructors are the last link between the prisoner-student and rehabilitation. "They don't ever want to leave the classroom," one teacher said.[58] Instructors who may initially be reluctant to teach inmates discover that they are easier to work with than traditional students because they are more committed to their education.[59]

Prison educators typically subscribe to the concept of behavior by expectation, as opposed to behavior by coercive rule, which is what inmates experience in prison. Coercive enforcement produces obedience, not cooperation, and not a desire to change. Rather than impose an idea on their students as to what is good for them (either for rehabilitation or for punishment), they inspire thinking. They help the prisoner-students discover what kind of behavior is really in their self-interest.

While mindful of why their students were sent to prison in the first place, attentive prison educators also remember that these same students will return to society. There, the students will have to care not only for themselves (as they've been used to doing in prison), but will also have to be concerned for the well-being of family members they will rejoin. In developing a sense of responsibility in these prisoners, educators may be helping their students find more constructive interests in life, interests that benefit others around them as well.

Despite the obstacles, which are very real, prison education programs can be very successful. Prisoners who once saw themselves as failures learn that their teachers are not patronizing them, and they start to realize they can do it. Their entire personalities change. Many—even those with life sentences—are eager for learning.

Education programs can flourish behind bars when there are dedicated educators supported by prison administrators and staff. It starts with planning and training and support for prisoners so that their education translates into employment and further education after release.

Key to their success are partnerships between the communities, the prisons, local educational institutions, and local business and industry, together with ties to political leadership.

Most people don't normally know about, or think about, prison life. But budget considerations and the social cost of over-incarceration make it critical that correctional administrators, policy makers, politicians and the general public understand that a sound investment in education can reduce costs, improve security and prisoner behavior inside our prison facilities, and contribute to a much safer, more prosperous world outside.

An Unlikely Environment

Prison is not an environment that encourages academic achievement. We have seen that it creates hardship for the instructors, and that is no less true for the prisoner-student who desires to learn. Inmates who want to study must do so with a constant blaring of noise, "voices and televisions reverberating off of metal surfaces."[60] Inmates express themselves in boisterous ways day and night, public address systems interrupt routinely, and security gates buzz piercingly. There are no quiet places to which one can escape to study.[61] Lacking quiet time to concentrate, students also lack the physical space to store books and other personal property. They have to work in small cells they share with one or more cellmates.[62] Or worse, they may live in a dormitory setting, with 50 or 100 other people in a room that is never quiet and where there is no privacy. Beyond all that, a reality of which people on the "outside" may be unaware is that within the prison culture, there are times when violence requires one to forget everything and focus entirely upon survival, times when personal safety is the priority.

Most prisoners have no internet access, no academic library, no access to tutoring, and are unable to find updated, relevant materials. Even simple supplies such as dictionaries, notebooks, pens, pencils, pencil sharpeners, highlighters, book lights, or sticky notes can be hard to come by.[63] There are, of course, no "office hours" and no way to call or e-mail professors with questions.

There are also usually restrictions on the number of books prisoners can keep in their cells and on the type of materials used for instruction. Federal prisoners are allowed to possess only five books at a time. To have more, even if needed for college correspondence courses, becomes risky. I, personally, was sanctioned with commissary loss for possessing too many books. (While not a pleasant situation, I would rather complete my assignments than eat well.) Nothing with a metal binding is allowed. Spiral notebooks, used by students universally, are barred because the metal binding can be undone for use as a weapon. Any equipment or substances that can be used as weapons or to manufacture drugs are barred. Therefore, obviously, no enrollment in chemistry lab courses is possible,[64] although a CD-ROM-based chemistry lab course might be authorized if the hardware and software were available, which it normally is not.

Whisked Away

Transfers are a major factor in prisoners being unable to complete courses. Overcrowded prisons and shortage of space cause frequent involuntary transfers of prisoners from one prison institution to another, even at times from one state to another.

This is one of the most difficult aspects of trying to obtain an education in prison: the fact that inmates are routinely transferred to other facilities involuntarily and with only days' or hours' notice. Transfers are disruptive to educational programs at any level. They interrupt coursework. Prisoners may be transferred to facilities with no college programming, which brings an abrupt end to earning credit or completing their degrees or certificate programs. Unfortunately, this frequently occurs regardless of how close they are to course or program completion. Their passport to survival when they are released goes up in smoke.

Completion of courses is key to the success of released prisoners trying to reintegrate productively into society and success in reducing the rates of recidivism. Therefore, until a system of coordination between prisons comes into existence, one that ensures educational continuity when prisoners are transferred from one facility to another, the hope of educating prisoners is dim.

One prison system working to correct the problem is in Virginia. The Virginia Department of Correctional Education is able to delay transfers of prisoners enrolled in education classes until they complete their coursework. On occasion, however, other factors (e.g., drug treatment) "trump" this agreement.

When considering these transfers, the Virginia DOC works closely with the Superintendent of the Department of Correctional Education to determine the best solution. Virginia's Department of Correctional Education also coordinates with contracting community colleges to ensure prisoners complete their coursework.[65]

North Carolina's Department of Corrections had also tried to address this problem by developing a prison education matrix. Based on a formula that factors in the length of a prisoner's stay at the facility, the matrix works to ensure that post-secondary prison education programs are offered only at prisons where prisoners would be able to finish them.[66] It may or may not work perfectly, but it is a laudable attempt to address a critical issue.

Policy Makers Play Politics

What prevents the necessary funding for prison education is the lack of support from policy makers and the voting public.[67] This is no doubt due to a lack of understanding of how this issue impacts the economic well-being and safety of our entire country. Until that support is there, higher education for most prisoners may be impossible.

Agencies Are Not Working on the Same Page

Complicating the development of effective educational programs is the fact that prison officials, prison educators, and higher education administrators often work for different agencies. These multiple agencies create additional layers of bureaucracy which may have conflicting priorities (security vs. education, for example). Without a strong, cooperative working relationship between these agencies, it is impractical to imagine a cohesive post-secondary prison education program.[68]

If the process were centralized, prison education programs could flourish. If, for example, the Department of Corrections and the State Board for Community and Technical Colleges worked together to create for-credit vocational certificate programs, or for-credit transferrable college-level courses from accredited schools, it could work in many systems. We've seen that it does work in North Carolina and other places that have initiated such cooperative contracts (see Chapter 5).

The Warden's Whim

In many prison facilities, the success or failure of educational programs depends entirely on a warden's or a superintendent's authority. If the warden does not believe in using public funds to offer post-secondary educational programs, there will be none—even if money is available. If a facility is currently offering post-secondary prison education and a new warden comes in, those programs may be shut down. Since there are usually no clear policies on the subject at the state or federal level, the warden makes the rules regarding the possession of textbooks, correspondence through the mail room, the use of the prison library, and other critical restrictions.[69]

Virtually every prison facility has the authority to allow or to not allow higher education programs and to negotiate with local colleges or universities to provide instruction. In the case of religious courses, approval must come from both the Education Department and the chapel. This may add extra layers of complexity to providing the course. To illustrate this, at one point I attempted to enroll in a theology course via correspondence, but was denied because it came from a religious school. It took two weeks of arguments with multiple staff members to gain approval. The issue wasn't the content of the course, but that policy didn't explicitly state that prisoners could take religious courses. So in the beginning I was given the default answer of "no." I had to work to gain a "yes." Because the policy is ambiguous, my facility, FCI Petersburg, now restricts prisoner-students from enrolling in post-secondary religious courses. Prisoners are not permitted to major in religious disciplines, such as theology or Christian studies, or even enroll at institutions which have a religious focus, such as the Moody Bible Institute, Brigham Young University, or Lee University.

Staff Support

Prison education might be able to overcome many of these challenges and function reasonably well if it had the support of prison staff to ease the way. Two states with the largest post-secondary prison education programs—Texas and North Carolina—have shown what can be accomplished when there is a statewide commitment to prison education and clearly defined policies that apply to all their prison facilities, policies that not only enable, but require prisons to offer higher education to prisoners. Sadly, this is not the case in most other states.

According to a study of the Institute for Higher Education Policy (and as observed firsthand by prisoners), prison staff often express resentment at the idea that prisoners would be offered educational opportunities which they themselves did not have.[70] In some facilities they are short-staffed and do not welcome the additional paperwork; in others, they are not encouraged to support such programs because their wardens don't believe in the benefits of inmate education.

"In 2003, a local chapter of the California Correctional Peace Officers Association undertook an active campaign to end state-funded post-secondary programs at two state prisons and was, in fact, able to persuade the warden at one facility to suspend the program."[71] Action like this on the part of prison staff to prevent post-secondary educational programming for prisoners is not unusual. Understandably, it can and does create real antagonism and frustration. In my own facility a severe reduction in ACE courses and teaching hours in 2012 was met with disappointment by inmate instructors and students alike.

An uncooperative prison worker can be extremely obstructive to educational programs at the post-secondary and other levels. Prison guards might, for example, refuse to release a prisoner from his or her cell to attend class. They might confiscate a prisoner's texts. They can do almost anything they want to thwart the efforts of prisoners who are capable of and eager for learning.

In various prisons where I have served time, what I have personally observed regarding some of the prison education staff and guards is lethargy. Many are unwilling to assist after class, and some appear completely uninterested in seeing prisoners become educated. They seem to be focused instead on when their shift ends and how to get by doing as little as possible until that time. This is sad, but well documented by those who study the prison environment. Two things can make a positive change here: a warden committed to post-secondary prison education and a dedicated educational coordinator.

5

Oases in the Desert

Despite the obstacles, which are very real, a few academic institutions offer higher education programs for prisoners that have proven to be extremely successful. According to the Federal Bureau of Prisons Program Statement 5354.03: Post-secondary Education Programs for Inmates (see Appendix I), all federal prisons "may offer on-site liberal arts and/or four-year college programs when feasible." However, whether educational programs exist in any specific prison depends on (1) whether the facility is geographically close to schools interested in participating, and (2) the whim of the warden at the specific prison. Sadly, administrators at most facilities have chosen not to.

Because state and federal governments do not spend money on higher education in prisons, the few success stories and college programs we describe below must rely on volunteers and the funding of private donors. These programs are the exception to the rule and represent isolated pockets of opportunity. But they do prove that education within prisons can achieve extraordinary results.

Education programs flourish behind bars when there are dedicated and qualified educators supported by prison administrators and staff, along with encouragement for prisoners to participate.[1] Incentives such as expanded access to visitation or commissary, good time credits that increase proportionately as the level of education completed gets higher, and recognition of the prisoner's efforts in the form of certificates, awards, and completion ceremonies go a long way. Yet experience shows that once prisoners are engaged in educational courses, they don't need incentives. They will do almost anything to be allowed to continue.

Following are programs we know of. Some have turned convicts into university professors and CEOs of successful companies; others provide academic college courses and vocational training in prisons, and still others focus on assistance with preparation for prisoners' release.

Prisoner-Professors Revolutionize Criminology

It is exciting to discover that a number of ex-prisoners who have gone so far as to earn their doctorate degrees have actually been appointed to permanent positions as faculty members at prestigious colleges and universities.

Not surprisingly, many former prisoners who teach at universities go to great pains to conceal their past record, fearing the reactions of their colleagues, university administrators, and the community—as well as concern about losing their jobs. Frank Tannenbaum, an ex-convict and professor at Columbia University in the 1930s, was an open exception who enjoyed a prolific career as a journalist, author, scholar, political activist, and organizer. However, most academic faculty members understandably felt a need to hide their history of incarceration—although this has become increasingly difficult, since virtually all states require criminal background checks for those who teach at publicly funded institutions.

In time, however, a group of these prisoners-turned-professors found themselves frustrated by criminology professionals, researchers, policy makers, and politicians who had no real understanding of crime, prison, or solutions. They decided, rather courageously, to "come out" for the first time in 1997, at the conference of the American Society of Criminology (ASC). They did so by presenting a seminar called "Convicts Critique Criminology."[2]

The seminar drew a large audience, including a great many from the media, and resulted in the publication of a book called *Convict Criminology*, which offered a new perspective in the academic field of criminology. These former prisoners, holders of Ph.D. degrees and academic faculty positions, felt that the academic literature on criminology never incorporated "what convicts knew about the day-to-day realities of imprisonment ... these works tended to gloss over the horrors of prison, inventing a sanitized presentation without the smell of fear and noise of desperation known so well by the men and women that live in cages ..." Many studies approached the subject abstractly, often without ever entering a prison or interviewing prisoners.[3] For the first time, this group of academics presented the true-to-life experiences of their own and of other prisoners in order to combat misrepresentations by scholars, media, and the government. They injected a view of reality and proposed innovative, less costly, more humane, and ultimately more effective solutions. So began a plethora of studies and media appearances.

Since 1997, the Convict Criminology group has organized nearly 50 sessions, panels, roundtables, and workshops at academic events in the U.S. and abroad. They are very active in analyzing public policy concerning felons, convicts, and ex-convicts.[4]

The "New School of Convict Criminology" is described on its website as a relatively recent and controversial perspective in the field of corrections and the academic field of criminology, challenging the way crime and its control are traditionally represented and understood. These professors provided insight from their firsthand knowledge of the prison world and opened up new dimensions to the study of corrections and criminology, jails, prisons, and the criminal justice system.

The Convict Criminology group has grown and continues to grow. More and more ex-prisoners complete degrees and become professors; more are rising in the ranks to earn tenure and contribute meaningful research. They mentor other prisoner-students and help them to secure academic faculty positions.[5] Today, studies and papers produced by the Convict Criminology group are included in textbooks and academic journals; their perspective has become an integral part of many university criminology courses.

Convict criminologists working in universities have the advantage of academic training in sociology, political science, criminology, and related disciplines, together with the empirical experience of having been prisoners or prison workers. Their stated goal is to make the public, academics, and policy makers aware of the realities of confinement and the social and psychological obstacles to a successful reentry into the community.[6] They are working to expose injustices faced by ex-prisoners when they study on college campuses, including Ph.D. students who are not permitted to defend their dissertations and professors (of whom ex-convicts are still very few) who are denied tenure and/or promotion. The Convict Criminology group recommends that all colleges and universities hire academic advisers who can serve felons, as they do for other minority groups.[7]

Additionally, ex-convict professors serve as role models, mentors, and advisors for prisoners and ex-prisoners who are completing college degrees in the social sciences.[8]

The book *Convict Criminology*[9] inspires prisoners and guides them in preparing a way to get themselves to college. Subsequently, the Convict Criminology group has also developed *Inviting Convicts to College,* a free, non-credit, college preparatory course from the University of Wisconsin's Oshkosh campus. Designed to help prisoners make wise decisions about enrolling in a college or university when they are released, the course teaches the academic skills convicts will need to succeed in college, as well as an introduction to the field of criminology studies. Faculty teaching the course come into the prisons from a number of various disciplines, including anthropology, business, English, psychology, and others.[10]

Serving as a bridge between prison and the university, the *Inviting Convicts to College* course costs the universities nothing, because it is taught by student interns and the universities do not have to deploy faculty. It costs the prisons nothing. And it costs the prisoners nothing, as well.[11]

Prisoners receive a certificate of completion, signed by a university dean and prison administrators, so that when released, they qualify for admission to a fully accredited college or university, as well as for financial aid.

Enrolling in a college becomes part of the prisoners' release plan. Often, when prisoners show their fellow convicts their letter of acceptance to a college, it inspires others to follow suit. Many of the prisoners who complete the course leave prison and enroll in universities. One prisoner said the course made him realize that being a convicted felon doesn't mean he can't succeed. Another said it was the first time he realized someone cared about what happened to him. It is a source of hope for people who have never had anybody care and an inspiration to start planning for a future.

The movement has evolved to a point where there has developed a divide among members. Some are more concerned with maintaining academic excellence in research, prison reform, and mentoring the incarcerated, while others want to focus more on activism and reform.

The original founders view themselves as academics, not activists. They believe that to be taken seriously, they must produce factual information and knowledge, not polemic. They caution that having had the prison experience is no substitute for carefully conducted research. "If time spent behind bars [were] the only criterion for being an authority, then every hospital patient would be an expert on the health care system."

They warn against members who focus more on airing personal grievances and disseminating unsupported statements or broad generalizations without a solid foundation of research and logic. The movement, they felt, had become infused with members who may be articulate and intelligent, but who lack the training for advanced degrees such as the Ph.D. and whose writings and discourse may not be able to meet the standards of a rigorous peer review.[12]

Founding members warn against the activist movement as "a dangerous development" that can destroy their hard-earned positive achievements. The academic route is slower, they claim, but has a better chance of enduring success. They fear that "sacrificing strict academic rigor for popular activism will spell the end of Convict Criminology as a creditable source of knowledge ..."[13]

More information is available from:

Dr. Stephen C. Richards
Professor, Department of Public Affairs
Criminal Justice Program

University of Wisconsin-Oshkosh
800 Algoma Boulevard
Oshkosh, Wisconsin 54901
Office: (920) 424–2179
Cell: (920) 904–3737
Office: scrichards@charter.net
http://www.convictcriminology.org

From Convict to Ceo: A Course in Success

Prison Entrepreneurship Program, P.E.P., is one of the most exciting prison education programs we have yet encountered. People ought to know about it because it is innovative, brilliant in its concept, and so effective in transforming the lives of murderers, gang leaders, and drug dealers. Today they are executives, MBAs, pastors, and professionals.

P.E.P. is built upon the belief that exceptional talent exists behind bars. Instead of sending released prisoners back on the streets to commit more crime, the program connects them with highly successful business people who can teach them legitimate skills and challenge them to maintain high standards for their lives.

P.E.P. brings some of the nation's top business executives, MBA students, and politicians together with prisoners who thrive on challenge and accountability. Uniting them through education, values-based entrepreneurial training, and mentoring, they create a positive life transformation for the executives and prisoners both.

And they do it with startling results. With more than 700 graduates since 2004, the P.E.P. program has an unusually high success rate. One ex-prisoner who had spent 15 years in prison for gang activity and murder said, "P.E.P. gave me the vision to succeed and reenter society. Now I can show society that I am a changed man and that I can make it."[14]

But it is not an easy ride. It is a tough program to get into and tough to stay. Eligible prisoners face a rigorous application process designed to eliminate those who "still act like criminals." Other applicants drop out because the intense study requirements and continuous homework assignments are more than they want to deal with. In the end only 15 to 30 percent of applicants remain in the P.E.P. program: those who are determined and motivated, who love the hard work, desire transformation, have a strong work ethic, and demonstrate entrepreneurial ability.

To qualify for entry into the P.E.P. program, prisoners must:

- be male,
- have at minimum a GED or high-school diploma,
- be within three years of release,
- have a clean recent disciplinary case history,
- have no history of sexual convictions,
- have no current gang affiliations, and
- be committed to personal change and willing to live in a positive environment.

For those who succeed in getting in and remaining in the P.E.P. program, its in-prison and post-prison offerings are comprehensive. They include:

- business education and training,
- proactive reentry support,
- job search assistance,
- continuing education,
- business development assistance,
- one-on-one mentoring, and
- employment.

Does it work? The proof is in the results:

1. The recidivism rate for P.E.P. participants is less than 5 percent!
2. 98 percent of program participants find jobs within one month of release![15]

Let's see how they do it.

P.E.P. Services in Prison

Business Training and Business Plans: P.E.P. offers a five-month in-prison program where participants learn both the theory and practical application of basic business concepts. With 18–20 class hours per week, inmates craft a plan for a business they might start when they are released from prison. P.E.P. advisors provide feedback regarding the concept, realism, feasibility, and grammar of the plans, and the prisoner-trainees rework their plans until they are excellent: not just business plans that are "good for a prisoner," but plans that rival those of an MBA-educated professional—Plans that will attract capital from investors.

Presentation Skills and Networking: During the five-month program, leading business executives from across the country come to the prisons to critique the aspiring entrepreneurs' sales pitches and presentations on why an investor should want to fund their business. Executives play the role of potential investors: some frugal, some distracted, others impatient, all of them asking difficult questions. What is important here is that participants not only learn to sell effectively, but they get to meet at least 100 business executives from the outside world while they are still in prison—executives who are there to provide valuable, substantial feedback and who also create a network which will be critical to the prisoners' success upon release.

In addition to business training, during the five-month program, prisoner-trainees learn decision-making skills using real-life situations to inspire integrity and moral excellence. These aspiring businessmen are taught to look and act like professionals, with instruction in the art of dress and dining etiquette. Prisoners are prepared for job searching after release with mock interviews where they are taught to present their qualifications effectively. The program also includes life lessons on fatherhood, substance abuse, marriage, dating, respect for authority, spirituality, and much more.

At the end of the five-month entrepreneurship training program, the prisoner-students make polished, 30-minute investment presentations on their completed business plan to a judging panel of executives. The competition, followed by a formal cap-and-gown graduation ceremony, is, for many of the prisoner participants, the greatest accomplishment of their lives and their first-ever graduation.

P.E.P. Services Post-Prison

Reentry Support: The most vulnerable time for a released prisoner occurs in the first 72 hours after stepping outside the prison walls. P.E.P. case managers are there the moment the program participant is released to the street. They pick up the trainee at the prison gate and transport him to their halfway houses. They provide transportation to parole offices, food-stamp offices, churches, drivers' license offices, and job interviews. Trainees get bus passes, phone cards and—through P.E.P.'s partnerships with private service providers—reduced-cost or free dental care, eye exams and glasses, medical care, and more permanent housing, once they have proven themselves accountable. P.E.P. case managers also assist with counseling, a support network, and emergency financial assistance.

In short, P.E.P. will do whatever is necessary to make sure their program participants do not fail.

Job Search Support: National statistics indicate that 89 percent of released prisoners who return to prison are unemployed at the time of arrest. To avoid the pitfall of unemployment, P.E.P. equips each participant with:

- professional resumes and cover letters,
- letters of reference,

- career counseling to determine industries of aptitude and interest,
- training in advanced interview techniques,
- assistance completing applications,
- job referrals,
- scheduled interview appointments,
- transportation to the interviews,
- introductions to business executives through networking events, and
- clothing for interviews and work.

P.E.P. circulates the trainees' resumes, together with reference letters, to their expanding network of executives and employment services providers. This network, comprising strong and carefully developed relationships with employers in the community, is key to the success of the trainees. It is the primary reason why an unprecedented 98 percent of program participants have jobs within the first month of release.

Entrepreneurship School and Executive Mentors: Having completed the five-month course while still in prison, released prisoners can attend P.E.P.'s weekly Entrepreneurship School at Rice University in Houston and at the University of Dallas. Courses in sales, marketing, business, and personal financial management are taught by CEOs of billion-dollar, publicly traded companies, venture capitalists at top-tier firms, and specialized university professors. When participants complete at least 20 workshops, they are eligible for small-business financing through P.E.P.'s network of "angel" investors.

When attending the Entrepreneurship School and proving themselves accountable to P.E.P.'s ethical and other rules, trainees are matched with executive mentors with whom they can meet weekly. P.E.P. provides training to the mentoring executives, as well as to the prisoner-participants, and they oversee all mentor/participant relationships to ensure a positive personal transformation and accountability. Mentoring executives provide:

- guidance for the trainees' reestablishment in society,
- a role model/father-figure who holds the participant accountable,
- assistance with job upgrades and networking with other executives,
- coaching through the Entrepreneurship School courses, and
- guidance in launching and growing a small business.

Business Development Assistance: When former prisoners actually start a business and become new entrepreneurs, they get a powerful kick-start from pro-bono consultation on nearly every aspect of their startup businesses from P.E.P.'s network of top-tier business experts. Moreover, they are able to acquire new clients through P.E.P.'s ever-expanding network of influential volunteers.

A Houston-based 501(c)(3) nonprofit established in 2004, P.E.P. was founded by Catherine Rohr, who had built a successful career in private equity as director of investment development for American Securities Capital Partners in New York City and as a venture capitalist at Summit Partners in Palo Alto, CA, working with more than 4,000 CEOs and generating $32 million in equity investments. Her belief in the potential business talent behind bars was so strong, even among prisoners who averaged a seventh-grade education, it moved her to abandon her career to develop that talent.

Rohr understood that teaching business and entrepreneurial skills in prison was not enough; the curriculum had to address the critical issues of men reentering communities from prison without even the most rudimentary resources. She devoted herself fully to building a program that responded to all the aspects necessary for a released prisoner's success.

At the conclusion of the first in-prison course, when 55 prisoners presented professional business plans complete with operating budgets and financial analyses to visiting executives, the impressive event was reported in the *Wall Street Journal.*

There is, however, one serious limitation to P.E.P. It functions currently only for male prisoners and only in Houston, Dallas, and Fort Worth, Texas. It has not yet expanded into other states, nor is it open to women. Rohr has started something similar called *Defy Ventures* in New York and, having built a network of supporters across the USA, she intends to take *Defy* nationwide. Hopefully, she will succeed in bringing it to many other parts of the country, because programs like this are our best hope for peace, compassion, and prosperity in our nation.

Employment with P.E.P.: P.E.P. is staffed with many expert free-world people with business backgrounds, including their volunteer governing and national advisory boards that comprise senior business professionals and influential executives. However, P.E.P. also employs graduates of the program upon their release from prison, tapping into the talent that exists behind bars.

P.E.P. employees are expected to demonstrate a strong work ethic and moral values. While it is not a faith-based organization, those who built the organization believe in the power of God to transform an individual, and their teaching incorporates spiritual attributes such as generosity, obedience, integrity, and purity. P.E.P. is available to prisoners of all faiths and incorporates the wisdom and expertise of executives from all faiths.

P.E.P.'s nonprofit organization, funded exclusively from private sources and not from taxpayer dollars, is particularly proud of the fact that 13 percent of all donations come from graduates of the P.E.P. program themselves.

Prison Entrepreneurship Program (P.E.P.)
P.O. Box 926274
Houston, TX 77292–6274
http://www.prisonentrepreneurship.org

Getting Ready for Work: Vocational and Trade Training

Post-secondary correctional education can be either academic or vocational. Both help prisoners reintegrate into society when released, but vocational programs focus specifically on trade skills.

Ex-offenders represent an untapped potential source of useful skills that could be a valuable resource to the nation. If employers get on board with reentry programs, they may discover a profitable pool of dedicated employees.[16] One visionary employer is the InterContinental Hotel Group in the UK, which provides training in catering and other work skills to prisoners while they are still incarcerated. Of the many skills that need to be taught, the most important is computer and internet literacy if a released prisoner is to survive in today's working world.[17]

Job sectors where released offenders might most easily obtain employment include: temporary help services, manufacturing, wholesale and retail trades, construction, and lodging and food services.[18] Temporary help requires competency in computer skills, reading, math, communication and other office skills. In construction, the highest demand is for carpenters, laborers, electricians, project managers, painters, maintenance, plumbers, pipefitters and steamfitters, engineers, equipment operators, sheet metal workers, cement finishers and concrete masons.[19]

When the Institute for Higher Education Policy (IHEP) conducted a 50-state analysis of post-secondary prison education policies,[20] it found that prison education programs had shifted away from the academic and trended increasingly toward vocational training, so that most prisoners who earned a degree or certificate in college classes were enrolled in vocational programs.[21] Only 28 percent were enrolled in an academic associate's degree program and a mere 3 percent were enrolled in a bachelor's or graduate degree program.

All federal prisons and most state prisons offer courses in basic life skills, literacy, and the high-school diploma equivalent (the GED). Beyond that, when it comes to vocational post-secondary prison education, only two states have significant programs: North Carolina and Texas. Both these states have shown a firm commitment to vocational prison education and have clearly defined policies that require all their prison facilities to offer post-secondary education to prisoners. It should be this way everywhere.

Texas: The Windham School District

Education is a key component of the rehabilitation program in Texas, which has one of the largest prison systems in the country. The majority of prison educational programs in Texas are vocational in nature.

As far back as 1969, the State of Texas has operated the Windham School District to provide post-secondary adult education programs within prison facilities of the Texas Department of Criminal Justice (TDCJ). The district operates with the motto: "Fighting Crime through Education," and it works well. As of 2006, the district was teaching 23 different occupational trades to roughly 60,000 inmates in approximately 90 facilities. Two-thirds of these worked toward an associate's degree, while others pursued vocational certificates. Texas had a 24 percent completion rate for its post-secondary education program, one of the highest in the nation.[22] A critical key to the success of this program is that eligible prisoners in a Texas facility that has no college program can apply for transfer to a facility offering the program of their choice.[23]

In 2000, after the Criminal Justice Policy Council evaluated the school district, it issued a report stating that only 16 percent of the participants were reincarcerated, as compared to an average of 68 percent in areas without the schools. "An overwhelming 84 percent did not recidivate."[24]

Windham was the first school system of its size to be established within a statewide prison system and one of the largest prison education systems in the nation. It had been funded with nearly $60 million per year from the Texas Department of Education. Almost all of that is allocated to basic, remedial, and lifestyle classes, while only $2.3 million per year goes to the college program (which formerly received additional funds from the now defunct "Youth Offender" grants).

The post-secondary education program in Texas works in cooperation with 15 two-year colleges and three universities that provide the instruction for prisoners. "When selecting educational programs to offer, Texas considers ... occupations in demand" and other factors to ensure the success of the programs.[25]

The programs are financially sustainable through Texas's creative reimbursement program. Released prisoners work with their parole officers to establish a manageable re-payment plan. Through payments averaging about $100 per month, thousands of ex-prisoners have paid their debts in full. The money is funneled back into the system to support more prison education programs and ensure their continuance for future prisoners in Texas.[26] For more information, contact:

Windham School District
P.O. Box 40
804 Bldg. B, FM 2821 West
Huntsville, TX 77320

North Carolina: Uniquely Successful

North Carolina operates one of the most comprehensive post-secondary correctional education programs in the United States, second only to Texas, educating more than 16,500 prisoners in 70 prisons each year. Beyond the GED, Basic Education and Life Skills, in North Carolina the emphasis is on vocational training.

What makes the North Carolina education program unique is that it reaches more than one-third of the state's prisoners each year.[27] That is an unprecedented and impressive number. One-third of the state's prisoners participate in an educational program so prisoners can function effectively when released back to the community.[28]

North Carolina prisons identify prisoners who have educational needs and would benefit from educational services. In some instances, the Department of Corrections goes so far as to refer prisoners to prisons where the educational program is commensurate with his or her skills and interests.

Another key to the success of the college-corrections partnership, and which ensures that prisoners enrolled in educational courses complete the program, is the "correctional education matrix." The matrix is a system to determine which prison facilities are permitted to offer which types of educational programs. It is based on a formula which takes into account the average length of time prisoners remain, in order to ensure that specific programs are offered only at prisons where inmates could finish them.[29]

Upon incarceration, all prisoners take tests to help case managers determine what kind of education—academic, vocational, and/or life skills—is most appropriate to the individual's background and aspirations. Typically, the NCDOC is supportive of prisoners who seek an education. Those who have no high-school diploma or GED or who score below sixth-grade levels of reading or math are required to enroll in educational programs. "Programs at the post-secondary level are optional and provided to inmates who meet eligibility criteria."[30]

The program, which began in 1987, has evolved over the years. By 1994, a statewide Prison Education Task Force created a system to match educational offerings at each prison facility with the prisoner's ability and length of stay.

The North Carolina Department of Corrections has been working closely for more than 30 years with the North Carolina Community College System, the University of North Carolina, and Shaw University to go beyond providing courses in basic skills (ABE), literacy, ESL, and the GED. The University of North Carolina provides limited on-site instruction, as well as courses through video and web conferencing and a comprehensive vocational training program for prisoners. Eligibility for UNC correspondence courses is tightly restricted and is funded by both the Education Welfare funds and, formerly, by the Incarcerated Youth Offender Grant (later named the Incarcerated Individual Program and now defunct). Shaw University is a historically black, four-year college offering associate's and bachelor's degrees at two of the facilities, assuming all financial responsibility for funding their program, which has strict eligibility requirements and limited enrollment.

The community college system is by far the primary provider and offers the vast majority of courses. It is the close partnership of the community college system and the Department of Corrections that develops the detailed policies and procedures for post-secondary correctional education to ensure the programs are of a quality to warrant using taxpayer funding. They also use a contact-hours system rather than student membership hours to ensure that the colleges receive their revenue and that students complete their courses.[31]

What is also unique in North Carolina is that post-secondary education is fully funded by the state. Unlike most states, which lay the costs of education upon the prisoners themselves, North Carolina uses state funding to pay for post-secondary correctional education and provides it to more than 10,000 inmates.[32] Prisoners receiving instruction from a community college pay no tuition. The community college system receives roughly $50,000 a year from the General Assembly to provide education and training to prisoners. Another source of funding is from the Inmate Welfare Fund collected from the prison canteens and prisoner telephone calls. These sources provide "equipment and supplies, including books, computers, inmate desks and chairs, and writing and project materials."[33]

The State of North Carolina's governing bodies made it mandatory that the same level of educational quality be maintained within prisons and on college campuses, so that there is no difference between them. All the degree and credit-bearing courses located on-site within the prisons are exactly the same as those offered to local residents.[34] Together the DOC and the community college system plan courses to ensure they reflect current educational technology and demands in the workplace.[35]

Furthermore, only courses that lead to a degree will be approved by the state board. When inmates are released from prison, they receive college transcripts that are identical to ones they would receive had they taken courses as non-incarcerated students. Their certificates, degrees, and diplomas are identical to those offered outside prison,[36] and because these courses are taught at a level and with a quality equal to that of regular students,[37] credits can be transferred to almost any community college or, for prisoners who earned an associate's degree, to any university in the state or throughout the country. That makes it much easier for prisoners who participate in these programs to continue on for a college degree upon release.[38]

The state does not make specific appropriations for prison education; rather, it counts prisoners enrolled in college courses together with regular students and funds them all equally. Both types of students receive the same amount of support.[39] However, before they will provide advanced-level academic courses, the community colleges require satisfactory library resources, support personnel, sufficient classroom space, and properly equipped laboratories, as well as an adequate number of qualified prospective students within the facility. Few facilities can meet these requirements.

Payment to the colleges in North Carolina is based not on the number of prisoners or students enrolled, but rather on the hours students are actually in attendance. This is to address the problem of inmates being removed, transferred, etc., before completion. It gives the colleges a way to ensure that the North Carolina Department of Corrections will work with them to ensure that prisoner-students complete their courses. "Given that revenue generation was a primary reason for the partnership between the North Carolina Community College System and the North Carolina Department of Corrections, if the ... college could not earn FTE for a course, it would not offer it within the local prison."[40] "FTE" is an acronym for "full-time equivalent." The FTE data reported on the rosters form the basis of funding formulas, so that the school's revenue is determined by reports of student enrollment and attendance and contact hours for each curriculum. Timely completion of attendance is necessary for the college to claim earned FTE. Unless the colleges are able to provide the courses, the prisons would have to find more costly ways to prevent inmate idleness.

North Carolina, the second highest provider of post-secondary correctional education (after Texas), takes a pragmatic approach to post-secondary prison education. The North Carolina Department of Corrections and North Carolina Community College System believe prisoners need programming that leads to immediate employment upon release. Said one Department of Corrections employee, "If we want an ex-prisoner to have any reasonable chance of going out and securing employment, we should be providing the type of training that will enable them to do that ... there's no magic bullet to this; it is common sense. Those fields are in the trades. They're in the technical fields."[41] Therefore, North Carolina's post-secondary prison education programming does not focus on advanced academics, but rather predominantly on vocational training. Prison industries designed to reduce prisoner idleness and help the state benefit from incarcerated labor include concrete pipe pouring, farming operations, and tailoring.[42]

Two issues remain problematic, even in North Carolina: one is the public perception of "unfairness" in providing free college education to prisoners when law-abiding citizens must fend for themselves. The other is a difficulty with the limitations of technology that attempts to utilize video-conferencing to deliver university-level courses. Distance education efforts are hampered by security concerns about inmates using the internet.[43]

All that notwithstanding, the coalition that brings together North Carolina's prison administrators, college educators, and business and industry advisors has all the elements for success. It not only taps the expertise of business and society leaders as members of a team effort, but it also elicits commitment from employers to hire former prisoners who were educated in the system they support. It is a commitment maintained statewide "because local communities, including prisons, colleges, and employers benefit from it."[44]

For more information, contact:

North Carolina Division of Prisons, Education Services
831 West Morgan Street
4264 MSC
Raleigh, NC 27699–4264
(919) 838–4000
or
North Carolina Community College System
5020 Mail Service Center
Raleigh, NC 27699–5020
(street address: 200 West Jones Street, Raleigh, NC 27603–1379)
(919) 733–7051

Michigan, New Jersey, North Carolina: Pathways from Prison to Post-secondary Education Project

Pathways, a recently launched program in Michigan, New Jersey, and North Carolina, puts prisoners into intensive vocational or college courses two years before their release and transitions them from their educational program into the job market.[45] It is a five-year experiment that will be evaluated by the RAND Corporation with the hope that the findings will motivate public investment in prison education.

States involved work closely with employers to obtain jobs for released prisoners who complete the program, and they provide mentoring and tutoring and parole policies that are supportive and collaborative, rather than merely enforcing rules. These states are also experimenting with technological access for prisoners, including controlled internet access.[46]

A highly innovative aspect of the program is that these states will house prisoner-students in a separate housing unit to stimulate positive reinforcement from peers.[47]

Pathways is sponsored by the Vera Institute of Justice and funded by prominent organizations such as the Bill and Melinda Gates, Ford, Kellogg, Open Society, and Sunshine Lady Foundations.

New Jersey and North Carolina already have post-secondary educational partnerships with community colleges and nearby universities, but for Michigan this is a fresh beginning.[48] In order to reduce the state's recidivism rates, Michigan's DOC is launching the pilot program in several prison facilities to a small number of inmates who are near parole. Some inmates taking the vocational training and college courses are learning skills to launch their own business after release to support their success on the outside and ensure they will not return to prison.[49]

The Pathways from Prison to Post-secondary Education Project in Michigan is funded with a four-year $1 million grant. Since 2012, Montcalm Community College has been providing correspondence courses to inmates throughout the state, and Jackson Community College has provided courses at Cotton Correctional Facility. Studies are partially funded by private grants, but inmates' families typically help with payments.[50] To learn more, contact:

Vera Institute of Justice
233 Broadway, 12th Floor
New York, NY 10279
(212) 334–1300

Colorado

It is well known by the Colorado Department of Corrections that the more education an inmate can get before being released, the higher the probability of that individual staying out of prison permanently.[51] Consistent with this understanding, Colorado prisons not only offer Basic Skills, High School, and GED courses, but they also provide a wide range of career and occupational training. A sampling of these courses includes:

- Apprenticeship
- CIOPP
- Correctional Library Services

- Career and Technical Education
  - Accounting
  - Barbering
  - Business Management and Technology
  - Canine Behavior Modification (Training)
  - Collision Repair Technology
  - Computer Application and Information Systems
  - Construction
  - Cosmetology
  - Custodial Training
  - Dairy Herdsman
  - Drafting Design
  - Electronics
  - Food Production Management
  - Graphic Media & Desktop Design
  - Heavy Equipment Operations and Maintenance
  - Landscaping
  - Laundry Operations
  - Machine Shop
  - Multimedia Video Production
  - Nurse's Aide
  - Printing
  - Radio & TV Broadcasting
  - Transportation
  - Upholstery
  - Welding
  - Wildland Firefighter
- Cognitive Education
- Career / Community Transition
- Gang Intervention
- Health
- Pre-Vocational Preparation
- Impact of Crime on Victims

All the listed course programs are approved by the Colorado Community College System (CCCS) so that credits earned are transferable to a community college for prisoners who want to work toward an Associate of Applied Science degree.

There is a long waiting list of prisoners wanting to make a positive transition back into the community through these courses. Prisoners with the closest release dates are often moved to the top of the list. To learn more, contact:

Colorado Department of Corrections
Colorado Educational Center
2862 South Circle Drive
Colorado Springs, CO 80906
(719) 226–4417

Oregon

Oregon law mandates a functional literacy program for all prisoners (except the mentally ill or those with life or death sentences). An average of 800 inmates per year complete their GED program.[52] In response to the abundance of existing research that shows "using prisons as educational correctional facilities, instead of punishing centers" is the most effective means of turning around young lives and reducing recidivism, two of the largest youth corrections facilities in Oregon—MacLaren and Hillcrest—have fully accredited high schools with a strong focus on career and technical education programs, quality course material and highly trained teachers.[53] These schools, created by a partnership of the Willamette Education Service District, the Oregon Department of Education, and the Oregon Youth Authority, have taken the lead in a statewide discussion geared to improving educational programs for juvenile offenders throughout the state.[54] Both schools have a full-time transition specialist to help with a successful reintegration into the community upon release. Their services include career counseling, job placement, finding housing, and the development of employability.[55]

The program is individualized, tailored to the assessed skills and knowledge level of the individual. While the first goal of these two schools is to have participants earn a high-school diploma, courses extend to work programs, career and technical courses, and college programs[56] provided by Chemeketa Community College at the Oregon State Penitentiary, Oregon State Correctional Institution, and Mill Creek Correctional Facility.

There have been 61 degrees awarded since 2007. Most of the participating inmates have gone on to work or continue college. None have gone back to prison.

As of 2010, 25 students earned associate's degrees in the first five years, and three earned Bachelor's degrees.[57] That number has undoubtedly increased today. Nearly all youth completing vocational programs, such as welding, cosmetology, etc. from these two correctional facilities have had success in securing jobs that pay decent wages.

Said ex-prisoner/professor Mitchell S. Jackson, "When they get out, they will move right next door to you, and what you want is for that guy to be a different and better person than the person who went to prison."[58]

Indiana

The Indiana Department of Corrections' studies confirm that offenders are far less likely to recidivate if they participate in correctional education. However, the DOC saw a need to shift their focus from academic to job-specific skills programs to effectively utilize limited educational funding for their inmates. They collaborate with seven state institutions of education to create post-secondary, job-oriented certificate programs in order to increase the employability of their inmates and reduce the recidivism rate. Of the prisoners who find employment upon release, they have found, those who participate in correctional education are typically higher paid than those who do not. Their studies further confirm that a reduction in recidivism results in a significant reduction in incarceration costs.[59]

Florida

Ashland Career Online High School in Pensacola, Florida, a project of Ashland University and Smart Horizons Career Online Education, offers an 18-credit high-school diploma and credentialed career certificates in fields such as Childcare, Transportation Services, Office Management, Homeland Security, Protection Services, and others.[60]

UNICOR's Federal Prison Industries, Inc.

While incarcerated in a federal prison, some inmates are fortunate enough to be able to participate in a UNICOR work program. For many prisoners who have never before held a job, this may be their first exposure to work skills and ways to keep constructively occupied during their time in prison. In addition to providing work on the factory floor or teaching computer and business skills to those working in the business office, Federal Prison Industries (FPI) claims to impart a good work ethic.

FPI offers more than 175 diverse products and services, encompassing over four million square feet of manufacturing space. They claim to create opportunity for a fresh start for nearly 22,000 skilled prison workers.

UNICOR was originally created 75 years ago to support our military needs in World War II. A captive labor force of 21,000 prisoners provided the Department of Defense with weapons and apparel, chemical gas detection devices, bomb components, protective goggles, transportation servicing and communications infrastructure. Today, UNICOR's wide-ranging products and services include clothing and textiles; electronics; fleet solutions (vehicle and vehicular components manufacturing); industrial products; office furniture; recycling; and services such as data and document conversion, digitizing, electronic imaging, printing and bindery, contact center and help-desk support, logistics, warehousing, and distribution.

The company now ranks as the government's 39th largest contractor and enjoys a special "mandatory source status" which requires federal agencies to buy its products—*even if they can be purchased cheaper elsewhere.* On the other hand, by limiting the for-profit prison factories to items which would otherwise be produced in off-shore sweatshops, the government can prevent these jobs and profits from going overseas.[61]

Sadly, the pressures of the general economy in recent years have also impacted Federal Prison Industries. Since 2008, more than 10,000 prisoners lost their jobs and, therefore, their training as well.

UNICOR operates at no cost to taxpayers, is entirely self sustaining, and receives no funds from Congress. For the few who are fortunate enough to get them, UNICOR jobs are the highest-paying of any prison assignments. UNICOR prisoners who earn more than $50 per month are required to contribute 50 percent of their work-related income to fulfill court-ordered restitution or fines. UNICOR claims that its prisoner-workers contribute almost $3 million of their earnings each year toward paying off their fines, child and family support, and/or victim restitution.

FPI awards occasional post-secondary school scholarships, as approved by the prison Supervisor of Education, to qualified prisoner workers who want to take business and industry courses or vocational training. In real life behind bars, however, even though FBOP policy allows FPI scholarship awards to its inmate workers, prisoners who inquire about it are typically discouraged and the information is usually difficult or impossible to obtain.

UNICOR programs might well be as their website describes them in many prisons. In the facility where I am incarcerated, however, they are not. Here, UNICOR workers sort clothes hangers that come from various large retailing chains. That's all they do for hours on end: sort hangers according to size, box them, and ship them out. It is hard to understand how this prepares an individual for a skill-based career. Hopefully, the UNICOR program in my facility is not typical.

Experiments in Academia

Prison doesn't have to be a hell hole. It can become a prisoner's center of learning. It can become a career training center. A seminary. Within its unpleasant confines, time spent in prison can be used to improve—and even turn around—a life.

Prisoners who want to pursue an education but cannot afford it or are otherwise not ready to enroll in credited classes, still have one advantage: they have *time* on their hands. They would be well advised to use that time to begin their education. To *read*. Reading is the best preparation for a higher education. Good literature and serious books provide a mind-expanding experience that can literally transport a prisoner beyond the concrete walls into another life.

If prisoners read national newspapers like the *New York Times* and the *Wall Street Journal* or news magazines like *Newsweek* and *Time,* they can gain an understanding of what is going on out there in the world to which they will one day belong again. They can learn about the issues people and politicians are dealing with, issues that may affect their future lives.

Prisoners can borrow good books from other prisoners who read. Or they can ask fellow prisoners who are taking college courses if they can read their old textbooks to get a leg up on preparing to enroll in school. And, of course, they should look through what is available in their prison library. Prison libraries are not generally known for the quality of their collections; still, if one looks through carefully, there could be a gem or two in there.

Prisoners can ask friends or family to check the Book Review section of the *New York Times* or other newspapers to see what is good out there and send books to them. Or they can write to their local public librarians and ask if they will donate good books (non-fiction and quality literature) to the prison's library.

Nothing Is Impossible

Despite the loss of Pell Grants for prisoners and all the obstacles to learning in prisons we have outlined above, a small handful of programs exists to offer a college education within prison walls, and these get an eager enrollment from about 10 percent of the prison population. "A lot of prisoners do their time and they don't think about bettering themselves.... They come to prison and become better criminals instead of better human beings."[62] But there are far more prisoners who do want to pursue an education, and for them there are isolated spots of light on the otherwise grim academic horizon. Experimental and innovative partnerships between individual prison systems and colleges are working to restore advanced academic opportunities to prisoners.

Prisoners and prison administrators alike are overwhelmingly enthusiastic about college programs offered on-site, inside prisons. Some of the prisoner-students in these classes had committed crimes as serious as murder and, initially, were far from "college material." Some had never even read a book. And some of them are now pursuing a Ph.D. Said one prisoner when he was accepted into the Bard program, "Oh, I was elated. I was elated! It was—it was almost like they told me I was going home ... it really was. I felt like it was a new chapter in my life—a chance to start over."[63]

For prisoners who want to pursue academic courses or a university degree, there are a few isolated experimental and innovative partnerships between individual prison facilities and colleges. Where these exist, one can see groups of prisoner-students seated at tables, holding animated discussions about Nietzsche's concept of aristocratic morality or about the nature of good and evil. These courses have rich layers of meaning for these men and women. Professors who teach them say the prisoner-students "want to drain every bit of information you have. They see books as full of gold. They ask every question they can squeeze in until the bell rings."[64]

Even though vocational programs are far more prevalent (66 percent of prisoners participating in post-secondary correctional education take vocational courses),[65] academic programs are beginning to gain advocacy.[66] College courses are grinding their way back within prison walls with the devoted labor of volunteer professors and graduate students. Many are sponsored by private religious institutions.[67] These programs are excellent, but they are few and far between.

Sixty-eight percent of the post-secondary prison educational programs that exist today are provided by state community colleges. The next largest provider group (16 percent) is that of the public four-year institutions. And the smallest provider group (4 percent) is that of the private, for-profit, educational institutions. In this chapter, we will not discuss distance-learning prison programs that prisoners find, enroll in, and pay for by themselves. Here we are looking only at advanced educational programs conducted on-site within prisons, without cost—or without much cost—to qualified prisoners.

Most of these courses are taught inside the prison facilities, although some use video or satellite instruction in part. In most jurisdictions, the use of the internet is still banned for security reasons. It is not banned, however, in New Mexico, the exceptional instance where the Department of Corrections has developed an innovative distance-education program using a secure internet connection. Since it has proven to be effective and affordable, we hope to see it spread to other prisons across the nation. Technology like this can open many doors now closed to prisoners seeking to better themselves through education.

We have listed below the most successful academic programs within prisons that we are aware of. However, the *Prison Studies Project* at Harvard University is compiling the first nationwide directory of post-secondary programs in U.S. prisons. Continually updated, the directory is an online, state-by-state listing of on-site degree-granting post-secondary education programs in prisons. To get the most complete and current listing of such programs in any particular state, visit http://prisonstudiesproject.org/directory.

The following are examples of prison education programs that work with great success through partnerships between prison facilities and educational institutions. Some of these programs are temporary and experimental; others are long-term. All have proven to be motivating and transformative for the prisoner-students.

New Mexico—Innovative and Successful!

Something very exciting and unique is happening in the prisons of New Mexico. The Department of Corrections is using secure-network, internet-based courses to deliver college education to its prisoners in nine prisons located in relatively remote areas. Eligible prisoners can earn an associate's, bachelor's, or master's degree in prisons equipped with laboratory space, computers, and a secure, high-speed connection to the university.

According to the Institute for Higher Education Policy (IHEP), no security breaches have been reported. They utilize "a WebCT engine, which is a closed-circuit Internet connection."[68] Additionally, the New Mexico Department of Corrections hired 14 full-time facilitators with college degrees to monitor the classes, answer questions, and provide communication between the prisoner-students and faculty when necessary.

New Mexico corrections officials are convinced, based on the success of the program, that internet-based education can and does work in prisons and that, managed correctly, it does not present a security threat. They are also convinced that this is an efficient use of state funds because it has been so successful in reducing recidivism and in ensuring that released prisoners contribute, and pay back to, the communities where they are released.[69]

In contrast to Texas and North Carolina, where post-secondary prison educational courses are predominantly vocational, New Mexico's post-secondary prison educational courses are predominantly academic. Although vocational programs are also offered on-site by the Department of Corrections' Bureau of Education, the focus is on expanding advanced academic courses through distance learning, courses with credits that will transfer to all of New Mexico's higher education institutions.[70]

Contracting with three post-secondary educational institutions, the New Mexico program offers 57 courses in business administration, computer information systems, and other university studies. "Eligible inmates can enroll at any of these three institutions to earn an associate's, bachelor's, or master's degree."[71] The most common program offered is the associate of arts in general studies, the core curriculum for a bachelor's degree. Consistent with all of New Mexico's higher education institutions, instructors are nationally certified, and these courses provide prisoner-students with the credits needed to further their education upon release.

Also unique to New Mexico are tactics used to ensure program completion:

1. If prisoner-students are transferred to another New Mexico facility through no fault of their own, this distance-learning format allows them to immediately enroll in the same course with the same instructor at the new facility and pick up where they left off with virtually no interruption.
2. Prisoners who complete an associate's degree while in prison can have four months taken off their sentences. If they earn a bachelor's degree, they can have six months taken off.
3. If the prisoner-student does not maintain a 2.5 grade point average, or is transferred to a higher-security facility for disciplinary reasons, that inmate must repay the cost of his or her tuition and books before being allowed to enroll in additional college-level courses.
4. Finally—and this is a unique approach, one that produces an extraordinary success rate—prisoners enrolled in New Mexico's post-secondary education program must sign an agreement that if they drop out before completing, the Department of Corrections is allowed to garnish their wages after release to help cover the cost of the program.[72]

While this policy may appear to be rather harsh, it has caused completion rates to rise from 50 to 90 percent!

The New Mexico Department of Corrections' Bureau of Education provides post-secondary prison educational services to almost all its state prisons and one private prison through contracts with a four-year university and two two-year community colleges. The state wants to expand this program, which is funded almost entirely by the Department of Corrections, to all its prison facilities.

New Mexico provides an outstanding model that can and should be emulated everywhere throughout the Federal Bureau of Prisons and all other state prison systems. The New Mexico program is empirical proof that there is a way, especially when prisons are located in geographically remote areas, making traditional post-secondary prison education programs prohibitively expensive. Now that federal prisons bureau-wide have implemented the Trust Fund Limited Inmate Communication System (TRULINCS), the FBOP has the infrastructure in place to install and employ a similar system of computer-based higher education. One would hope this infrastructure will be put to constructive use to expand internet-based distance learning in prisons throughout the nation. Write to learn more:

> Pete Sandoval
> Casa Nor Este Bldg.
> 3415 Pan American Fwy NE
> Albuquerque, NM 87107
> (505) 841–2476
> Pete.Sandoval@state.nm.us
> http://corrections.state.nm.us/programs/education.html

New York State: A Beehive of Creative Academic Programs

Some of the most exciting developments in prison education are taking place in New York State. Authorities in the NY Department of Correctional Services believe—and their experience proves—that education changes the lives and outlook of prisoners and improves public safety. As a result, they have developed some forward-looking coalitions among New York prison facilities, institutions of higher education, community groups, and charitable foundations to sponsor college programs as an integral part of the DOC's reentry initiatives.

Here is a sampling of prison education programs in New York:

BARD PRISON INITIATIVE

Bard College, an elite private school at Annandale-on-Hudson, initiated the privately funded *Bard Prison Initiative* to offer an associate's and/or bachelor's degree in philosophy, history, literature, art history, writing, and many other fields within several New York prison facilities. The highly successful *Bard Prison Initiative* serves as a national model for independent, privately financed education programs in prisons.[73] As of 2012, this rare free college education for inmates had 250 incarcerated people enrolled, and 175 have graduated through its program.

Prisoner-students are held to the same standards as on-campus Bard College students,[74] and the quality of instruction equals that of classes offered to traditional campus students in courses such as "Greek Tragedy," "American Intellectual History," and "Human Biology."[75] "Bard seeks to prepare inmates for life after prison by providing them the ability to function as more reflective citizens and social beings."[76]

Bard sends its faculty directly to the prisons to teach, but the admissions process for prisoners is rigorous, determined by the inmates' level of enthusiasm and proven ability to do college-level work.[77] One out of 10 applicants is admitted based upon, among other things, a three-page essay about a reading. Bard is looking for ambition, curiosity, and drive.[78]

Each prisoner-students works with an advisor. There is a strong emphasis on college-level writing and grammar. Classes in literature, foreign language, history, philosophy, social sciences, math, science, and art all require that prisoner-students turn in "long final papers on topics ranging from U.S. policy toward Cuba to the ideas of literary critic Northrup Frye." In addition, participants must complete a senior thesis.[79] Success is measured by the capacity for critical thinking and self-reflection, fluency of expression, interest in current events and social connectedness.

Bard provides "a rigorous experience that leaves many of its graduates eager and ready for further education and all determined to lead productive lives after release."[80]

Bard also facilitates a wide variety of pre-college opportunities, from GED mentoring to courses in theology, workshops in the arts, and more. And for prisoners who possess a GED or high-school diploma, Bard works in partnership with Episcopal Social Services to offer a complete credit-bearing college education and a true liberal arts degree inside three long-term, maximum-security prisons and two medium-security prisons.[81]

Undergraduate student volunteers travel from the campus to the prison to provide tutoring to inmates, an interaction that has proven as beneficial to the campus students as it is to the inmates.[82] In fact, having volunteer students visit regional prisons is said to have also had a profound impact on the intellectual life of the Bard College campus.

The impact of Bard prisoner-students is felt throughout the prison. They bring their readings and discussions back to their cells, and as students congregate in the yard to discuss what they're reading, they often engage non-students[83] in their excitement over varying interpretations of literature or history.

The camaraderie and respect among prisoners and between faculty and students is a new experience for many.[84] Formal education helps connect prisoners to the world and enhance their sense of civic mission. They come out wanting not only to get a job, but also to pay back to their communities.[85]

The age of prisoner-students averages in the mid-twenties, but some are as old as 45. Most had not graduated from high school before prison and received their GED while incarcerated. Almost none flunk out, although some are prevented from completion by prison transfers. Almost none ever return to prison. Most are reunited with their families and hold responsible jobs.[86]

Bard's success is due to (1) its admissions process, (2) its approach to skill development, and (3) a blurring of the lines between academic and vocational education.[87] Their program is driven by three goals:

1. engage the moral action of the students in a positive environment,
2. respect and develop their dignity, and
3. encourage a critical observance of social structures.

What is particularly hopeful is that a number of alumni of the Bard Prison Initiative have gone on to organize similar volunteer programs across the country. Expanding to operate five satellite campuses in New York, the success of Bard's program grew into a three-institution consortium that includes Grinnell College in Iowa and Wesleyan University in Connecticut, institutions to which Bard has donated more than $300,000 to begin their pilot programs in an effort to jump-start a national expansion of their model. Bard hopes to expand its consortium to ten institutions in ten states.[88] However, financial uncertainty beyond the initial seed money can jeopardize the future of these newer programs.

Unfortunately, the Bard program, like so many others, is threatened with insolvency. Major philanthropic organizations that invest generously in higher education do not include prison college programs in their portfolios. To learn more, contact:

Bard College
PO Box 5000
Annandale-on-Hudson, NY 12504–5000
bpi@bard.edu
(845) 758–7308
http://www.bard.edu/institutes/bpi

College and Community Fellowship (CCF)

Also in New York is the College and Community Fellowship (CCF), an organization created by the City University of New York. CCF works with released prisoners (women, mostly) who want to continue their education, helping those who have had criminal convictions overcome social and personal barriers to academic advancement. The CCF website claims to guide these women through various stages of higher education while promoting their leadership, self-advocacy, artistic expression, civic participation, and long-term economic security. "We see limitless possibilities beyond reentry for our participants, their families, and their communities," their website says. "We expect what others deem impossible, and the results are incredible!"

Two-thirds of CCF released prisoners attend schools within the City University of New York. Most participants pursue degrees in human services, but some pursue various other fields of study, including business administration, sociology, urban education, public policy, theology, and women's studies.

Students who sustain at least a 2.5 GPA can receive $600 per semester after their first 12 college credits. Almost all of the women participating earn their associate's and/or four-year bachelor's degrees. Some have gone all the way to earn their Ph.D.s.

The College and Community Fellowship has a stunning record of success: almost 70 percent of participants receive four-year degrees within four years of joining the program. Clearly, the connection between prison-based and community-based educational programs is one of the most exciting areas for innovation in the larger reentry movement.[89] Need proof? CCF participants have a recidivism rate of less than two percent.[90] Find out more at:

College & Community Fellowship
365—5th Avenue
Suite 5113
New York, NY 10016
Tel: (212) 817–8906 Fax (212) 817–1573
Email: info@collegeandcommunity.org
www.collegeandcommunity.org

Bedford Hills College Program (BHCP)

The Bedford Hills Correctional Facility is a New York State maximum-security prison for women where prisoners receive not only the usual ABE Basic Education and GED programs, but can also enroll in academic courses for a bachelor's or a master's degree.

At Bedford, prisoners must take classes to reach a 9th-grade level of reading and math before moving on to the GED program, where they will focus on courses such as algebra, science, reading, and written expression. Bedford's GED program is intense, cramming four years of study into three months. Students attend class three hours a day, five days per week. Unless prisoners have a high-school diploma, the course is mandatory.

When the women arrive at the facility, they take an exam to determine their mathematics and reading proficiency so they can be placed in classes at an appropriate level. For women who test at the college level, the Bedford Hills College Program (BHCP), offered in conjunction with Marymount Manhattan College, offers non-credited college-preparatory courses and credit-bearing courses leading to an associate of arts degree in social science and a bachelor of arts degree in sociology.

The Marymount Manhattan College website clearly states the college's philosophy on the subject of prison education. While acknowledging the public's anger about crime and realizing that prison is first and foremost a punishment for crime, the college also believes that when prisoners are able to work and earn a higher education degree, they are empowered to pay back their debts to society by working toward repairing some of what has been broken.

The Bedford prison facility supplies the needed classroom space and a learning center with a computer lab and on-site library staffed by dedicated volunteers from the Bedford community. To fulfill their requirements for a Marymount Manhattan College degree, prisoner-students take the same courses as those offered on campus, including basic required courses and a wide variety of electives in art, history, creative writing, computer systems, and the sciences.

At Marymount's college program in Bedford Hills, New York, a new twist is that students on the inside and outside are now taking classes together. "Inside students must meet the same admission criteria, take the same required courses and pass the same tests as their outside counterparts, but often have to work harder because they have access to fewer resources." One outside student said he experienced some of the most stimulating debates and conversations in his college career with prisoner-students.[91]

The Bedford Hills College Program is supported by Doris Buffett's Sunshine Lady Foundation, an organization that has contributed $8.5 million to more than 20 in-prison college programs.[92] Students receive a quality education while in prison, but the greatest benefit for these women comes when they are released. New worlds of experience and opportunities await them. Other women, released while still pursuing their degrees, are permitted to complete their degrees at the Marymount Manhattan campus. Prison-students in this program have praised the New York prison system for bringing meaning to their lives, even in such restricted circumstances.[93] Find out more from:

The Bedford Hills College Program
Marymount Manhattan College
221 East 71st Street
New York, NY 10021
(212) 517-0400
http://www.mmm.edu/study/resources/academicachievement/bhcp.html

The Cornell Prison Education Program

At the maximum-security prison in Auburn, New York, as well as at the nearby medium-security Cayuga Correctional Facility (CCF) in Moravia, the *Cornell Prison Education Program* is designed to build an academic community within prison walls. According to executive director James Schechter, "There are a lot of talented, smart people in prisons ... these guys hang onto everything you say, and they'll challenge you. They turn you into a better teacher and a better thinker."[94] Instructors found the students hungry for education and grateful for their efforts. "They are very, very well behaved in the classroom and they ask really good questions."[95]

Credit courses offered at Auburn include economics, constitutional law and individual rights, creative writing, genetics, medical anthropology, international human rights, and poetry. Noncredit courses include writing, math, and Asian meditation. A course in ancient philosophy is also taught at the Moravia facility. "With funding and collaboration with the community college, it's plausible to have all the disciplines represented," Schechter said.[96]

A cooperative effort of Cornell University, Cayuga Community College, the Auburn Correctional Facility, and the Cayuga Correctional Facility, the Cornell program offers 12 courses each semester, and Cornell waives tuition and fees so the program is free of charge to prisoners, who can work toward an associate's degree from Cayuga Community College.[97] Largely supported by an annual grant from Doris Buffett's Sunshine Lady Foundation, this program provides instructors, books, school supplies, and administration.[98] Volunteer faculty and teaching assistants from Cornell University deliver the courses in a for-credit liberal arts curriculum.

Auburn's prison administration approved Schechter's proposal to host a computer room with equipment donated by a campus group that recycles university hardware. Publishers donate or significantly discount current textbooks for the program, and the Friends of the Tompkins County Public Library donate boxes of dictionaries. "This is a phenomenal opportunity," said a prisoner who had taken Cornell courses at Auburn since 2003. "By all rights, this is a real Cornell education."[99]

McGraw Hall, Room 101
Ithaca, NY 14853
jas349@cornell.edu
(607) 255–2852
http://www.cornell.edu/outreach/programs/program_view.cfm?ProgramID=2281

Hudson Link

This program grants college degrees, operating in partnership with Mercy College in the Bronx and Nyack College in New York. It began at Sing Sing, a maximum-security prison in Ossining, New York, and later expanded to Fishkill Correctional Facility in Fishkill, New York, and to the Taconic Correctional Facility in Bedford Hills, New York, where students from Vassar College also participate in courses on family, law, and social policy. Typically, the first hands to go up in response to the instructor's questions are those of inmates in attendance.

One Vassar student said the women prisoners bring their unique perspectives to the class, not only as inmates, but also as wives, mothers, and grandmothers. She said they are exposed to life experiences not ordinarily found in a normal college classroom. Topics include domestic violence, welfare policy, and other family-related issues.

Students are graded on weekly papers and a final paper. One Vassar instructor proudly affirms that the program improves reentry success for these women and also improves their individual lives. Prisoner-students expressed a sense of extraordinary accomplishment at the idea of having completed a Vassar college course.[100]

Hudson Link for Higher Education in Prison
P.O. Box 862
Ossining, NY 10562
Tel: (914) 941–0794
info@hudsonlink.org
http://www.hudsonlink.org/joomla/index.php

Inside Out Center Classes

Also at the Taconic Correctional Facility in Bedford Hills, New York, is one of many programs from Temple University's Inside Out Center. With leadership provided by the College and Community Fellowship,[101] this is a weekly class in which participating prisoners and students from Vassar College come together to study "Gender, Social Problems, and Social Change." The Vassar students use teaching techniques that put the prisoner-students at ease and encourage participation, including sitting in a circle so students can all see, and speak directly to, one another. Weekly oral and written reports on the readings are returned to students with comments that deepen their connection to the instructors and to the course material.

Prisoner-students said the class inspired them to continue their education and that of their children. One wrote, "I'd always been afraid of going to college.

This class opened my eyes to a whole new way of learning, and built my confidence in a way I never could have imagined!"[102]

College Connections: Higher Education for Women in Prison

Another program at the medium-security Taconic Correctional Facility (TCF) in Bedford Hills, New York, offers both non-credit and credit-bearing college-level courses to women through Nyack College, a private religious school. Courses come at no cost to prisoners because instructors volunteer their time, and textbooks and materials are all donated, either by individuals or publishers. More information is available from:

Nyack College and Alliance Theological Seminary
1 South Boulevard
Nyack, NY 10960
(845) 358–1710
http://www.nyack.edu

Religious Studies Programs in New York Prisons

Rising Hope, an all-volunteer organization that provides one year of college-level education to men in prison, operates in six New York State prisons: Sing Sing, Green Haven, Arthurkill, Fishkill, Mid-Orange, and Woodbourne. Since 1995, more than 700 men have graduated with a Certificate in Ministry & Human Services. There is no charge for tuition, professors all volunteer their time, and students can borrow needed textbooks. *Rising Hope* asks graduates to use their newly developed academic skills and spiritual maturity to build up the community wherever they live, whether in prison or after release on the outside, as a way to discharge their debt by serving others.

Rising Hope, Inc.
P.O. Box 906
Croton Falls, NY 10519
(914) 276–7848
Email: RisingHopeInc@optonline.net
http://www.risinghopeinc.org/

The Master's of Professional Studies, a non-accredited certificate in Christian Ministry, is a two-year program of college-level academic studies taught by the New York Theological Seminary at Sing Sing to enable prisoners to prepare for achieving a master's degree and a profession. After graduation, prisoner-participants are required to make a one-year commitment to carry out a self-designed program or activity.

> New York Theological Seminary
> 475 Riverside Drive
> New York, NY 10115–0083
> (212) 870–1211
> http://www.nyts.edu/programs/276-new-york-theological-seminarys-mas ters-of-professional-studies-program-at-sing-sing-correctional-facility

Seeking to expand post-secondary education programs for their prison population, the NY Department of Correctional Services works cooperatively with the NY State Education Department, State University of New York (SUNY) Community Colleges, the U.S. Department of Education, the John Jay College of Criminal Justice Prisoner Reentry Institute, Bard College, and the College and Community Fellowship Program at the City University of NY Graduate Center.

Massachusetts

Boston University's Prison Education Program

For more than three decades, Boston University has demonstrated a strong commitment to serve the Massachusetts prison population, understanding that study gives prisoners an intellectual ability to see themselves in a different light and leave prison equipped to make a positive contribution to their families and their communities.

Boston University offers what may be the oldest and largest of the College-in-Prison programs[103] with more than 600 courses in a variety of disciplines, including accounting, English composition, ancient Greek and Latin, biology, sociology, marketing, acting, opera, and language courses in Spanish, French, and Greek. Those who successfully complete the program earn a bachelor's degree in liberal interdisciplinary studies.

Having replaced the now-defunct Pell Grants with its own funding, Boston University has brought all the necessary undergraduate coursework for the bachelor of arts and master of arts degrees into prisons for incarcerated students. The university donated the cost of its faculty instructors, some of whom are very prominent (political commentators Marshall Goldman and Christopher Lydon among them, having taught at MCI-Norfolk). BU also supplies prisoner-students with tuition, textbooks and materials. Additional funding comes from business partners like McGraw-Hill; Addison-Wesley; Partakers, a faith-based organization; the Massachusetts Department of Corrections; and private contributions.

Teaching 180 prisoner-students at any given time in three prisons at Norfolk, Framingham, and the Bay State Correctional Center, Boston University previously had awarded both bachelor's and master's degrees, but currently offers only the bachelor's degree due to funding limitations.

The Massachusetts Department of Corrections provides support and guidance to the Boston University instructors, as well as to the prisoner-students, who (unless serving mandatory sentences) receive "good time" credits for attending the classes, up to 2 ½ days per month (Massachusetts General Laws Annotated, chapter 127, § 129).

Admission to the Boston University Prison Education Program requires that entering students already have a high-school diploma or GED, pass an entry exam, and have completed some first-year college-level work. Once in the program, they must maintain a GPA of 2.5 or higher.[104] Nevertheless, prisoner-students who complete the *Boston University Prison Education Program* generally do very well. According to the BU website, "some continue with their education at Boston University or at other schools, completing their undergraduate work or enrolling in graduate school. Others go to work and develop careers..."[105]

Boston University invites the inquiries of people who are looking for guidance to launch similar programs. This, more than anything, can help to spread prison education to other states and prison systems everywhere. Contact:

Robert Cadigan, Director
Boston University Prison Education Program
808 Commonwealth Avenue, room 237
Boston, MA 02215
(617) 353–5945
rcadigan@bu.edu
or
Jenifer Drew, Program Coordinator
1844 Commonwealth Avenue
Newton, MA 02466
(617) 243–2196
jdrew@lasell.edu

PARTAKERS—COLLEGE BEHIND BARS PROGRAM

Working closely with Boston University, this faith-based nonprofit supports prisoner-students with sponsors, mentors, GED test preparation, and correspondence courses.

Available at minimum-security facilities and pre-release centers for prisoners with short-term sentences, the College Behind Bars Program has a rigorous curriculum and a positive impact on students, as well as high retention rates. Partakers donate the salary of one faculty member, and they sponsor courses; they provide typewriters and tutoring services to prisoner-students and help prepare them for qualifying exams.

PARTAKERS—ALTERNATIVES TO VIOLENCE PROGRAM

This is not an academic program, but it is extremely effective in helping prisoners deal with conflict without resorting to violence. In these prison workshops, prisoners learn to care for one another, even within the prison environment, which tends work against the concept of friendship. The community they build is a rare and profound gift. Participants practice new-found communication skills, a sense of community, and experience of transformation to peacefully resolve potentially violent situations.

Partakers
230 Central Street
Auburndale, MA 02466
(617) 795–2725
information@partakers.org
http://www.partakers.org/sponsor.html

Northern California's Prison University Project at San Quentin

"San Quentin, California's oldest prison, with its fortress-like facades and 1890s-era wrought-iron front gate" offers the state's only on-site college degree-granting program in all of California's prisons.[106] (Another, offered by San Diego City College, has been discontinued due to lack of funds.)

Founded in 2004 at San Quentin prison as an extension of Patten University, an accredited independent university in Oakland, California,[107] the *Prison University Project* serves as an in-prison higher education model for rehabilitation. The *Prison University Project* offers 20 courses per semester leading to an accredited associate of arts degree, with the intention to expand to a four-year bachelor's degree program.[108] Hundreds of participating student-prisoners have earned at least a GED.[109]

Comprising three stages (college preparatory, a two-year associate's degree, and a pre-release advisory program), "about 250 prisoners enroll each semester in Associate of Arts courses in the humanities, social sciences, math, and science, foreign languages and independent study, in addition to intensive college preparatory courses in math and English."[110]

At San Quentin, prisoner-students in the Prison University Project pay no fees or tuition. However, because no state or federal funding is available for prison higher education in California, the program relies entirely on donations from private individuals and foundations. All textbooks (most of which are donated by the publishers) and school supplies are provided by the Prison University Project.[111] Teachers and tutors are all volunteers from colleges and universities in the Bay Area of California,[112] including U.C. Berkeley and Patten University. Even after the Pell Grants disappeared in 1994, volunteer teachers at San Quentin chose not to quit, so courses have continued.

So far, 74 men have completed their associate of arts degrees through this program, and many others, released before they could finish, have completed their degrees on the outside. Death-row prisoners receive their diplomas by mail, while those in the general prison population participate in a commencement ceremony with traditional caps and gowns in the prison chapel, complete with family and friends in attendance.[113] Here is how a class at San Quentin was described: "Inside the class, past the various security checkpoints, it's possible to forget that this is a medium-security prison. These men are here to learn, to discuss what they are reading, to engage one another in what may be the prison's only racially integrated environment, and to study history.

"We learn from our mistakes and we learn from our successes," says a prisoner who is one of the students. "We all hear about the rise and fall of the Roman Empire, but we want to know: how did it rise and how did it fall?"

Besides the college program at San Quentin, the Prison University Project provides guidance and information about prison education to students, the media, academic researchers, and members of the state and federal legislatures, as well as to individuals interested in developing similar programs at other institutions, prisoners at institutions other than San Quentin, and friends and family members of people in prison. To learn more, contact:

Prison University Project
Post Office Box 492
San Quentin, CA 94964
(415) 455–8088
http://www.prisonuniversityproject.org/pages/programs/san-quentin-college-program.html

Southern California: A Disaster

While state budgets have been slashed mercilessly (see Chapter 4), and prison education programs are now almost nonexistent in Southern California—certainly there are no post-secondary courses offered—there remains a handful of isolated individuals who attempt to maintain hope. In Southern California's Camarillo College, for example, nine students visit the Ventura Youth Correctional Facility on Thursday and Friday evenings to tutor, teach, and mentor a dozen prisoners, providing advice on college life and teaching such basic skills as taking notes and writing a short essay. These young tutors say they've gotten more out of the experience than the prisoners they mentor. They hope to create a culture of learning in which the few inmates they can reach will inspire others. They also hope to expand the program to other campuses and colleges. For the class that will begin next semester, 60 prisoners so far have expressed interest.[114] There is also the Inland Empire Prison Education Project, a new program introduced in 2012 to help fill the need for a basic level of educational programming for the prison populations of the California Institution for Men (CIM) at Chino, the California Institution for Women (CIW) in Corona, the California Rehabilitation Center (CRC) in Norco, and the Ventura Youth Correctional Facility (VYCF) in Camarillo.

In these facilities, graduate and undergraduate college students deliver orientation presentations, literacy and math classes in the Basic Education course, and life-skills classes for resume writing and interview techniques, and they try to foster aspirations for higher education. Formerly affiliated with Cal Poly Pomona, the Prison Education Project is currently affiliated with Transcendence Children & Family Services.

Southern California has a long way to go to get their prison population past a basic level of education into higher, post-secondary courses. The one glimmer of hope that we know of is the Youthful Offender Program, championed by filmmaker Scott Budnick with the help of staff at Ironwood State Prison in Blythe, and the California Rehabilitation Center in San Bernardino County. Budnick created a unique learning environment where young inmates live in a dormitory set aside exclusively for those enrolled in college.

In addition to the young inmates who enroll the day they arrive at an adult prison, approximately 600 prisoners under the age of 35 and within seven years of parole are taking college courses at Ironwood, the California Rehabilitation Center, and the California Institution for Men (CIM) in Chino.

In 2012, the California Rehabilitation Center recorded 17 associate's degrees and 207 course completions achieved by inmates. At Ironwood, 37 inmates received associate's degrees. Of the 75 participants who have graduated from the college program at the California Rehabilitation Center, a mere three percent have returned to prison. Some of the inmate participants have gone on to attend Loyola Marymount University, Morehouse College in Atlanta, and the University of California-Los Angeles after their incarceration.

New Jersey

The New Jersey Scholarship and Transformative Education in Prisons Consortium (NJ-STEP)

Operating in partnership with the New Jersey Department of Corrections and state parole board, *NJ-STEP* was launched in August, 2012, with two grants totaling $4 million to provide college courses to prisoners and help them continue with their education after release. The program, housed in the Rutgers School of Criminal Justice, also involves Drew University, Essex County College, Mercer County Community College, and the College of New Jersey to serve 1,200 to 1,500 inmates at 11 correctional centers.[115]

Rutgers School of Criminal justice
Center for Law and Justice
Newark NJ 07102–3094
(973) 353–3311/3292
rscj@newark.rutgers.edu

WOMEN'S RE-ENTRY INITIATIVE FOR TRAINING AND EDUCATION

At the Edna Mahan Correctional Facility in Clinton, New Jersey, this group provides higher education and occupational training programs for women in prison. Write:

Office of Educational Services Department of Corrections School District
Whittlesey Road
Trenton, NJ 08625
(609) 292–8054
http://www.localschooldirectory.com/district-schools/218502/Office-of-Educational-Services-Department-of-Corrections-School-District/NJ

PROJECT INSIDE

At the same facility, Edna Mahan, Project INSIDE operates a program for juvenile offenders and women under the age of 26 to provide credit-bearing, college-level courses that count toward a certificate in Small Business Administration from Union County College.

Also at this facility, New Jersey's only state prison for women, a partnership between the Inside-Out Prison Exchange Program and Raritan Valley Community College offers a joint AA/BA degree program for female prisoner-students (see "Inside-Out" below).

Prison to Community Project

Still another innovative program at the Edna Mahan Correctional Facility is the Prison to Community Project, which provides computer and academic education to hundreds of incarcerated women. The program prepares these prisoners for successful entry into the working world upon release and follows them from incarceration to halfway housing all the way to enrolling in a community college or landing a productive job. With help from Rutgers University, the women get online courses in math, writing, English, and the major Microsoft Office applications. Instructors are volunteers from the Essex County Community College and the Women's Reentry Initiative for Training and Education. Said one of the incarcerated participants, "It helps by giving me something to look forward to ... it gives a lot of women here hope." Participants in the Prison to Community Project, compared to the national average, proved to be 78 percent less likely to recidivate.[116]

Partners in the initiative include the Nicholson Foundation, the project's main funding source; Essex County Community College; the Mahan Correctional Facility; and several state agencies including the Department of Corrections, the Department of Labor and Workforce Development, and the Parole Board.

South Carolina's Prison Initiative Program

Working with Columbia International University (a Christian, faith-based school), the South Carolina Department of Corrections provides an accredited two-year associate of arts degree with no charge to prisoners—including texts and materials. These are not correspondence courses (although CIU offers those, too, at the normal fee); these courses are taught inside the prison, with face-to-face faculty-student interaction.

According to Dr. David C. Osterlund, the director of the CIU Prison Initiative, prisoners who are accepted into the program are transferred from the 26 state institutions to the Reception and Evaluation Center in Kirkland, South Carolina, where they become residents, and going to school becomes their job.

Prisoners attend classes daily, and the instruction is conducted by top-quality professors who travel to Kirkland to teach. In two classrooms that comfortably handle 15 men each, the center is equipped with PowerPoint, whiteboard, and desks or tables. There is also a library with 2,400 books and a 14-station computer lab. There is no internet access, but the men do most of their work at a computer. For those who have never sat at a keyboard before, Osterlund says they have programs to assist with computer limitations.

Supported by donations from businesses, churches, and private individuals, these courses include English, math, creative writing, psychology, and history, as well as faith-based courses such as Bible survey, evangelism, Romans exegesis, ethics, discipleship, etc. Additionally, participants receive two-week sessions in hospice training and comparative religions.

Once released from prison, ex-prisoners can choose to continue on and pursue a full bachelor's, master's, and/or doctorate program on campus. For more information, contact:

Columbia International University
7435 Monticello Road
Columbia, SC 29203
(803) 807–5064 or (800) 777–2227 (ext. 5064).
Email: prisoned@ciu.edu
http://www.ciu.edu/prison-initiative

Missouri's Saint Louis University

Funded partly by the Hearst Foundation, this program originally offered only courses in theology, but it has expanded into an associate's degree, with plans to offer bachelor's degrees.[117] Saint Louis University works with the medium-security Eastern Reception Diagnostic and Correction Center (ERDCC) in Bonne Terre, Missouri. Utilizing some of the elements in the Bard and Boston programs, ERDCC adds a whole new component, addressing the needs of prison employees and offering degree programs to them, as well as to the prisoners. This is crucial, because the prison is located in a very low-income area of St. Francois County, where only about 10 percent of adults have college degrees, and no educational institution is geographically accessible.[118]

"For the prisoners that will someday be paroled, the hope is that the education will help them transition back into the world and aid them in finding employment. For prisoners serving life sentences, the hope is that they will mentor younger prisoners at the facility, encouraging them to turn their lives around, rather than continuing their lives of crime."[119]

Connecticut's Wesleyan University Center for Prison Education

A high-caliber liberal arts education for selected members inside prison walls is functioning at Connecticut's Cheshire Correctional Facility for men and York Correctional Institution for women, provided by Wesleyan University's Center for Prison Education. There, paid faculty members teach humanities, natural science, politics, and sociology courses for which prisoner-students receive credit toward a bachelor's degree. Due to the program's resounding success, it earned authorization to continue through 2014.

Prisoner-participants must meet rigorous entrance requirements. The primary criterion for admission is academic potential, since the courses offered in prison are the same as those taught on Wesleyan's campus, and they uphold the same high standards of academic excellence. The length of sentence to be served and past criminal conduct, however serious, are not factors considered in deciding admission.

Prisoners are eager to participate in the program. Some 120 of them at Cheshire applied to fill 19 open spots in the classes. Finalists write essays and submit to personal interviews. Students selected into the program must be approved, of course, by the prison administration.

Prisoner-students take courses on expository writing and sociology and must submit essays on weighty matters like Frantz Fanon's view that "language helps support the weight of a civilization," or Sigmund Freud's thoughts on happiness. Other courses include chemistry and politics.

Privately funded with a $300,000 grant from the Bard Prison Initiative,[120] and a $5,000 grant from the Hartford Foundation to finance it through 2013, the program provides diverse research and volunteer opportunities. More importantly, it provides hope. Students at Wesleyan hold drives to donate books and provide tutoring to prisoners—an experience which is proving to be as beneficial for traditional Wesleyan students as for the prisoner students.

Wesleyan University
Middletown, CT 06459
(860) 685–2000
http://www.wesleyan.edu/cpe/

Washington State's Post-Prison Education Program

The Post-Prison Education Program provides educational opportunities to the incarcerated and to recently released prisoners in Washington State.[121]

Through their *Bridge to College Program,* they help felons transition successfully to college and the work force by providing

- scholarships,
- academic advising and career counseling, and
- advocacy and mentoring.

The program admits only individuals who are at significant risk of recidivating based on their extensive prison sentences. They make presentations inside prisons and give intensive support upon release, mentoring and guiding students and their families so they can obtain resources to become sustainable and contributing members of society.

The Post-Prison Education Program will help by removing "any obstacle that gets in the way of further education. That could mean paying tuition ... rent, running interference with various bureaucracies ... [or] tutoring."[122] The program provides mentoring and volunteers to help prisoners succeed in breaking the cycle of incarceration and create safer communities. They do this by offering financial aid, linking participants with post-secondary education, building mentorship relationships, and delivering support services such as assistance with housing, legal representation, mental health counseling, or tutoring. The program spends only a fraction of the costs of prosecution and incarceration, but it has succeeded in dramatically reducing recidivism and increasing public safety, ensuring that prisoner-students have stable jobs, strong family ties, and productive lives.

New England's ABE-to-College Transition Project

For prisoners who graduate from literacy classes and who want to prepare for post-secondary education,[123] this program, conducted within the prison facilities of Norfolk County House of Correction in Dedham, Massachusetts, and Webster Correctional Facility in Cheshire, Connecticut, is taught by instructors from four Massachusetts community colleges: Massasoit, Mass Bay, Gateway, and Quincy. Students who successfully complete the program are encouraged to continue their education when released from prison by enrolling in the collaborating colleges.

The ABE-to-College Transition Project is a partnership between the New England Literacy Resource Center at World Education and 23 adult learning centers in six New England states. For more information, contact:

NCTN/ World Education, Inc.
44 Farnsworth Street, Boston, MA 02210

Email: nctn@worlded.org
Phone: (617) 482–9485
http://sabes.org/resources/publications/fieldnotes/vol12/f21patton.htm

Georgia—Louisiana—Mississippi:
The Leavell College Extension Center

At Phillips State Prison in Buford, the New Orleans Baptist Theological Seminary created the Leavell College Extension Center to provide Georgian prisoners a two-year associate's degree and a four-year bachelor of arts in Christian ministry. These fully accredited college degrees prepare students for ministry within the Georgia state prison system.

Prisoner-students in the program must have a high-school diploma or GED and must submit a statement of religious experience with their application. The program comprises time-consuming reading and writing assignments, 15 hours of in-class lecture, and at least 30 hours of study per week. To maintain accreditation, the classes are taught and graded at a college level.

Eligible prisoners must have at least five years of remaining prison time, must not have had any disciplinary reports within the previous twelve months, and must not request early release or parole while enrolled in the seminary program.

Funded by the Georgia Baptist Convention, this program is offered in locations other than Buford, as well. It is also found at Angola Penitentiary in Louisiana and the Parchman State Prison in Mississippi, where prisoners can also earn a college degree, minister under the direction of the chaplain while in prison, and return to their communities with a college degree in their hands that will open doors to a future vastly different from their past. For more information:

New Orleans Baptist Theological Seminary
3939 Gentilly Blvd. | New Orleans, LA 70126
(800) 662–8701 | (504) 282–4455
http://educationjustice.net/pipermail/list_educationjustice.net/attachme
nts/20080612/38314261/attachment–0003.pdf

PROJECT RETURN

Project Return in Louisiana, like many others around the country, was forced to end its prison education program because of the current trend in reduced funding for such programs.

Colorado's Youthful Offender Post-Secondary Program

In Colorado, college-level distance-learning courses are available to prisoners 25 years of age or younger who have a realistic probability of being released. Adams State College works with the program to deliver courses leading to an associate's degree. For more information, contact:

Adams State College
208 Edgemont Blvd.
Alamosa, CO 81102
(800) 824–6494 or (719) 587–7011
http://www.adams.edu/gs/students/grenemyer/grenemyer.php

Washington, D.C.: The Prison Outreach Program

In DC-area jails and prisons, Georgetown University offers weekly classes to prisoners in critical reading, writing, narrative discourse, Appalachian literature, and prison literature. Designed to enhance the inmates' critical thinking and written and oral communication skills, the program also provides prisoners with one-on-one tutoring weekly sessions. Contact:

Patricia O'Connor
(202) 687–7622
or write
P.O. Box 44325
Fort Washington, MD 20749
(202) 347–3239
prisonoutreach@georgetown.edu
http://studentorgs.georgetown.edu/prisonoutreach/?Action=Announc
ements

Pennsylvania's Inside-Out Program

This program, created at Philadelphia's Temple University, trains and sends undergraduate college students into prisons to conduct courses, not only in Pennsylvania, but in dozens of Inside-Out classes all over the country. One example is the University of Oregon Honors College course, taught at the Oregon State Penitentiary. To learn more, contact:

The Inside-Out Center
Temple University
Suite 331, MB 66–10

1810 Liacouras Walk
Philadelphia, PA 19122
Tel: (215) 204–5163
Email: insideout@temple.eduhttp://www.insideoutcenter.org

Indiana

Indiana State University was offering two-year and four-year degree programs at five prisons within the state because, says corrections department spokesman Doug Garrison, "lawmakers like the lower recidivism rates they produce."[124] In recent years, they have shifted their focus to vocational programs (see "Getting Ready to Work" below). For more information, write to:

Tirey Hall, Room 134J
Indiana State University
(812) 237–2334

Maryland

The Goucher Prison Education Partnership, a division of Goucher College, offers courses at the Maryland Correctional Institution for Women and the Maryland Correctional Institution-Jessup. There is no public funding for this program; it is supported entirely by private grants and donations. Contact Amy Roza, program director, at 410–337–6033 or at amy.roza@goucher.edu.

Alabama

The *Alabama Prison Arts and Education Project* has grown since its beginning in 2001 to serve 12 prisons in the state, with 80 writers, artists, and scholars providing classes in poetry, creative writing, southern literature, photography, African-American literature, and others. Classes are based on introductory college courses and run for 14 weeks. While no credit is earned, they motivate prisoner-students to continue on with their education. Instructors found that incarcerated students often apply more effort than ordinary students and show a genuine thirst for education.[125]

Arizona

Rio Salado College partners with the state corrections department to provide on-site post-secondary education in the prisons, although courses requiring lab materials, special software or other elements not consistent with the prison environment are not offered. Student eligibility is based upon having earned a GED or high-school diploma, age, academic history, time to release, and the inmate's behavioral record.[126]

Wisconsin's Transforming Lives Network

Prisons in Wisconsin partnered at one time with the Correctional Education Association (CEA) and the Milwaukee Area Technical College (MATC) to create a distance-learning project that uses the satellite services of the CEA's Transforming Lives Network. Starting as a pilot program in five Wisconsin prisons, this "College of the Air" expanded to prisons throughout Wisconsin, Virginia, Tennessee, Minnesota, Maine, Louisiana, Hawaii, and Alaska. Credits for these courses were transferrable to colleges and universities everywhere. These programs were also available to the corrections staff for their development.[127] These courses, however, were not free; inmates had to pay per credit.

Sadly, this program has had to close down because funding is no longer available.

Kansas

In 2001, the Lansing Correctional Facility Program in Lansing, Kansas, started to provide an on-site program leading to an associate's degree from Donnelly College. As of 2013, 325 inmates have taken courses and 14 have earned an associate's degree. Students pay one third of the tuition fee, while Donnelly College raises the balance.[128] For more information, contact:

Donnelly College
608 N. 18th Street
Kansas City, KS 66102
(913) 621–8700

Wyoming

The Department of Corrections was granted $242,000 through the American Recovery and Reinvestment Act to strengthen the educational infrastructure within Wyoming prisons and serve prisoners who are within one to six months of release, prisoners needing a GED, and those who need English-speaking skills. Contact:

Wyoming Department of Corrections
1934 Wyott Drive, Suite 100
Cheyenne, WY 82002
307-777-7208
http://corrections.wy.gov/services/education.html

The Correctional Education Association (CEA)

The CEA, a non-profit, professional association of educators and administrators, does not specifically involve prisoners in its activities; however, it is an organization worthy of attention. As the largest affiliate of the American Correctional Association, the mission of the CEA is to:

- prepare prison students for successful reentry into society, equipping them with academic, career/technical, and personal/social skills;
- support the professional skills development of prison educators; and
- increase community awareness and legislative support for prison education through public relations and legislative advocacy.

For more information, write or call:
Correctional Education Association
8182 Lark Brown Road, Suite 202
Elkridge, MD 21075
Phone: (800) 783-1232
Stephen Steurer, Executive Director—ext. 11
Erica Houser, Assistant Director—ext. 10
http://www.ceanational.org/index2.htm

Post-secondary prison education is rare and extremely difficult for prisoners to obtain, but the experimental programs we've been looking at prove it can be done, with outstanding results.

Some prisoners are determined to get an advanced education. And a few prison systems (New Mexico, North Carolina, Texas, etc.) are developing innovative strategies for overcoming the many real barriers that keep prisoners from learning.

Our challenge now is to find out how we can make education at all levels an integral part of prison rehabilitation—how it can become the standard, rather than the exception.

Reentry Preparation Programs

Too many prisoners, after being released and returned to their old neighborhoods, are soon led back to prison. For this reason, the Second Chance Act of 2008 directed the Justice Department to step up research on reentry issues and established a national Reentry Resource Center to promote training for successful reintegration into society.

A new model for reentry preparation is described in a new publication, "Reentry Education Model; Supporting Education and Career Advancement for Low-Skilled Individuals in Correction" from the Office of Vocational and Adult Education. It is an interdisciplinary effort between corrections and education professionals who determined that education is a vital part of preparation for release and that the incarcerated person should use prison time to get schooling to survive the challenges of society. The authors of the reentry model encourage education providers within prisons and those out in the community to work together.[129]

The president's 2014 budget has added $3 million to continue and expand this work.[130] But the Second Chance Act and the new model study notwithstanding, public programs to assist prisoners in preparing for their release are very few. Several states, however, are making an attempt. Here are some successful examples:

Massachusetts: The Sheriff's After-Incarceration Support Services (AISS) Department

In 1997 the Hampden County Sheriff's Department secured a $150,000 grant to provide vocational and career guidance to help prisoners transition from prison education courses to adult education programs in the community and to ensure follow-up and support for them in pursuing college-level instruction after release. According to the Hampden County Sherriff, "Correctional programs ... significantly helped us in managing our record overcrowding numbers."[131]

Before a prisoner's release, the Hampden County Sheriff's Department requires that he or she prepare a detailed plan for his or her housing, mental health, substance abuse, and education. Any prisoner who expresses an interest in continuing with education is invited to meet one-on-one with an education reintegration counselor and get help with creating a follow-up plan.

At the time of release, the counselor schedules an enrollment appointment for the recently released prisoner and also arranges for the released prisoner to meet with a mentor from the community. The mentor is an employee of the Hampden County Sheriff's Department—and also a former prisoner! If the student stops attending classes or has other support requirements, the mentor is there to provide what he or she needs.[132]

A key component to the success of the program is that the prison program coordinator remains in communication with both the prisoners and with the providers of adult education programs in the community. The coordinator explains the reintegration concept and solicits support for it from educational institutions and their teaching staff. Because there has been overwhelming support, it becomes easy to make referrals for newly released prisoners.

Inside the prison facility, there are monthly "Student of the Month" ceremonies at which the coordinator talks to the prisoner-students about opportunities for education upon release and where community educators come into the prison facility to discuss available educational programs.

Prisoner-students need to understand that continuing the education they began behind bars can lead to a world of satisfying careers. Prior to this reintegration program, only about 30 percent of prisoners expressed interest in pursuing formal education after their release. After the reintegration program began, a full 75 percent expressed a desire to further their education. They can, indeed, go for it.[133]

To learn more about the program, contact:

Hampden County Pre-Release Center
325 Alabama Road
Ludlow, MA 01056
(413) 547–8000, ext. 2802
PRC@hcsdmass.org
or
Hampden County Sheriff's Department
736 State Street
Springfield, Massachusetts 01109
(413) 733–5469 ext 8311

Washington State's Bridge to College

This is a post-prison education program designed to help released prisoners transition to state community colleges. It was founded in 2005 with the understanding that with the necessary tools and human support, a true academic education—not merely vocational training—empowers released ex-prisoners to find meaningful employment and succeed in the community, thereby reducing recidivism, economic crime, and prison overcrowding.

A creation of the state's Post-Prison Education Program and the Department of Corrections, the Bridge to College reentry program provides social and financial support to help released prisoners bridge the cultural gap between prison life and college life. Various community groups and the Department of

Corrections reinforce each other's efforts by matching educational opportunities during prison with educational opportunities after prison.

Post-Prison Education Program
810 Third Avenue—Suite 205
Seattle, WA 98104–1651
For Mailing: Post Office Box 45038
Seattle, WA 98145–0038

Michigan's Prison Reentry Initiative

Michigan has initiated a multi-phased program. Phase I covers the time of imprisonment and begins with assessing the prisoners' risks, needs, and strengths, then assigns them to appropriate programs, including correctional education.[134] Phase II is preparation for a transition to community at the time of a parole decision. At this point a reentry plan is developed to address the challenges of housing, jobs, education, training, substance abuse, health care, family reunification, etc. The third phase begins with the prisoner's release and continues until discharge from parole supervision. In the last phase, the released prisoner works with a transition team of local service-providing agencies to integrate back into society and implement his or her plan.

New Jersey's Safe Streets and Neighborhoods Initiative

Supported by public and private funds and partnerships, including the Nicholson Foundation, two of this program's segments specifically serve female offenders. One, the Computer-based Learning from Prison to Community Program, begins during incarceration and continues after release, at which time a computer is provided to each participant in halfway houses, and participants get employment and training in relevant skills from the New Jersey Department of Labor and Workforce Development.[135]

Another program in New Jersey's reentry initiative is Opportunity Reconnect, a one-stop center facilitating access to post-secondary education and college courses, training, employment, housing, substance abuse treatment, health care (physical and mental), and academic and personal counseling.[136] There is more information at:

New Jersey State League of Municipalities
222 West State Street
Trenton, NJ 08608
(609) 695–3481

or

The Office of the Attorney General
(609) 292–4791

Indiana's Allen County Reentry Court Project

With the goal of lowing recidivism rates in Allen County, this program begins with assessing an offender's needs, making recommendations for a reentry plan, and providing education, job training, and treatment services. Participants, as well as the friends and family they live with, must sign an agreement accepting the terms and conditions of the Reentry Court. It is funded by the Indiana Department of Correction and by reimbursements from participating released offenders, either in cash or community service. For more information, contact:

Allen Superior Court
213 S. Calhoun, Rm. 302
Fort Wayne, IN 46802
(260) 449–7583
Email: jsurbeck1@earthlink.net

Computer Skills Needed for Job Hunting

Released prisoners can access computers for free at most public libraries. If they are comfortable getting information and tutorials online, the *Fair Shake Reentry Resource Center* provides information on resources for job training, housing assistance, health programs, food assistance, voting rights, licensing, volunteer opportunities, and more. They are there to help ex-convicts succeed on the outside. A tour of the website is provided at http://www.fairshake.net/new_to_fs

Fair Shake Inc.
P.O. Box 63
Westby, WI 54667
(608) 634–6363
http://www.fairshake.net

Another online resource is the website of the Federal Bureau of Prisons. It provides a list of employment resources to assist ex-prisoners with job hunting. There is a wealth of information on these and other websites, all accessible at no charge in public libraries. It should be noted, however, that it takes a lot of time and patience to dig into all the links. No one can expect to get all of it at once. The released prisoner must prepare to spend several weeks, at least, to peruse, absorb, and apply all the information accessible on this site: http://www. bop.gov/inmate_programs/itb_references.jsp. It can be helpful, but only if the searcher is not overwhelmed.

Further, there are numerous job-hunting websites for positions open in both the private sector (www.monster.com, www.CareerOneStop.org, http://j obcenter.usa.gov,) and in the public sector (www.usajobs.opm.gov, www.statel ocalgov.net). These and dozens of other sites can assist the job-seeking released prisoner if he or she is sufficiently computer-savvy to navigate them, to create pages on LinkedIn and Facebook, and to submit professional-looking online resumes.

Other Resources

Living as a prisoner, incarcerated, surrounded by incessant noise and violence is for many a lonely and frustrating existence. Everyone needs community, and prisoners are no exception. It helps to know that like-minded people experience the same issues, have the same questions, and want to reach out and communicate with one another.

The restrictions of prison life make this difficult. One way to break through the isolation and create community is by reading publications specifically written by prisoners and for prisoners wherein prisoners can get current news that affects prison life, share one another's experiences, and build relationships through correspondence. It is important, however, that prisoners verify regulations governing inmate-to-inmate correspondence policies at their facilities prior to writing to other incarcerated individuals. In some prison systems it is prohibited.

A number of publications written for prisoners can open the door to community. Some provide news and information relevant to prison life and the justice system; others provide a creative or analytical outlet for prisoner expression. And still others address special-interest groups within the prison community (religious, political, legal, ethnic, etc.). Prisoners who subscribe to these publications, or to the several prisoner pen-pal clubs that exist, can widen the narrow horizons of prison life and connect in a meaningful way with others in the world behind prison walls. (See Appendix II for a list of these publications.)

6

Options for Distance Learning

Distance education means doing schoolwork away from campus. Most distance education is conducted via the internet. Obviously, in the case of prisoner-students, that medium is not accessible; prisoner-students must pursue their education by mail. The school sends the prisoner-students instructions in a study guide, along with a list of required books, materials, and assignments through the mail. Prisoner-students may have to rely on family members or friends to locate and purchase required textbooks online, ensuring that they are the correct edition, and have it mailed to them. The student follows the study guide on what to read, what assignments to do, what research papers to submit, and what to mail back to the school. The instructor at the school then reviews, corrects, and returns the assignments, with comments, to the student. After finishing a stipulated number of assignments, the student might take a midterm exam or a final exam when the course is complete. This exam usually has to be proctored or monitored, so someone from the prison's educational department must be willing to be there (and some are not) for required exams.

In most facilities, prisoners must fill out extensive paperwork to get authorization to pursue college courses and receive books. Every prison is different; every warden and educational supervisor has his or her own point of view. Some are very supportive; others put up roadblocks.

Prisoners who want to pursue a formal education must almost always first have completed either a GED or a high-school diploma. That will be the first order of business for many. Once that requirement is fulfilled, they can decide which educational path is best suited for their life goals. There are pros and cons to each of the available options:

- academic and other college-credit courses (two-year or four-year programs),
- career or vocational courses (trade schools),

- personal enrichment courses, and
- religious studies (free and fee-based, Bible studies, etc.).

Academic College Education

Of the one-third who enrolled in academic programs, most pursued an associate's (two-year) degree. Of these, only a small percentage completed. If a college education is the direction a prisoner chooses, unless incarcerated in one of the very few prisons that have an on-site college program, that person is on his or her own. When we consider how long it takes to complete degree requirements under acutely adverse conditions, it is not surprising that only a very few—three percent of prisoners nationwide—enrolled in programs leading to either a bachelor's (four-year) or graduate (more advanced) degree.

The academic track is the longest and the hardest road to education, and it isn't for everyone. On the other hand, as one prisoner said who was enrolled in a four-year program, "A vocational training program will teach you how to do something [and qualify you] to have a job, but it doesn't teach you how to think ... that's the problem a lot of men in prison have, is that they're not thinking, they're reacting. So [while] a vocational program might give you the skills to have a job, an academic program will give you critical thinking and problem-solving skills, skills, in other words, to have a life."[1]

Some people complete the two-year associate's degree with the intention of later transferring to a four-year college where they will focus on a specialized area of study for the last two years and earn a bachelor's degree in Sociology, Business Administration, Criminal Justice, Engineering, Political Science, or other fields. Some do it because a two-year community college is much less expensive; others do it because they cannot meet the entrance requirements at a four-year college. It's a practical way to start—*if* they are diligent about finding out in advance the credit-transfer requirements of the four-year university at which they will later study, and *if* they have verified that the two-year college is properly accredited, and *if* they have satisfied other entrance requirements, such as foreign language proficiency, etc.

College through correspondence cannot compare to on-site classrooms and lecture halls, but the academics are tough and it is still challenging and mind-expanding. Prisoners pursuing a liberal arts degree often study five or six hours per day to make the grade. It may take time, a lot of time, for a prisoner to complete a bachelor's degree. That's all right. If it isn't completed before release, the prisoner will be in a good position to enroll at a college or university and continue on after release. The important thing is to get started. And some individuals, those who really work at it, do succeed in completing degrees while still incarcerated. It can be done. It has been done.

Vocational or Technical Schools

Trade schools take less time to complete and are less expensive than academic studies at colleges and universities. They are also more likely than colleges or universities to offer payment plans that can be very attractive to prisoners.

Trade schools provide work-related skills prisoners can use immediately upon their release. Plumbers, electricians, and construction specialists are needed everywhere, as are people who know computers and information technology, health care, and hospitality. Since most jobs require technical skills, technical and vocational schools help one to get a good job more quickly.

Vocational classes can include everything from dog training to retail management, from drug-abuse counseling to automobile mechanics or paralegal training. Vocational schooling does lower recidivism rates because it increases an ex-prisoner's chance to find good employment with a decent wage, especially for-credit vocational courses in community colleges that lead to an associate's degree or career training which includes an apprenticeship.[2] This is why support of vocational education may be more "palatable" to legislators.

As of 2003–2004, two-thirds of the prisoners enrolled in post-secondary prison education took for-credit vocational certificate programs that lead to work skills in the shortest time possible: in other words, to a *job*.

Religious studies and enrichment courses are often offered without cost. They can be very beneficial, personally, but they do not lead to employability.

Looking Carefully into the Pitfalls

Before selecting a school or educational program, there are many factors a prisoner must take into consideration, factors that require the prisoner do research—without the normal research tools most of us take for granted. To select the right school, prisoner-students will want to verify:

- the variety and quantity of course offerings,
- the format of learning materials (electronic or web-based courses are not permitted in most prisons, nor are courses requiring chemicals),
- completion deadlines,
- the availability and cost of deadline extensions,

- degrees offered,
- solidity of the correspondence program, and
- the school's experience with prisoner-students.

Most importantly, they must verify that the school providing the courses is properly accredited. Without proper accreditation, the hard-earned degree may not be considered legitimate or accepted within the prisoner's chosen profession. Without accreditation, credits may not transfer to other schools at which the prisoner might want to advance.

All this must be determined without access to a computer or the internet, or even easy access to a telephone.

Even more treacherous for the prisoner-student are the academic scams that abound. Not all accreditation agencies are legitimate. Not all are nationally recognized. And some are outright frauds. There are bad schools out there, too, schools we call "diploma mills" or "degree mills" that boldly and falsely claim accreditation when they are not accredited or when they are "accredited" by an inauthentic accreditation agency that they, themselves, have created.[3] There are also fraudulent "lost diploma replacement services" that will—for a fee, of course—mail a document attesting to any degree one claims to have earned.

If a school costs far less than usual and grants degrees requiring little or no work—some will even confer a diploma for a price—it is most likely not legitimate. "Degree mills" that offer a fast path to a degree offer a fast path to nowhere. Too many prisoners have been fooled. They have put their hard work into earning a diploma that isn't worth the paper it is printed on.

It's bad enough that dishonest companies sell phony degrees. What's worse, and what keeps them in existence, is that people really do buy them and pass themselves off as skilled professionals. "A lot of fakes and frauds are out there right now, practicing medicine, teaching classes, practicing law, counseling troubled families, building bridges, pulling teeth, and keeping books without benefit of a degree, a license, or proper training."[4] These colleges advertise heavily and make it sound easy to obtain a degree. Prisoners need guidance so that they aren't suckered.

Prisoners must also be aware that some professions are forever closed to them and not waste their time or money studying to work in certain areas of education, social work, nursing, medicine, or law. They might earn a degree, but will probably not be allowed to practice. On the other hand, business degrees, such as those in accounting and finance, are a mixed bag. While it might be difficult to secure a position which involves the management of money, for prisoners who want to start and operate their own business, this is where they'll get the information needed to do it successfully.[5]

One area where prisoners can put real-life experience and first-hand knowledge to good use is a career in criminology. They may not ever be able to work in law enforcement, prisons, or probation and parole departments, and it may be uncomfortable studying in a classroom full of students planning to be policemen, eager to get out there and lock up all the bad guys. But they have several options in this field: they can teach criminology and justice in a community college or university, they can work with juveniles or prisoners, and they can do research. Another promising field is in substance abuse treatment; since crime is sometimes a consequence of drug or alcohol abuse, a prison record can add credibility. Many in this field have criminal histories that have not created a barrier to success.

Cost: A Hard Reality

Money, money, money. Alas, education is expensive. And if one can't pay for the courses, they are of no use. Prisoners who earn between $5.25 and $20 per month cannot afford college courses. A small handful might make up to $100 or $150 a month, but it takes years and years to climb the ranks to reach that level. So covering the cost of education by themselves is almost impossible for most prisoners.

In addition to tuition fees, students must pay application fees, registration fees, shipping expenses, textbooks (books are the second largest expense after tuition) and, if one is lucky enough to get there, even graduation fees. Earning a degree through correspondence can cost anywhere from $25,000 to $50,000.

Federal financial aid to students is *not* available to incarcerated students, at least not until after they are released. There are three or four privately funded scholarships for prisoners that can help maybe 20–45 prisoner-students per year (assuming the prisoner-student can locate them). At one time there was the Federal Incarcerated Youth Offender (IYO) grant for prisoners under the age of 35 and within seven years of release. This was later changed to the Incarcerated Individual Program (IIP), which had been available in a limited number of state prisons. The IIP was most commonly used to assist prisoners with educational costs and to provide employment counseling and other related services.[6] The Incarcerated Youth Offender (IYO) grants were awarded not to individuals, but to institutions. Therefore, prisoners who qualified could not apply directly; they had to inquire at their facility's Education Department. Since 2012, however, this source of assistance has been defunct. It no longer exists.

In Virginia, the Elizabeth Kates Foundation, Inc., formed by the first female warden in Virginia, provides a scholarship to cover the tuition of approximately 10–15 women each semester.[7]

Also in Virginia, inmates who are veterans can apply to receive state veteran education benefits, but only about 10 to 15 typically qualify. Those who do qualify must be able to pay up front for the courses from personal funds and then apply for reimbursement.[8] That makes these benefits inaccessible to most prisoners.

Prisoners incarcerated in Texas who are honorably discharged veterans can take their chances and apply to the Hazelwood Act for a grant, as well as to the Texas Public Education Grant, which is a needs-based program.

Inmates who are veterans may also be eligible for the Montgomery GI Bill if they signed up while on active duty and made the required $1,200 contribution. If so, they can apply for aid as an inmate in a federal prison. (It should be noted, however, that inmates receive educational aid in amounts less than veterans who are not incarcerated. Also, a "fugitive felon," one who has an outstanding warrant for a felony or has violated a condition of probation or parole by committing a felony, is not eligible to use the GI Bill. As for the Veterans Educational Assistance Program, veterans in prison and parolees must contact a VA regional office to determine eligibility. VA benefits will not be provided to any veteran or dependent wanted on an outstanding felony warrant.)

The only other scholarship known to be specifically dedicated to prisoner-students was the Prison Scholarship Fund. However, demand has been so high and donations so low that they can no longer respond to requests.

That's it. A drop in a waterfall. So, the two main sources of assistance for the incarcerated are families (for those who can) and in-prison courses, if one is fortunate enough to be in one of the few prisons where they are offered.

Released ex-prisoners can find more in the way of support through scholarships and grants. For the 1.7 million children who have a parent in prison, the Creative Corrections Education Foundation works to reduce crime in subsequent generations by helping them receive either vocational or academic educations if they have applied for a Pell Grant and have good references from their schools.

But the bottom line is this: Financial help for the incarcerated is next to nothing.

In-prison, on-site education is the only practical solution. However, prisons have budget problems, too. State and federal funding for prison education has been reduced and even eliminated in some states. Unless something changes, and until people and politicians realize it is not only for the benefit of prisoners, but for the benefit of society that we educate the prison population, the downward spiral of a world polluted by crime and impoverished by exponentially expanding prison systems will continue.

7

Too Late, Too Old?

Older prisoners are seldom motivated to pursue a college education. From a practical view they might ask, "What's the point?" My former cellmate, a man in his early 60s who will be released when he is 70 or 71, refused my offer to pay his tuition if he were to enroll in college. He declined the gift; he was simply not interested. He had lost his ability to envision or care about any kind of a future.

It is understandable, but how sad! A life isn't over until it's over. At any age—even as a "lifer" who has no hope of release—education is a way to make something meaningful of the years one spends behind bars—a way to redeem the previous wasted seasons of a life shaped by poor decisions. It is an opportunity to pay something back to society and to make a positive difference.

If they became educated and developed communication skills, older, long-term prisoners could start a school to teach the younger prisoners. They could inspire and motivate the younger ones to turn their lives around—their own lives, their children's lives, and the lives of others in the communities to which they will return.

Newly incarcerated or long-term, all prisoners would do well to ask themselves, "How much time have I wasted in my life because of poor decisions?" I would encourage them, "Do something positive now and don't waste a single minute more! You've got time on your hands, plenty of it. Make it work for you. Use it to read about subjects of interest. Reading isn't a burden; it's an exciting adventure."

Adult learners perform as well as, or even better than, traditional-age students. They are often more focused, more purposeful, and more motivated. So there is no reason for prisoners to fall back on advancing age as an excuse or to look for reasons why they cannot succeed; rather, they must look for ways they *can*. All of us—incarcerated or not—have only so much time. To throw any of it away when we could be making a difference is a travesty.

"But four years from now, that prisoner will be × years old!" one might protest. True. But, four years from now, whether that person gets a degree or not, he or she will still be × years old. And they will still need resources.

Prisoner-Students: An Oxymoron?

While it is true that some prisoners are initially reluctant to participate in mandatory basic education classes,[1] most likely because of bad experiences with school in earlier years, many seem to turn around quickly and embrace education enthusiastically. Instructors discover how much prisoners desire education, and prisoners have proven to be excellent students. Instructors observe that "inmates enrolled in correctional educational programs nationally can and do make significant progress in learning"[2] and usually achieve significant increases in grade level.[3] At the New Hampshire State Prison, for example, inmates who completed a one-year educational course in technology improved their initial scores as much as four grade levels. These findings were also borne out by inmates surveyed by Daniel Lawrence at a facility operated by the Oklahoma Department of Corrections. His research found that inmates "caught up" at the rate of one academic year for every three months of study."[4] Moreover, prisoner-students were found to earn higher grades than non-incarcerated students taking the same courses on campus.[5]

"The National Adult Literacy Survey, conducted by the U.S. Department of Education in 1992 and 2003, included both federal and state prisoners. One finding was that prisoners with a GED scored higher in reading skills than persons in the general population with the equivalent education. The analysis is also consistent with research which finds that prisoners can and do achieve at levels equal to, or higher than, members of the community."[6] Dozens of studies with large samples and multi-state designs or meta-analyses indicate the academic performance of inmates is as competent, or more so, than students in the community.

A few examples: In a University of California extension program at San Quentin, 57 percent of the prisoner-student papers received a grade of A; less than 1 percent received an F.[7] University authorities rated San Quentin prisoner-student work as of a higher quality than that of community students. In a University of Wisconsin extension program at Wisconsin State Prison, inmate students again had both higher completion rates and higher grades than their traditional-student counterparts.[8]

At the college level of academic study, inmates did not generally score higher than their community counterparts, but they did perform at the same level. Ball State University faculty evaluated inmate students as having academic ability equal to campus students and, taking the course with the same curriculum and texts, as having put greater effort into their studies than campus students.[9] "Over the years, incarcerated men and women have demonstrated astonishing potential and real talent within a structured learning environment."[10]

One would typically expect campus college students perform at higher levels than their prison counterparts because they have greater resources. On the other hand, prisoner-students, knowing they have very limited post-secondary opportunities, are highly motivated. Inmates say they are driven by career goals, personal satisfaction, intellectual stimulation, and enhanced post-release employment opportunities.

The public policy implication is that investments in correctional education can provide a broad range of social gains, as well as personal benefits for prisoners.[11]

Ex-Cons Excel on Campus

Entering students who are older than traditional high-school graduates are a growing population on campuses and are not as unusual as some might think. Some older students come back to school after a career crisis, a divorce, military service, or time in prison.[12] Even though many enter college ill prepared by having failed in urban schools in earlier years,[13] former prisoners and parolees who pursue an education on the outside have proven to be committed students and serious learners, strong at overcoming adversity.

But we must not gloss over some realities.

It is easier if prisoners complete their education *before* leaving prison, for both financial and social reasons. First of all, former prisoners are an undesirable demographic for many higher education institutions, wary of potential liability that may ensue for admitting a known former prisoner. Colleges concerned with issues of social stigmatization and risk management may limit opportunities for former prisoners seeking an education after their prison terms have ended.

Prisoners do not enjoy legal protection in pursuing educational opportunities as a minority group under civil rights law, and universities can exclude them with impunity.[14] Ex-prisoners, you might say, are an invisible minority. On most campuses there are special advisory services for women, gays, the disabled, and veterans, but there are none for ex-prisoners. Because they come in many colors and ethnic groups, the ex-prisoners are not immediately obvious as a minority group. Especially since most of them attempt to hide their criminal pasts. Who can blame them if they want to put the stigma behind them and be able to study like other students?[15]

There may be questions about felonies on applications. Some colleges or universities conduct background checks and may eliminate an applicant with a criminal history. Some discriminate against convicted felons, denying financial aid, campus employment, and/or housing. And within the college or university, a prison record may mean that certain majors or schools, such as social work, medicine, nursing, law, or business, are off limits to ex-convicts.[16]

Most colleges collect their information about criminal records primarily through self-disclosure on the application, although some (particularly the private and four-year schools) do background checks. A student admitted with a criminal record may be supervised. Not all colleges, however, consider criminal records in their admissions process. And studies show that schools that do not collect criminal justice information appear to be equally safe. Crimes on campus are typically committed by people without criminal records. Therefore, "barring people with criminal records ... does not improve campus safety, but does undermine public safety in the larger community."[17]

Also difficult is the fact that ex-prisoners walk around a campus surrounded by students who typically grew up in solid families and came straight from high school to college. They don't know much about the streets or courts, jails or prisons, and do not understand what the ex-prisoner has experienced.[18] So the ex-offender may suffer a sense of isolation on campus.[19]

It can be a catch–22. It is understandable that these individuals want to interact as students, not as formerly incarcerated individuals. On the other hand, non-disclosure makes it difficult to obtain resources and assistance.[20]

The College Initiative

In New York, at the City University of New York (CUNY), a program called the College Initiative (CI) was created as an outgrowth of the Bedford Hills in-prison programs. Its purpose is to assist former prisoners with their pursuit of an advanced education, helping them to become "transformative leaders within their own communities," to find employment, and serve as engaged citizens working for a safer city, providing a role model for youth.[21] College Initiative staffers believe—and have proved—that former prisoners succeed if they can navigate the barriers and challenges they face when trying to further their education. Although released prisoners are eligible for financial aid, that alone does not guarantee their success. College Initiative offers support services at stressful transition points that include orientation and assessment at pre-release facilities, tutoring, financial aid counseling, peer support, and connection to other reentry services for housing, public benefits, employment, etc.[22]

College Initiative utilizes an individual counseling approach and has been successful in helping prisoner-students overcome bureaucratic barriers that prevent them from advancing. However, CI's limited staff found they could not keep pace with the growing need for its services, as almost 6,000 college-eligible individuals come to New York from prison facilities every year.[23] Working closely with the City University of New York, CI staffers have expanded their capacity to serve by coordinating relationships they have forged with on-campus organizations, other educational institutions, the criminal justice system, and the reentry community. In so doing, they minimize unnecessary duplication of effort and create synergy. Graduate CI students work to support released prisoners who follow, further increasing the impact of a small organization.

In fact, College Initiative can serve as a model on a national level to show how an organization can accomplish a great deal with a small staff. They have created a multi-level problem-solving strategy utilizing root-cause analysis to address problems beyond the individual level, problems that occur at a systemic level and affect broader groups which can be solved with changes in institutional or public policies.[24] Some of these problems stemmed from insensitivity or lack of awareness of what a former prisoner is facing.

As of 2010, the recidivism rate was as low as 3.2 percent for CI participants enrolled in just one semester of college. Out of 2,000 who signed up for support services as of that time, 12 have earned associate's degrees, 51 attained bachelor's degrees, and 27 completed their master's degrees. All performed on par with the traditional CUNY student population.

It is crucial that not only the prisoners themselves, but also faculty and administrators of educational institutions, understand that education is the key to prisoner reintegration. Many ex-prisoners do not feel deserving of a college education or believe it exists for them. On campus, subtle signals from the campus may indicate they are not welcome and reinforce that feeling.

CI works to help formerly incarcerated prisoners bear a more positive self-image as students and responsible citizens. Many CI students become leaders and speakers on criminal justice policy and reform issues. Some become CI leaders.

Ex-prisoners entering college need time to adjust to their new situation. It may be intimidating to fill out financial aid applications or register online. Taking a required placement exam and attending one's first classes can produce anxiety. They need to know how to navigate opportunities for research, professional development, and employment.[25] Like most new and unfamiliar things, it can be intimidating. College is unknown territory, but it is also a grand adventure.

If a released ex-convict is too timid for adventure, that person may be too timid for real life.

Both prisoners and ex-prisoners have proven to make good students. Teachers at San Quentin say, "They complete reading assignments and homework and ask insightful questions."[26] They value a rigorous curriculum of literacy, writing, math, and cognitive therapy.[27] Imprisoned students apply what they learn to their lives and their environment, seeking "to understand, not regurgitate," and are more concerned with ideas than grades.[28] They are serious about learning, and their motivation may be more powerful than that of traditional students because they are working toward nothing less than a total transformation of themselves, their minds, and their lives. For them, education is the key to freedom in a brand-new world.[29] "These students bring a level of drive and focus to their academic and professional development that distinguishes them from many traditional college students."[30]

It isn't easy. Some prisoners fail, just like people on the outside fail. But inside or outside, determined people reach their goal.

The Prisoners' Perspective

Before enrolling in a prison education program, prisoners often have a view of the world as a deck stacked against them. Many come from a life of poverty, racial discrimination, poor schools, and often violent, abusive homes. They have no vision of anything that can improve their circumstances and no concept of options, choices, or actions that could alter the course of their lives.[31] Looking back, some prisoners regret wasting the opportunity to learn when they had it, often citing drug use as a major factor. Sometimes that regret will motivate them to attend classes when or if they are available in their prison facilities.[32]

It is interesting to note that prisoners, as a rule, do not blame the school system or former teachers, but typically they take responsibility for their previous failures. Said one inmate, "You can learn if you want; it's up to you. It's not up to the teacher or ... other people, just do you want to learn?"[33]

For the most part, these are people for whom public education did not work the first time, but prisoners who move from Adult Basic Education (ABE) to earning a GED and on to college acquire more than new skills; they acquire a different view of the world and higher expectations of themselves.

It is not surprising that 94 percent of prisoners surveyed said they do want education to improve their skills and chances of post-release success. What a remarkably strong statement of motivation to seek a better life![34] The *Police Journal* has reported the same thing, that prisoners emphatically want more educational programs.[35] In fact, prisoners placed education above all other life-essential services.

Yet despite the well-known eagerness on the part of prisoners and the documented positive outcomes, the percentage of prisoners who participate in post-secondary correctional programs is low.[36] Enrollment can be prevented by many factors, including prison policies and program availability. Of course, individual drive and determination also make a huge impact on whether an individual pursues an education. The question remains: Why do some participate and succeed while others do not?[37] On the federal level, the low percentage of participation, according to some researchers, may partially be due to inaccuracy in BOP's Education Data System.[38]

It is interesting to note that prison staff tend to believe prisoners would be motivated to attend classes more by cash awards and other material incentives,[39] but more relevant is what the prison-students themselves had to say about why they enrolled in courses. One common response was that they wanted to avoid "dead time" while incarcerated, sitting and doing nothing. Prisoners know time goes a lot faster when working in a meaningful, positive way. Studying for classes provides an "escape" from the stifling confines of prison or, as one prisoner put it, "blowing the roof off confinement."[40]

Said Sarah, a college student who had served for eight years,

"When you're in college it takes you away from the prison ... it's like, you're opening your mind to a whole different experience ... you're still in prison, but once you're in that class it's like you're not in prison, you know? You're here getting an education ... I didn't know anything about India and China and the opium war ... And it took me to go to [prison] to take up that class in order for me to learn that ... I didn't know about Sigmund Freud, none of that! But reading the books and writing ... I'm telling you, it was just so amazing for me, I was like bugged out, because I ... I never would've known. To me, [college] puts you on a higher level."[41]

Some prisoners enroll out of loneliness, to be with people they can talk to and to be part of a safer, more positive, cooperative environment. Prisoners, like everyone else, need community. For them, the classroom becomes a refuge, a sanctuary from the brutal realities of prison, a place where geniality between teachers and students prevails.[42] "Even when we're out of the classroom, everybody is still respecting and helping each other."[43]

Prisoners said they view their college education as a lifeline, as a way to develop the mind, promote personal growth, and keep their social support networks alive. And many feel the need to go beyond an elementary grade level. They said that reading was the basis for all other learning, so it scored as the single most important educational skill. They also emphasized the need for writing skills to communicate both legally and socially, and math was needed for work (measuring square footage, accounting records, and so on).

Education is a prisoner's hope for getting out and staying out. It's the ticket to a good job and the ability to support a family. It is a second chance at life. And they know it.

The First Step

Earning a GED is often the first step toward the world of higher education. Debra, incarcerated at Bedford Hills, failed the test on her first try and worked hard to pass it a second time. Like so many of her fellow inmates, seeing her name on the diploma brought tears.

"So I got the envelope. I opened it and a copy of my diploma fell out, and I just started crying. Tears just started coming to my eyes. I was like 'Oh! I got it! I finally ... ' I was so happy. I made so many copies. I sent it to my grandfather, to my son, to my daughter, to everybody! To let them know, you know, that I was in school and just, you know, I may be away but I'm doing something to better myself while I'm here. My grandpa was so proud."[44]

Obtaining a GED is a step away from drugs and from life on the streets; it is a leap toward further education and a more meaningful, productive life. It changes the way many prisoners feel about themselves. "At last I was more than just a felon incapable of doing anything positive; I had become a legitimate person."[45] The diploma brings with it a pride in accomplishment. "I feel really good that I accomplished something. And it's made my family look up to me. They are proud of me."[46]

Another prisoner interviewed said that having experienced achievement, he now gets frustrated when he doesn't do his best. And the heady sense of accomplishment typically awakens a desire to encourage relatives and children to also pursue a diploma, to show that they can do it, too.[47]

Advanced post-secondary education requires prisoners to take on serious academic work. For college programs, prisoner-students must satisfy the same enrollment criteria as students on the outside, including passing rigorous entrance exams. Once accepted, most prisoner-students strive to complete a degree, to the extent possible, before leaving prison.[48]

"I've always been afraid of going to college. This class has opened my eyes to a whole new way of learning, and built my confidence in a way I never could have imagined!"[49]

Prisoners who were fortunate enough to be incarcerated at facilities that have on-site advanced education expressed the importance of one-on-one assistance from teachers. They said teachers who expressed interest in their success inspired them to commit the necessary time and energy to their education.[50]

Responsibility and Giving Back

At the heart of most post-secondary prison education programs are requirements for participation and giving back, often in the form of tutoring and mentoring. This creates a culture of peer support in which prisoners come to see themselves as part of a larger social context.[51] College graduates "give back" by developing in-prison and community-based programs such as anger management, substance abuse, health care, domestic violence, sexual abuse, and parenting skills.

"After having time to reevaluate how many people were hurt and the ridiculous choices I made ... my remorse turned into wanting to make amends. Wanting to make things better. Helping others not make the same mistakes ..."—Rayla[52]

"When I was ... in the [Bedford] college program, I learned about the importance of giving back. I had a lot of time inside to think about what I had done and the many people who paid a price for my behavior. I decided that I had to commit myself to helping others, my children and other people who are going through hard times ... I know what I have to do. It isn't always easy. You can't just pop back into your life or your kids' lives. You've changed and so have they. But having the chance to find our way has been—well, I have never done anything so rewarding."—Victoria[53]

Said Rose, a college graduate, serving 25 years to life:

"And that's what happens in here, in this very dark place. We are educated. We go to college and we learn new things. And we have a lot of confidence. Not only our self-esteem, but we even have something to offer others."[54]

Some prisoners attribute a growing sense of responsibility for their crime to their college experience. They begin to connect with their victims and victims' families, to their children, and the communities from whom they are separated, as well as to fellow students and to social change.

"Education softens you too. It's made me soften. I think about things more. I appreciate things more. People. Their feelings. And it made me feel differently about the crime. Before, I was stupid. I had that thug mentality. That street thing. That hard thing. But now, you can do anything to me, and I'm not going to react like that. I'm not going there."—Francine[55]

If our prisons become a place for intellectual, emotional, and social growth that, for these people, would not have been experienced on the outside, wouldn't prisoners and all of society be better off?

Education Transforms

What may be hard for prisoners to articulate, but is clearly evidenced, is the powerful liberation that comes when they learn to reason logically and analytically. Education and the act of writing open a prisoner's world to the freedom of expression, of healing, and of giving voice to the self who was silenced. Education, many prisoners said, is a way to preserve one's sanity and release creativity that is therapeutic and rehabilitative.[56] "I was in a much bigger prison before I got here, but I didn't know it."[57]

The core elements of education, reflection, and inquiry create critical thinkers who take responsibility for their past and future actions and view themselves as actively engaged in the betterment of society.[58] Many advanced educational programs are structured to (1) stimulate intellectual and personal growth for students; (2) build a supportive community of learners among the prisoners in the college; and (3) encourage a sense of personal responsibility and a commitment to giving back, both to the prison community and later to the outside community post-release.[59]

Those who participated in classes—whether academic, arts, or other—felt they had grown as individuals and as part of the prison community. Take the example of Denise, a college student and mother of three:

"When I first came [to prison], I was a chronic disciplinary problem, getting tickets back to back. I had a very poor attitude as well. I was rude and obnoxious for no reason; I did not care about anything or anyone.... Then I became motivated to participate in a number of programs, one of which was college. I started to care about getting in trouble and became conscious of the attitude I had that influenced my negative behaviors.... College is a form of rehabilitation, one of the best."[60]

It is undisputed: education changes people. And that's what prisons should do. Education changes minds, teaches people how to think and how to respond in a positive, constructive way to circumstances.[61] If we allow education to shape moral thinking and promote pro-social attitudes,[62] it will alter the prisoners' values and beliefs so that they become productive, law-abiding, and loyal to their country.[63]

But college alone will not do it for them. Prisoners enrolled in an educational program understand that change has to come from within, that one must be open and ready for that change.

Moreover—and this is significant for the long-term impact on society—when one person breaks out of the cycle of poverty and crime, and when that person experiences the transformational realization of self-worth that an education brings, that person has a rippling effect on the people around him or her.

If education will change the way people think and exist, prisoners who benefit from these programs will no longer threaten community safety or drain our economic resources when they are released from prison. If we facilitate their access to education, they will come out of prison willing and ready to be a positive influence in their community.

Brilliance Behind Bars

A number of imprisoned intellectuals have made a powerful impact upon society and the political or social order. Among some of the unforgettable are Thomas More, Mahatma Gandhi, William Reich, George Jackson, Eldridge Cleaver, Malcolm X, Nelson Mandela, Martin Luther King, and Antonio Gramsci (founder of the Italian Communist Party).[64] There is much one can do to contribute, even behind bars. One can advocate, spread ideas and fight for a better world. Imprisonment is not an excuse.

And how many people realize that from inside prison walls has come some of the world's finest and most enduring literature? World-renowned writers like Miguel de Cervantes (*Don Quixote*); Fyodor Dostoevsky (*Brothers Karamazov*); Alexandre Dumas (*The Count of Monte Cristo*); Aleksandr Solzhenitsyn (*Gulag Archipelago*); and Leo Tolstoy (*War and Peace*) were imprisoned. The list goes on and on. It includes literary giants like Oscar Wilde, Voltaire, Paul Verlaine, Ken Kesey (*One Flew Over the Cuckoo's Nest*), William Burroughs, and O. Henry. We can fill many pages with the work of incarcerated writers and artists, the point being that there is a pool of talent—sometimes extraordinary talent— that we cannot ignore or allow to waste.

8

No Guts, No Gain

Without question, the single *smartest* thing prisoners can do is to get an education. A degree is the ticket to wherever they want to go.

What is not so easy is making it happen. In their given situation, this could be the single *hardest* thing they will ever have to do in their lives. How many are up to it?

We must not kid ourselves: This is not a route for cowards. It is fraught with obstacles, frustrations, and defeats.

With very few exceptions, American prisons do not offer courses beyond literacy and very basic education. So prisoners interested in advanced education have to pay for it on their own (except for free self-help courses available to them), study on their own, and take the tests on their own. This is something prisoners have to do for themselves; in most cases, no one will help.

No Easy Way

Prison is a tough place. It can be degrading, painful, and caustic.[1] Cages restrain people in a mean-spirited system staffed with workers who are not always held accountable. In most jurisdictions, neither prisons nor jails are designed for reform or rehabilitation.

For prisoners trying to pursue a post-secondary education on their own, it is a tough road to travel. But obstacles must not mean defeat. If prisoners are aware of the difficulties, they can prepare for them financially, logistically, psychologically, and emotionally. Here are some of the pitfalls inmates are up against when seeking to become educated:

- Information is hard to find about what kind of higher education is available and where it is. Most prison libraries have no college catalogs, no listing of schools or courses that exist. Therefore, determined prisoners have to find college addresses, write to each one, and apply on their own. When they do find the right courses and enroll, they must discipline themselves to concentrate, do the assignments, turn away from distracting activities, and put in the time. No one else cares if they succeed; they will find little, if any, support from prison staff.

- Distance learning programs are expensive, and money is hard to come by, especially since the Pell Grants and most student loans are no longer available to the incarcerated.

- Prisoners cannot study online; most have no internet access. But almost all distance-learning programs are provided through the internet, so none of the 2,500 online colleges and universities are available to prisoners. For prisoners, they don't exist. And, what is worse, fewer and fewer schools offer courses by mail as more and more of them go exclusively online each year.

- There are snafus in prison mail rooms. In most prisons, the mailroom can, at its own discretion, withhold all or parts of packages and correspondence, even prepaid correspondence courses and materials. It can limit enclosures, prohibit receiving stamps, and increase restrictions that further isolate prisoners from the outside world.[2] Peter Collins tells of one prisoner-student who had sent away for information on Black Panthers and the Native American movement. He was not able to receive it.[3] Prisoner-students walk a delicate political line.

Receiving books and texts can take weeks, if they are delivered at all. Packages may be rejected because the mail room misplaced a form. Theoretically, when a package is rejected, the recipient prisoner should be notified, but usually is not, so he or she is left to wonder why the books and lessons have not arrived after weeks or months of waiting. The prisoner is also entitled to be notified of his or her right to appeal the rejection of the package, but rarely does the mailroom staff provide such notification.

In my personal experience, the mail room has rejected books, Bible courses, career courses, personal-enrichment courses, high-school courses, and college courses that were mailed to me. Filing grievances against the mailroom for these rejections, which I do, is typically an exercise in futility.

- If a prisoner-student is required to submit a synopsis of a book to obtain purchase approval, this creates a "catch–22," because prisoners do not have access to bookseller catalogs. Without access to book descriptions, they can't write a synopsis and, therefore, cannot get the book.

- Support is frequently lacking from wardens and prison administrators. They do not always encourage prisoners who are trying to pursue a higher education because of the extra paperwork and processing it imposes upon them. Even guards have vast discretionary powers, and the prison environment often brings out the hostile, aggressive, and abusive sides of their characters.

Beyond "not supportive," sometimes prison administrators deliberately create barriers. One prisoner described educational events being cancelled on a moment's notice for "security reasons." He had seen guards flex their muscle and return men to their cells with no provocation, just to undermine the educational process. He said prisoners were treated with disrespect and left with little or no avenue for defense.[4]

Personnel on the prison staff can change. All kinds of things can happen, one expert warns,[5] so prisoners have to be prepared and flexible. Prisoner-students are advised to get approval for their studies in writing and to keep records of all paperwork, whether from the prison administration or from their school—enrollment confirmations, receipts, notes from teachers, anything related to their education. They should document everything, make allies on the staff, and remain on their best behavior. If they anger or annoy the guards, they pay the price. Irritated guards can make a prisoner's life very difficult.[6]

- Prisoners are often involuntarily transferred from one facility to another for a variety of reasons, an event that prevents prisoner-students from completing their studies.[7] Sometimes it happens just prior to completion of a degree.[8] And while taking courses may be helpful, the completion of a degree is of much greater importance, not just for the psychological satisfaction, but because a degree is crucial for employment prospects, and employment is the key factor in reducing recidivism.[9] Even when not transferred, inmates can be barred from study by frequent lockdowns, meetings with their attorneys, or other events beyond their control. Jobs can prevent them from attending educational programs, so those who must work to earn money for essential items like shampoo or toothpaste have to drop out of courses that interfere with work assignments.
- Filling out long and complex application forms for schools is difficult for anyone in the best of circumstances, but prisoners who are likely to be transferred, or have courses interrupted, may have to do it over and over again, starting each time from the beginning.
- The overcrowded prison environment is noisy and distracting; one can find no quiet place for study and concentration.
- An educated individual becomes a critical thinker and is more likely to dissent. But in prison, dissent—even perceived dissent—causes

problems. Any challenge to the status quo or to authority can be taken as a threat, and prisoners can be silenced in harsh ways. For example, if an official is irritated by the subject matter of a term paper, the prisoner's books, files, pens, typewriters, and school materials can be confiscated with an excuse as flimsy as calling them "a fire hazard."[10]

I, myself, was reported as "causing a fire hazard" when a staff member said I had "too many books and paper-based research materials" in my cubicle. The guards dumped my neatly filed and organized paperwork out of my locker onto the floor. They opened and emptied every envelope and file and confiscated my highlighters, paper clips, and book lights.

My efforts as a prisoner-writer have been marked by conflict. The manuscript for this book was confiscated numerous times during the writing and editing process. Officials at my prison simply stopped incoming and outgoing copies of the manuscript—and would not notify me of the confiscations. In one two-month period, 27 envelopes containing various revisions were either never delivered to me or, after I had red-lined the manuscript, never reached my editor. The problem had become so bad that every time a manuscript was mailed to or from me, it had to be sent via certified mail.

In another instance, four prisoner-students requested that their college program director add an ethnic studies course and create an advisory committee that represented their various cultural, political, and social views for determining future courses. When the prison authorities heard about it, their cells were searched, correspondence was confiscated and, shortly thereafter, the four were barred from all courses and extracurricular programs. Two were transferred out to other prisons, and three found themselves in solitary confinement for a very long time.[11]

Prisoner-writers whose thoughts displease prison officials may experience retribution by having parole denied, losing good time credit, physical threats, cell searches, confiscation of manuscripts, time spent in solitary confinement, or disciplinary transfers to other prisons.[12] According to *Farrow v. West*, 320 F.3d 1235, 1248 (11th Cir. 2003), "the First Amendment forbids prison officials from retaliating against prisoners for exercising the right of free speech." Nevertheless, prisoners typically have no right and no way to prevent such retaliatory actions; they are completely at the mercy of the prison system in this respect.[13]

No doubt about it: Prison is not a picnic, and prisoner-students have a tough time of it. Thousands of inmates experience the same thing. But despite the nearly complete shutdown of higher education classes in prisons across the country when Pell Grants were denied to prisoners, determined prisoners are enrolling in independent study courses, and many have done so with surprising success—success achieved in spite of, rather than because of, the system.

Tales of Tenacity

Canadian lifetime prisoner Peter Collins was giving seminars on how to become eligible for parole and stay out of prison. During the years of Collins's imprisonment, he had earned many certifications as a tutor and counselor. Documents he wrote on HIV/AIDS protection were widely used in prison health and safety education and in training seminars around the world. His art and writing have been published, with most of the proceeds donated to charities. Collins has won numerous awards and received several written offers of employment, should he ever be released.

Collins claims the Canadian prison system prevents prisoners from engaging in academic or vocational education that would develop employable skills. Even families, he said, are not permitted to send educational books to prisoners, and he described the prison libraries as dismal.[14]

"Prisoners pay a serious price for speaking critically about ... [the Canadian prison system] practices. Most prisoners keep their heads down and their voices silent because they are cowed."[15]

With good reason. Collins's seminars were barred. He was also denied permission to take art classes, although his relentless campaign of letter writing won him the support of an Anglican Bishop who, after almost three years, helped get permission for Collins to take the art classes. Once he was enrolled, however, prison officials confiscated his art supplies and course materials and prevented him from buying others. Then he was involuntarily transferred several times. "An art course that should have taken a couple of years to complete," said Collins, "took me from 1990 till 1998."[16] Eventually, his persistence earned him an honors diploma in graphic, commercial, and fine arts.

Collins next set about studying how to start a small business with his art, and he created a business plan. At that point, he encountered more obstacles, including a "censorship board" which had been created to deny permission for his cartoons and political work. (Parenthetically, in the United States, federal prisoners are not required by the FBOP to have their art or writing preapproved as they are in Canadian prisons. According to Program Statement 5350.27, Inmate Manuscripts, manuscripts, cartoons, etc. may be produced "without staff approval.")

Despite all his positive achievements, Collins's past prison record keeps his security status high. He is under tight scrutiny and is a sad reminder of how talent, eagerness to contribute, and brilliance behind bars are often suppressed. What could have been a significant national asset has been relegated to a significant national waste.

Having shot and killed an innocent man, Arnie King, now in his late 50s, has been at the Walpole State Prison since the age of 19. "I try each and every day to do something that communicates remorse and to make atonement for the life I took," he wrote in an article called "Reflections from Inside."[17]

King tells us that "Prison life sucks! Work detail ... consists of menial jobs requiring little or no skill. Janitorial tasks, kitchen assignments, maintenance, and industry factories. Most jobs pay one to two dollars per day, and unemployment is always very high.... Therefore, I have concentrated on academic studies and rehabilitative programming."[18]

For Arnie, the most significant and meaningful job he had in prison was as an assistant teacher in the ABE program. "Walpole Prison was chaotic and violent, with daily assaults and monthly murders. The school area was a relatively safe environment and the ABE director hired me to work with older adult prisoners."[19] With only a GED and a few college courses, he was instructing men in numbers and the alphabet. Some days he assisted other prisoners with reading, or writing a letter to family, or filling out an institutional form to request medical services.

King continued to work in prison education at Walpole, Norfolk, and Bridgewater state prisons. He observed that it was more typical for prisoners to receive assistance from other prisoners in an informal way than from within a structured classroom setting. He discovered how rewarding it was to help others, especially when he saw that basic education created fundamental changes in the lives of his fellow inmates.

Teaching others required that King pursue advanced courses to become a positive example. He went on to earn an associate's degree in business and, from Boston University, a bachelor's degree in liberal studies and a master's degree in liberal arts. King was also accepted to postgraduate programs at Union Institute and the University of Massachusetts–Boston. Sadly, however, the wall of prison bureaucracy has prevented further advancement for this talented individual.

Arnie King's story, which touches upon the controversial issue of providing education to "lifers," speaks for many. King noted that there are some already with life sentences in the Massachusetts prison system who hold Boston University degrees. He suggested the prisons provide workshops and training for these more educated convicts and transform them into peer educators to teach the ABE, GED, and ESL programs. That way, prisoners "convicted of murder will be able to offer a humanitarian gesture to society and to other human beings from the cell-block." They will play an important role in helping released prisoners return to their communities with less hostile attitudes, more inclined to contribute to the well-being of their neighborhood.[20]

The majority of prisoners enter the "big house" without a GED or diploma. In fact, a large percentage have never been to high school. "Education is very important for individuals to ... function in our society," King wrote. "Without the fundamentals, it's clear that one is destined to be unsuccessful.... The world expands beyond the 6 × 9 cell as one increases [one's] understanding of the environment outside. It has become evident to me that authentic rehabilitation will not occur without including education in the formula."[21]

Unfortunately, King observed, as highly successful as the ABE, GED, ESL, and other educational programs have proven to be, they are given very low priority in the prison system. "In the end," he wrote, "most prisoners are eventually released without adequate skills to function in the community as law-abiding citizens. The challenge is to prepare the prisoner for release while [still] incarcerated by providing the tools and the ability to use them."[22]

"I never thought I would see the day when 'correctional officers' would work in concert to suppress a prisoner's education, especially one which the prisoner is paying for through his own means," wrote Scott Steffler[23] who is serving a life sentence at the Oregon State Penitentiary.

For the first year, as Scott pursued a degree in psychology, it went fairly well. Then came a series of obstacles in receiving his textbooks, having his exams proctored (half the time he was refused), and delays because of years in solitary confinement. He describes the violent behaviors and "megalomaniac and tyrannical personalities personified as 'correctional officers'" who caused him to live with constant anxiety about missing class deadlines and not meeting other course requirements. So much depended upon the discretion of the guards.

Steffler wrote a stream of letters expressing his grievances and complaints to the state governor, which earned him an exception so he could finish his courses and avoid flunking out of college after he was released from solitary. However, after 17 months in "the hole," he was transferred to a maximum-security penitentiary where he had to reorder a complete new set of courses. When they arrived, the materials he had personally paid for were again confiscated—because, they told him, a new policy had been established which barred anyone who had been in prison for more than eight years from taking courses.

Steffler filed additional grievances and, after another five months, was allowed to finish the courses that had arrived. After that, however, there came another 20 months in solitary confinement when he was again denied course materials. "We have insufficient staff and resources," they told him. Then he was permanently barred from taking any additional courses.

Steffler requested a transfer to the Federal Bureau of Prisons or to a California prison where inmates were encouraged to enroll in college courses. His requests for out-of-state transfer were denied.

Steffler has educated himself in psychology, history, science, and foreign languages. He is now writing novels and submitting appeals. But Scott Steffler remains barred from further study. His education, together with a $25,000 grant he had received, is defunct. In the real world, said Steffler, "not even the President of the United States has the authority to force someone to flunk out of college; yet in prison, 'correctional officers' can do it on a whim."[24]

As a teenager, John Keith Irwin was dazzled by outlaws. Born in 1929 to a modest but honest family, his father managed a candy store and sold insurance, while his mother remained at home managing the household affairs. Irwin grew up in Los Angeles when it was known for the glamour of Hollywood and had no smog. Giving into his fascination, Irwin fell into burglary, car theft, and armed robbery, which landed him in prison.

The living conditions of the prison environment shocked and dismayed Irwin to the point where he made a conscious decision to abandon his criminal pursuits and obtain an education. During his five years in prison, he accumulated 24 college credits and, when released, he enrolled at UCLA to earn a baccalaureate degree.

For Irwin, that was just the beginning. He earned a doctorate in sociology at the University of California at Berkeley, then joined the faculty at San Francisco State University. A prolific author who wrote seven books and many academic articles, Irwin dedicated the rest of his life to teaching and writing about prison reform until he passed away in 2010.

Dr. Jon Marc Taylor: A Profile in Courage

Dr. Jon Marc Taylor's story is one of determination and productivity. Having served most of his life in prison, and currently incarcerated in Missouri, Taylor has overcome extreme obstacles to complete his undergraduate and graduate university degrees all the way up to his Ph.D. Perhaps even more significant, he has pioneered the pathway of education behind prison walls, and it is to him that I owe a great deal in producing my own work.

Taylor's writing on the elimination of Pell Grants in American prisons contributed an important voice to the national debate on prison education—but it incurred serious repercussions. Quickly transferred to the maximum-security Crossroads Correctional Center in Cameron, Missouri, Dr. Taylor spent 220 days in solitary confinement on the basis of fabricated charges against which he continues to defend himself in court. Reprisals like this would silence a less determined voice, but they have not been able to deter Jon Marc Taylor from the cause of education for prisoners, or keep him from achieving his own educational accomplishments.

A recipient of numerous writing awards, including the Robert F. Kennedy Journalism Award and the Nation/I.F. Stone Journalism Award for his reporting on "Pell Grants for Prisoners," Taylor has authored more than 100 articles, many of which are about the need for prison education and how a prisoner can get it, and he is the author of the ground-breaking *Prisoners' Guerrilla Handbook to Correspondence Programs in the U.S. & Canada,* published by *Prison Legal News* in 2009.

My Own Journey

My name is Christopher Zoukis. I am a prisoner, a student, and an educational advocate at FCI Petersburg, where I have embarked on an intense, self-directed educational program to pursue a college degree and, at the same time, where I am writing about the subject of prison education. In presenting the issue, I draw not only upon research in the field, but also upon my firsthand experience inside the world of prison where I live.

In many countries around the world, large categories of citizens are denied education. In our country, it is prisoners who are denied—or if not denied, made to travel a hard, sometimes impossible road to gain access to an education. Prisoners cannot use computers, so they are unable to do research or take courses on the internet. Anything they write, they do it the old-fashioned way: with pen and paper. If they are lucky enough to have a typewriter, they may not be able to afford the supplies needed to utilize it.

Several members of the educational staff at prisons where I have been incarcerated have shown no interest in either rehabilitation or education for the incarcerated students in their prisons. They appear, rather, to be focused on enforcing rules and avoiding additional work. I understand that's not an objective statement; it is merely what I have personally observed. And it is sad. People in the educational profession should be working as much for passion as for a paycheck.

For the prisoner who longs to learn, the frustration and defeat compete with joy and victory—three steps forward, two back. But it is worth it. It is an investment in one's future.

As a prisoner, I feel that the world generally perceives me as worthless—as the lowest of the low. It would be depressing if it weren't for the projects I engage in to keep busy. And it would really take a toll on me if I didn't believe I was doing something to turn myself around, something to create a better future for myself and my family.

Within the confines of prison, so much of who we are, our individuality, is stripped from us—Sometimes even our sanity. Education is my escape. My studies carry me beyond prison gates to a world of exploration, discovery, challenge, and deep satisfaction. When I focus on developing my mind, rather than on my surroundings, I travel outside the prison world on a road to transformation. I'm becoming a different person, a better person. Education makes me feel as if I'm on my way to contributing something positive to society. With the skills I am developing through education, I hope to redeem myself.

I'm not sure what drives me to perform well in my studies. Maybe it's a need for validation or a hope for something better than this. Maybe it's a desire to be the man my parents want me to be. But it is the struggle, the need to work for what I achieve, that makes the journey meaningful and life-changing. So I'll do what it takes to stay focused and overcome the obstacles to earn a college degree and a life worth living.

I was born in 1986 and grew up in a wealthy, professional home where I was loved, provided for, and sent to very good schools. Despite all these advantages, I made bad decisions. I lived in a haze of alcohol and drugs, the fast lane, the "fun" lane. Most of my relationships were toxic, but I couldn't see it.

My parents cared deeply and tried everything to change the destructive path I was on, including expensive drug and alcohol abuse rehabilitation centers, but I was oblivious to their love, sacrifice, and concern. I continued to live, lost in a wasteland of selfishness.

So here I am, in prison since high school. And it's no one's fault but my own.

Before my arrest, I had made a lot of stupid, drug-fueled choices, and I dropped out of school when my troubles with the law began. At that time, I was too drugged to give education a thought. But once incarcerated and surrounded by people who did bad things, really bad and evil things, people who didn't have the opportunities I had been given, I knew I had hit the bottom of the barrel. I had to find a way up and out.

I was eighteen, a senior in high school, when I was confined in the North Carolina Department of Corrections for 15 months. At first, I was thrown directly into the fire at the Polk Youth Detention Center, a very rough state prison for 18- to 24-year-olds. After the mandatory eight months, I was sent to Morrison Correctional Institution, another hellish youth facility, where I remained until I turned 21 and was transferred, mercifully, to Sandford Correctional Center, a normal adult prison with a comparatively non-violent environment.

At Sandford, I completed the work for a GED and started looking for college classes. Of course, college courses did not exist in the prison; there were only the GED program, proctored by Central Carolina Community College, and a two-month brick masonry class taught by a volunteer.

I expected to be released after two years. Instead, I found myself in the McDowell County Detention Center for almost a year, facing federal charges. That year was tough; in fact, a real nightmare. Isolated in "the hole" because of an altercation that I did not initiate, the only human contact allowed to me was with preachers on Sunday mornings and my 15-minute telephone calls home. I could receive no newspapers, books, magazines, or any sort of internet-printed or news-related material. Only personal letters, Bibles, and Bible-study course materials. These were my shelter in the storm, my only contact with the outside world.

Exposed to the concept and the beauty of the Christian faith, my eyes, ears, and heart opened to the message of love. Hungry to know more, I took on an in-depth study of the Bible and was amazed at how much I could learn from its eternal wisdom. In hindsight, the isolation and Bible study at McDowell were a gift. The faith I embraced transformed my mind and my very being. Today, I can say gratefully, I am a changed man.

From McDowell, I was transferred to Federal Correctional Institution Petersburg in Virginia, a medium-security prison, where I remain today. During the first five years, I learned to survive in a violent and socially deadening prison society. But these years of hell also made me determined to use my prison time in a productive way, so that it will never happen again in my lifetime.

I sought every possible way to further my education. I studied for and earned a real high-school diploma, not just a GED; continued my Bible studies; and completed paralegal and other legal courses which I use to work in the law library and help fellow prisoners who cannot afford to pay for legal assistance. These courses only served to whet my appetite. I want more—a lot more. I want a college education and a career.

I wrote letters to every college and university I could find an address for. Brochures and catalogs came in and piled up in stacks under my bunk. These materials opened my eyes to the possibility of a college education via correspondence. Today I am working toward a bachelor's degree in sociology.

Education is the focus of my life, preparation for making a contribution when I am released. My parents are totally supportive of my efforts, and I'm driven to succeed, not just for my own sake, but also for theirs.

It hasn't been easy, however. Here at FCI Petersburg, the "Education Department" may be a misnomer. The educational staff act more like prison guards concerned primarily with security. When I said I wanted to earn a high-school diploma, my college coordinator actually scoffed. Can you imagine an educator deliberately discouraging a student from finishing high school? I was embarrassed about my lack of education and, like most prisoners, feeling pretty worthless. Educational staffers like this one are effective at reinforcing a negative self-image and squelching possibilities for change.

The college coordinator was also not helpful when I was researching colleges. He made it very clear he didn't want to be bothered with questions about schools. In fact, he posted a sign outside his office saying that he had no college catalogs or other college information. The sign directed inquiring prisoners to the prison library, where, however, there was only a single book listing some community colleges (which did not offer correspondence courses). My personal experience with this individual, along with experiences told to me by others, confirmed that when it came to pursuing an advanced education, we were on our own.

Worse than on our own: Sometimes we were obstructed. On one occasion, the college coordinator did not fill out paperwork properly for my midterm examination. In another instance, he refused to telephone my school to resolve a problem with missing coursework. I had to go to the supervisor of education who, after an argument with the college coordinator, directed him to make the call.

Lest I appear unfair, I will admit there are occasional college coordinators who support education-minded prisoners. There was one in our facility for a brief time who was willing to pick up the phone on my behalf and work out problems with the school when they occurred. She was a breath of fresh air, and with her came a cautious hope for a better post-secondary educational environment at FCI Petersburg. Unfortunately for the prisoner-students, she was promoted to another position and her replacement is just like the first: an obstructionist. She reduced the ACE program and fired the inmate ACE instructors. Why? We'll never know.

Not all problems come from the education department. The mail room, too, can cause a fair share. Sometimes they reject college correspondence courses for which a prisoner had received approval by filling out appropriate Package Authorization forms. When they reject a package arbitrarily and do not inform the recipient, the prisoner-student cannot complete the work within the allotted time and may fail the course. Even worse, sometimes mail-room employees lie to cover up their mistakes. One time, when my rejected package was returned to the sender, the school assumed I was no longer at the same address. Six weeks passed, and I wondered why my course material never arrived. My family called the university and discovered the package had been returned. So I went through the process again from the beginning.

Again the package didn't arrive. I asked the college coordinator to call my academic advisor at the university, and we discovered that the English course had been returned again. Now, having had a second package returned, Ohio University assumed it was my fault, that I had done something improper to cause the package rejection.

For a third time I filled out the package authorization form and asked Ohio University to mail the same English course to me. By now I had been attempting to receive the same course for four months. This time, however, we did not use the prison mailing address; we used the address for the adjacent warehouse, and the course arrived.

In the prison setting, what can happen, will. Things do not go as planned, and often we never find out why.

I am more fortunate than others here. My parents are extremely supportive, financially and emotionally, while I pursue my education. Even so, studying is difficult. I can't pick up a phone and ask a question, can't go to a real library and dig further into a subject. Within BOP institutions, inmates cannot have more than five books in their possession. And, of course, we cannot do research on the internet.

Then there is the noise. Inmates scream, beat on tables, slam trash cans, and even dance on tables. Rowdy sports fans yell at the TV. I am fortunate to have a quiet cellmate who goes to bed early, but in many other cells people stay up, screaming to their friends through the vent all night. While trying to study, the decibel level is deafening.

Our small cell (7½ by 9 feet) houses two grown men with a sink, toilet, two lockers, and a bunk bed. This is an improvement. I used to live in a cell the same size with two other men, a broken vent no one would fix, and a bunk three beds high. I slept on top. If I sat up too quickly, I hit my head on the ceiling. In a minimum-security state prison, we lived in dormitories housing 80 to 100 other inmates. There, the noise and distractions were infinitely greater. There was not a single quiet corner. And you had better not take your eyes off the other prisoners because of the systematic violence and rampant theft.

In the medium-security prison where I live now, my two-man cell is locked at 9:00 p.m. I sit at the desk, put on my headphones, and turn on my book lights, and my cellmate knows I mean business. He is considerate about letting me work. And work I do. I spend the quieter late-night hours studying, writing, completing course assignments, and preparing classes (when I was teaching). I utilize book lights instead of the overhead fluorescents so my cellmate can sleep.

Everything came to a screeching halt in 2012. My work on this text and my activities as an advocate for prison education landed me in solitary confinement for five months, with a loss of e-mail, telephone, and commissary privileges, as well as a loss of good time credits (time taken off the sentence for good behavior). The BOP claimed that my activities constituted a "business," a violation of BOP policy, and tried to transfer me to a maximum-security prison. I had to retain attorneys to fight the charges (at considerable expense to my family). Eventually, I was found to be innocent and it was determined that the accusations were false. I was absolved of all the fabricated disciplinary charges. But that didn't erase five months of confinement and isolation and anxiety, not knowing how or when this would end in "the hole." And, because I could not sit for exams, I had to withdraw from the college courses I was taking, forfeit the fees they had cost, and lose the coursework I had completed. I was no longer permitted to teach. My record and reputation were restored, but at a considerable price.

I made an effort to return to normalcy. Like many other prisoner-students, I am totally immersed in reading, writing, and Bible lessons. It keeps us focused on intellectual thoughts, rather than on our surroundings. It is a means of escape, a vehicle to a much more interesting, more sane world. Our studies give us purpose; a reason to live and wake up each day. It is our hope for a different tomorrow.

I make the most of my time. In addition to working on my degree and writing about prison education, I also write science-fiction, poetry, essays, articles, and book reviews, as well as legal articles for *Prison Legal News* and columns for three websites: PrisonEducation.com, PrisonLawBlog.com, and Christopher-Zoukis.com. Two of my stories won awards from the PEN American Center.

Teaching is another one of my passions. I had been teaching a weekly class on "Writing and Publishing" to help prisoner-students put their thoughts on paper in a constructive and appropriate manner. Sadly, I was no longer permitted to hold classes when the fabricated disciplinary procedures commenced. But students continue to ask when the classes will be available again, so I continue, individually, to help edit my former students' writings and provide private instruction to fellow inmates who sincerely want to learn.

Prisoners are people, too. People who have made mistakes and poor choices and live with the consequences daily. And like other people, prisoners are unique individuals with different talents and personalities. Some have a criminal mentality that may never change. Others strive for transformation and a new life. I am one of those trying to make restitution, to pay something back, to make amends. Education is my conduit to a meaningful and productive future. This is one train I must not miss!

I will spend the rest of my life trying to bring college programs into prisons with qualified professors, quiet places to study, and an educational staff that offers support, mentorship, and encouragement. For our sake, for yours, for the fiscal benefit of our nation, for the safety and welfare of our society, we must educate our prisoners and reduce the prison population. It is simply the right thing to do.

9

What the World Knows

In other countries, European ones in particular, it is understood that educating prisoners makes good sense. In 1987, the Council of Europe put forth an alternative approach to the punitive model of imprisonment that, they believe, holds a denigrating view of incarcerated individuals. The recommendations of the EPEA (European Prison Education Association) emphasize the need for and the importance of prison education for rehabilitation (see Appendix VII). The alternative approach was adopted in the *European Prison Rules,* and their rules have been adopted by many European countries since 1989.[1]

Education, as recommended by the European Council, should include normal classroom subjects, vocational education, creative and cultural activities, physical education and sports, and social and library facilities.[2] Research has made it clear to the Europeans that humanities courses are more effective for reducing recidivism rates than courses addressing offending behavior. That is not to say that teaching about substance abuse, anger management, thinking skills, parenting, etc. is not helpful, but it is not sufficient to rely entirely upon such basic programs.[3]

According to the Council of Europe, the primary goals for prison education are: (1) to "normalize" to some extent the damage done to prisoners by the often brutal environment of prison, (2) to address their educational disadvantages, (3) to teach employable skills, and (4) assist those who want to turn away from crime by emphasizing personal development and building confidence.[4]

To derive maximum effectiveness from educational activities in prison, the Council of Europe report "Education in Prison" (1990) suggests that offering a wide variety of high-quality "learning opportunities" to prisoners will attract a larger number of them into educational programs and will also better address the needs of "the whole person."[5]

The Council of European Prison Rules

The *European Prison Rules,* adopted by the Council of Europe in 1987, can be summarized as follows[6]:

- Incarceration within prison conditions is punishment in itself; prison authorities, therefore, will not aggravate the suffering inherent in this;
- Living conditions should be compatible with human dignity and community standards, minimizing the differences between prison life and community life, protecting self-respect and a sense of personal responsibility. Toward this end, prisons are encouraged to strengthen healthy ties with families and develop skills that improve the chance of successful reintegration into society upon the prisoners' release[7];
- Every prison shall seek to provide educational programmes to all prisoners which are as comprehensive as possible and which meet their individual needs and aspirations;
- Remuneration for work within prisons should be equal to remuneration for the same work outside[8];
- Educational priority shall be given to prisoners with literacy and numeracy needs and those who lack basic or vocational education;
- Education shall have no less status than work within the prison regime, and prisoners shall not be disadvantaged financially or otherwise by taking part in education;
- As far as practicable, the education of prisoners shall:
  - be integrated with the educational and vocational training system of the country so that after release they may continue their education and vocational training without difficulty; and
  - it shall take place under the auspices of external educational institutions.[9]

Eastern Bloc countries were required to agree with and accept these principles in order to be accepted into the European community.[10]

In 1995, the first international seminar on the topic of prison education was organized by the UNESCO Institute for Education. In 2002, the CONFINTEA V meeting in Bangkok pronounced an "urgent need" to develop an international initiative to recognize every person's right to education in a democratic society. "Education," conference leaders agreed, "is a passport for a type of citizenship that has not yet finished discovering all its potentiality."[11]

When reading the literature produced in Europe by those who study prison issues, we find Europeans are dealing with the same problems that we are, and they are coming to the same conclusions about the solutions. Namely, they see education as the most effective means to reducing recidivism. However, even in many European countries where general and vocational education is free, higher education comes with a fee. This discourages prisoner participation in higher education,[12] because very few prisoners have money.[13]

In the Federal Bureau of Prisons, the highest pay scale is with UNICOR jobs ($0.23 per hour to $1.15 per hour), but these are rare. My own wage, currently, is $5.25 a month. Most prisoners have to use their wages to pay for soap, toothpaste, toothbrushes, and shampoo.

Reentry into society upon release also appears to pose the same problems in many countries around the world. Released prisoners face the same challenges and the kind of reentry assistance needed is the same.

In Europe, it is generally recognized that there are two very different approaches to prison policy:

- The Scandinavian-Nordic approach, which leans toward humanizing and rehabilitating the incarcerated, and
- The Anglo-American approach to incarceration, which is associated with the punitive model.[14]

The Scandinavian, or Nordic, Approach

Criminal justice systems in Scandinavia, famous for their humane efforts, are regarded internationally as models for the rest of the world. Nordic prison systems regard prisoners as people. They afford them respect as individuals and as members of the larger society. Therefore, in the Scandinavian prison systems, the goal and purpose of education is much more than merely to reduce recidivism. It is also to satisfy a requirement that prisoners be treated with dignity, that they minimize the negative effects of prison life, and that they sustain their ties to the outside world.

Sweden

Sweden incarcerates 69 people per 100,000, as compared to the USA where we incarcerate 716 people per 100,000—more than 10 times as many!

In Swedish prisons, education is one of the primary tools for successful prison management. Furthermore, the need for prisoners to be provided with suitable work is evident in Sweden's 1994 Prison Treatment Act, designed to establish "positive foundations for offenders' lives leading to successful reintegration back into society."[15]

In 2005, the Nordic Council of Ministers determined that another key to prison management is the "normalization" principle, which includes the need for prisoners to be given suitable work and educational programs comprising academic, vocational, and social skills.[16]

Preparation for an inmate's release in Sweden begins the day he is confined to prison. The Swedes have shown the world that when these programs are tailored to the culture of the local society and to each individual prisoner, education not only reduces recidivism but, having effected changes in the individual's attitudes toward life, and arming him with employable skills, better prepares the prisoner for integration into the real world after release, so that there is no need to commit further offenses.[17]

Education is most effective, they find, when combined with meaningful work, treatment programs, and other positive activities. Tutoring provided for inmates in basic reading, writing, and arithmetic creates a positive attitude toward education and a higher sense of self-esteem.[18] Moreover, in Swedish prisons, inmates who are motivated to study are allowed to do so in peace and quiet.

There is a concerted attempt to re-socialize the prisoner to the outside world and counteract the harmful effects of incarceration.[19] "If we want humans to behave as humans," said William Rentzmann, deputy director-general, Department of Denmark's Prisons and Probation, "we must treat them like humans. If you treat prisoners as plague-ridden, it only ensures that they do indeed become a plague." As such, Swedish criminal justice professionals continually search for improved educational methods and humane treatment of prisoners. Prisoners are considered citizens. When they have done wrong and paid their debt to society, the prison and probations services are required to support a positive outcome.[20]

Prisoners can participate in these activities eight hours a day, five days per week, but participation in prison educational programs is voluntary, with priority given to those with the greatest economic need.[21] Ninety-eight percent of inmates surveyed said they wanted to be involved in studies.

Swedish prison education, designed by professional educators, comprises:

- life skills: study circles, parenting, anger and abuse, library, creative activities, sports, and social skills, etc.,
- primary and lower levels (including Swedish language for immigrants),
- upper secondary school,
- vocational education (mechanical engineering, industrial wood products, sheet metal work, welding, and electrical engineering), and
- university and other higher education.[22]

Teaching is outsourced to adult education centers. Most education in Swedish prisons is web-based, which allows it to be individualized and flexible. If inmates are transferred to other facilities, they can continue classes they have started. Security requirements are not minimized, but the new technology reduces the cost of teachers' salaries.[23]

Efforts to "normalize" prison life include extended periods of stay away from prison for participation in drug treatment, vocational training or military service, work-study or community programs, placement in rural families, etc. Prisoners have full citizens' rights to services.

In Nordic prison systems, generally acknowledged as among the best in the world, authorities acknowledge the wisdom of Rule 65 of the *European Prison Rules*, which focuses on minimizing the negative effects of prison life.[24] In Sweden, the modern view is that, preferably, people ought not to be locked up. It is believed that the most effective way of getting offenders to lead crime-free lives is by keeping them within the community. Furthermore, they say, non-institutional care is both more humane and less expensive than care in prison.[25]

Denmark

Similar to Sweden and other Scandinavian countries, prison philosophy in Denmark is focused on normalization (making prison life as close as possible to outside life), openness, and personal responsibility, as outlined in the *European Prison Rules*.[26] Only prisoners considered dangerous are initially placed in closed prisons. Normally prisoners are placed in open prisons as close to their homes as possible, and they get weekend leave once every three weeks.[27] Security in open prisons relies upon the self-discipline of inmates. Those who abuse the trust can be transferred to a closed prison.

Prison has its negative effects: broken families, loss of work, loss of involvement in organizations of their choice, loss of property ownership, etc. The freedom to go where they want is limited by incarceration. But in Denmark, prisoners can have their own furniture and personal effects in their cells and wear their own clothes if they prefer.

Visits from family and friends are encouraged as often as possible. Visits, either in the prisoner's cell or in a visiting room that is comfortably furnished, are private enough for sexual activity. As a result, sexual assaults in Danish prisons are a thing of the past. Moreover, the tone of communication between inmates and prison personnel is consistent with that of communication between citizens on the outside.[28]

The *European Prison Rules* stipulate provision for leave from prison for low-risk individuals to accommodate medical, educational, occupational, familial, and other needs, which could include weddings, birthdays, funerals, a job or housing search, or attendance at educational courses. Those who leave the facility without problems earn more leave. Those who present a problem when away from prison relinquish their right to leave. It was found that when inmates get a "breather" like this, it is easier to accept their imprisonment and they become less aggressive.[29]

Danish prisons encourage personal responsibility and self-reliance by requiring inmates to buy and cook their own nutritious food (for which money and instruction are provided), manage their personal hygiene, wash and repair their clothes, etc. They have a wage system with a fixed amount for board and hygiene, in addition to pay for work performed.[30] This system is designed to involve the inmate more actively in things they have to do for themselves when released. And to avoid the boredom that leads to drugs and other illicit endeavors, inmates engage in activities that ordinary citizens enjoy for a more constructive use of their free time.[31]

Prison education programs in Denmark are taught with the same curricula, materials, and methods used in community schools. Since prisoners typically have a lower educational level and have had bad experiences with education in their past, there is an emphasis on teaching basic study skills, cognitive abilities, life skills, and to creating opportunity for "victories."[32]

Finland

Similarly, Finnish prison managers know that recidivism is tightly linked to a lack of drug treatment, education, and employment. Finland offers courses in reading, writing, vocational training relevant to market demands, and sometimes advanced degrees to prisoners who are interested and motivated. Rates of recidivism are fairly low, around 25 percent, in Finland. Prisoners with short sentences have been found to have the highest recidivism rates because they are not incarcerated long enough to complete educational courses.

KRIS Tempere is a community-based organization working to reduce recidivism and reliance upon incarceration. The Finish penal system helps only about 20 percent of released prisoners with reintegration into society. To be effective, they recognize, it has to start with prison programming from the time the person enters prison, in addition to services prior to and after release.[33]

The idea of normalization in prison management, as emphasized in the *European Prison Rules,* has spread in the 1990s from the Scandinavian prison systems to those of other European countries. This includes promoting interaction with the community (a very high priority of the Council of Europe, according to their report, "Education in Prison"[34]) and integrating prison education with the educational standards of the country.

The Anglo-American Approach

The Scandinavian way of dealing with prisons and prisoners runs totally counter to the punitive philosophy of prisons in the United States, Canada, Britain, and other Anglo countries, where primacy is given to security measures.[35] In the Anglo systems, prisoners are seen as one-dimensional: they are offenders. Their personalities, complexities, problems, and qualities disappear.

England And Wales

In response to prison disturbances in England and Wales in the late 1980s, the education program for prisoners was improved and more prisoners were given access to basic educational services. Although education is a relatively new phenomenon in the English and Welsh penal system, by the 21st century, education had become an integral part of prison life. It served partly as a practical control mechanism and partly as a more altruistic ideal.

Research in Britain as far back as 1993 reported that prison education will cause a drop in recidivism, as well as help to build social, artistic, and other skills if programs are directed by well-trained staff and have relevance to the outside world.[36] Until 1993, the management and delivery of education and training in prisons was carried out by local education authority staff. Since that time, responsibility for education has been contracted out to organizations such as the Staff College, other universities, and private training organizations.[37]

Today, "the UK prison service is legally obliged to offer educational opportunities to all prisoners" from literacy to postgraduate study, with students ranging in age from 15 to over 65. However, priority is given to basic skills (literacy, numeracy, social and life skills) and vocational education, utilizing various types of teaching methods. Access to higher education, perceived as an "elite" activity, still remains difficult.[38] The future for lower-level prison education in England and Wales seems secure, and it is likely to play an increasingly central role in prison reform efforts.[39]

Basic education takes place in classrooms within the prisons and is contracted out to educational institutions. There are also some distance-learning courses in vocational and academic programs. Employability is the main focus, with higher education a minority interest.

Issues related to prison education in the U.K. are almost identical to those we face in the U.S. (restricted internet access, environmental distractions, transfers, security requirements, etc.). But in the U.K., they are working on internet platforms that can offer safe access to online education.[40] Constrained budgets make it mandatory to create individual learning plans based on assessments of inmates' learning needs and ability to benefit from education and training, especially for higher academic learning.[41]

Unfortunately, the issue of education has been eclipsed by overcrowding and sentencing severity that currently dominates public debate. But the agency responsible for prison education is reaching out to employers to facilitate opportunities for released offenders.

"Prison is an expensive way of making bad people worse," said David Waddington, British Home Secretary. In the United Kingdom, prison policy makers are not as forward-thinking as the Scandinavian prison authorities, but as compared to the American emphasis on punishment, deterrence, and protecting society from potentially dangerous individuals, they show a greater focus on rehabilitation and education of prisoners. It is no surprise, therefore, to learn that the rate of recidivism for released prisoners in the U.K. is notably lower than the recidivism rate in the U.S.

One provider of education to the incarcerated population of 6,300 in prisons throughout the U.K. is Strode College in Somerset County. Approximately half the prisoners engage in classes that include literacy, numeracy, ICT, and vocational skills,[42] as compared to only three percent in U.S. prisons who participate in correctional education programs.

"The College provides curricula which meet the needs of the prisoners based on the twin principles of raising the level of basic skills and providing courses which assist prisoners to gain employment on release. The College employs over 250 full- and part-time qualified teachers in the prisons and delivers 166,000 teaching hours per year." In some prisons, the college provides training courses on site for prison service staff, as well.

Educational programs within the prisons are externally accredited by awarding bodies because the same standards of college quality, personnel, financial policies, and practices are fully applied to the teaching in prisons.[43]

Ireland

Participation in courses from basic literacy through college is voluntary in Irish prisons. There is a strong emphasis on the creative arts. Prisoners can also enroll in distance-education courses from the Open University where pre-release courses and support for released prisoners are provided.[44]

Scotland

In Scottish prisons, despite legitimate security concerns, technological developments have made it possible to facilitate web-based prison learning[45] which highlights the role of the arts to engage hard-to-reach prisoners.

When a prisoner begins an educational course, a learning plan is drawn up. Learning plans vary dramatically with the individual prisoner-students. Progress is monitored regularly and reviewed every six months. To be successful, these plans must include post-release support services.[46]

Australia

The correctional system in Western Australia is currently focusing more on rehabilitation. Therefore, education and training, combining work, study, and behavior management, is expected to increase.

Australia embraces community partnerships to ensure that prisoners are trained during incarceration and also reintegrated and employed after their release into society.[47]

Since the 1970s, Western Australian governments have made efforts to incorporate vocational education at all security levels of prisons (minimum, medium, and maximum) to help prisoners acquire occupational skills. Their emphasis is on courses and apprenticeships of 10 to 12 weeks' duration so they can be completed.[48]

In 2001, a national strategy for vocational education and training for prisoners was adopted, with an effort to ensure continuity for prisoners transferred into different prisons. That training is linked to current employment opportunities in the labor market. Many of the courses are provided through partnerships with technical schools and colleges.[49] Accredited courses inside Australian prisons are recognized by schools on the outside.

Each prisoner is screened to determine his or her level of literacy after incarceration. Each one has an individual plan that is reviewed every three to six months to monitor progress and make any required changes. For example, it may be specified that a prisoner must take courses in substance abuse and/or anger management. Prisoners not enrolled in educational courses at first may decide later to enroll.[50] The Western Australian Department of Justice's Education and Vocational Training Unit ensures that courses are widely available and rewarding for prisoners, but participation is always voluntary.

In general, prisoners do want to develop skills. In fact, prisoner demand for educational training exceeds the capacity of Australian prison facilities to provide it for all who wish to participate.[51]

Similar to American prisoners, many Australian inmates have low levels of education and limited work experience prior to incarceration. And prison work (most of which is related to prison maintenance) is not perceived as helpful to attaining a career upon release; inmates view studying and apprenticeships as having more value.[52]

Australian prisoners face the same issues upon release as prisoners in the U.S. (hostile communities, etc.). As in the U.S., having a prison record is a barrier to many employment and housing opportunities.[53] The Department of Justice has been working successfully to build industry and employer networks that allow qualified ex-prisoners to gain employment. After release, with the cooperation of businesses and institutions in the community, prisoners are regularly placed in workplaces for apprenticeships and further training As of 2009, 45 percent of Western Australian prisoners engaged in work while incarcerated, and 30 percent engaged in education and vocational training,[54] percentages which far exceed prisoner participation in the U.S.

Western Europe

Germany

The Prison Library Support Group (Förderverein Gefangenenbüchere-iene) is an advocacy organization that promotes books and AV materials (where permitted) to help connect prisoners to the outside world and make their time in prison more productive to prepare for a more successful reentry when released. Their "Library as a Partner in Education" project, recently introduced by the state of North Rhine-Westphalia, inspired a new level of cooperation between the Prison Education department and the prison library.[55]

Belgium

The Belgians have not yet systematically incorporated individual education plans into their prison education programs, but one prison manager stated a strong opinion that it is very necessary.[56] In Belgian prisons, prisoners are prevented from taking courses because they need to give their time to work and earning opportunities. In-prison education is free of charge in Belgium, but if prisoner-students lose income in order to take courses, it is costly to them.[57] For prison education to be successful, it cannot be an either-or situation.

Spain

Spanish law tends to impose the shortest and least restrictive sentences and provides educational opportunities to prepare for reintegration into the community. The Spanish constitution and correctional legislation maintain the right of prisoners to access culture and pursue personal development, and they elaborate on the requirements for inmate training and education.[58] The "new" approach is more humanitarian; education and reading are seen as important not just for the acquisition of knowledge, but also for moral improvement and as an escape from harsh prison reality. Enhanced reading and writing, it is believed, help prisoners adapt to new social patterns and connect with the rest of the world.[59]

Spain experiences a high rate of recidivism and an average sentence length of four to eight years, if there have been multiple crimes. As in our country, most inmates come from violent backgrounds with an educational level far below the national average and a high rate of illiteracy. Many have learning difficulties, language deficiencies, a gang mentality, and psychological disorders.

Professional librarians are part of the prison staff to maintain quality libraries and promote reading.[60] A 2005 Reading Promotion agenda created "Reading Initiation" teams in prisons to promote reading clubs, support education courses, and report on library activities. In prisons, the role of the library is also a social one; it is a site that facilitates informal interaction among inmates.[61]

In 2008, the concept of reintegration centers became more important, together with open prisons that allow inmates to serve their sentences on weekends, with no loss of freedom.

In Spain, inmates can access computers and the internet for educational and training purposes. Such use requires approval by an instructor and supervision by staff. One innovative use of the internet is the award-winning Bloggers from Prison project. It started in 2006 in a Barcelona youth prison, with the collaboration of the University of Barcelona and the Catalan government's Omnia office. Bloggers from Prison demonstrates how, in a closed and marginalized environment, information technology can still be a tool for learning and social readjustment. With this project, the internet has become a social space for artistic creation and communication where prisoners establish relationships, share experiences, and learn together. They find it affirming and confidence-building when strangers read their postings and respond to them. They begin to feel like citizens again.[62] At the same time, inmates are learning to use a computer and improving their vocabulary and language skills. They learn to use a dictionary and increase their reading skills in order to debate, to express their feelings, and to get involved in topics not typical of prison culture.

Greece

Historically, Greece has had one of the lowest crime rates in Europe. In theory, its mission is to prevent perpetrators from committing new crimes, and it does this through an emphasis more on rehabilitation than on what it considers cruel punishment (solitary confinement, capital punishment, etc.). The focus, especially with juvenile offenders, is said to be on education, vocational training, and productive labor to create a "right-thinking citizen." EPEA Hellas, an official branch of the European Prison Education Association, is dedicated to establishing education within prisons and to the professional development of incarcerated individuals. They have created a virtual school that offers diplomas equal to that of universities.[63]

Professional social workers and psychologists provide reentry services to help find employment upon release. NGOs (nonprofit organizations working for human welfare and operating separately from any national government) help prisoners with after-release services, such as housing, medical care, and continuing education, etc. Some are faith-based, and almost all are privately funded.

The unfortunate reality, however, is that Greek prisons suffer from extreme overcrowding (exacerbated by pretrial detentions as long as a year), poor conditions, and inadequate implementation of stated goals. If this continues, the Greek penal system may face punitive measures from the European Court of Human Rights.

Eastern Europe

Russia

The Russian government would like to transform penitentiaries into centers of social rehabilitation; therefore, some of their prisons provide higher education through correspondence for prisoners willing to pursue a degree. Unfortunately, however, most prisons are still poorly equipped or not equipped to support distance education.[64]

To engage prisoners with low levels of motivation, Russian prisons try to offer a curriculum that includes expressive arts and active learning. They might, for example, involve students in a play, such as *Hamlet,* or one where prisoners can write the script themselves; they might involve inmates in decorating the school, organizing the performances, or making costumes, etc.[65]

Hungary

Hungarian prison managers also espouse the idea of creating individual education plans; however, it has not yet proven to be a pervasive aspect of the Hungarian prison system.[66]

Romania

In Romania, too, it is mandated that "education for persons in detention must be in all respects [of equal] quality to [that of] adults in society."[67] Schools that function in Romanian prisons operate under the Ministry of Education, Research, Youth and Sports, and are included in the network of schools of the national education system. Authorities believe that educational and vocational training are priority activities that contribute to social reintegration opportunities for the inmates. Training courses held in prisons are conducted in accordance with law. Furthermore, "persons sentenced with a custodial sentence may attend university in the form of reduced frequency or distance learning within accredited higher education institutions."[68]

Also within Romanian prisons, there must be a library for the use of detainees, libraries whose contents and quality must meet established standards. In addition, the prison administration must provide free newspapers and publications, as well as sufficient reception of national and local radio and television programming.[69]

Upon the prisoners' release, county employment agencies collaborate with the prisons to provide information, counseling, mediation, and employment training to increase the inmates' chances of social reintegration.

Serbia

Serbian prisons are overcrowded. There are almost double the number of occupants recommended by the *European Prison Rules.* Nevertheless, according to Serbian law, all prisoners have certain rights. Cells must be of standard size, clean and dry with windows, and heated in winter. Prisoners may wear their own clothes, can make phone calls, have visitors, practice their religions, and receive medical care and education. If the prisoner is married, special rooms for family visits exist.

Recent legislation in Serbia ensures the educational rights of inmates to achieve positive changes in behavior, self-image, and relationships with other inmates, as well as literacy and vocational training in order to prepare them to function successfully in society upon release.[70]

Solitary confinement exists for inmates who represent a threat to prison security or other prisoners. These rooms are much smaller than their cells, and they lack natural light and ventilation. The maximum time a person can spend in solitary is one month.

While the primary focus of a Serbian prison is security, socialization is also an important aspect for avoiding behavioral problems, but it is felt that privacy in prisoners' cells allows a person to think about his crime, repent, and develop independence. Experiments have shown the Serbs that prisoners living in groups manifest worse behavior than prisoners who have private space.[71]

Estonia

As an incentive to participate in prison education, prisoners have an opportunity to live in a separate section of the prison where students have a little more freedom. In the educational section, relations are different, topics of conversation are different, and inmates feel less like prisoners and more like students.[72]

An educational development plan is prepared for each prisoner based on an individual risk assessment. If, for example, the person's educational level is low, that person must be persuaded to study. If the person doesn't speak Estonian, the prison offers language classes to help him or her fare better upon release. What is missing from the Estonian educational development plan, however, is the prisoner's active participation in the design of the plan and taking ownership of the goals.[73]

Prisoners also participate in programs intended to develop their social skills: family relations, anger management, addiction cures, etc. They are encouraged to participate in hobbies, sports, music and art, publishing a prison newsletter, etc. Some prisoners record books for the blind, and others enjoy attending the recording sessions.[74]

Lithuania

In this country, access to higher education in prison is almost impossible; there is little to no opportunity.[75]

Asia

Singapore

The Singapore Prison Service embraces the philosophy of prison as a learning school with the motto "Rebuilding Lives and Awakening Hope." The government established a prison school, the Kaki Bukit Centre Prison School, built on the principles of "Rehabilitation, Renewal, and Restart," offering academic and vocational classes and support for prisoners who prove they want to change.[76]

The management style of KBC is that of a school first, a prison second. Posters with encouraging and motivational messages fill the corridors. Staff members who do not subscribe to the shared vision are asked to transfer out. Prisoners who are not motivated or continue to have behavioral problems are transferred. Prison officers serve as advisors and role models to help inmates clarify what is important in their lives and develop individual life plans based on personal aspirations.

The system involves a team of professionals, including prison officers, teachers, counselors, psychologists and volunteers.[77] More advanced inmates serve as mentors to those struggling to catch up. The prison school has 11 classrooms, 3 computer labs, a science lab, a library, and an electronics lab.[78] The curriculum includes IT and web design, social studies, and activities such as music, games, sports, and drama. As of 2011, 5,094 inmates participated in training, with a 93.4 percent completion rate.

Inmates take courses appropriate to their competencies and interests. On the vocational track, they take classes to develop practical skills that lead to jobs. Also offered are treatment programs on family, sexuality, violence, aggression, and substance abuse while developing reasoning, problem-solving, and social skills.[79] Exploration of one's internal images and preconceptions on how the world works helps prisoners learn to be responsible toward themselves and others and how to make restitution. A "Reflective Thinking" course has them look at their misdeeds and learn there are consequences to both right and wrong choices. A system of privileges encourages good conduct.

Learning is done in teams through dialogue and discussion. The principal shares his thoughts daily with the school; individual inmates do the same in an open forum, as well as in writing. Prisoners develop reading habits and have access to a full library and reading clubs. They are taught to feel connected to others and to life itself and to work with forces of change, rather than resisting them.[80]

Most prisoners show a real commitment to doing well in their courses and to contributing to the school community. Key to this commitment is a built-in shift of control from prison officers to the inmates themselves. The prisoners plan and run activities, organize games, clubs, celebrations, and competitions; they put out a monthly newsletter and manage the library.

Security is still considered extremely important and is not neglected, but the corrections staff tries not to stifle rehabilitation.[81] Prisoners are searched after every activity.

While these are the stated principles of KBC, the daily reality is not always consistent with the vision and mission. Some of the officers are reported to be condescending or disrespectful of the prisoners. Despite the imperfections, however, recidivism rates among KBC prisoner-students are very encouraging, with the rates decreasing as the education levels rise. "More praiseworthy, however, is [the goal of] changing people's lives so that they become more responsible, respectable and caring; so that they build stronger character and are able to care for their families and themselves."[82]

Thailand

Authorities in Thailand understand that education is the best strategy for modifying prisoners' behavior so they become better citizens and members of society.[83] In 1949, Thailand began to incorporate education programs in prisons, ranging from functional literacy and life skills to vocational training and bachelor's degrees for those who completed their secondary schooling. Teachers may be prison officers or volunteers or outsourced staff,[84] and courses are offered to all inmates according to their ability and need. But the higher education courses are offered only at the prisoners' expense, some with partial scholarships.

When first confined, prisoners meet with psychologists or religious teachers to help them deal with the tension and fear brought about by incarceration.[85]

Japan

We find a completely different system in Japan. To begin, there are very few people incarcerated in that country: 55 per 100,000, as compared to 149 in Britain and 716 in the U.S. In Japan, also, recidivism is very low. And there has never been a riot in a Japanese prison since the Second World War, nor have there ever been attacks on prison staff. Escapes are rare and drugs almost nonexistent. In Japanese prisons, there is remarkable order.

Japanese prisons, however, operate with "draconian rules." Talking is not permitted, except on breaks. Unpaid work is a duty, not a choice. Solitary confinement is widespread, and conjugal visits are banned, so marriages break down. They operate with what we would consider a violation of fundamental human rights, far afield from international standards.[86] But Japanese corrections officials take pride in their differences from Western prisons; they believe their system works perfectly.

10

Thinking Inside the Box
to Make It Happen

To recap the issue in a nutshell: Our society is endangered by approximately 725,000 prisoners released each year to the streets. They are often angry and ill-equipped to survive without resorting to crime or violence. Our economy is undermined by the fact that most of them return to crime and prison, so that more and more of our state and national budgets go to building and operating prisons. Unfortunately, in the last decade the concept of prison reform has been replaced by policy that is punitive and favors long-term incarceration.[1]

It is not working.

Cutting funds for prison education is a bad decision. Virtually every existing academic and professional study unanimously finds that the one proven method for rehabilitation and for the reduction of recidivism and crime is *education*. Education prevents more crimes than increasing incarcerations and lengthening sentences—and costs far less.

Paradoxically, in the face of that knowledge, prison education has been systematically eliminated over the years, and federal funding for prisoner-students has been cut. Institutional programming to develop marketable skills and critical thinking is not available. If prisoners never left prison, this would be of lesser consequence. However, 97 percent of all prisoners are eventually released and will hit the streets again.[2] We cannot pretend it isn't so.

America has to catch up with the rest of the world. It is time—it is way past time—to open the gates of education to American prisoners. We need to stop the revolving prison doors and transform criminals into productive, tax-paying citizens. The formula is simple: The more advanced the education we provide behind bars, the lower the crime rate. It is proven.

The big question is, "How?"

The U.S. Department of Justice works with several national foundations, including the Pew Center on the States, the Open Society Institute, and the

Joyce Foundation, to help states create policies to lower recidivism rates and save taxpayer funds.[3] Some states continue to build more prisons despite their budget constraints. However, a growing number are working to identify effective strategies and practices, including community-based correctional education (see Chapter 5), to improve the reentry process.[4]

Areas that were deeply affected by the cuts, in addition to education, were staffing and health-care services.[5] Among ways being considered to reduce corrections budgets is to identify individuals who can safely be released after serving shorter terms and by reexamining mandatory and lengthy sentencing policies, especially for drug offenders.[6] State policy makers now question the effectiveness of harsher sentencing that has created the largest prison population of any country in the world, especially when we consider that nearly 25 percent of all those incarcerated are there on nonviolent drug convictions.[7]

A Model Prison

In 1994, the prevailing philosophy was that prisoners must not be "coddled," that prisons must be stripped of anything that can be construed as recreational and, as the Massachusetts governor of that time so aptly stated, prisons should be "a tour through the circles of hell."[8] This resulted in some drastic measures, among them the "Take Back the Streets" act and the disastrous repeal of Pell Grants for prisoners. By 1995, prisons around the country were making life as tough as possible for the incarcerated.[9] Alabama, for example, had reinstated the chain gang, with inmates doing hard labor in leg irons for up to ten hours a day.

This attitude on the part of the public made it hard for the rest of the country, too, since the 1994 crime bill made for longer and mandatory sentences that drove prison costs through the roof.

Flying in the face of current thinking was a federal prison warden named Dennis Luther at the McKean prison facility in Bradford, PA. Luther took seriously the studies he read. They showed that to the degree education and vocational training programs were cut, prison violence increased. So, at a time when American prisons were intensely brutal places breeding hatred and violence, rather than remorse, Warden Luther did the unthinkable: he set about educating his prisoners.

His approach was based on an "unconditional respect for the inmates as people." His inmates earned TV and telephone and family picnic privileges if they kept order in their cells and demonstrated consistent good behavior. Staff members were encouraged to make suggestions for improvement. He made sure there were sufficient recreational activities because, he believed, if there was less recreation, there would be more fights, more health problems, and more trouble.

Luther operated on the belief that if "you create Spartan conditions, you're gonna get gladiators."[10] He knew that long-term goals keep inmates sane and less inclined to violence. His educational programs served not only to slash recidivism rates, but made his prison easier and less expensive than most others to operate. That's right: his costs ran about two thirds of what it normally requires to run a prison, and there were, he reported, "no escapes. No homicides. No sexual assaults. No suicides." Even violent inmates who transferred to McKean from other prisons appeared to calm down. Because of his educational and recreational programs, Luther said, McKean needed fewer officers on staff, which kept operating costs down.

Inmates at McKean created a mentoring group to teach one another and the "I Care" group to deal with issues of prison life.[11] They kept busy with studies or work training. In Luther's prison, there was an unprecedented 47 percent enrolled in classes, earning certificates and licenses to help find employment after release. Many of McKean's released prisoners went on to work in social services and treatment programs.

Not surprisingly, McKean earned one of the highest ratings possible from the American Correctional Association as the best-managed prison in the country.[12]

A Working Solution

Stephanos Bibas, professor of law and criminology at the University of Pennsylvania and author of *The Machinery of Criminal Justice,* asks why we allow prisoners to spend their days in endless TV watching, weight-lifting, or socializing and not put them to work? "Productive, law-abiding citizens work for a living. We encourage schoolchildren to work and study hard to grow into responsible adults. We expect able-bodied welfare recipients to work for their bread. Why, then, do we house convicted criminals in state-sponsored idleness at enormous taxpayer expense?"[13]

We impose no responsibility on prisoners to make restitution to their victims or to support families they've left behind, Bibas observes. We simply force them to remain inert.[14] Unless they are seriously disabled, Bibas says, they should be required to work. Money they earn should forcibly go to victims and to their families so they can get off welfare and other social "handouts," or it can go to the government, helping to defray the "cost to taxpayers of investigation, conviction and incarceration." If they were to accept responsibility and offer an apology, it could also help to heal victims. Furthermore, the work experience would prepare them to be self-supporting when released, through lawful jobs. Prisons, therefore, should make drug treatment, job training, and education absolutely mandatory—steps not to be considered as "privileged treatment, but as steps toward becoming law-abiding citizens."[15]

Historically, Bibas tells us, labor unions suppressed the cheaper competition of prison labor, so that by 1940 Congress outlawed interstate commerce in prison-made goods and, by 1979, private firms could only hire inmates at prevailing wages. "Thus, there was little reason to hire inmates, given their low skills and the security costs incurred." Today, as a result, prisoners do little to make restitution or to prepare for lawful employment when released back to their communities.

We could even, Bibas suggests, draft convicts into the military—at lower ranks and with lower wages than ordinary enlistees. They could wear different uniforms and be given fewer privileges or benefits. But "whether in prison industries or in the military, inmates ... should be held accountable. Punishment should be tough, but it should also be productive and socializing."[16]

Making It Successful: What the Experts Say

By now it is well established that correctional programs can increase post-release employment and reduce recidivism; however, it can do so only if the programs are well designed and implemented.[17] Throwing information at inmates is not sufficient. In-prison education requires an infrastructure to ensure effectiveness and success.

States that have minimal educational programs and low rates of inmate participation should learn from the successes of other states and adapt their methods to fit local circumstances.

One often overlooked cause of prison overcrowding is the poor quality of public education delivered to impoverished communities. The need to equalize education in less fortunate areas is, studies tell us, as important as getting education into our prisons, "for it is those schools that are, unfortunately, often the pipelines to prison."[18]

Except for prisoner-students independently enrolled in correspondence courses (which they pay for fully themselves), most post-secondary education is delivered through on-site instruction, which poses logistical challenges and is limited by security considerations. The two key factors that will facilitate a broader reach of education within prisons across the country are (a) the use of technology and (b) funding.[19]

Technology and Safe Access to the Internet

One cost-effective approach, proven very successful in New Mexico (see Chapter 5), is the secure use of online distance-learning programs for prisoners. New Mexico prisons illustrate how we can rapidly expand higher education programs throughout our state and federal prison systems and reduce or eliminate waiting lists for education (including college courses) in prison.

Most states prohibit access to the internet for inmates due to concerns relating to the integrity of prison security, contact with the public at large, and unwanted contact with victims and victims' families.[20] But these restrictive regulations were enacted before technology was refined to enable limiting the users' access to specific sites. Consequently, to respect security requirements, distance-learning tools that do not require access to the web, such as videoconferencing (satellite or closed-circuit instructional television), CDs, DVDs, or virtual private networks (VPN) would be most appropriate and would allow us to bring a wide range of courses to prisoner-students.

By developing firewalls that limit access to the online learning system and library, as well as e-mail communications to instructors, which can be monitored, pilot programs have proven how successful it can be. Naturally, it would incur initial investment costs to create the technology for these distance-learning programs, but these costs are far lower than the cost of traditional classroom instruction.[21]

Typically, we calculate the cost of prison education based on teaching one classroom with one instructor. Online distance education enables one instructor to teach multiple classrooms at the same time. It significantly reduces the cost of obtaining instructors to come into the prisons and expands the number of prisoners we are able to reach with education. Of course, even if it is not necessary to have a professor on site, a proctor is still needed in the classroom, as well as guards to transport prisoners to and from their classes and supervise them while there.[22]

Today, in an economy where employment opportunities exist mostly for skilled workers, inmates have to be educated beyond a high-school level.[23] The most cost-effective method of educating inmates and preparing them for useful employment upon release is to expand on-line education within appropriate security parameters.

Current technologies also offer "adaptive learning systems," or individualized teaching to match a student's reading level and interests with articles and content from the web.[24] They can enhance reading comprehension with automated word look-up to expand vocabulary.

Limited internet access for online distance learning has proven very successful in New Mexico, Arizona, and Australia, where the inmates' use of computers provided to them is closely monitored.[25] In addition to the academic or vocational content of the courses, inmates are learning computer skills, which are also critical to surviving and succeeding in society.

Many colleges and universities provide constantly improving electronic distance education courses, but outside New Mexico, none of them are being utilized to bring higher learning into prisons.[26] To continue the current restrictions on internet access creates a critical challenge to prison education.[27] Experts in the field urge corrections policy makers to revise regulations and support the development of internet-based delivery of courses. Secure systems, they are convinced, can resolve many of the obstacles.

It should be noted that the Federal Bureau of Prisons has recently installed TRULINCS, a computer system that allows prisoners to manage their phone number and mailing lists, send internal e-mails to staff, view their commissary account balance, and send e-mails to approved people on the "outside" through a monitored e-mail service. This might serve as an initial phase in building the needed infrastructure, but prisoners still do not have access to the internet, and they can only e-mail approved persons. Plus, it costs five cents per minute to do so, which many cannot afford.

Correctional institutions that have not yet built the infrastructure for technology-based education will be faced with the necessity to do so. "To truly reduce recidivism and provide ex-offenders with the best chance to successfully integrate back into a technology-based society, fundamental changes in educational delivery are not negotiable."[28]

Hopefully, the profound impact of budget deficits upon inmate training and education will "drive leaders to consider policy changes that were unthinkable in the past."[29]

Following is a combined summary of recommendations for success with creating prison education programs from organizations that have been studying the issue and publishing their findings about it for many years, such as:

1. the Institute for Higher Education Policy (IHEP) in its extensive study of post-secondary correctional education throughout the nation[30];
2. the John Jay College of Criminal Justice, Urban Institute;
3. the Post-Prison Education Program of Seattle [www.postprison edu.org];
4. the Eighth International Women's Policy Research Conference[31];
5. the Correctional Education Association;
6. the U.S. Department of Education, Office of Correctional Education;

   7. Convict Criminology;

   8. the National Association for the Advancement of Colored People
(NAACP);

   9. the Texas State Department of Criminal Justice;

  10. the Urban Institute, Justice Policy Center;

  11. the American Correctional Association;

  12. the City University of New York;

  13. the Women's Advocacy Project 2009, created by women in the criminal justice system; and

  14. the North Carolina Department of Corrections.

These scholars in the field of corrections and many others (see Appendix
III for additional recommendations for maximally effective correctional education programs) all agree that prison education will prepare inmates for employment, help families escape poverty, and reduce recidivism. They agree also on
a number of steps to take if we are ready to utilize education to reduce recidivism.

Assessment and Monitoring

We must start with a systematic procedure for proper screening, assessment,
and evaluation of inmates' abilities at intake in order to determine their eligibility
for educational programs appropriate to their needs and interests. Assessment
would take into account the prisoner's age, reason for incarceration, test scores,
and length of sentence, as well as the individual's desire, motivation, and readiness.[32] It is important that offenders' backgrounds, personalities, and attitudes
be matched with educational and other programs offerings that are suitable to
them. Assessment allows us to select offenders who can truly benefit from school
and who are not likely to be transferred to facilities without educational programs.[33] Furthermore, accommodation can then be made for the needs of disabled prisoner-students.

Once placed into an appropriate educational program, each prisoner's
progress and achievement should be monitored. It is important that we document and track both successes and failures so that, upon their release, inmates
can be provided with reentry preparation suitable to their level of achievement.

States that offer academic advisors and evaluation of prisoners' educational
levels are more likely to succeed, but they also must carefully monitor the current
demands of the local labor market, as well as to track and document whether
in-prison training and education result in employment in those areas of training.
This will help shape the programs so that they produce maximum benefits. This

will also motivate prisoners,[34]and it will allow us to fund only those programs that are proven to be cost-effective and successful.[35]

- Programs should have clearly defined recruitment and hiring processes for instructors and policies that identify what constitutes qualified program staff. Instructional staff should have access to professional development opportunities and support services.
- Programs should have comprehensive student recruitment and orientation components. Before the inmate's participation, staff should assess the goals, skill level, and needs of each student and develop an individual learning plan based on these assessments.
- Programs should be provided in environments supportive of learning in which students feel physically safe and comfortable. Programs should use materials and activities that have been designed specifically for adult learners and that are relevant and appropriate to the living environment of prisoner-students. In addition to printed materials, programs should use computers and individual tutoring.
- Programs should have appropriate staff-to-student ratios and avoid mixing different skill levels in the classroom.
- Programs should have well-defined roles within their communities, governing bodies composed of community stakeholders, and open lines of communication with important local agencies. Additionally, strong management systems should incorporate data collection and evaluation processes to ensure program effectiveness and accountability.

Additional recommendations from the Urban Institute, John Jay College of Criminal Justice, for maximally effective correctional education programs suggest that they incorporate certain principles from general education practices (not necessarily specific to correctional education).[36] How realistically feasible all of these are within the unique conditions of a prison facility depends on the extent of commitment we, as a society, have to their success.

Support from Prison Culture and Staff

Prison education will not work unless we have institutional commitment to ensure a culture of support for education in the state and federal prison systems. Correctional authorities should enforce, even mandate, the provision of Basic Education (including instruction on health, mental health, parenting, and addiction counseling) and GED programming. Prison managers should seize the opportunity to provide a wide variety of in-prison work assignments and vocational training with equipment that is current and relevant in the workplace outside. And they should not only give prisoners greater access to higher education, including college courses, but academic tracks should be *encouraged*, not discouraged, as they often are. A detrimental factor in the prison culture is that there is palpable resistance from guards and other staff members to educational opportunities for prisoners. This has been observed and documented in prisons across the country. Prison authorities need to prohibit guards and prison staff from refusing to grant release from work details to prisoners enrolled in any educational or college program. Educational programs should not have to compete with work assignments, visitation, or other necessities.

As a solution to this prevailing obstructionist attitude, the Institute for Higher Education Policy proposes that education programs offered to prisoners should also be offered to prison employees. There would be very little extra cost involved, since they would be using instructors, textbooks, class space, and equipment already in use on the premises. This would allow our prison systems to offer professional development to their existing staff and motivate that staff to function more effectively in their roles. In so doing, we will see prison staff members more eager to support prisoner attendance in their educational courses.[37] Beyond a supportive attitude, qualified and credentialed staff who are committed and accountable can actually provide instruction to prisoners.

Participants should be able to work towards an A.A. degree and transfer credits if they wish to move on to a four-year college or university and, when necessary, there should be provision for remedial educational opportunities.

Academic and vocational records should be made an integral part of the prisoner's master file and transferred when the inmate is moved to another facility.

Prison libraries should be comparable in quality to public libraries and participate in inter-library loan programs with public libraries. Use of the library by prisoners should be encouraged. A qualified staffer or volunteer can coordinate library services and have access to a professional librarian. And, as part of the library services, prisons should have to provide academic advisory services and information about colleges prisoners can access, just as high schools do. How else can prisoners be informed about, and aware of, college programs and requirements for enrollment?

Eligibility for Pell Grants and Other Funding

One unanimous call from all the experts and organizations focused on our correctional system is that we immediately reinstate Pell Grant eligibility, as well as restore and expand state and federal grants and scholarships to specific categories of incarcerated individuals. In other words, make inmates who are most likely to succeed eligible for need-based financial aid.

Recommendations call for the restoration of both federal and state funding for higher education in all prisons, including on-site college programs. In addition, they suggest we allocate state and federal funds to colleges and universities that provide instruction in prisons, some of which can be applied to grants for low-income inmates. States that provide budgeted support reflect a commitment essential to the survival of in-prison educational programs. Without state support, we will not see innovative programs like New Mexico's secure internet distance-learning initiative.

Recommendations also include restoration and expansion of the federal Incarcerated Youth Offender grant with a higher age limit and without the annual per-student spending cap, as well as active campaigns to solicit resources from foundations, private colleges, universities, corporations, and private individuals to support post-secondary education in our prisons.

Partnerships with Community Colleges

The connection between prison-based educational programs and community colleges is one of the most promising avenues for success in the reentry movement,[38] as illustrated in North Carolina and elsewhere. Community colleges are valuable allies in the effort to educate prisoners, and experts all encourage corrections departments to build partnerships with colleges or universities in the community.

However, most of the programs offered to inmates by community colleges are basic education, literacy, and non-credit vocational programs generally taught by prison staff rather than qualified instructors.[39] What is needed now are more of the credited vocational and advanced academic programs.

Prison systems that partner with colleges enjoy resources that they may otherwise not be able to afford. They can provide incentives to college faculty members who are willing to teach prisoners and share a staff of highly qualified instructors, placement testing, remediation strategies to prepare prisoner-students for post-secondary courses, software licensing, learning systems, technological hardware, and the ability to confer degrees.[40]

By using the already existing educational, financial and political resources of the community college systems, we do not have to reinvent the wheel or create new expenses. Such partnerships promote buy-in from the community and avoid wasted funds and duplication of efforts. Partnering with nearby schools and colleges may also create the best source of recruiting full-time, on-site teachers. Further savings can be realized if prisons enlist retired professors and instructors to volunteer for teaching in the prisons and have them assisted by qualified volunteers from the community and other prisoners.

Partnerships can be centralized, as in North Carolina, where they are governed by a state body comprising representatives from the community colleges and corrections systems, and where the governing body ensures that courses provided to prisoners are equal in quality and content to those offered to the general public. Or they can be decentralized, whereby the prisons contract with the individual colleges. The disadvantage to decentralized programs is that course credits are less likely to be transferable between prisons and colleges, or that they will not be recognized by business and industry. In either case, though, it is important that the programs offered in prisons lead to real job opportunities, that they can be completed during the average length of the inmates' stay, and that they be recognized by state colleges and universities so that credits and degrees can be transferred.[41]

In order to qualify for federal grants (those that used to exist before the budget cuts), educational programs in prisons had to ensure they were provided by an accredited educational institution. Community colleges are a natural partner, since providing access to post-secondary education for everyone—and that includes the incarcerated—is their mission. (One community college, the J.F. Ingram State Technical College, is an accredited, state-supported school in Alabama and perhaps the only one dedicated specifically to educating prisoners.)

To be successful, these partnerships between the community colleges and prison systems have to be effectively managed and must generate a positive perception on the part of the general public.[42] Instruction has to be appropriate to the prisoner's level of education, and it must be at a level equivalent to that of education in the community so that it is accepted by employers and other educational institutions. Instruction must also be responsive to the demands of the job market.

In New Mexico, for example, post-secondary education follows the standardized curriculum of an associate's degree in the public colleges. North Carolina has a business advisory council to ensure their prison vocational programs prepare returning prisoners for jobs available in local economies. In other words, it is important to align prison education programs with state education systems and with local workforce needs so that credits are readily transferable and further education or employment can be pursued. Otherwise, the entire effort may be a waste of money.

Basic to all of this, of course, is adequate funding. States that allocate state funds to public colleges and universities that provide instruction in prisons reflect real support and commitment.

Partnerships with the Community and Local Employers

To encourage prisoners' participation in studies and make it possible for released prisoners to secure jobs, the state can provide incentives to employers who will hire former prisoners who have enrolled in college-in-prison programs.

Certain jobs can be set aside for felons, jobs like building maintenance, park services, street repair, etc. By allowing released prisoners to earn money immediately upon their release to pay for food and shelter, we help them support further vocational training or academic education. Most ex-prisoners will turn away from the underground street economy if they have a better way to live than resorting to crime, and if they have money to pay for school and their goals for a better life.

When prison education programs teach skills that are applicable to the current job market, such as office administration and computer technology, and when they partner with employers, non-profit reentry assistance groups, and community organizations, they help prisoners access the widest possible variety of jobs and learning opportunities. In New York, organizations like the College Initiative and the College and Community Fellowship (see Chapter 5) help released prisoner-students enroll in colleges to complete their education.[43]

Also helpful would be apprenticeship programs where prisoners are given in-prison work experience corresponding to their vocational studies, so that their skills are not lost before their release. The Federal Bureau of Prisons and Virginia and North Carolina are making attempts to do this.[44] Even better would be to have businesses from the private sector engaged in the training and employment of offenders prior to their release, with the goal of linking these prisoners to employment when they return to the community.[45]

Reentry Initiatives

We discussed earlier the numerous problems newly released prisoners face when "dumped" without resources back onto the streets. Without follow-up and assistance, without a support network or any assurance that prison programming is followed by reentry services upon release, we are condemning ex-cons to a return to crime and prison—at taxpayers' expense.

Release preparation, to be effective, must begin the day a person enters prison with the preparation of a detailed plan, and it must continue until the day of release. Prisoners need assistance with, and instruction on, financial planning, obtaining social security cards, drivers' licenses, and medical care. Newly released ex-prisoners who leave the protection of prison walls alone, with no one to meet or transport them, need sufficient "gate money" to guard against desperation and relapse. And, at the time of release, prisons must ensure that ex-prisoners are sent out with sufficient identification documents and the paperwork necessary for the next step in their employment plans. These documents should include transcripts of credits earned and certifications granted during their time in prison.

Everything helps. Reentry programs might consider subsidized childcare for ex-prisoners attempting to complete their education.

There is a real need for reform in the parole system so that the primary focus is on helping newly released prisoners secure a job, housing, medical treatment, and education. This could help prevent "technical" violations of parole which have proven to be so costly because the only solution is to send them back to prison.[46] Many probation and parole workers may be better placed in Community Resource Centers that work to find jobs, train for new skills, enroll in school, locate affordable housing, and readjust to family life.

Another recommendation, put forth by the founders of Convict Criminology, is that we allow eligible prisoners an earlier release if they participate in educational and vocational programs, as well as in drug and mental health treatment.

For certain inmates, Residential Treatment Centers (RTCs), which are much less expensive to operate than prisons, can substitute for incarceration near the end of a prison sentence to facilitate a return to the community. If some prisons were converted to RTCs, they could treat thousands of people at a time and prove to be economically viable.[47]

And, if we want to see ex-convicts pursue completion of their education and become respectable, contributing citizens, we need to eliminate discrimination in college admissions and financial aid after an inmate is released, as well as to close the criminal records of ex- offenders if they haven't committed another crime in a specified number of years.

A Separate Space

All specialists seem to agree that an important factor associated with educational program success rates is the prison facility's ability to keep the program separate from the rest of the prison routine.[48] It would help to dedicate and maintain a safe and quiet place conducive to learning where students can study away from noise, threats and interruptions. Better still would be a student-only dorm.

It requires a new way of thinking, a different set of priorities, to establish a separate space with dedicated resources such as a library, a computer lab, and space for volunteer tutoring.[49] States could even fund services by ex-convicts who hold college degrees in social work, medicine, and related fields.

Sense in Sentencing

As a nation, we incarcerate five to ten times as many people per capita than any other Western democracy. It would make more sense to reserve imprisonment, as others do, for serious crimes and dangerous criminals. Since 50 percent of prisoners are incarcerated for mental health and drug use issues, studies show it would make economic sense to divert these individuals who would otherwise serve a mandatory prison term to drug and medical treatment centers, where we can then divert the money budgeted for prison facilities.

Course Completion

A problem faced in prisons where classes are offered is how to keep inmates enrolled until courses are completed. To start, correctional authorities would have to ensure prisoner-students will not be involuntarily transferred before completion of a class while enrolled in vocational and college courses, except for disciplinary reasons. In Washington State, for example, where prisoners may enroll in a state-funded one-year vocational program, completion rates have been very low because of involuntary transfers. There has been an attempt to standardize curriculum and course materials in the community and technical colleges to help alleviate the problem, but progress has been slow. Texas, on the other hand, will rarely transfer prisoners who are enrolled in college courses. When it happens, it is easy to get transferred back quickly.

To keep inmates enrolled until courses are completed, prisons in both Virginia and Texas have made agreements with the DOC to reduce interruptions caused by transfers. North Carolina's DOC matches educational programs to a prisoner's length of stay.[50] Some states provide incentive to complete courses and earn degrees with reduced sentences. Recognition of achievement also serves as an incentive, as do pay, access to preferred jobs, and special privileges. In New Mexico, the incentive to complete courses is exceptionally strong: prisoners have to pay for the program if they fail to complete it.[51]

Education of the Public

Nothing will change until the people demand it. And people won't demand prison education until proponents communicate effectively to the public how prison education benefits not just prisoners but, in a multitude of ways both financial and social, all of us in communities throughout America. It is important that legislators understand it is their constituents who will benefit most from reduced recidivism.

The issue of prison education has not had much attention since the denial of Pell Grant eligibility in 1994, and there is very little understanding among the public about post-secondary education for prisoners. People are generally not aware of how such programs reduce recidivism and save tax dollars. They don't understand that released prisoners who can find jobs are less of a threat to the safety of citizens in their communities. And they may not be aware that higher education would not in any case be available to any and all prisoners, but only to those who would meet stringent eligibility requirements.[52]

We must educate our legislators and publicize the findings of studies and the benefits that will result so that policy-makers and the voting public will approve funding initiatives for prisoner rehabilitation, reentry preparation, and higher education.

Agency Coordination

Sometimes various government agencies that impact prison educational programs operate with conflicting goals and priorities. It will smooth the way if we can establish informed, open, and cooperative working relationships among state agencies that are responsible for corrections, prison education, and higher education. According to a report from the Council for Advancement of Adult Literacy, "the offices of Vocational and Adult Education and the Office of Corrections are physically separated in the Federal Government; they are not in the same building and their staffs are not in touch. Correctional education requires coordinated input from both."[53]

Legal Barriers

We must repeal repressive and backward laws and regulations, such as those which restrict academic instruction in prison, and create restorative justice programs. These may be less effective, perhaps, with hardened criminals or those with multiple crimes, but if young or first-time offenders were made to repair the damage they have done to victims, it might turn them around and help them appreciate the personal pain their actions have caused. This, after all, is what restorative justice is about.

According to IHEP, 66 percent of Americans want our criminal justice system to put more of an emphasis on rehabilitation than on "warehousing" prisoners. As evidenced by our high recidivism rates, many people believe the prison system has failed.[54]

Hopefully, this represents a shift in public opinion. Hopefully voters will support legislators who will dare to do what is right: right for society, right for the economy, and right for people both inside and outside prison walls.

Funding Sources and Reentry Assistance

The first indication of a shift in political thinking and an acknowledgment of the need for reentry support services to help ex-offenders begin a new life was the Second Chance Act of 2008. Its authorized funding for reentry services is recognition of the challenges released prisoners face when they return to their old neighborhoods and an attempt to keep them from coming back into prison.[55] The Act also recognized the need for post-secondary education in our prison systems and authorized $165 million per year to initiate more schooling and drug treatment while prisoners remained incarcerated. Once prisoners are released, the Act was to provide aid for housing, medical care, job training, placement services, and guidance for building family ties and productive lives in society.

President Bush said, "Our government has a responsibility to help prisoners to return as contributing members of their community." But he was quick to add that government cannot do it alone. We must also rely on faith-based and community efforts to help returning prisoners reclaim their lives. "It will help our armies of compassion use their healing touch, so lost souls can rediscover their dignity and sense of purpose."[56]

"If properly funded," said Assemblyman Jeffrion Aubry, Justice Center board member and chair of the New York State Assembly Correction Committee, "this legislation will increase public safety, improve lives, and make more effective use of taxpayer dollars."[57]

The need for post-secondary education in our prison systems to enhance employment opportunities and an individual's ability to function in society is the primary focus of the Second Chance Act.

The Second Chance Act of 2008 was partially responsible for several states initiating improvements in their prison education programs. Arkansas's prison system had the largest graduating class to date. Instruction plans were being developed for Pennsylvania's prisoners, and women in Tennessee prisons began earning college credits.[58]

In 2011, the Second Chance Reauthorization Act extended the original grant program for an additional five years and incorporated several amendments to ensure that federal dollars would be spent in a cost-effective manner. The amendments promoted stricter accountability measures and transparency regarding compensation for nonprofit executives.

Other Sources

There are a few state prison systems where state appropriations provide limited funding for educational programs. Oklahoma utilized supplemental sources to assist Native American prisoners with Tribal Council grants. In Texas, prisons received educational funding from Texas Public Education Grants and from the Hazlewood Act, which provided tuition and fees at colleges and universities for Texas military veterans.

In Virginia and some other states, instruction is provided with private donations or scholarships from private colleges. Massachusetts is a prime example of this: the entire post-secondary correctional education program for the state is funded by Boston University (see Chapter 5).

In New York, there used to be state funding for post-secondary correctional education through the Tuition Assistance Program, which awarded educational grants to low-income individuals. This program kept education going after prisoners became ineligible for Pell Grants; however, this grant, too, was ended for prisoners in 1995.

A unique situation is that of North Carolina's state-funded post-secondary correctional education program (see Chapter 5). Fully funded by the state and reaching an extraordinary 33 percent of the North Carolina prison population, this program could serve as a model for states throughout the country. How do they do it?

Classes offered by community colleges in prisons are funded by the North Carolina legislature. The legislature assists all full-time students, without differentiation between prisoner-students and regular students. In 2006, there were 10,516 North Carolina prisoners out of a total population of 37,725 (28 percent) enrolled in college courses.[59] Today, despite the fact that IYO grants no longer exist, attendance in post-secondary correctional education in North Carolina remains above 30 percent.

A small handful of private endeavors, such as the Carl D. Perkins Vocational-Technical Education Act and The Nicholson Foundation, fund all or part of numerous reentry programs. They help to find additional financial resources for programs that reduce recidivism, strengthen families, improve neighborhoods, and enhance public safety.[60] These courageous efforts on the part of specific individuals are wonderful, but they are a drop in the bucket and insufficiently supported throughout the nation.

Innovative thinking will cut costs, as well. In the Boston University program, prisoner-students work after graduation to help coordinate and administer the in-prison programs. In this win-win scenario, the organization benefits from experienced assistants that cost them far less than employees from the "free world," and the prisoners benefit from a much better-paying job than one can usually find in a prison.[61]

One very innovative and effective source of funding comes from Inmate Welfare Funds, which the North Carolina Department of Corrections collects from prison canteens and prisoner telephone calls. These funds can be used only for the direct benefit of prisoners, and they are sufficient to meet the entire budget for educational equipment and supplies, including books, computers, student desks and chairs, and writing and project materials.[62]

All this said, however, the bottom-line reality is that funding for prison education has been drastically decreasing since 2009. Increasing pressure on state budgets makes it difficult for states to maintain funding commitments to post-secondary correctional education[63]and, sadly, there still remain a number of states which specifically forbid the use of state money to fund post-secondary education for prisoners.[64]

Smart Money: Shifting the Burden of Payment

Prisoner accountability, responsibility, and restitution may be the way to overcome public resistance to the concept of education behind bars. Rather than thinking about advanced education as a "reward" for having committed a crime, which is how many people tend to think of it, we can use advanced education as a way to make prisoners take responsibility for self-improvement while incarcerated and as a way for them to make restitution to society after their release. In other words, we build into the program a system of prisoner accountability.[65]

Payback

A most innovative suggestion, one that might really earn public acceptance, comes from the Institute for Higher Education Policy (IHEP). They propose that when prisoners are released and employed we make them pay back to the state what it had cost to house and feed and educate them while they were in prison. Texas is the only state, to my knowledge, that currently requires prisoners to reimburse the state for the cost of their education after their release from prison.[66] The repaid money ($250,000 in 2004) is used to fund post-secondary educational programs for other inmates within the Texas prison system (see Chapter 5).

In this way, we shift the burden of payment for prison education back to the prisoners themselves. Normally, prisoners have little money and few family resources. But if our prison systems provided them with education so they can obtain good jobs and earn a living wage, they will be in a position to pay it back when they are gainfully employed after release.

It Is Time—Way Past Time

Is education a form of coddling prisoners, or does it make sense because it enhances public safety? This was the question posed by a California agency charged with improving government efficiency. "We think better education is consistent with being anti-crime."[67]

The decrease in educational programs, combined with "get tough" strategies (longer and mandatory sentences, isolated supermax prisons, etc.) that create ever-increasing prison populations is creating serious problems.[68] Around the country, academic and professional voices are calling for prisons to no longer function as warehouses for violent, dangerous people who will be let out and sent back into our streets; calling for prisons to become centers of rehabilitation that transform prisoners into responsible citizens.

Will your voice be one of them?

Prison education is a concept whose time has come. It is time to stop studying the issue and stop discoursing. It is time to start the ball rolling and *do* something about it.

Appendix I: Federal Bureau of Prisons Program Statements

Post-secondary Education Programs for Inmates

U.S. DEPARTMENT OF JUSTICE
FEDERAL BUREAU OF PRISONS

PROGRAM STATEMENT

OPI: FPI/EDU
NUMBER: P5354.03
DATE: 12/17/2003
SUBJECT: Postsecondary Education Programs for Inmates
RULES EFFECTIVE: 12/19/2003

1. [**PURPOSE AND SCOPE §544.20. The Bureau of Prisons offers inmates the opportunity under its postsecondary education program to participate in post-secondary education courses (courses for college credit other than those courses which pertain to occupational education programs), which have been determined to be appropriate in light of the institution's need for discipline, security, and good order. Participation in postsecondary education courses which are part of occupational education programs is governed by the provisions of the Bureau's occupational education program (see subpart F of this part).]**

Postsecondary education is defined as courses for college credit other than courses that are a part of an occupational education program as defined in the Program Statement on Occupational Education Programs.

This Program Statement's provisions do not apply to the Advanced Occupational Education program.

2. **SUMMARY OF CHANGES.** The language pertaining to occupational education courses that are college accredited was removed. The section on Advanced Occupational Education (AOE) was removed.

The inmate's responsibility for postsecondary education tuition costs is clarified.

3. **PROGRAM OBJECTIVE.** The expected result of this program is:

Inmates will be provided with the opportunity to enroll in postsecondary education programs.

4. **DIRECTIVES AFFECTED**

   a. **Directive Rescinded**

   P5354.02 Postsecondary Education Programs, Inmates (5/7/97)

   b. **Directives Referenced**

   P4100.03 BOP Acquisitions (9/16/96)

   P5300.21 Education, Training and Leisure-Time Program Standards (2/18/02)

   P5353.01 Occupational Education Programs (12/17/03)

   P8120.02 FPI Work Programs for Inmates (7/15/99)

   Federal Acquisitions Regulations (FAR)

   c. Rules cited in this Program Statement are contained in 28 CFR 544.20–21.

5. **STANDARDS REFERENCED**

   American Correctional Association 3rd Edition Standards for Adult Correctional Institutions: 3–4410

6. [**PROCEDURES §544.21**

   a. The Warden or designee must appoint a postsecondary education coordinator (ordinarily an education staff member) for the institution. The postsecondary education coordinator is responsible for coordinating the institution's postsecondary education program.]

   Ordinarily, the supervisor of education is delegated authority to designate the Postsecondary Education (PSE) Coordinator. The PSE Program Coordinator or designated education staff member will coordinate course offerings, class schedules, and graduation requirements with the representative from the postsecondary education service provider.

   The PSE Coordinator will also be responsible for maintaining and updating program records.

   [**b. An inmate who wishes to participate in a postsecondary education course must apply through the postsecondary education coordinator. If the postsecondary education coordinator determines that the course is appropriate in light of the institution's need for discipline, security, and good order, the inmate may enroll provided that:**

   (1) The inmate meets eligibility requirements for the course which have been set by the course provider, and

   (2) The inmate is responsible for payment of any tuition either through personal funds, community resources, or scholarships available to the inmate.]

   Other resources available to inmates include UNICOR scholarships, veteran benefits, and other sources.

   Tuition will not be paid from Trust Fund or Salaries and Expenses appropriations.

   The inmate will incur all costs, including tuition, books, materials, and all other related fees, associated with correspondence courses.

   [**(3) The unit team determines that the course is appropriate for the inmate's apparent needs.**]

7. **TYPES OF POSTSECONDARY EDUCATION PROGRAMS**

a. **College Programs.** Institutions may offer on-site liberal arts and/or four-year college programs when feasible. Programs must meet all the following criteria:

    (1) An appropriate number of inmates requesting the program.

    (2) Inmates have the funds to pay tuition and books.

    (3) The space is available to conduct classes.

b. **Correspondence Courses.** Inmates are *encouraged* [author's emphasis] to enroll in PSE programs. If courses of study are not available on-site, inmates may enroll in programs through correspondence.

Inmates must receive approval from the PSE Coordinator before enrolling in any correspondence program. Institutions will establish written approval and enrollment procedures.

Tuition for correspondence courses will not be paid from Trust Fund or Salaries and Expenses appropriations.

[Author's note: With regard to this statement on correspondence courses, what I and many other prisoners have personally observed and experienced is different. In practice, College Coordinators only advise inmates on how to obtain correspondence course materials and how proctored examinations work. I have yet to see a College Coordinator provide an inmate with a school's correspondence program catalogue or assist with class schedules or with an understanding of graduation requirements. My personal observation is that the task of the prison College Coordinator is to record which students enroll in correspondence courses and the institutions from which the courses originate.]

8. **EDUCATION RECORDS.** Education staff will enter PSE program enrollments and completions into the SENTRY Education Data System (EDS) under the postsecondary group code and assignment category. At the Supervisor of Education's discretion, education staff may enter correspondence courses into the EDS system if an inmate required staff assistance.

9. **SELECTION OF EDUCATION SERVICE PROVIDERS.** The supervisor of education will select postsecondary education service providers competitively and they will award contracts according to applicable procurement procedures as required by the Federal Acquisition Regulations and the Program Statement on BOP Acquisitions.

    [Author's note: Religion-based correspondence courses can be difficult for the prisoner to enroll in because the FBOP Education Department requires that religious training go through the Religious Services Department, which has no system in place for handling correspondence studies. This creates a "Catch–22" for the inmate.]

                              /s/

                         Harley G. Lappin
                         Director

Education, Training and Leisure Time Program Standards

U.S. DEPARTMENT OF JUSTICE
FEDERAL BUREAU OF PRISONS

	OPI: FPI
	NUMBER: 5300.21
PROGRAM	**DATE:** 2/18/2002
STATEMENT	**SUBJECT:** Education, Training and
	Leisure Time Program
	Standards

1. [**PURPOSE AND SCOPE** §544.80. **In consideration of inmate education, occupation, and leisure-time needs, the Bureau of Prisons affords inmates the opportunity to improve their knowledge and skills through academic, occupation and leisure-time activities. All institutions, except satellite camps, detention centers and metropolitan correctional centers, shall operate a full range of activities as outlined in this rule.**]

Satellite camps, detention centers (to include the federal transfer center), and metropolitan correctional centers are exempt from providing full education programs; however, those exempted must have, at a minimum:

- General Educational Development (GED),
- English-as-a-Second Language (ESL),
- continuing education,
- library services, parenting, and
- recreation programs.

Independent camps should provide the full range of education programs specified in this Program Statement.

The Bureau requires that uniform standards must be followed in the operation of the Bureau's education, training, and leisure-time programs. Uniform standards are necessary for program accountability and evaluation, and for resource allocation. In addition, experience suggests that clearly defined standards contribute to effective program management and thereby enlarge inmate education, training, and leisure activity opportunities.

2. **SUMMARY OF CHANGES.** This revision clarifies program offering requirements for the Federal Transfer Center, Oklahoma City, and professional training requirements for education and recreation staff and allows credit for some training received from operational/program reviews, correspondence courses, and the Management and Specialty Training Center (MSTC), Aurora, Colorado.

It requires education staff to include the literacy provision of the Violent Crime Control and Law Enforcement Act (VCCLEA) and the Prison Litigation Reform Act (PLRA) in the Education Handbook so inmates can be better informed of the impact of satisfactory progress in the literacy (GED) program on their Good Conduct Time (GCT).

It also clarifies the role of inmate tutors/aides, the SENTRY data-reporting requirement for apprenticeship training programs, and the trade advisory committee's purpose for occupational training programs.

3. **PROGRAM OBJECTIVES.** The expected results of this program are:

a. Inmates will be advised of and afforded appropriate opportunities to improve their knowledge and skills through academic, occupation, and leisure-time programs.

b. Accurate and timely records and reports will be maintained about inmates, education staff, individual programs, and the education/training/leisure time programs' overall operation.

c. Each inmate who completes a program will receive a certificate of completion (and/or otherwise have that completion recorded in his or her file) and will receive other appropriate recognition (for example, graduation ceremonies).

d. Each education/recreation department will operate at a high level of professionalism through continuous self and supervisory evaluation, staff development, and communication.

e. Half-day work/education/recreation programs and the number of inmate participation in those programs will increase.

f. Inmate idleness will decrease.

4. **DIRECTIVES AFFECTED**

   a. **Directive Rescinded**
   PS 5300.17 Education, Training and Leisure-Time Program Standards (9/4/96)

   b. **Directives Referenced**
   PS 5251.05 Inmate Work and Performance Pay Program (12/31/98)
   PS   5300.18 Occupational Education Programs (12/23/96)
   PS   5322.11 Classification and Program Review of Inmates (3/11/99)
   PS   5325.05 Release Preparation Program (7/18/96)
   PS   5350.24 English-as-a-Second Language Program (ESL) (7/24/97)
   PS   5350.25 Literacy Program (GED Standard) (9/29/97)
   PS   5355.03 Parenting Program Standards (1/20/95)
   PS   5370.10 Recreation Programs, Inmates (2/23/00)

   c. Rules cited in this Program Statement are contained in 28 CFR 544.80–83.

5. **STANDARDS REFERENCED**

   a. American Correctional Association 3rd Edition Standards for Adult Correctional Institutions: 3–4150, 3–4264, 3–4381, 3–4401, 3–4410, 3–4410–1, 3–4411, 3–4412, 3–4412–1, 3–4413, 3–4414, 3–4415, 3–4416, 3–4418, 3–4419, 3–4421, 3–4422, 3–4422–1, 3–4426, 3–4428, and 3–4447

   b. American Correctional Association 3rd Edition Standards for Adult Local Detention Facilities: 3-ALDF-5A-02, 5B-01, 5B-02, 5B-03, 5B-04, 5C-01, 5C-02, 5C-06, 3D-24, and 2E-04

   c. American Correctional Association 3rd Edition Standards for Administration of Correctional Agencies: 2-CO-5B-01, 2-CO-5C-01, and 2-CO-5F-01

6. [**PROGRAM GOALS §544.81. The Warden shall ensure that an inmate with the need, capacity, and sufficient time to serve, has the opportunity to:**
   a. Complete an Adult Literacy program leading to a General Educational Development (GED) certificate and/or high school diploma;]

An Adult Literacy program completion is the achievement of minimum scores for issuance of a high school diploma, or equivalency credential, by the state from which the individual inmate will obtain it.

- Need is defined as not having achieved a verifiable high school diploma or equivalency certificate.
- Verification is established when an inmate furnishes a copy of the credential or official GED scores, or when the achievement is verified officially in a presentence investigation report.

[**b. Complete one or more levels of English-as-a-Second Language;**]

The English-as-a-Second Language (ESL) program offers limited English-proficient inmates the opportunity to improve their English skills.

- An ESL completion is the achievement of at least a score of 225 (eighth grade proficiency) on the Comprehensive Adult Student Assessment System (CASAS) Reading Certification Test and a score of 215 on the Listening Comprehension Test, respectively.
- Need is defined as a score of less than 225 and 215 on the CASAS Reading Certification Test and Listening Comprehension Test, respectively.

[**c. Acquire or improve marketable skill through one or more programs of Occupation Education (OE);**]

The need for occupation training will be based on the inmate's previous education and work history. When there is no demonstrated stable work history, or no specialized education or training record to demonstrate a marketable skill, an inmate will need some form of training. Program participation restrictions may be applied in accordance with the Occupational Education Program Statement.

Programs of occupation counseling, work experience, and/or formal training may be used (independently or in combination) to satisfy the identified need.

Ordinarily, an inmate does not receive compensation for participating in any Occupation Education program. When compensation is received (for example, during Apprenticeship Training), it may not exceed the amount appropriate for participation in institution or UNICOR work assignments.

An Occupation Education enrollment is to be entered into the SENTRY Education Courses (EDC) category when the inmate begins a program of study in any formal occupational skills training program. Final action will be entered in the SENTRY EDC system when an inmate exits that program.

Successful completion is when one of the following criteria is met:

(1) **Exploratory Training.** Achieving written criteria the institution established and approved by the Supervisor of Education.

- Exploratory programs are designed to provide an introduction to a specific occupation or a "cluster" of related occupations.
- Ordinarily, programs are less than 100 hours; however, completing predefined criteria rather than attendance must be demonstrated before awarding an exploratory level completion.

(2) **Marketable Skill Training.** Achievement of marketable skills, marketable at least at the normal entry level for a specific occupational title or cluster of titles; and completion of at least 100 hours of program attendance.

- Concurrent academic education requirements such as GED completion or GED enrollment may be established for marketable skill training programs.
- Ordinarily, inmates may not be enrolled in any marketable skill-training program if they have not met academic requirements previously or if they do not maintain concurrent GED enrollment.

Individual exemptions may be made, e.g., an inmate who is exempt from the GED continuing participation/promotion requirements because of **documented special learning needs**, but has the capability to learn the marketable job skills with **reasonable accommodations**.

(3) **Apprentice Training.** Achievement of the Joint Apprenticeship Committee's requirements for a journeyman's certificate in a U.S. Department of Labor, Bureau of Apprenticeship and Training registered program.

The start date for tracking apprenticeship-training hours in the SENTRY-based Education Courses (EDC) category is the actual date when the state or local apprenticeship training bureau or council accepts an inmate into the apprenticeship program.

Education staff should use the SENTRY-based Periodic Review/Withdrawal Record (PERW) to document training hours from another institution and/or other relevant training history.

[d. Complete one or more Postsecondary Education activities;]

A Postsecondary Education program completion is receiving a passing grade in a course an accredited postsecondary education institution has approved for postsecondary credit.

[e. Complete one or more Adult Continuing Education activities;]

Adult Continuing Education (ACE) activities are those formal instructional classes that are of special interest such as:

- Typing
- Financial planning
- Parenting
- Refresher training in a basic skill
- Consumer education, or
- Computer literacy.

Continuing education is completed when an inmate meets the participation and achievement standards established for that activity.

[f. Participate in one or more leisure, fitness, wellness or sport activities;]

All inmates are considered to have a need for informal recreation and leisure activities. Certain inmates may benefit, because of existing medical, physical, or emotional needs, from involvement in a more formal program.

- Such needs will be considered at initial classification meetings or when recommended by a member of the unit, psychology, medical, or recreation staff.

Completions of leisure and wellness activities will be reported on the Education Data System (EDS) when they meet established performance criteria.

[g. Participate in a Release Preparation program; and]

Release Preparation is a multi-disciplinary program that assists the inmate with specific and broad-based preparation for release back into society. Completion of **education** portions of the release preparation program is achieved and documented in the EDS when an inmate attends and completes release preparation courses as outlined in the Program Statement on the Release Preparation Program.

All education courses entered into EDC RE** in the release preparation program must meet the requirements outlined in the Program Statement on the Release Preparation Program and be approved by the Supervisor of Education.

[**h. Participate in Career Counseling.**]

Career Counseling will be an ongoing activity throughout the inmate's incarceration. Individual needs will be determined by a combination of factors, e.g.,:

- educational level,
- work history,
- aptitude and interest inventories,
- specific job skills, and
- unit team recommendations.

Inmates with career counseling needs can participate in a self-help program that assists them with career planning and development.

[**Staff shall encourage each inmate to accept the responsibility to identify any specific education needs, set personal goals, and select activities, programs and/or work experiences which will help to reach those goals.**]

7. [**GENERAL PROGRAM CHARACTERISTICS §544.82**

a. **The Supervisor of Education shall assure that the following minimum criteria are met for the institution's education program set forth in §544.8l.**]

28 CFR 544.81 refers to Section 6 of this Program Statement. These criteria must be met before the program can be reported into the SENTRY EDC:

[**(1) There is a written curriculum which establishes measurable behavioral objectives and procedures.**]

The Supervisor of Education must approve and teachers must follow the curriculum.

- The curriculum must be reviewed annually and updated as necessary. The review will be documented. A copy of the curriculum and its review records are to be kept in the Supervisor of Education's office. These requirements should not apply to activities entered into EDC RN**

[**(2) There are clear criteria which establish minimum expectations for program completion, as well as provisions for the assessment of student progress.**

(3) There are provisions for periodic review of the relevancy and effectiveness of the program.

(4) Unless unusual circumstances (e.g., college credit courses) exist, all programs should allow for open entry and exit, at least on a monthly basis.

(5) The Supervisor of Education may establish other requirements necessary to assure that the stated goals of the program are achieved.]

When questions exist, the Supervisor of Education is to consult with the Regional Education Administrator and document any approved deviations from minimum standards.

[**b. Upon an inmate's completion of a program specified in §544.81, staff may issue and/or review and file a certificate when it contributes to an inmate's future plans in such a way that it validates the inmate's education and training; supports the inmate's chances of securing employment; improves the inmate's acceptance for advanced education; or enhances the inmate's opportunity for success in any other activity the inmate chooses to pursue. The certificate will confirm that the inmate has completed the requirements to receive a certificate that fits one or a combination of the following categories:**]

28 CFR 544.81 refers to Section 6 of this Program Statement.

[(1) Accredited certificates—high school diplomas and occupation training certificates approved or issued through local school districts, state departments of education, or other recognized accrediting educational organizations;

(2) Postsecondary certificates and transcripts—postsecondary degrees or course certificates approved or issued through a sponsoring accredited educational institution;

(3) General Educational Development tests—programs sponsored by the American Council on Education;

(4) Private certificates—outside agencies, private business and industry, other than those stated in paragraph (b)(1) of this section;

(5) Institutional certificates—approved general education, occupation training, recreation, adult continuing education and social education certificates, issued to an inmate who completes a program, and when the institution cannot provide a certificate as provided in paragraphs (b)(1) and (4) of this section; or]

[(6) Transcripts—issued to an inmate who completes general education programs, formal occupation training, on-the-job and apprentice training and work assignments. With the inmate's consent, transcripts may be sent to schools and colleges, business, industries and other agencies.]

    c. Each institution is to provide programs for bilingual and bicultural inmates.

- Reasonable efforts will be made to obtain bilingual teaching materials and resources.

    d. Standard competency based curricula must be supported by appropriate instructional materials and classroom resources.

- Instructional objectives are to be stated in terms, which allow the performance to be observed or assessed.

Emphasis is to be placed on individual student progress and evaluation based on performance, according to established criteria.

- Instructors must provide and maintain individual student progress charts corresponding to the competencies identified in the curriculum.

    e. Reasonable classroom space and supplies of necessary equipment, including desks and chairs, audiovisual, materials, and other relevant instructional materials, should be provided for all academic, occupation, and leisure-time programs.

    f. Each Supervisor of Education is to ensure that academic, occupation, and career counseling is provided to individual inmates. Counseling should provide assistance, encouragement, and feedback regarding the inmate's education and occupation program plans while incarcerated and post-release goals.

Individualized assessment procedures (e.g., education interview, program recommendations) should be conducted during the Admission and Orientation (A&O).

    g. A graduation ceremony will be held at least annually in each institution to recognize inmates for program accomplishments, including those in ESL, GED, occupation training, postsecondary education, leisure-time activities, and other programs. Additional recognition ceremonies may be held as needed.

8. HALF-DAY WORK/EDUCATION/RECREATION PROGRAM

OPTION. At the Warden's discretion, all sentenced inmates may be placed in the education programs stated in Section 6 in a half-day work/education/recreation programming option.

- A half-day work/education/recreation assignment is defined as approximately three to four hours of continuous education/recreation or related programming in the morning or afternoon.

- Ordinarily, inmates with half-day programming are assigned to regular work assignments for a half-day and to education/recreation, or a related program, for the remaining half-day.

Ordinarily, inmates in half-day work/education/recreation programs do not receive compensation for the education/recreation portion of half-day work/education/recreation programs.

- However, local institutions may elect to pay inmates for participating in half-day education/recreation (e.g., apprenticeship training program) if resources permit.

When compensation is received, it may not exceed the amount appropriate for participating in institution or UNICOR work assignments.

9. [**INMATE TUTORS** §544.83. **Institutions may establish an inmate tutor/aide program. Guidelines shall be developed regarding the training and supervision of inmate tutors/aides where such programs are available.**]

When implemented effectively, an inmate tutor/aide program provides an effective alternative to combat inmate idleness and to promote positive use of the inmate labor force.

When feasible, institutions are encouraged to establish an inmate tutor/aide program to use as many inmate tutors/aides as needed.

At a minimum, guidelines should address:

- The supervision, training, and certification of inmate tutors/aides,
- Performance pay for inmate tutors/aides,
- Position description for inmate tutors/aides, and
- Other concerns as identified locally.

Inmate tutors/aids cannot serve as the primary instructors for the GED or ESL programs. They can only assist Bureau staff or contract instructors with instruction delivery.

- However, working under the general guidance and supervision of Bureau staff or contract instructors, inmate tutors/aids can teach adult continuing courses (ACEs) and other self-improvement classes.

10. **PROGRAM STANDARDS.** The following standards apply to education programs and full-time Civil Service and contract teachers:

a. **Instruction Time.** All full-time teachers and education specialists must spend at **least** 75 percent of their 40-hour workweek in instruction or in work related to instruction, with a minimum of 50 percent of their work hours spent in direct classroom instruction.

- Full-time test administrators are not expected to meet the 50 percent direct classroom instruction requirement.

b. **Adult Continuing Education.** Adult continuing education classes are organized differently in different institutions. Additionally, non-education staff members sometimes share responsibilities for developing and supervising these activities. [In my experience, almost all ACE courses in most federal prisons are taught by educated inmates. A staff member is responsible for the ACE program but rarely, if ever, actually teaches the course.]

Therefore, no national standards are established for class size. However, when full time staff or fully funded contractors provide instruction, ordinarily at least 15 students should be considered necessary to justify program continuation.

c. **Accreditation.** Whenever feasible, education and occupation programs are to be accredited by a state or other recognized accreditation association or agency. When a regional branch of the American Association of Colleges and Schools provides for the accreditation of "optional" or "special" schools, institutions should be accredited by that agency, if it can be achieved cost effectively.

When there is no feasible method of accrediting the entire department, special efforts should be made to gain independent certification for each occupation-training program. (It may be officially encouraged that programs obtain accreditation; however, in reality it is rare.)

Certification tests from organizations (e.g., National Occupational Competency Testing Institute, American Service of Excellence) may also be administered to individual inmates upon completing of a specific occupational training program.

- However, the individual skill competency certification should not replace a training program's certification.

d. **Schedule.** The education program will operate on a 12-month basis with minimum break periods for holidays.

e. **Program Hours.** Education activities are to be scheduled at least eight hours per day, Monday through Friday. (The hours need not be consecutive; e.g., 8:00—11:00 a.m. 12:30—3:30 p.m. and 6:00—8:00 p.m. are acceptable).

- Friday evening education activities may be eliminated when there are eight hours of combined Saturday or Sunday education activities.

Recreation activities will be programmed at least eight hours per day, Monday through Friday, to include both afternoons and evenings and at least 12 hours per day on weekends.

- Special weekday morning recreation supervision may be required when a significantgroup of inmates would not have access to exercise areas in the evening because of work assignment conflicts.

f. **Mandatory Education Program Hours.** Each mandatory education class session (literacy and ESL), to include special learning needs (SLN) class, must meet a minimum of one and one half hours per day. Daily class sessions may be longer, contingent upon local institution resources and needs. Program hours should be consistent with the Literacy and ESL Program Statements.

g. **Weekend Programs.** Weekend education service operation is encouraged when staff resources and the facility's location permit.

h. **Teacher Evaluations.** The Supervisor of Education shall ensure that annual formal class observations are conducted for all teachers. The Supervisor of Education shall provide feedback to the teacher about the overall quality of the classroom environment. This may include descriptive comments about classroom structure and discipline, student participation and motivation, and lesson preparation.

i. **Staff Training.** The Supervisor of Education and the Supervisor of Recreation are to ensure that at least 48 hours of training are provided every three fiscal years to the appropriate education/recreation staff members as described below.

- This 48-hour requirement may include the 8-hour per year, discipline specific training incorporated in Annual Refresher Training. All other mandatory training will not be counted toward the 48-hour requirement.

The training should be in two broad areas, with 20—28 hours in each area, for a total of 48 hours every three fiscal years. Regional training in education/recreation services can be applied to both areas.

(1) **Professional development which specifically relates to the education/recreation discipline.** The intent of this type of training is to ensure that education and recreation professional staff stay abreast of the current thinking and trends in their discipline's professional community.

This can be accomplished through department-wide retreats, off-site training, correspondence courses, or other appropriate methods.

• When department-wide retreats are conducted to provide this type of training, the training must be provided by outside speakers or Bureau staff knowledgeable of current education or recreation theories and practices.

• The subjects covered at these department-wide training sessions must relate to broad education or recreation professional development, not Bureau policies and practices. Subjects may include:

- learning styles and assessments,
- tournament organization and management,
- vocational training standards,
- language acquisitions, and
- other appropriate current theories and practices of education and recreation service delivery.

Departmental-wide retreats to develop strategic plans or to provide SENTRY training will not be counted toward the 20–28 hours in this professional development area, but they can be counted toward the Bureau policies and procedures subsection (2) below.

Correspondence courses provide a viable way to keep abreast of current theories and practices in education and recreation professional fields. With the Supervisor of Education and the Employee Development Manager's approval, selected correspondence courses may be counted toward the 20–28 professional training hours.

• Mandatory Bureau training that is not related specifically to the education/recreation discipline may not be applied to this 20–28 hours of training in this area.

• However, mandatory training courses offered at the MSTC that are related specifically to the education/recreation discipline such as teacher development, recreation/sports specialist training and education/recreation management training can be counted toward the 20–28 training hours in this area of training.

Cross development training in Education/Recreation Services taken by the new education and recreation staff and Spanish Immersion and Inmate Job Placement training taken by education/ recreation staff can be applied to meet the requirement in area (1).

Professional education/recreation staff must have 20–28 hours every three fiscal years relating to professional development.

Clerical and support staff are encouraged to acquire training in relevant professional areas.

(2) **Bureau policies/procedures which specifically relate to the education/ recreation discipline.** This training's intent is to ensure that **all** education/recreation staff members are fully trained in relevant Bureau policies and procedures pertaining to education/recreation disciplines. Examples of acceptable training include:

• SENTRY training for the VCCLJEA and PLRA procedures,

• participation in **education/recreation** operational and program reviews. The maximum amount of hours within a three fiscal year period from both types of review is **24** hours,

• GED test security procedures, or

- recreation-based security procedures, etc.

All education/recreation staff must complete 20–28 hours of training in this area every three fiscal years.

j. **Unit Team Participation.** An education or recreation staff member must be assigned to serve as an education advisor on each unit team as outlined in the Program Statement on Inmate Classification and Program Review.

k. **Admission and Orientation Handbook.** Each Education Department must develop an education handbook and make it available to all inmates during Admission and Orientation.

- Handbooks are to be updated at least every two years.

The handbook should give a brief overview of all education and recreation programs, the incentives and achievement awards system, and other pertinent information and include the VCCLEA and PLRA's literacy provisions.

A foreign language version of the education handbook (for example, Spanish) may be produced when 10 percent of the institution's inmates speak that foreign language and do not speak English.

l. **Trade Advisory Committee.** A trade advisory committee is required when occupational training programs are not offered by outside accredited education institutions or are not certified or accredited by outside accrediting or certifying agencies. When an entire education department is accredited or certified by an outside accrediting agency/organization, a trade advisory committee still is required to ensure individual program quality.

The trade advisory committee's size and composition may vary according to local needs, but must include at least two active members who are not regular employees or institution contractors.

The intent is to include representatives from trade organizations, accredited training institutions, or potential employers.

- These committees are to meet at least twice a year with at least one meeting conducted at the institution.
- Minutes from the trade advisory committee are to be prepared and maintained for three years.

At least once a year, the committee members will assist the training instructor to review the curriculum, instructional delivery, equipment, and other relevant areas to ensure that the training program is comparable to community standards. The review findings must be documented and maintained for three years. This review process can be part of the meeting conducted at the institution.

11. **ATTENDANCE.** The Supervisor of Education will monitor both unexcused and excused absences from school.

- Inmates are expected to attend class unless officially excused.
- The Supervisor of Education must watch for and correct patterns of program interruptions due to work details, sick calls, and other call-outs.

The Supervisor of Education is to ensure that all teachers maintain current class rolls. Inactive class rolls are to be dated and archived for three years. Institution and regional education staff will use these rolls for routine data maintenance and periodic program reviews.

12. **INMATE EDUCATION RECORDS.** An electronic education record is to be created and maintained to document inmate participation in education programs. An education record consists of:

a. **Interview Record.** Documents inmate education level, program interests, and related areas. An interview record is not required for pretrial inmates.

b. **Program Review/Withdrawal Record.** Documents the periodic reviews of inmates participating in literacy and other education programs.

c. **Justification of Exemption Record.** Where applicable, documents program exemptions.

d. **Test Scores.** Where applicable, documents literacy and ESL test scores.

Appropriate certificates and diplomas, as specified in Section 7.b., may be issued to inmates to document their achievements in and completions of education programs.

13. **PROGRAM REPORTS MID DEPARTMENT MEETINGS.** By February 15th of each fiscal year, Supervisors of Education must submit an annual education program report to the Wardens of their institutions reflecting achievement of strategic goals in meeting the inmate population's education and program service needs.

- Copies are sent to the Central Office Education Administrator and Regional Education Administrator.
- A copy of the institution's education handbook and class schedules are to accompany each annual education program report.
- The Education Department is to maintain a copy of the annual education report for 10 years.

The Supervisor of Education must hold monthly education/recreation staff meetings.

The Supervisor of Recreation is to hold monthly staff meeting when recreation is a separate department.

- Minutes from these meetings will be sent to the Regional Education Administrator, the Central Office Education Administrator, the Warden, and the appropriate Associate Warden via BOPNet GroupWise.

Minutes may also be sent via Groupwise to other Supervisors of Education or Supervisors of Recreation in the region.

- A copy of staff meeting minutes is to be maintained in the Education/Recreation Department for three years.

14. **REVIEW OF STANDARDS.** As part of the annual review and certification process, Central Office education staff must review these standards and definitions periodically (no less than once every year) and ensure that they are revised and updated, as necessary.

15. **EDUCATION DATA SYSTEM (EDS).** Supervisors of Education (or Supervisors of Recreation where Recreation is a separate department) are responsible for accurate and timely reporting of the department's program activities in accordance with the most current EDS guidelines. Supervisors of Education (or Supervisors of Recreation where Recreation is a separate department) must provide EDS training for all department staff.

Regional Education Administrators are responsible for monitoring the EDS data's validity and accuracy from their respective regions and for promoting the EDS' managerial use.

/s/
Kathleen Hawk Sawyer
Director

Appendix II: Prisoner Publications and Pen-pal Clubs

General Interest Publications

What might be considered by many the most important of the publications is *Prison Legal News*. *PLN* is a top-quality monthly newspaper distributed in prisons throughout the country, originated by Paul Wright, formerly a U.S. Army military policeman, then a convicted murderer who became a jailhouse lawyer and, subsequently, a prisoners' rights advocate. Battling public and private prison operators to gain reform and attention for human rights for prisoners, *PLN* has focused on the need for protection against violence by other prisoners or guards, the right to adequate medical care, and to freedom of expression. The publication provides detailed information about political issues and news that affect the incarcerated directly, reporting on relevant court cases and educating prisoners about how to fight their legal battles to achieve their legal rights.

Editor Wright has been battling prison censorship for a long time and has filed more than 20 lawsuits to preserve the publication in American prisons. Why does he put himself at risk to provide this information to prisoners? "Because," said Wright, "no one else will." An annual subscription is $24 for prisoners, $80 for attorneys and institutions, and $30 for other individuals. To subscribe, contact:

Prison Legal News
P.O. Box 1151
Lake Worth, FL 33460
Phone: (561) 360–2523
www.prisonlegalnews.org

Of equally significant importance is *The Journal of Prisoners on Prisons* (*JPP*). The Canadian-based non-profit is a distinguished academic journal publishing the work of convicts and ex-convicts since 1988. JPP earned its reputation as a clearinghouse of knowledge and academic studies produced by imprisoned writers to enlighten the public about the current state of prison institutions. It creates an educational forum that allows "criminalized" men and women to develop research that concerns them directly.

Each issue focuses on a specific theme, such as Education in Prisons or Women's Issues. To maintain its high standards of quality, all writing submitted for publication undergoes a stringent peer-review process to select the finest articles from prisoners with strong academic backgrounds or advanced educational degrees.

The editors believe definitions of deviance are traditionally put forth, with few exceptions, by social scientists, media representatives, politicians, and people in the legal community who have no experience of prison life. Too often, *JPP* claims, their understanding of the people participating in those defined acts are sadly lacking, and their analyses exclude the voices of the people most affected. Such a lack of understanding, the editors feel, may facilitate repressive and reactionary penal policies and practices. *The Journal of Prisoners on Prisons* serves, therefore, as a fresh, new source of information that counteracts popularly held stereotypes and misconceptions about those who face the deprivation of liberty. To subscribe, contact:

> The Journal of Prisoners on Prisons
> c/o University of Ottawa Press
> 542 King Edward Avenue
> Ottawa, Ontario, Canada
> K1N 6N5
> (613) 562–5246
> Email: jpp@uottawa.ca
> www.jpp.org

The Prison Journal is the international and interdisciplinary Sage Publications periodical that presents a diversity of views from distinguished experts who explore various aspects of correctional punishment, new and progressive theories, research, policy, and practice. *The Journal* provides news about innovative programs, state-of-the-art surveys, and legal and historical analysis.

Special issues regularly supplement *The Prison Journal's* coverage with articles offering an in-depth analysis of a single topic, such as "Women in Prison and Jails," "Education in Correctional Settings," and "Drug-Involved Offenders." Other topics include criminal justice administration and law, health and mental health, history, political science, psychology, public administration, public policy, and sociology.

Originally published by the Pennsylvania Prison Society, America's oldest prison reform organization, founded in 1787, *The Prison Journal* continues to gather vital insights and professional opinions on emerging trends, innovations, and developments in the rapidly changing world of corrections and alternative sentencing. Available from:

> SAGE Publications
> 2455 Teller Road
> Thousand Oaks, CA 91320
> (800) 818–7243

Another *Prison Journal* is quite different. Edited by John and Ann Worley, this *Journal* publishes poetry, short essays, and art from prisoners with the intention of providing an outlet for creative expression. It is the belief of the editors that "the presence of God resides in all people, and that everyone, even those incarcerated, can transform their lives in a positive direction." With no restrictions on professional standards except that the work be original, they invite submissions from inmates all over the country. To subscribe, contact:

> The Prison Journal
> c/o John Worley
> 6041 Watch Chain Way

Columbia, MD 21044–4107

Email: theprisonjournal@gmail.com

Cry Justice News is a newsletter publishing serious articles on imprisonment, poetry, and occasional art. One policy paper they published, "Calling for Sheepskins" by Dr. Jon Marc Taylor, had considerable influence in getting attention and initiating a grassroots lobbying campaign for allocating several million dollars a year to post-secondary correctional education for prisoners from the Inmate Collect Calling Phone System. Legislation was introduced into three General Assembly sessions of the Missouri Legislature. Although it was approved by committee, it was not passed by the full assembly. This is most unfortunate, because it would have been such an easy way to pay for getting on-site college programs back into that state's prisons. Moreover, had it been successful, it could have worked for prisons in many other states, as well. To subscribe, contact:

Cry Justice News

P. O. Box 2525

New Bloomfield, MO 65063

Cell Door Magazine is written mostly by prisoners who describe the incarceration experience and how the ex-prisoner fares once back on the street.   Content runs the gamut from poetry to short stories, from art to op-ed commentary. Selected for quality and educational or entertainment value, the editors introduce the men and women behind bars. Articles range from self-help and self-pity to current topics, insight, empathy, and pathos. But the primary focus is always on how living behind bars affects a human life, revealing to those who don't already know that prisoners can be intelligent, personable, and talented human beings. To subscribe, contact:

Mid-September to June:

Cell Door Magazine

12200 Road 41.9

Mancos, CO 81328

publisher@celldoor.com

www.lairdcarlson.com/celldoor/01002

July to mid–September:

Cell Door Magazine

6 Tolman Rd

Peaks Island, ME 04108

publisher@celldoor.com

www.lairdcarlson.com/celldoor/01002

The Pen, a publication originally created to gives voice to the silenced, was similar to *Cell Door Magazine* in that it published prisoner-students expressing their trials, tribulations, hopes, dreams, frustrations, and fears, both in writing and through art. However, we do not know if this publication still exists, as no information can be currently located and no address can be found.

Of interest to prisoners, but not actually targeted to an incarcerated readership, is the *Journal of Correctional Education*. Published by the Correctional Education Association for professionals in the field of penal education, its articles concern post-secondary education, as well as ABE, ESL, pre-GED, and GED classes offered in prisons. The organization does not focus specifically on advanced academic education; however, it does emphatically support the concept of prison education as the most effective means to rehabilitation.

From the Association website:

"Since 1990, the literature has shown that prisoners who attend educational programs while they are incarcerated are less likely to return to prison following their release. Studies in several states have indicated that recidivism rates have declined where prisoners have received an appropriate education. Furthermore, the right kind of educational program leads to less violence by prisoners involved in the programs and a more positive prison environment. Effective education programs are those that help prisoners with their social skills, artistic development and dealing with their emotions."

To subscribe, one must be a member of the Correctional Education Association. Annual membership fee is $65 for an individual. Contact:

Correctional Education Association
8182 Lark Brown Road
Suite 202
Elkridge, MD 21075
(800) 783–1232
Email: office@ceanational.org
http://www.ceanational.org/publicat.htm

The *Corcoran Sun*, a newsletter originally published from a California state prison cell, publishes poems and short literary prose written by prisoners and includes news, prison legal news, jokes, self-help articles, and advertisements of interest to the prisoner population. Each issue costs six stamps, or $2.76 (as of August 2013). There are usually three to four articles per issue, as well as monthly excerpts from the novels of editor-in-chief Dave Babb. To subscribe, contact:

Corcoran Sun
c/o Freebird Publishers
P.O. Box 541
North Dighton, MA 02764
www.freebirdpublishers.com

FAMM-gram, published three times a year, is the e-mail newsletter of Families Against Mandatory Minimums (FAMM), advocating for fair state and federal sentencing. Its colorful pages provide reports on FAMM's work to reform mandatory minimum sentencing laws and information about injustices resulting from mandatory minimum laws.

Articles are informative, ranging from the new crack law to the rumors of federal prisoners receiving increased time off for good behavior. The *FAMM-gram* is free and does not accept prisoner submissions. At the current time, the printed newsletter is no longer sent to prisoners.

FAMM
1612 K Street NW, Suite 700
Washington, D.C. 20006
famm@famm.org
www.famm.org

Fortune News, published by The Fortune Society, is a quarterly dedicated to education, advocacy, and successful reentry. Each issue includes "Justice Beat," a summary of research in the field; "Lentes Latinos" ("Latin Lens"), a Spanish-language column about criminal justice issues faced by the Hispanic community; "New & Noteworthy Prison Programs," a feature that highlights programs around the nation that are doing good work; "Center Stage," a selection of poetry, comics, drawings, and other creative works from incarcerated or formerly incarcerated individuals; and more.

Sample topics in past issues have included "Reentry," "Immigration and Detention," "Giving Back," "Crystal Meth," "Aging in Prison," "Alternatives to Incarceration," "Prison Conditions," "The Cost of Incarceration," "Shattered Families," "The Job Search," "Hepatitis C: The Silent Epidemic," "Voices from Death Row," and "Youth." The magazine is free to prisoners.

Founded in 1967, the Fortune Society is a Long Island, New York-based nonprofit social service and advocacy organization with a mission to support successful reentry from prison and promote alternatives to incarceration. If you would like to learn more about Fortune's programs and services, you are welcome to write, to call, or just drop in and talk.

Fortune News
29–76 Northern Boulevard
Long Island City, NY 11101
(212) 691–7554
Email: info@fortunesociety.org
www.fortunesociety.org

Prisoner Express appears once a year in print and online from the Durland Alternative Library at Cornell University. Designed to promote creative self-expression amongst prisoners, it publishes writing and educational projects for prisoners who sign up through their newsletter. To subscribe at no cost, contact:

Cornell University
127 Anabel Taylor Hall
Ithaca, NY 14853
(607) 255–6486
Email: alt-lib@cornell.edu
www.prisonerexpress.org

Prison Living Magazine is a magazine published four times per year for prisoners of all faiths. It offers articles that are both practical and inspirational to assist with living better in prison, as well as after-release issues such as reintegration into society, finding jobs, and resources available to the ex-prisoner. Numerous articles are dedicated to entertainment, including a sports section, crossword puzzle, comics, and trivia. To subscribe, $12 per year. Write or call:

Prison Living Magazine
10645 N. Tatum Boulevard, Suite 200–661
Scottsdale, AZ 85254
(800) 419–2891
http://prisonministry.net/plmag.

Prison Voices is a community outreach program, not a publication, but is listed here as another outlet where prisoners can give expression to their experiences. Originally an outgrowth of the Bay State Correctional Center (BSCC) community services program at Norfolk, MA, carefully screened prisoners meet with small groups of high-school students, college students, or other interested members of the community. The prisoners speak candidly about their lives, the events that led them to prison, and what the incarceration experience has been like for them.

Community members gain insight into the prison system and other criminal justice issues from this alternative information resource. For prisoners, it is an opportunity to serve the community while completing the remainder of their sentences.

The *Prison Voices* website features only a pen-pal program to create a bridge between prisoners and people outside. For more information about the Prison Voices program contact:

>Derek Estler or Jaileen Correira
>Bay State Correctional Center
>P. O. Box 73, Norfolk, MA 02056
>(508) 668–1687, ext 211.
>www.prisonvoices.com

ACLU National Prison Project Publication List

From the ACLU (American Civil Liberties Union) come several publications to address areas of interest to prisoners:

Journal is a biannual newsletter featuring articles, reports, legal analysis, legislative news, and other developments in prisoners' rights. An annual subscription, normally $35, is only $2 for prisoners.

The Prisoners' Assistance Directory includes contact information and descriptions of services for over 300 national, state, local, and international organizations that provide assistance to prisoners, ex-offenders, and families of prisoners. It also includes a bibliography of informative books, reports, manuals, and newsletters of interest to prisoners and their advocates.

A sampling of ACLU's other publications would include: *Breaking the Addiction to Incarceration; ACLU Commentary on DOJ's Proposed Standards to Prevent, Detect, and Respond to Prison Rape; States Aim to Make the Grade When It Comes to Shackling Pregnant Prisoners; Bradley Manning's Treatment Is Just the Tip of the Iceberg;* and many others.

To order any of these publications, send a check or money order to:
National Prison Project Publications
915 15th St., NW, 7th Floor
Washington, D.C. 20005
(212) 549–2500
http://www.aclu.org/prisoners-rights/aclu-national-prison-project-publication-list

CURE Newsletter is a national publication from Citizens United for Rehabilitation of Errants (CURE) that advocates for less incarceration and more rehabilitative opportunities for offenders. Their goal is to reduce crime through criminal justice reform. To subscribe, write:

>CURE
>P.O. Box 2310
>National Capitol Station
>Washington, D.C. 20013
>(202) 789–2126
>www.curenational.org

Razor Wire Newsletter, published quarterly by the November Coalition, reports on drug war-related issues, releasing prisoners of the drug war, and restoring civil rights.

A yearly subscription is $6 for prisoners and $25 for all others. Contact:

November Coalition
282 West Astor
Colville, WA 99114

Bureau of Justice Statistics Bulletin is published by the U.S. Department of Justice. It is exactly as the title suggests: 40+ pages of tables with statistics related to felony cases, providing data on demographics, criminal history, pretrial processing, adjudication, and sentencing. It is not for the casual reader. But if you want it, write to:

U.S. Department of Justice
Office of Justice Programs
Bureau of Justice Statistics
Washington, D.C. 20531

Special-Interest Publications

As there are in the "outside" world, there are numerous publications in the prison world geared to readers with a specific area of interest.

DEATH-ROW AND LIFETIME PRISONERS

Compassion is a bi-monthly newsletter written by death-row prisoners. Various subscription rates are available based on personal circumstances. To subscribe, write:

Compassion
c/o St. Rose Peace and Justice
140 W. South Boundary Street
Perrysburg, OH 43551

Lifelines is the publication of the National Coalition to Abolish the Death Penalty. It is published every four months. For more information, contact:

Lifelines
c/o National Coalition to Abolish the Death Penalty
1750 DeSales Street, NW, Fifth Floor
Washington, D.C. 20036
(202) 331–4090

Lifer-Line, a monthly online publication available in both English and Spanish, focuses on issues of interest to life-term prisoners. It is available free for those outside prison and mailed to prisoners as resources allow. For more information, contact:

Lifer-Line
c/o Life Support Alliance
P.O. Box 277
Rancho Cordova, CA 95741
(916) 402–3750
http://www.lifesupportalliance.org/Publications.html

EDUCATION FOR PRISONERS

The *Education Behind Bars Newsletter* (EBBN) is a free, bi-monthly publication directed toward prisoner-students and prison educators. It is founded on the belief that by educating prisoners we can make a huge impact on reducing recidivism and significantly reduce the national budget while promoting a safer, more prosperous nation. EBBN publishes writings from prisoner-students and prison educators on topics relating to prison education and prisoners rights. EBBN is published by Middle Street Publishing. For more information, contact:

Education Behind Bars Newsletter
c/o Middle Street Publishing
3900 Pelandale Avenue, Box 319
Modesto, CA 95356

To receive free news updates three times a week, prisoners with access to Corrlinks. com/TRULINCS computers can add news@prisonlawblog.com to their contacts list. These updates focus on prison education, prison law, and prisoners' rights.

Those outside prison can view the electronic edition of EBBN online at www.PrisonEducation.com and read *Prison Education News* at www.PrisonEducation.com/prison-education-news. Middle Street Publishing also operates the *Prison Law Blog* at www. PrisonLawBlog.com, where prison law and prisoners' rights are given coverage.

HEALTH-RELATED PRISONER PUBLICATIONS

CorrectCare is a quarterly newspaper which covers correctional health care. Prison libraries may subscribe to this publication by contacting:

CorrectCare
c/o National Commission on Correctional Health Care
1145 W. Diversey Parkway
Chicago, IL 60614
(773) 880–1460
www.ncchc.org/pubs/correctcare.html

Damien Center Newsletter is a free, bi-monthly publication focused on AIDS-related issues. For more information, contact:

Damien Center Newsletter
c/o Damien Center
26 N. Arsenal
Indianapolis, IN 46201
(317) 632–0123

Dispatch is a quarterly newsletter focused on AIDS-related issues. For more information, contact:

Dispatch
AIDS Delaware
100 W. 10th Street, #315
Wilmington, DE 19801
(302) 652–6776

INNOCENT AND WRONGFULLY CONVICTED PRISONERS

Innocence Denied offers advice and assistance to people wrongly incarcerated and their loved ones and will support and join forces with organizations that support the freeing of innocent victims of our justice system.

Innocence Denied is also a strong advocate for education, music, art, and skills acquisition for anyone incarcerated, but especially for those who are wrongfully imprisoned.

Innocence Denied does not address prison conditions, nor complaints about various aspects of cases wherein the prisoner is not innocent. Nor does the publication provide prisoner-to-prisoner contact, as in pen-pal services. The focus is on the editorial belief that "there should be massive protests on an innocent individual's behalf. There should be massive media coverage concerning the illegal confinement of the innocent. Judges and prosecutors who knowingly convict innocent individuals should be forced to resign [and] ... prosecuted.... Sadly, in reality this never happens." Subscriptions for prisoners are $6 per year; $15 for others. To subscribe, contact:

Innocence Denied
P.O. Box 18477
Pittsburgh, PA 15236
www.innocencedenied.org
innocencedenied@ymail.com

Justice Denied is a magazine focused on exposing wrongful convictions and how and why they occur. Six issues: $10 for prisoners, $20 for others. $3 for sample issue.

Justice Denied
P.O. Box 68911
Seattle, WA 98168
(202) 335–4254
www.justicedenied.org

LEGAL INTERESTS AND LITIGATORS

For litigators on behalf of prisoners and prisoners who are interested in the legal aspects of crime and the justice system, there are three monthly legal newsletters. All three provide case citations, updates on prison policy, news articles, and explanations of relevant legal issues (ex: habeas corpus relief or new U.S. sentencing guidelines). In addition, there is a circuit-by-circuit review of positive case law.

The Update: Federal Criminal & Immigration Law

This newsletter focuses on federal criminal and immigration law and is sponsored by Yvette M. Mastin, Attorney at Law, licensed to practice in Minnesota, Texas, and the U.S. Court of Appeals. Ms. Mastin provides representation in immigration trials, motions to reopen/reconsider, appeals to the Board of Immigration, and petitions for review in the circuit courts. With her extensive knowledge of how criminal charges affect the status of non-citizens, Ms. Mastin represents individuals facing deportation and criminal prosecution. For legal assistance you can reach her at:

Law Offices of Yvette M. Mastin
P.O. Box 572140
Houston, TX 77257
(832) 251–3662
Email: mastinlaw@yahoo.com
www.yvettemastin.com

The following two newsletters are sponsored by D. Craig Hughes, an attorney who has been Board Certified in Criminal Law by the Texas Board of Legal Specialization since 2000. A graduate of Rice University in 1985 and of the University of Texas School of Law in 1988, Mr. Hughes was a prosecutor with the Harris County, Texas, District Attorney's Office prior to becoming a defense lawyer. For legal assistance, he can be reached at:

D. Craig Hughes, Esq.
7322 Southwest Freeway, Suite 1100
Houston, TX 77074
(713) 535–0683
Email: dcraighughes@msn.com

State and Federal Criminal Law Review provides information about criminal law on both state and federal levels, and

Texas Criminal Law Review which is relevant to prisoners in Texas.

All three of the above publications can also be read online at www.federalcriminalparalegal.com.

Craig M. Coscarelli is the editor and producer for all three newsletters. Prior to earning a B.S. degree in telecommunications and film from San Diego State University, Craig had trained to be a paralegal during his seven years in federal prison, where he fought—and won—his own case and was released. After release, he was immediately hired as a paralegal by a high-profile criminal defense law firm in Houston, Texas, where he has worked for the last 10 years.

To subscribe or for further information on any of these three publications, contact:

Craig M. Coscarelli
9211 West Road, Suite–143–149
Houston, Texas 77064
(832) 814–1050
info@federalcriminalparalegal.com

Correctional Law Reporter is a bi-monthly law publication which covers recent court decisions and legislative developments in the correctional law realm. Subscriptions are $179.95 per year. For more information, contact:

Correctional Law Reporter
c/o Civic Research Institute
P.O. Box 585
Kingston, NJ 08528
(609) 683–4450
orders@civicresearchinstitute.com
www.civicresearchinstitute.com

Justice Quarterly is a quarterly publication, published by Routledge, which contains academic articles approved by the Academy of Criminal Justice Services. Subscriptions are $75 per year and come with a membership to the Academy of Criminal Justice Services. For more information, contact:

Justice Quarterly
c/o Routledge Customer Service
325 Chestnut Street, 8th Floor
Philadelphia, PA 19106
(800) 354–1420
support@tnfonline.com
www.acjs.org

WOMEN

The Fire Inside is a biannual print and web newsletter providing a space where women prisoners and their supporters communicate with one another and the broader public about the issues and experiences faced specifically by women prisoners. The publication prints articles, editorials, art, and poetry, some of which are translated into Spanish. Available at no charge from:

California Coalition for Women Prisoners
1540 Market St., Suite 490
San Francisco, CA 94102
(415) 255–7036 ext. 4.
Email: info@womenprisoners.org
http://www.womenprisoners.org/fire/

JUVENILE

The Beat Within presents a forum of writing and artwork from juvenile prisoners across the country and editorial commentary on every published piece. Available weekly online and monthly in print, it is free to prisoners, teachers, counselors, and correctional staff. Others are asked for a donation to Pacific News Service in the name of *The Beat Within*. Write to:

275 Ninth Street
San Francisco, CA 94103
(415) 503–4170
Email: beat@pacificnews.org
www.thebeatwithin.org

Religious

Inside Journal, published by Prison Fellowship, is a newspaper that reaches thousands of incarcerated men and women with the hope of the Gospel, explaining the Gospel in a way that makes sense to prisoners. *Inside Journal* includes both inspirational stories of lives transformed through Jesus Christ and practical-resource articles to help prisoners make the most of their time behind bars, whether they are close to release or incarcerated for life.

The editors believe the best way to transform our communities and make them safe is to transform the people within those communities, and that restorative change comes only through a relationship with Jesus Christ. They believe that prisoners can become productive ambassadors for Christ, both in prison and beyond. To subscribe, contact or have your prison chaplain contact:

Prison Fellowship
44180 Riverside Parkway
Lansdowne, VA 20176
(800) 251–7411
Email: insidejournal@pfm.org
https://www.prisonfellowship.org/pf-resources/resources-officialas-chaplains

Crossroad Journal of the Arts is published by the Crossroad Bible Institute with art, articles, and poetry by prisoners for prisoners to enjoy. Subscribe or submit your work to:

Crossroad Journal of the Arts
Senior Editor: H. David Schuringa
P.O. Box 900
Grand Rapids, MI 49509

Joy Writers' Good-News Letter sent out to encourage prisoners in their faith with poems and articles by prisoners and others. Submit your work or subscribe at:

The Joy Writers' Ministry
2001 Liberty Square Drive
Cartersville, GA 30121

Yard Out, a publication of the Prisoners for Christ Outreach Ministries, comes out three times a year with prison-related stories, articles, and poems. Write to:

Yard Out
c/o Prisoners for Christ
P.O. Box 1530
Woodinville, WA 98072
www.pfcom.org

BUDDHIST OR DHARMA

Dharma Garden, a quarterly publication, accepts submissions of articles, artwork, poetry, fiction, and reviews. To submit or subscribe, write to

Dharma Garden Newsletter
1 Fairtown Lane
Taneytown, MD 21787
www.facebook.com/DharmaGardenSangha
Dharmagardensangha@gmail.com

CHRISTIAN

The Fishers of Men Prison Ministries Newsletter is a monthly Christian publication available in print or online. The newsletter welcomes nonfiction and fiction stories, personal essays, and poetry about God from prisoners. Free. Send subscription requests and submissions to:

5403 N. Second Street
Loves Park, IL 61111
(815) 633–7508
http://prisonministry.net/fompm
Email: (form available on website)

MUSLIM

Prisonworld Magazine is a multi-state Muslim tabloid that presents itself as "the preferred prison entertainment magazine." Published six times a year with a format similar to the *National Enquirer,* the publishers also own a record company, video blog site, merchandising company, and radio network, addressing both the incarcerated and the outside world communities. All proceeds from *Prisonworld* go toward their prison outreach programs, which are unspecified in nature.

Dawah International LLC
P.O. Box 380

Powder Springs, GA 30127
(678) 233–8286
www.prisonworldmagazine.com
dawahinternationalllc@gmail.com

Revolutionary Politics

4strugglemag, produced three times a year, is a joint project between political prisoner Jaan Laaman and organizers of the Toronto Anarchist Black Cross. They publish
writing by political prisoners, prisoners of war, and their friends and family. Unapolo-
getically "anti-imperialist," they support "progressive national liberation" and the strug-
gles of the black, Mexican, Puerto Rican, and Native American "nations," which they
regard as "controlled by U.S. imperialism." *4strugglemag* advocates for their view of "justice, equality, freedom, socialism, protection of the Earth, human rights and peace." In
each issue, in addition to three or more main topics, they also publish poems, graphics,
essays, and announcements. More information is available at:

4strugglemag
P.O. Box 97048
RPO Roncesvalles Avenue
Toronto, Ontario, M6R 3B3 Canada
Email: jaanlaaman@gmail.com
www.4strugglemag.org

Resist Newsletter is a bi-monthly publication focused on social justice issues. The
suggested donation is $25 per year, but they will mail copies to prisoners for free if the
prisoner doesn't have the requisite funding. For more information, contact:

Resist Newsletter
c/o Resist
259 Elm Street, Suite 201
Somerville, MA 02144
(617) 623–5110
Email: info@resistinc.org

State-Specific Prisoner Publications

CALIFORNIA PRISONERS

Prison Focus is a biannual magazine produced by the group California Prison
Focus. Issues focus on a specific theme, such as: "Survival in Prison," "International
Imprisonment," and "Children of Prisoners." In this magazine one finds prison-related
news from newspapers and human-rights organizations. The editors print and encourage
article submissions from prisoners, as well as evaluations of conditions at Pelican Bay
State Prison in California. Cost for four issues: $5 for prisoners, $20 for others. Contact:

2940 16th Street #B-5
San Francisco, CA 94103
(415) 252–9211
Email: contact@prisons.org
www.prisons.org/publications.htm

California Lifer Newsletter may be found in your prison law library. If not, a year's subscription (six issues) is $25 or 80 postage stamps. Issues provide a comprehensive (70+ pages) reporting of cases litigated and news or events of interest to California's prisoners serving indeterminate sentences. Together with attorneys and his staff, Donald ("Doc") Miller, a former physician and lifer who got his law degree while in prison, works to consult with lifers and help to provide litigation and administrative appeals.

California Lifer Newsletter
P.O. Box 277
Rancho Cordova, CA 95741
(916) 402-3750

DELAWARE PRISONERS

Delaware Center for Justice Commentary is a free, quarterly newsletter of interest to prisoners in Delaware state prisons. For more information, contact:

Delaware Center for Justice Commentary
100 West 10th Street, #905
Wilmington, DE 19801
(302) 658-7174
www.dcjustice.org

LOUISIANA PRISONERS

The Angolite is a magazine published bimonthly "by and for the inmates" of the Louisiana State Penitentiary. It features current events, religion, and sports sections, as well as a legal Q&A from prisoners. $20 for one-year subscription. Write to:

The Angolite
c/o Cashier's Office
Louisiana State Penitentiary
Angola, LA 70712
Email: support@prisontalk.com
www.corrections.state.la.us/lsp/angolite.htm

MARYLAND PRISONERS

Maryland CURE Newsletter is the quarterly publication of Maryland CURE, covering legislative, prison system, and criminal justice news relevant to prisoners incarcerated in Maryland. Subscriptions are fulfilled through CURE membership at $2 for prisoners, $10 for individuals, and $15 for families. For more information, contact:

Maryland CURE Newsletter
c/o MD CURE
P.O. Box 23
Simpsonville, MD 21150
marylandcure@comcast.net

MICHIGAN PRISONERS

Michigan CURE Newsletter is the quarterly publication of MI-CURE, covering legislative, prison system, and criminal justice news of interest to prisoners incarcerated in Michigan. For more information, contact:

Michigan CURE Newsletter
c/o MI-CURE
P.O. Box 2736
Kalamazoo, MI 49003–2736
www.mi-cure.org
(802) 257–1342

Minnesota Prisoners

The Prison Mirror is a monthly newsletter of interest to prisoners incarcerated within the Minnesota Stillwater Correctional Facility. For more information, contact:

The Prison Mirror
c/o Pat Pawlak
970 Pickett Street North
Bayport, MN 55003–1490
(651) 779–2700

Northwestern States: Oregon, Washington State, Idaho, Montana, Utah, Nevada and Wyoming Prisoners

Justice Matters is a quarterly newsletter from the Partnership for Safety and Justice that reports on criminal justice issues in northwestern states. A subscription is $7 per year for prisoners and $15 for others. Write to:

Partnership for Safety and Justice
P.O. Box 40085
Portland, OR 97240
(503) 335–8449
www.safetyandjustice.org

Ohio Prisoners

Against All Odds is a newsletter from CURE-Ohio which publishes information of interest to Ohio state prisoners. Write to:

Against All Odds
c/o CURE-Ohio
P.O. Box 4080
Columbus, OH 43214
www.cure-ohio.org

Pennsylvania Prisoners

Graterfriends is a monthly publication that provides an opportunity for prisoners incarcerated in a Pennsylvania state prison to voice their opinions and concerns about prison legislation and criminal justice issues. The newsletter strives to facilitate communication between prisoners and correctional staff and between prisoners and the outside community. Submit articles to Dee Johnson, Managing Editor, telephone extension 112.

An annual subscription is $3 for prisoners and $15 for others. To subscribe write:

Attention: "Graterfriends" Subscriptions
Pennsylvania Prison Society
245 North Broad Street, Suite 300
Philadelphia, PA 19107
(215) 564–6005, ext. 102
www.prisonsociety.org/pubs/gf.shtml

Virginia Prisoners

Inside Out is the quarterly newsletter of Virginia CURE, which regularly covers legislative, prison, and criminal justice issues of interest to Virginia state prisoners. Subscriptions are fulfilled through CURE membership. Membership dues are $2 for prisoners (or six stamps), $15 for individuals, $25 for families, $50 for supporting members, $150 for life members/ organizations, and $250 for benefactors. For more information, contact:

Inside Out
c/o Virginia CURE
P.O. Box 2310
Vienna, VA 22183
www.vacure.org
(703) 272–3624

Veterans

The Veterans Advocate is a newsletter which focuses on veterans' law, advocacy, and lifestyles. Subscriptions are $80 for one year or $120 for two years. To subscribe, contact:

The Veterans Advocate
c/o National Veterans Legal Services Program
P.O. Box 65762
Washington, D.C. 20035
(202) 265–8305
www.nvlsp.org

Unlisted or Discontinued Publications

The *Coalition for Prisoners' Rights Newsletter* had been published for 34 years, but as of June 2009 had to cease mailing due to lack of funding. The Real Cost of Prisons Project now posts the C.P.R. Newsletters online in PDF format starting with the July 2009 issue. The newsletter can be downloaded from http://www.realcostofprisons.org/coalition.html and sent to prisoners.

Prisoners can also send the "Coalition for Prisoner's Rights Newsletter" a large self-addressed, stamped envelope and request up to 12 issues at a time. Write to:

Coalition for Prisoners' Rights
P.O. Box 1911
Santa Fe, New Mexico 87504–1911

There are a number of other publications whose continued existence is uncertain and for which no information could be found. They include *Prison News Service*, a publication by and for prisoners in Canada and the U.S.; *Voices from Prison*, offering poetry, prose, art, and more from U.S. prisoners, *Inner Voices*, a magazine publishing literature, poetry, essays, and plays by prisoners; *Prison Poetry* by Robert R. Reldan, a prisoner at the New Jersey State Penitentiary writing to deal "with the madness of prison life"; and *Deadman Talking*, essays about life on death row written by a prisoner waiting for execution in California's San Quentin Prison.

Pen-pal Clubs

Cyberspace Inmates
9700 NW Louis Dr.
Cameron, MO 64429
InmateConnections.com

ConvictPenPal.com
465 NE 181st, #308
Portland, OR 97230

Inmate Scribes
P.O. Box 371303
Milwaukee, WI 53237

LoveAPrisoner.com
P.O. Box 5563
Thibodaux, LA 70302

PenACon.com
P.O. Box 1037
Edna, TX 77957

Prison Inmates Online
8033 W. Sunset Blvd., #7000
Los Angeles, CA 90046

Prison Pen Pals
PO Box 120074
Ft. Lauderdale, FL 33312

WriteAPrisoner.com
P.O. Box 10
Edgewater, FL 32132

www.PrisonerPenPals.com
P.O. Box 19689
Houston, TX 77224

> (Note: Although prisoners cannot go online, they can write to this group, which will then post pen-pal profiles online. Online readers can send messages to prisoners via postal mail or through the service.)

Lists of Pen-pal Clubs

The Pampered Prisoner can provide more information about developing pen pals. Send an email to email@thepamperedprisoner.com or write:

PO Box 141
Okotoks, AB., Canada T1S 1A4

or

PMB #120—9220 SW Barbur Blvd. Suite 119
Portland, OR 97219

Appendix III: Funding for Correctional Education

Funding for correctional education comes from several sources and varies from system to system. At the state level, funding may come from general fund appropriations to state departments of corrections, labor, or education, or special revenue sources such as "inmate welfare" funds or prison industry profits. States can also access various sources of federal funding to be used for education in state prisons and in some cases jails. Federal funding sources include:

- funding for adult basic and secondary education, English literacy classes, and special education under Title II of the Workforce Investment Act (WIA), one of the largest federal sources of financial support for correctional education;
- money for vocational and technical training through the Carl D. Perkins Vocational and Applied Technology Education Act;
- grants for academic and vocational post-secondary education through the Workplace and Community Transition Training for Incarcerated Individuals State grant;
- funding geared toward juveniles and incarcerated youth (up to age 21 in some cases) such as Title I State Agency Neglected and Delinquent Program under the Elementary and Secondary Act; and
- funds for educating youth (up to age 21) with disabilities from the Individuals with Disabilities Education Act.[1]

As states face increased budget pressures, the amount spent on correctional education may drop, and there is less federal funding available than in the past to fill the gap. The trend in recent years has generally been toward reduced federal spending on education for incarcerated populations. For example, the Adult Basic Education Act previously required that at least 10 percent of its allocated funds be used for correctional education; the Workforce Investment Act that replaced it in 1998 states that now a maximum of 10 percent of the funds can be used for this purpose.

Perhaps the most widely discussed reductions in federal funding have been in post-secondary education, specifically the 1994 elimination of access to Pell Grants for students incarcerated in state and federal prisons. Up to that point, Pell Grants had been the primary source of funding for higher education programs in correctional facilities. In the year following the ban, the number of incarcerated individuals receiving post-secondary education dropped 44 percent.[2] Some states responded by developing new funding streams or offering loan programs to fill the gap.[3] A recent national assessmentfinds that the percentage of incarcerated individuals enrolled in post-secondary education has returned to pre–1994 levels. However, many more of these students are now enrolled in vocational rather than academic courses.

Trends in Federal Funding for Correctional Education

In 1964, Title II B under the Economic Opportunity Act authorized the first federally funded adult basic education program through the Adult Basic Education Act (ABEA). The Adult Education and Family Literacy Act (AEFLA), Title II of the Workforce Investment Act (WIA), replaced the ABEA in 1998 and remains one of the largest sources of federal funding for correctional education. While ABEA required that a minimum of 10 percent of appropriated funds be used for correctional education, WIA changed this to a maximum of 10 percent. Because of the statutory language, in actuality only 8.25 percent of the total appropriation may be allocated to correctional education. In 2004, $30 million in WIA funding was allocated for programs in correctional facilities.

The Carl D. Perkins Vocational and Applied Technology Education Act is another source of federal funding for correctional education programming. Before 1998, the Perkins Act required states to use a minimum of one percent of the funds toward correctional education programs. However, in 1998 the Perkins Act was amended, and states can now spend no more than one percent of funds on correctional education.

Federal funding streams are also available to states to fund post-secondary educational programs in correctional institutions. One such program is the Workplace and Community Transition Training for Incarcerated Youth Offenders State grant, now the Workplace and Community Transition Training for Incarcerated Individuals State grant. Once reserved for individuals age 25 and younger who were within five years of release, these funds were subsequently extended to include incarcerated individuals up to the age of 35 who are within seven years of release. Despite this expansion of eligibility, funding for the program was cut by 25 percent between 2008 and 2009 and eliminated completely in 2012.

Appendix IV: Free and Discounted Books for Prisoners

This list includes free general books, free religious books, and organizations from which prisoners may order books.

We are not sure if all the companies listed are still in business. If you have updates or changes to this list, please contact the author, Christopher Zoukis, at PrisonEducation.com.

General Interest Books

The Aleph Institute
9540 Collins Avenue
Surfside, FL 33154
(305) 864–5553
Website: www.alephinstitute.org
Free books for Jewish inmates and regular monthly literature, holiday offerings, and family programs.

American Correctional Association
Publications Department
8025 Laurel Lakes
Laurel, MD 20707–5075
Books to prisoners, no religion or legal (all states except OR).

Appalachian Prison Book Project
P. O. Box 601
Morgantown, WV 26507
aprisonbookproject.wordpress.com
Sends books to KY, MD, OH, TN, VA, WV. Cannot send to TX.

Arizona Read Between the Bars
c/o Daily Planet Publishing
P. O. Box 1589
Tucson, AZ 85702
Sends books only to prisoners in Arizona.

Asheville Prison Book Program
c/o Downtown Books and News
67 N. Lexington Avenue
Asheville, NC 28801
www.main.nc.us/prisonbooks/main.html
Sends free books to prisoners in NC, SC, TN, and GA. Cannot send to TX inmates.

Book 'Em
P. O. Box 71357
Pittsburgh, PA 15213
Sends books to Pennsylvania and New York prisons only.

Books for Prisoners
P. O. Box 2143
Colorado Springs, CO 80901

Books 4 Prisoners
c/o Hobo Bookstore
4040 Hamilton Avenue
Cincinnati, OH 45223
Sends books to inmates in Ohio, Indiana, and Texas prisons only.

Books Through Bars—Ithaca
c/o Autumn Leaves Bookstore
115 The Commons—2nd Floor
Ithaca, NY 14850
Sends free reading material to inmates in ME, VT, NH, MA, RI, CT, NY, NJ, DE, MD.
Does not send books to Texas inmates.

Books Through Bars—NYC
c/o Bluestockings Bookstore
172 Allen Street
New York, NY 10002
booksthroughbarsnyc.org
Sends free reading material to inmates in all states except AL, FL, LA, MA, MI, MS,
NC, PA and OH, with a priority for NY. Specializes in political and history books. Also
sends literary fiction and other educational books. Does not send religious literature.
Donations of stamps and cash are appreciated.

Books Through Bars—Philadelphia
4722 Baltimore Avenue
Philadelphia, PA 19143
Email: info@BooksThroughBars.org
www.BooksThroughBars.org
Sends free progressive political and educational materials to state and federal prisoners
in PA, NJ, DE, NY, MD, VA, WV. Does not send books to Texas inmates.
No catalog. Request books by topic and specific subject areas (for example: novels, self-
help, American history, etc.). You may request specific titles or authors; however, we
may not be able to provide these. No legal books. Donations, including stamps, are
greatly appreciated. Please send information regarding prison regulations for reading
material being sent in.

Books to Oregon Prisoners
P. O. Box 11222
Portland, OR 97211
http://www.bookstooregonprisoners.org
Free books to Oregon prisoners only.

Books to Prisoners
c/o Left Bank Books
92 Pike Street, Box A
Seattle, WA 98104
Email: bookstoprisoners@cs.com
www.bookstoprisoners.net
An all-volunteer, nonprofit organization that sends books to prisoners founded in the early 1970s and sponsored by Left Banks Books. BTP provides 3 books at a time and delivers to all states in the USA.
Please send a list of topics you are interested in. No legal or religious books. BTP receives over 1,000 requests for books each month. Volunteers work two evenings a week opening letters, finding books in our collection that correspond to the request, and wrapping and mailing parcels. Because of a continuing backlog of requests, prisoners sometimes wait up to six months to receive their books and have to be very patient. Friends and family writing to request books for their relatives are welcome to make a donation to help with costs.

Books 2 Prisoners
P. O. Box 791327
New Orleans, LA 70179
Louisiana prisoners only.

Books to Prisoners—Vancouver
c/o Joint Effort
P.O. Box 78005
Vancouver BC V5N 5W1
CANADA
Canadian prisoners only.

Books to Prisons—D.C. Area
P.O. Box 5243
Hyattsville, MD 20782
(301) 699–0042
Email: bookstoprisoners@quixote.org
http://bookstoprisons.org
Books to Prisons offers free educational as well as a wide selection of fiction and non-fiction reading material to prisoners around the United States free of charge. Please send requests for your general interests.

Boston Prison Book Program
1306 Hancock St. Suite #100
Quincy, MA 02169
Sends books to all states except CA, MI, MD, NV, TX, and Graterford, PA. Does not offer computer books, horror, romance, textbooks, true crime, or white supremacist materials. Publishes the National Prisoner Resource List free to prisoners nationwide on request.

California Coalition for Women Prisoners
1540 Market St., Suite 490

San Francisco, CA 94102
(415) 255–7036
Email: info@womenprisoners.org
SDCCWP sends books to women prisoners on various women's and political issues. Please
write to request a free book list. Stamp donations are appreciated to pay for shipping.

Chicago Books to Women in Prison
c/o Beyond Media Education
4001 N. Ravenswood Ave. #204C
Chicago, IL 60613
Sends books to female prisoners in CT, FL, IL, IN, MS, and OH.

Claremont Prison Library
Project PMB 128
915-C W. Foothill Blvd.
Claremont, CA 91711
Sends books to all states. Free books on self-help, personal and spiritual growth, wellness,
and metaphysical topics. No law books, technical, or GED. No catalog. Free resource
guide on request.

Cleveland Books 2 Prisoners
P.O. Box 602440
Cleveland, OH 44102
Sends books only to prisoners in Ohio.

Cody's Bookstore
2454 Telegraph Avenue; Berkeley, CA 94704
(510) 845–7852 and
1730 Fourth Street, Berkeley; CA 94710
(510) 559–9500
www.codysbooks.com
U.S. (800) 995–1180
CA (800) 479–7744

DC Books to Prisons Project
P.O. Box 34190
Washington, D.C. 20043–4190
www.dcbookstoprisoners.org
You can request titles, but prioritized subjects of interest preferred. List prison restrictions. Stamps appreciated. Lacks postage money to respond to all requests and puts lower
priority on the following: New England, OR, WA, PA, OH, NY, NJ, WI, and IL. Please
limit requests to once per 5 months.

FIRM (Furnishing Inmates Reading Material)
Attention: Don Bowman
7 West Lake Drive
St. Simmons Island, GA 31522
Sends books/materials to prison chaplains.

Gainesville Books for Prisoners
P.O. Box 12164
Gainesville, FL 32604
Sends books to prisoners throughout the United States.

The Granite Publishing Group
P.O. Box 1429
Columbus, NC 28722
(828) 894–8444
Email: info@granitepublishing.us
http://granitepublishing.us
Inmates may write to receive free books on subjects that support the cultivation of planetary consciousness. The metaphysical/transformational subjects of our books range from Native American spirituality to the extraterrestrial presence. Please send postage if possible.

Inside Books Project
c/o 12th Street Books
827 West 12th Street
Austin, TX 78701
insidebooksproject.org
Sends free reading material to inmates in Texas. One request every three months. Inside Books Project also publishes the handy Resource Guide.

Internationalist Prison Books Collective
405 W. Franklin Street
Chapel Hill, NC 27516
www.prisonbooks.info
Sends free reading material to inmates in AL, MS, and LA. Does not send books to Texas inmates.

Loompanics Unlimited
P.O. Box 1197
Port Townsend, WA 98368
Legal books and prisoner issues.

Louisiana Books 2 Prisoners
1631 Elysian Fields Avenue, #117
New Orleans, LA 70117
lab2p.wordpress.com
Sends free books prisoners in the following states: AL, AR, FL, GA, KY, LA, MO, MS, NC, TN, SC, VA, WV. Women and LA prisoners are prioritized. Does not send books to Texas inmates.

Louisiana Books to Prisoners
831 Elysian Fields #143
New Orleans, LA 70117
books2prisoners@riseup.net
Ships free books to prisoners all over the U.S., but focuses primarily on those in Louisiana.

Maoist Internationalist Ministry of Prisons
P.O. Box 40799
San Francisco CA 94140
prisoncensorship.info
Free books on Marxism, politics, history, law, dictionaries and other reference. Free anti-imperialist newsletter and political study groups for prisoners.

Midwest Books to Prisoners
c/o Quimby's Bookstore

1321 North Milwaukee Ave. PMB #460
Chicago, IL 60622
www.freewebs.com/mwbtp
Free books to Midwest prisoners.

The Midwest Pages to Prisoners Project
c/o Boxcar Books and Community Center
408 E. 6th St.
Bloomington, IN 47408
(812) 339–8710
www.pagestoprisoners.org

Sends free reading material to inmates in AZ, AR, FL, IN, IA, KS, KY, MN, MO, NE, ND, OH, OK, SD, TN, and WI. Does not send books to Texas inmates.

Sends up to three books at a time. Books can be requested every two months. Sends all subjects of fiction and non-fiction reading material. Priority is given to people requesting books from women's and youth facilities.

Open Books Prison Books Project
1040 N. Guillemard St.
Pensacola, FL 32501
www.openbookspcola.org

Sends free reading material to inmates in Florida. Does not send books to Texas inmates.

Pen Writing Program
588 Broadway
New York, NY 10012
(212) 334–1660

Write and request their *Prisoner Educational Catalog, Prisoner Resource List*, and *Handbook for Writers*. All are free to prisoners.

Prison Book Program
c/o Parsons Bookstore
1306 Hancock St. Suite 100
Quincy, MA 02169
(617) 423–3298 (No collect calls)
Email: info@prisonbookprogram.org
www.prisonbookprogram.org

Sending free books to prisoners in all states except CA, MD, MI, NV, OR, PA, or TX since 1972. You can request topics or titles: there are limited legal materials, educational, social, political, fiction, and books in Spanish. They do not offer computer books, horror, romance, textbooks, true crime, or white supremacist materials. Publishes the National Prisoner Resource List free to prisoners nationwide on request.

Prison Book Program, Redbook Store
92 Green Street
Jamaica Plain, MA 02103

Books cannot be sent to the following states: KS, NE, IA, MI, or CA.

Prison Book Project
c/o Food for Thought Books
P.O. Box 396

Amherst, MA 01004–0396
(413) 584–8975 ext. 208
prisonbookproject@riseup.net
www.prisonbooks.org

Cannot serve prisoners in Texas. Request books by topics of interest or title. No mailing list or catalogue. No hardback books.

Prison Library Project
915-C West Foothill Boulevard
Suite C 128
Claremont, CA 91711
prisonlibraryproject.org

Free books and educational material to inmates nationwide except HI, ME, MI, NE, NV, WI, PA, and VA. Book topics include self-help, personal and spiritual growth, wellness, and metaphysical books. No law books, technical, or GED. No catalogue. Free resource guide on request.

Prison Mindfulness Institute
11 South Angell St. #303
Providence, RI 02906
(401) 941–0791
www.prisonmindfulness.org
www.prisondharmanetwork.net

Sends free books on mindfulness practices, Buddhism, and other contemplative paths. Offers an online Directory of Prison Dharma Organizations, useful for prisoners seeking mentors, pen-pals, and other resources.

Prisoner Express
127 Anabel Taylor Hall
Cornell University
Ithaca, NY 14853
www.prisonerexpress.org

Free books to prisoners nationwide. Must send eight stamps or $3.50 for postage. Specify subjects of interest.

Prisoners Literature Project
c/o Bound Together Bookstore
1369 Haight Street
San Francisco, CA 94117
Email: prisonlit@yahoo.com
www.prisonersliteratureproject.com

Offers free books to prisoners; also has a prisoner resource address list free. You may request types of books—not specific titles. Topics include: Black studies, Chicano history, basic math/writing/science, books in Spanish, novels, politics, history and more. No Christian, Islamic, horror, romance novels, or legal books. Stamps or donations are greatly appreciated but are not required. Main types of books usually requested: dictionaries, ethnic studies, basic educational books. Sorry, no Texas prisoners.

Providence Books Through Bars
c/o Paper Nautilus Books
5 Angell Street
Providence, RI 02906

info@providencebtb.org
www.providencebtb.org
Sends free reading material to inmates nationwide including targeted self-help and inspirational books upon request.

Read Between the Bars
c/o Daily Planet Publishing
P.O. Box 1589
Tucson, AZ 85702–1589
readbetweenthebars.com
Sends free reading material to inmates in AZ. Does not send to Texas inmates.

The Readers Corner
Prison Book Program
31 Montford Ave.
Asheville, NC 28801
prisonbooks31@hotmail.com
www.main.nc.us/prisonbooks
Sends free books to prisoners in North and South Carolina, Georgia, and Tennessee only.

San Diego Books for Prisoners
c/o Groundwork Books
0323 Student Center
La Jolla, CA 92037
Sends books nationwide.

UC Books to Prisoners
P.O. Box 515
Urbana, IL 61803
www.books2prisoners.org
Sends free reading material to inmates in IL. Does not send to Texas inmates.

Urbana—Champaign Books to Prisoners Project
c/o Spineless Books
P.O. Box 515
Urbana, IL 61803
www.books2prisoners.org
ucbtp@yahoo.com
Sends all types of books to state and federal prisoners in Illinois. Has a large selection
of novels, but tries to stock popular genres such as African American history and literature, as well as dictionaries, although they're hard to maintain.

Wisconsin Books to Prisoners
c/o Rainbow Bookstore Co-operative
426 W. Gilman Street
Madison, WI 53703
(608) 262–9036
www.madisoninfoshop.org/wbtp/
Free books and reading material to prisoners in Wisconsin only.

Women's Prison Book Project
c/o Arise Bookstore
2441 Lyndale Ave. South

Minneapolis, MN 55405
www.prisonactivist.org/wpbp
Ships to all states except OR, MI, CO, and WV. Free books to women prisoners only. No county jail requests. Does not ship hardback books. Free resource guide for women and transgender prisoners. Encourages women and transgender prisoners to write articles for their newsletter. Write for more details.

Free Bibles and Religious Books

American Bible Society
1865 Broadway
New York, NY 10023
Free Bible upon request.
Free Bibles, including large-print and study guides. They can be sent through a chaplain.

American Muslim Foundation
1212 New York Avenue NW Suite 525
Washington, D.C. 20005

Arm the Spirit
P.O. Box 6326—Stn. A
Toronto, ON, M5W 1P7
Canada

Association for Research and Enlightenment
67th and Atlantic Avenue
P.O. Box 595
Virginia Beach, VA 23451
Books on spiritual growth and Edgar Cayce. Prisoners may receive two free books per month. Request books by topic, not titles.

Bible Says
P.O. Box 99
Lenoir City, TN 37771
Provides several packets of religious books.

Bibleingo.com®
P.O. Box 19039
Spokane, WA 99219

Bibles for America
P.O. Box 17537
Irvine, CA 92623

Chapel Library
2603 West Wright Street
Pensacola, FL 32505
Provides free Christian materials and Bibles.

Coalition for Jewish Prisoners
1640 Rhode Island Avenue NW
Washington, D.C. 20036

Free Bible Ministry
19603 Arroyo Lane
Cordes Lakes, AZ 86333

Healing Tao Center
P.O. Box 471
Revere, MA 02151
Books on Taoist yoga methods.

Human Kindness Foundation
P.O. Box 61619
Durham, NC 27715
humankindness@humankindness.org
(919) 383–5160
Two free books, or catalogue of other hard-to-find spiritual books.

International Bible Society
P. O. Box 35700
Colorado Springs, CO 80935–3570
Free Bible upon request.

International Prison Ministry
P.O. Box 130063
Dallas, TX 75313–0063
Free Bible upon request.

Islamic Center
22551 Massachusetts Avenue NW
Washington, D.C. 20008
Free Koran and study guides. Can be sent through a chaplain.

Prison & Outreach Ministries
Rev. David J. Dostiglio
World Christianship
238 Stagg Street
Stratford, CT 06615

Prison Fellowship
P.O. Box 2204
Ashburn, VA 20146–2204
Provides several free Christian books.

Rev. David J. Dostiglio
World Christianship
Prison & Outreach Ministries
238 Stagg Street
Stratford, CT 06615

United Prison Ministries International
P. O. Box 8
Verbena, AL 36091
Provides several free Christian books.

Books Discounted for Prisoners

Any bookstore, online or otherwise, will sell books to you if you send in an order and a check. However, the following are listed because they claim to be particularly relevant to prisoner issues or because they sell to prisoners at a discount.

ACLU
132 W 43rd Street
New York, NY 10036
ACLU Handbook on Prisoner's Rights $5.

A.K. Press
PO Box 40682
San Francisco, CA 94140–0682
40 percent discount on books to prisoners. Distributes thousands of books on all subjects. Write for a catalogue of books for sale.

F&W Publications
1507 Dana Avenue
Cincinnati, OH 45207
Write for a catalogue of books for sale.

Groundwork Books
0323 Student Center
La Jolla, CA 92037
Phone: (858)452–9625
Email: groundwork@libertad.ucsd.edu
Books are 40 percent off for those who can afford to pay. We will send two free books per person for those who are cannot afford to pay.
Send your request, specifying your interests, and we will send you a detailed booklet for that area of interest. Subjects: Africa, African-American, Asia, Asian-Pacific Islander, Chicano/a, China, CIA, FBI, Police, Cultural Criticism, Ecology, Education, Feminist Theory, Labor, Latin America/Caribbean, Native American, Political Theory, Racism, U.S. History, Political Economy and Imperialism and much more, including spirituality, dictionaries, social criticism, and select novels. Stamp donations are appreciated but not required.

Oceana Publications
75 Main Street
Dobbs Ferry, NY 10522
Books on legal information for prisoners.

South End Press
7 Brookline Street #1
Cambridge, MA 02139–4146
Write for a catalogue of books for sale.

Valley Merchandisers
P.O. Box 1271
Hagerstown, MD 21741–1271
Discounted books to inmates and their families, also do out-of-print book searches. Write to us for further information.

Appendix V: Federal Financial Aid for Incarcerated Individuals FAQ

1. Is a prisoner eligible for federal student aid while incarcerated?
Individuals who are currently incarcerated have limited eligibility for federal student aid. Individuals incarcerated in federal or state institutions are eligible only for Federal Supplemental Educational Opportunity Grants (FSEOG) and Federal Work-Study. Those incarcerated in local institutions are eligible for Pell Grants, FSEOG and Federal Work-Study. However, upon release, you are eligible for all types of aid. For more information, contact your institution's education coordinator or the financial aid administrator at the school where you plan to enroll.

2. Are prisoners eligible for loan consolidation while incarcerated?
No; incarcerated individuals may not receive federal consolidation loans.

3. Can a prisoner's student loans be deferred while incarcerated?
Prisoners may be able to have their loans deferred, but they must apply for a deferment and meet the eligibility requirements for the deferment. The chart below explains the steps to take to apply for deferment.

> **Federal Perkins Loans:** Contact the school that made your loan or the school's servicing agent.
>
> **Direct Loans or Direct PLUS Loans:** Contact the Direct Loan Servicing Center at **1-800-848-0979** or online at www.dl.ed.gov.
>
> **FFEL Loans (includes FFEL PLUS Loans):** Contact the lender or agency holding your loan. For thephone number of the agency in your state, call 1-800-4-FED-AID.

4. Is an individual recently released from prison eligible for federal student aid?
Once released, a former prisoner is eligible to receive all types of federal student aid, including grants, loans and work-study. However, eligibility may be limited if the individual had been convicted of a drug-related offense. (See question 6.)

5. Is a released prisoner eligible for aid if currently on probation or residing in a halfway house?
Yes; once the individual is no longer incarcerated, he or she is fully eligible to receive federal student aid, unless they have a drug conviction and have not completed the necessary steps to regain eligibility. (See question 6.)

6. **What types of convictions will affect eligibility for federal student aid?**
   A student convicted of the possession or sale of illegal drugs may have eligibility suspended if the offense occurred while the student was receiving federal student aid (grants, loans or work-study). Complete the Student Aid Eligibility Worksheet for the drug conviction question on the FAFSA to determine if the conviction affects the individual's eligibility for aid. As an alternative to waiting until the end of the period of federal student aid ineligibility, one can complete an acceptable drug rehabilitation program to regain eligibility for federal student aid. For additional assistance, call the Federal Student Aid Information Center at **1-800-4-FED-AID** or call FSAIC at **319-337-5665**. TTY users (for the hearing impaired) can call **1-800-730-8913**.

7. **How does one apply for federal student aid?**
   To apply for federal student aid, one must complete the *Free Application for Federal Student Aid* (FAFSA^SM). Contact the prison's education coordinator or the financial aid administrator at the school one plans to attend for more information.

8. **What address does a prisoner provide when applying for federal student aid?**
   When applying for federal student aid while incarcerated, inmates must use their current institution's mailing address. However, once released, they can update their permanent mailing address by using *FAFSA on the Web* (www.fafsa.ed.gov) or by calling 1-800-4-FED-AID.

9. **How can an ex-prisoner get assistance applying for federal student aid?**
   If one has any additional questions about federal student aid, application procedures or other federal student aid topics, they can contact their prison's education coordinator or call 1-800-4-FED-AID.

10. **How can one receive publications about federal student aid?**
    To receive a FAFSA or any Federal Student Aid publications, contact the prison's institution's education coordinator or call **1-800-4-FED-AID**. Also, check out the publications section at **www.FederalStudentAid.ed.gov** for financial aid guides, brochures and fact sheets.

Appendix VI:
Numbers Tell a Story

Facts About Prisons and Prisoners

The Growing Corrections System

- The number of inmates in state and federal prisons has increased seven-fold from less than 200,000 in 1970 to 1,524,513 by 2009. An additional 760,400 are held in local jails, for a total of 2.3 million.
- Between 2000 and 2008, the state prison population increased by an average annual rate of 1.5 percent, the federal population by 4.5 percent, and the jail population by 3.0 percent.
- As of 2009, 1 of every 135 Americans was incarcerated in prison or jail.
- The number of persons on probation and parole has been growing dramatically along with institutional populations. There are now more than 7.2 million Americans incarcerated or on probation or parole, an increase of more than 290 percent since 1980.
- One in nine black males ages 25–29 was in prison or jail in 2009 as were 1 in 27 Hispanic males and 1 in 60 white males in the same age group.
- Nationally, 131 females per 100,000 women were in prison or jail in 2009; 1,398 males per 100,000 men were in prison or jail.
- The 2009 United States' rate of incarceration of 748 inmates per 100,000 population is the highest in the world.

Who Is in Our Prisons and Jails?

- 93 percent of prison inmates are male, 7 percent female.
- As of 2009, there were 201,200 women in state and federal prison or local jail.
- 39 percent of persons in prison or jail in 2009 were black, 21 percent were Hispanic, and 34 percent were white.
- 62 percent of jail inmates in 2009 were unconvicted and awaiting trial, compared to 51 percent in 1990.
- Of those persons incarcerated in state prisons in 2008, half (53.8 percent) had been convicted of a violent offense, and just under half for a drug, property, or public order offense.

- 1 in 4 jail inmates in 2002 was in jail for a drug offense, compared to 1 in 10 in 1983; drug offenders constituted 18 percent of state prison inmates in 2008 and 51 percent of federal prison inmates in 2009.
- Black males have a 32 percent chance of serving time in prison at some point in their lives; Hispanic males have a 17 percent chance; white males have a 6 percent chance.

The number of prisoners in the USA 2011 is by far more than any other country in the world.

	Country	Number of Prisoners	Prisoners per Capita (per 100,000 people)	
1	United States	2,019,234	USA	715
2	China	1,549,000	Russia	584
3	Russia	846,967	Belarus	554
4	India	313,635	Palau	523
5	Brazil	308,304	Belize	459
6	Thailand	213,815	Suriname	437
7	Ukraine	198,386	Dominica	420
8	South Africa	181,944	Ukraine	416
9	Mexico	172,888	Bahamas	410
10	Iran	163,526	South Africa	402
11	Rwanda	112,000	Kyrgyzstan	390
12	Pakistan	87,000	Singapore	388
13	Indonesia	84,357	Kazakhstan	386
14	Poland	80,467	Barbados	367
15	United Kingdom	78,753	Panama	354
16	Germany	74.904	Trinidad / Tobago	351
17	Bangladesh	74,170	Thailand	340
18	Philippines	70,383	Estonia	339
19	Japan	69,502	Latvia	339
20	Turkey	64,051	Saint Kitts / Nevis	338

Source: (June 2011). U.S. Department of Justice, Office of Justice Programs, Bureau of Justice Statistics

Appendix VII—Prison
Education in Europe

Council of Europe Recommendation No. R(89)12 of the Committee of Ministers to Member States on Education in Prison

(Adopted by the Committee of Ministers on 13 October 1989 at the 429th meeting of the Ministers' Deputies, as updated Monday, 02 April 2007)

The Committee of Ministers, under the terms of Article 15.b of the Statute of the Council of Europe–

- Considering that the right to education is fundamental;
- Considering the importance of education in the development of the individual and the community;
- Realizing in particular that a high proportion of prisoners have had very little successful educational experience, and therefore now have many educational needs;
- Considering that education in prison helps to humanise prisons and to improve the conditions of detention;
- Considering that education in prison is an important way of facilitating the return of the prisoner to the community;
- Recognising that in the practical application of certain rights or measures, in accordance with the following recommendations, distinctions may be justified between convicted prisoners and prisoners remanded in custody;
- Having regard to Recommendation No. R(87)3 on the European Prison Rules and Recommendation No. R(81)17 on Adult Education Policy, recommends the governments of member States to implement policies which recognise the following:

1. All prisoners shall have access to education, which is envisaged as consisting of classroom subjects, vocational education, creative and cultural activities, physical education and sports, social education and library facilities;

2. Education for prisoners should be like the education provided for similar age groups in the outside world, and the range of learning opportunities for prisoners should be as wide as possible;

3. Education in prison shall aim to develop the whole person bearing in mind his or her social, economic and cultural context;

4. All those involved in the administration of the prison system and the management of prisons should facilitate and support education as much as possible;

5. Education should have no less a status than work within the prison regime and prisoners should not lose out financially or otherwise by taking part in education;

6. Every effort should be made to encourage the prisoner to participate actively in all aspects of education;

7. Development programmes should be provided to ensure that prison educators adopt appropriate adult education methods;

8. Special attention should be given to those prisoners with particular difficulties and especially those with reading or writing problems;

9. Vocational education should aim at the wider development of the individual, as well as being sensitive to trends in the labour market;

10. Prisoners should have direct access to a well-stocked library at least once per week;

11. Physical education and sports for prisoners should be emphasised and encouraged;

12. Creative and cultural activities should be given a significant role because these activities have particular potential to enable prisoners to develop and express themselves;

13. Social education should include practical elements that enable the prisoner to manage daily life within the prison, with a view to facilitating the return to society;

14. Wherever possible, prisoners should be allowed to participate in education outside prison;

15. Where education has to take place within the prison, the outside community should be involved as fully as possible;

16. Measures should be taken to enable prisoners to continue their education after release;

17. The funds, equipment and teaching staff needed to enable prisoners to receive appropriate education should be made available.

Appendix VIII—Reentry Facts

From the **National Reentry Resource Center**, a project of the Council of State Governments Justice Center, http://www.nationalreentryresourcecenter.org/facts.

- Federal and state corrections facilities held over 1.6 million prisoners at the end of 2009—approximately one of every 199 U.S. residents.[1]
- At least 95 percent of state prisoners will be released back to their communities at some point.[2]
- During 2009, 729,295 sentenced prisoners were released from state and federal prisons, an increase of 20 percent from 2000.[3]
- Approximately 9 million individuals are released from jail each year.[4]
- More than 5 million individuals were on probation or parole at the end of 2009.[5]
- In a study that looked at recidivism in over 40 states, more than four in 10 offenders returned to state prison within three years of their release.[6]
- In 2009, parole violators accounted for 33.1 percent of all prison admissions, 35.2 percent of state admissions, and 8.2 percent of federal admissions.[7]
- Twenty-four percent of adults exiting parole in 2009—131,734 individuals—returned to prison as a result of violating their terms of supervision, and 9 percent of adults exiting parole returned to prison as a result of a new conviction.[8]

Mental Health

The incidence of serious mental illnesses is two to four times higher among prisoners than it is in the general population.[9]

In a study of more than 20,000 adults entering five local jails, researchers documented serious mental illnesses in 14.5 percent of the men and 31 percent of the women, which taken together, comprises 16.9 percent of those studied—rates in excess of three to six times those found in the general population.[10]

Substance Abuse

Three quarters of those returning from prison have a history of substance use disorders. Over 70 percent of prisoners with serious mental illnesses also have a substance use disorder.[11]

In 2004, 53 percent of state and 45 percent of federal prisoners met *Diagnostic and Statistical Manual for Mental Disorders* (DSM) criteria for drug abuse or dependence. Nearly a third of state and a quarter of federal prisoners committed their offense under the influence of drugs. Among state prisoners who were dependent on or abusing drugs, 53 percent had at least three prior sentences to probation or incarceration, compared to 32 percent of other inmates. At the time of their arrest, drug dependent or abusing state prisoners (48 percent) were also more likely than other inmates (37 percent) to have been on probation or parole supervision.[12]

In 2002, 68 percent of jail inmates met DSM criteria for drug abuse or dependence. Half of all convicted jail inmates were under the influence of drugs or alcohol at the time of offense. Inmates who met substance dependence/abuse criteria were twice as likely as other inmates to have three or more prior probation or incarceration sentences.[13]

Only 7 to 17 percent of prisoners who meet DSM criteria for alcohol/drug dependence or abuse receive treatment in jail or prison.[14]

Housing and Homelessness

More than 10 percent of those entering prisons and jails are homeless in the months before their incarceration. For those with mental illness, the rates are even higher— about 20 percent. Released prisoners with a history of shelter use were almost five times as likely to have a post-release shelter stay.[15]

According to a qualitative study by the Vera Institute of Justice, people released from prison and jail to parole who entered homeless shelters in New York City were seven times more likely to abscond during the first month after release than those who had some form of housing.[16]

Health

The prevalence of chronic illnesses and communicable diseases is far greater among people in jails and prisons.[17]

In 1997, individuals released from prison or jail accounted for nearly one-quarter of all people living with HIV or AIDS, almost one-third of those diagnosed with hepatitis C, and more than one-third of those diagnosed with tuberculosis.[18]

At year-end 2008, 1.5 percent (20,231) of male inmates and 1.9 percent (1,913) of female inmates held in state or federal prisons were HIV positive or had confirmed AIDS. Confirmed AIDS cases accounted for nearly a quarter (23 percent) of all HIV/AIDS cases in state and federal prison. In 2007, the most recent year for which general population data are available, the overall rate of estimated confirmed AIDS among the state and federal prison population (0.43 percent) was 2.5 times the rate in the general population (0.17 percent).[19]

Education and Employment

Two in five prison and jail inmates lack a high-school diploma or its equivalent.[20] Employment rates and earnings histories of people in prisons and jails are often low before incarceration as a result of limited education experiences, low skill levels, and the prevalence of physical and mental health problems; incarceration only exacerbates these challenges.[21]

A large, three-state recidivism study found that less than half of released prisoners had secured a job upon their return to the community.[22]

Families

An estimated 809,800 prisoners of the 1,518,535 held in the nation's prisons at midyear 2007 were parents of children under age 18. Parents held in the nation's prisons—52 percent of state inmates and 63 percent of federal inmates—reported having an estimated 1,706,600 minor children, accounting for 2.3 percent of the U.S. resident population under age 18.[23]

Since 1991, the number of children with a mother in prison has more than doubled, up 131 percent. The number of children with a father in prison has grown by 77 percent.[24]

Twenty-two percent of the children of state inmates and 16 percent of the children of federal inmates were age 4 or younger. For both state (53 percent) and federal (50 percent) inmates, about half their children were age 9 or younger.[25]

Women and Reentry

At the end of 2009, federal and state correctional facilities held 113,462 women, and increase of 22 percent since 2000.[26]

An additional 740,253 women were on probation and 98,432 women were on parole at yearend 2009.[27]

According to an analysis of recidivism data from 15 states, 58 percent of women released from state prison in 1994 were rearrested, 38 percent were reconvicted, and 30 percent returned to prison within three years of release.[28]

Compared to men, women are more likely to be incarcerated for drug and property crimes, and less likely to be incarcerated for violent crime. In 2008, 53.8 percent of sentenced ale prisoners were convicted for violent offenses, compared to 35.6 percent of sentenced women prisoners. 29 percent of women were convicted of property crimes, compared to 17.7 percent of men. 26.9 percent of women prisoners were convicted of drug offenses, compared to 17.8 percent of men.[29]

Chapter Notes

Introduction

1. Benjamin Todd Jealous, Roslyn M. Brock and Alice Huffman, "Misplaced Priorities: Over Incarcerate, Under Educate," a report of the National Association for the Advancement of Colored People, Baltimore, MD, 2011.

2. Gregory A. Knott, "Cost and Punishment: Reassessing Incarceration Costs and the Value of College-in-Prison Programs," *Northern Illinois University Law Review*, Vol. 32 (2012).

3. Cal Thomas, "Jailbroken: 5 Ways to Fix USA's Prisons," *USA Today*, July 14, 2011.

4. James Ridgeway and Jean Casella, "No Budget Cuts for Federal Prisons," *Prison Legal News* (June 2012).

5. Ibid.

6. G. Knott 2012, op. cit.

7. Robert Allen, "An Economic Analysis of Prison Education Programs and Recidivism," Emory University, Department of Economics (2006).

8. Jon Marc Taylor, "Pell Grants for Prisoners: Why Should We Care?" *Journal of Prisoners on Prisons*, Vol. 17, No. 1 (2008).

9. Marcia Johnson, Katherine Bauer, and Elizabeth Tagle, "Proposal to Reduce Recidivism Rates in Texas," *ECI Interdisciplinary Journal for Legal and Social Policy*, Vol. 1, No. 1 (2011).

10. J. Ridgeway and J. Casella 2012, op. cit.

11. "Education as Crime Prevention," Open Society Institute, Criminal Justice Initiative, Research Brief Occasional Paper Series No. 2 (September 1997).

Chapter 1

1. "State of Recidivism, the Revolving Door of America's Prisons," The Pew Charita-

ble Trusts, The Pew Center on the States (April 2011) and Scott C.S. Hayward, "The Fiscal Crisis in Corrections: Rethinking Policies and Practices," Vera Institute for Justice (2009).

2. Tracey Kyckelhahn, "State Corrections Expenditures," U.S. Department of Justice, Bureau of Justice Statistics (2012).

3. "State of Recidivism..." 2011, op. cit. and Laura E. Gorgol and Brian A. Sponsler, "Unlocking Potential: Results of a National Survey of Post-secondary Education in State Prisons," Institute for Higher Education Policy (May 2011).

4. J. Garmon, "Higher Education for Prisoners will Lower Rates for Taxpayers," *Black Issues in Higher Education* (January 2002).

5. "State of Recidivism..." 2011, op. cit.

6. Christopher E. Pauls, "Student Perceptions of the Charter School Experience at Metro Detention Center," Master's Thesis, University of New Mexico, 2011.

7. "State of Recidivism..." 2011, op. cit.

8. Marc De Maeyer, "Are Prisons Good Education Practice?" *Convergence (International Council for Adult Education)*, Vol. 42, Nos. 2–4 (2009).

9. V. Beiser, "The Jail as Classroom. Why Los Angeles County's Top Cop Wants to Offer an Education to Tens of Thousands of Prisoners," *Miller-McCune*, Vol. 4, No. 3 (2011).

10. Emily Deruy, "What it Costs when We Don't Educate Inmates for Life After Prison," ABC News, accessed March 14, 2012, http://fusion.net/justice/story/us-fails-educate-inmates-life-prison-11751/.

11. Scott Harris Conlon, Jeffrey Nagel, Mike Hillman, and Rick Hanson, "Education: Don't Leave Prison Without It," *Corrections Today* (February 2008).

12. "Partnerships Between Community

Colleges and Prisons: Providing Workforce Education and Training to Reduce Recidivism," U.S. Department of Education, Office of Vocational and Adult Education, Office of Correctional Education (2009).

13. E. Deruy, op. cit.

14. Jeanne Contardo and Michelle Tolbert, "Prison Postsecondary Education: Bridging Learning from Incarceration to the Community," monograph presented at the Reentry Roundtable on Education, convened by The Prisoner Reentry Institute at John Jay College of Criminal Justice in cooperation with The Urban Institute, April 2008.

15. Michelle Fine, M.E. Torre, I. Bowen, K. Boudin, D. Hylton, J. Clark, M. Martinez, R.A. Roberts, P. Smart, and D. Upegui, with the New York State Department of Correctional Services, "Changing Minds: The Impact of College in a Maximum-Security Prison: Effects on Women in Prison, the Prison Environment, Reincarceration Rates and Post-Release Outcomes," City University of New York (2001).

16. C. Pauls 2011, op. cit.

17. M. Clarke, "Michigan DOC Rehabilitation Programs Emphasize Education, Reentry Support," Prison Legal News (June 2012).

18. C. Pauls 2011, op. cit.

19. L. E. Gorgol and B. A. Sponsler 2011, op. cit.

20. Ibid.

21. J. Contardo and M. Tolbert 2008, op. cit.

22. Jeanne B. Contardo, Providing College to Prison Inmates (El Paso, TX: LFB Scholarly Publishing LLC, 2010).

23. S.J. Meyer, L. Fredericks, C.M. Borden, and P.L. Richardson, "Implementing Postsecondary Academic Programs in State Prisons: Challenges and Opportunities," The Journal of Correctional Education, Vol. 61, No. 2 (2010).

24. Contardo 2010, op. cit.

25. G. Granoff, "Schools Behind Bars: Prison College Programs Unlock the Keys to Human Potential," Education Update Online, accessed March 13, 2012, http://www.educationupdate.com/archives/2005/May/html/FEAT-Behind-Bars.html.

26. Patrick A. Langan and David J. Levin, "Recidivism of Prisoners Released in 1994," Bureau of Justice Statistics Special Report (2002).

27. H.J. McCarty, "Educating Felons: Reflections on Higher Education in Prison," Radical History Review, Vol. 96 (2006).

28. S.J. Meyer, et. al. 2010, op. cit. and M. Clarke 2012, op. cit.

29. Stephen J. Meyer, "Factors Affecting Student Success in Post-secondary Academic Correctional Education Programs," The Journal of Correctional Education, Vol. 62, No. 2 (June 2011).

30. J. Gerber and E.J. Fritsch, "Prison Education and Offender Behavior: A Review of the Scientific Literature," Prison Education Research Project: Report 1, Sam Houston State University/Texas Dept of Criminal Justice, 1993.

31. Lawrence S. Mears, D.P. Dublin, and G.J. Travis, "The Practice and Promise of Prison Programming," The Urban Institute, Justice Policy Center (2002).

32. Shakoor A. Ward, "Career and Technical Education in United States Prisons: What Have We Learned?" The Journal of Correctional Education, Vol. 60, No. 3 (2009).

33. M. Martin, "What Happened to Prison Education Programs?" Prison Legal News (June 2009).

34. John Linton, "United States Department of Education Update," The Journal of Correctional Education Vol. 64, No. 2 (May 2013).

35. "Education as Crime Prevention" 1998, op. cit.

36. "Education as Crime Prevention," Open Society Institute, Criminal Justice Initiative, Research Brief Occasional Paper Series No. 2 (September 1997); E.R. Meiners, "Resisting Civil Death: Organizing for Access to Education in our Prison Nation," DePaul Journal for Social Justice, Vol. 3, No. 1 (2009); H. McCarty 2006, op. cit.

37. Stephen J. Steurer, Linda Smith, and Alice Tracy, "OCE/CEA Three State Recidivism Study," United States Department of Education, Office of Correctional Education (September 2001); J. Vacca, "Educated Prisoners are Less Likely to Return to Prison," The Journal of Correctional Education, Vol. 55, No. 4 (December 2004); "Lift State Ban on Higher-Education Funding for Prison Inmates," Editorial, Seattle Times, March 4, 2013.

38. M. Johnson, et. al. 2011, op. cit.

39. Ibid.; M. Martin 2009, op. cit.

40. Ibid.

41. Laura Winterfield, Mark Coggeshall, Michelle Burke-Storer, Vanessa Correa, and Simon Tidd, "The Effects of Post-secondary Correctional Education: Final Report," Urban Institute Justice Policy Center (2009).

42. P. Case, "Predicting Risk Time and Probability: An Assessment of Prison Education and Recidivism," presented at the Confer-

ence of the American Sociological Association, Montreal, Quebec, 2006.

43. Sherry E.M. Heiser, "Student Perceptions of a College Distance Learning Program at a Maximum Security Prison," Master's thesis, Humboldt State University, 2007.

44. K. Mentor, M. Bosworth, eds., "College Courses in Prison," draft submission to the *Encyclopedia of Corrections*, July 2011.

45. "Education as Crime Prevention," 1998, op. cit.

46. Robert Allen, "An Economic Analysis of Prison Education Programs and Recidivism," Emory University, Department of Economics (2006).

47. S. Ward 2009, op. cit.

48. John H. Esperian, "The Effect of Prison Education Programs on Recidivism," *The Journal of Correctional Education*, Vol. 61, No. 4 (December 2010).

49. Gerald G. Gaes, "The Impact of Prison Education Programs on Post-Release Outcomes," monograph at the Reentry Roundtable on Education, convened by The Prisoner Reentry Institute at John Jay College of Criminal Justice in cooperation with The Urban Institute (April 2008).

50. John Britton, "Government Reduces In-Prison Education Even Though It Helps Lower Recidivism," *Neiman Watchdog*, Neiman Foundation, 2004).

51. S. Kimmitt, "The Impact of Community Context on the Risk of Recidivism among Parolees at a One-, Two-, and Three-Year Follow-ups," Honors Thesis, Ohio State University, 2011.

52. Ibid.

53. Contardo 2010, op. cit.

54. Ibid.

55. S.J. Meyer, et. al. 2010, op. cit.

56. Ibid.

57. Kate Musgrove, N. Derzis, M. Shippen, and H. Brigman, "PIRATES: A Program for Offenders Transitioning into the World of Work," *The Journal of Correctional Education*, Vol. 63, No. 2 (September 2012); T. Fabelo, "The Impact of Prison Education on Community Reintegration of Inmates: The Texas Case," *The Journal of Correctional Education*, Vol. 53, No. 3 (2002).

58. S. Bahn, "Community Safety and Recidivism in Australia: Breaking the Cycle of Reoffending to Produce Safer Communities Through Vocational Training," *International Journal of Training Research*, Vol. 9, No. 3 (2011).

59. R. Allen 2006, op. cit.

60. Karen Lungu, "Colorado Prison's 'Education Row' A Boon for Inmates," *The Durango Herald*, April 26, 2010.

61. S. Soferr, "Prison Education: Is it Worth It?" *Corrections Today* (October 2006).

62. Miles D. Harer, "Recidivism among Federal Prisoners Released in 1987," Federal Bureau of Prisons, Office of Research and Evaluation (1994).

63. S. Heiser 2007, op. cit.

64. G. Banks, "Learning Under Lockdown," *ColorLines* (March 15, 2003).

65. S. Steurer, et. al 2001, op. cit.

66. "Inmates Receive College Education from San Quentin," *Jet*, Vol. 102, Issue 17 (October 14, 2002).

67. G. Gaes 2008, op. cit.

68. R. Allen 2006, op. cit.

69. K. Mentor and M. Bosworth 2011, op. cit.

70. W. Erisman and J.B. Contardo, "Learning To Reduce Recidivism: A 50-State Analysis of Postsecondary Correctional Education Policy," The Institute for Higher Education Policy (IHEP) (2005).

71. G. Banks 2003, op. cit.

72. S. Richards, D. Faggiani, J. Roffers, R. Hendricksen, J. Krueger, "The Dynamics of Race and Incarceration: Social Integration, Social Welfare, and Social Control," *Convict Criminology* 2 (2008).

73. "Few Prisoners Enrolling in Available College Classes," a report from the Institute for Higher Education Policy (IHEP) (2005).

74. V. Munoz, "Report to the Special Rapporteur on the Right to Education," presented at the United Nations Human Rights Council, April 2, 2009.

75. J. Garmon, "Higher Education for Prisoners will Lower Rates for Taxpayers," *Black Issues in Higher Education* (January 2002).

76. Gregory A. Knott, "Cost and Punishment: Reassessing Incarceration Costs and the Value of College-in-Prison Programs," *Northern Illinois University Law Review*, 32 (July 2012).

77. J. Garmon 2002, op. cit.

78. "Education as Crime Prevention," 1998, op. cit.

79. Richard J. Coley and Paul E. Barton, "Locked Up and Locked Out: An Educational Perspective on the U.S. Prison Population," Educational Testing Service (2006).

80. Ibid.

81. M. Fine, et. al., 2001, op. cit.

82. John Linton, "U.S. Department of Education Update," *The Journal of Correctional Education*, Vol. 63, No. 2 (September 2012).

83. C. Nink, R. Olding, J. Jorgenson, and M. Gilbert, "Expanding Distance Learning Access in Prisons: A Growing Need," *Corrections Today*, Vol. 71, No. 4 (2009).

84. Brazzell, Crayton, Lindahl, Mukamal, and Solomon, "From the Classroom to the Community: Exploring the Role of Education During Incarceration and Re-entry," The Urban Institute, Justice Policy Center, John Jay College of Criminal Justice (2009).

85. Jon Marc Taylor, "Pell Grants for Prisoners: Why Should We Care?" *Journal of Prisoners on Prisons*, Vol. 17, No. 1 (2008) and S. Soferr 2006, op. cit.

86. "Education as Crime Prevention," 1997, op. cit.

87. E.R. Meiners 2009, op. cit.

88. M. Johnson, et. al. 2011, op. cit.

89. M. Fine, et. al. 2001, op. cit.

90. R. Coley and P. Barton, 2006, op. cit.

91. T. Fabelo 2002, op. cit.

92. P. Case 2006, op. cit.

93. Benjamin Todd Jealous, Roslyn M. Brock, and Alice Huffman, "Misplaced Priorities: Over Incarcerate, Under Educate," a report of the National Association for the Advancement of Colored People, Baltimore, MD, 2011.

94. L. E. Gorgol and B. A. Sponsler 2011, op. cit.

95. M. Fine, et. al. 2001, op. cit.

96. C. Pauls 2011, op. cit.

97. P. Case 2006, op. cit.; T. Fabelo 2002, op. cit.; Steve Aos, Marna Miller, and Elizabeth Drake, "Evidence-Based Public Policy Options to Reduce Future Prison Construction, Criminal Justice Costs, and Crime Rates," Washington State Institute for Public Policy (2009); M. Martin 2009, op. cit.

98. V. Beiser 2011, op. cit.

99. M. Fine, et. al. 2001, op. cit.

100. Ibid.

101. Lauren Sieben, "Liberal-Arts Colleges Reach Minds Behind Bars," *Chronicle of Higher Education*, Vol. 57, No. 23 (2011).

102. S. Aos, et. al. 2009, op. cit.

103. *Seattle Times*, March 4, 2013, op. cit.

104. "State of Recidivism..." 2011, op. cit.

105. S.J. Meyer, et. al. 2010, op. cit.

106. Cindy Borden, P. Richardson, and Stephen Meyer, "Establishing Successful Postsecondary Academic Programs; A Practical Guide," *The Journal of Correctional Education*, Vol. 63, No. 2 (September 2012).

107. "Education as Crime Prevention" 1998, op. cit.; Contardo 2010, op. cit.

108. W. Erisman and J.B. Contardo 2005, op. cit.

109. M. Johnson, et. al. 2011, op. cit.; "Three Year Outcome Study of the Relationship between Participation in Windham School System Programs and Reduced Levels of Recidivism," Windham School District, Texas Department of Criminal Justice TR 94–001 (1994).

110. Jack Beck, "Education from the Inside, Out: The Multiple Benefits of College Programs in Prisons," transcript of testimony at The Correctional Association of New York's Hearing of the Assembly's Corrections Committee, 2012.

111. "Justice Beat: Education from the Inside, Out," report of the Correctional Association of New York, *The Fortune News*, Vol. 43, No. 2 (June 2010).

112. G. Gaes 2008, op. cit.

113. Gregory A. Knott 2012, op. cit.

114. S. Heiser 2007, op. cit.

115. K. Mentor and M. Bosworth 2011, op. cit.

116. D. Skorton and G. Altschuler, "College Behind Bars: How Educating Prisoners Pays Off," *Forbes* (March 25, 2013).

117. G. Granoff 2005, op. cit.

118. G. Gaes 2008, op. cit.

119. Ibid.; and J. Taylor 2008, op. cit.

120. "Education as Crime Prevention" 1998, op. cit.

121. K. Mentor and M. Bosworth 2011, op. cit.

122. "Education as Crime Prevention" 1998, op. cit.

123. Jenifer Warren, "One in 100: Behind Bars in America," The Pew Charitable Trust Center (2008).

124. W. Erisman and J.B. Contardo 2005, op. cit.

125. "Education as Crime Prevention" 1997, op. cit. and P.W. Greenwood, K.E. Model, C.P. Rydell, and J. Chiesa, "Diverting Children from a Life of Crime: Measuring Costs and Benefits," Rand Corporation (1998).

126. V. Beiser 2011, *op. cit.*

127. Audrey Bazos and J. Hausman, "Correctional Education as a Crime Control Program," *UCLA School of Public Policy and Social Research* (2004).

128. J. Ridgeway and J. Casella 2012, op. cit.

129. R. Coley and P. Barton 2006, op. cit.

130. J. Piché, "Barriers to Knowing Inside: Education in Prisons and Education on Prisons," *Journal of Prisoners on Prisons*, Vol. 17, No. 1 (2008).

131. B. Jealous, et. al. 2011, op. cit.

132. E.R. Meiners 2009, op. cit.

133. B. Jealous, et. al. 2011, op. cit.
134. Ibid.
135. K. Mentor and M. Bosworth 2011, op. cit.
136. B. Jealous, et. al. 2011, op. cit.
137. "Partnerships Between Community Colleges and Prisons..." 2009, op. cit.
138. Ibid.
139. Ibid.
140. Editor, "Prison Break," *The New Republic* (October 2002).
141. Jeffrey Ian Ross and Stephen C. Richards, *Beyond Bars* (New York: Alpha/Penguin, 2009).
142. "Education as Crime Prevention" 1998, op. cit.
143. S.J. Meyer, et. al. 2010, op. cit.
144. J. Linton 2013, op. cit.
145. Jon Marc Taylor, "The Education of Ivan Denisovich," *The Journal of Correctional Education*, Vol. 48, No. 2 (June 1997).
146. L. Winterfield, et. al. 2009, op. cit.
147. Karen Lahm, "Educational Participation and Inmate Misconduct," *Journal of Offender Rehabilitation*, Vol. 48 (2009).
148. Ibid.
149. Robert A. Hall, "Technology Education & the Felon (Teaching High School Behind Prison Walls)," New Hampshire State Prison Adult Vocational Training Center (1990).
150. D. Skorton and G. Altschuler 2013, op. cit.
151. G. Spangenberg, "Current Issues in Correctional Education. A Compilation and Discussion," paper presented to the Council for Advancement of Adult Literacy, 2004.
152. J. Esperian 2010, op. cit.
153. R. Allen 2006, op. cit.
154. S. Heiser 2007, op. cit.
155. G. Banks 2003, op. cit.
156. Miles D. Harer, "Prison Education Program Participation and Recidivism: A Test of the Normalization Hypothesis," Federal Bureau of Prisons, Office of Research and Evaluation (1995).
157. Ibid.
158. Ibid.
159. Gregory A. Knott 2012, op. cit.
160. G. Granoff 2005, op. cit.
161. Brazzell, et. al. 2009, op. cit.
162. "Education as Crime Prevention" 1997, op. cit.
163. "Justice Beat: Education from the Inside, Out," 2010, op. cit.
164. Ibid.
165. Brazzell, et. al. 2009, op. cit.

166. S. Heiser 2007, op. cit.
167. J. Gerber and E. Fritsch, 1993, op. cit.
168. W. Erisman and J.B. Contardo 2005, op. cit.
169. Jeremy Travis. "Rethinking Prison Education in the Era of Mass Incarceration," delivered at the Conference on Higher Education in the Prisons, John Jay College of Criminal Justice, City University of New York, February 2011.
170. Bruce R. McPherson and Michael Santos, "Transcending the Wall," *Journal of Criminal Justice Education*, Vol. 6, No. 1 (Spring 1995).
171. C.A. Winters, "Inmate Opinions Toward Education and Participation in Prison Education Programmes," *Police Journal*, Vol. 68, No. 1 (January-March 1995).
172. W. Erisman and J.B. Contardo 2005, op. cit.
173. L. Winterfield, et. al. 2009, op. cit.
174. Ibid.
175. Luis Urrieta, Karla Martin and Courtney Robinson, "'I Am in School!' African American Male Youth in a Prison/College Hybrid Figured world," *Urban Review*, Vol. 43, No. 4 (2011).
176. Ibid.
177. Ibid.
178. Ibid.
179. S.J. Meyer, et. al. 2010, op. cit.
180. C. Pauls 2011, op. cit.
181. J.C. Moore, "Camarillo College Students Help Educate Youth Offenders," *Ventura County Star*, April 10, 2013.
182. C. Pauls 2011, op. cit.
183. Daniel W. Lawrence, "Inmate Students: Where Do They Fit In?" Oklahoma Department of Corrections (1994).
184. C. Pauls 2011, op. cit.
185. M. Fine, et. al. 2001, op. cit.
186. C. Pauls 2011, op. cit.
187. "Justice Beat: Education from the Inside, Out," 2010, op. cit.
188. S. Ward 2009, op. cit.
189. W. Erisman and J.B. Contardo 2005, op. cit.
190. S. Heiser 2007, op. cit.
191. J. Piché 2008, op. cit.
192. S. Nagelsen, "Writing as a Tool for Constructive Rehabilitation," *Journal of Prisoners on Prisons*, Vol. 17, No. 1 (2008).
193. J. Taylor 1997, op. cit.
194. D. Skorton and G. Altschuler 2013, op. cit.
195. S.J. Meyer, et. al. 2010, op. cit.
196. Jon Marc Taylor, "Piecing Together a

College Education Behind Bars," *Prison Mirror*, Vol. 115, No. 10–13 (May-August 2002).

197. H. McCarty 2006, op. cit.

198. J. Gerber and E. Fritsch 1993, op. cit.

199. V. Beiser 2011, op. cit.

200. J. Esperian 2010, op. cit.

201. G. Knott 2012, op. cit.

202. G. Banks 2003, op. cit.

Chapter 2

1. Susanna Spaulding, "Borderland Stories about Teaching College in Prison," *New Directions for Community Colleges*, Vol. 155 (2011).

2. Richard J. Coley and Paul E. Barton, "Locked Up and Locked Out: An Educational Perspective on the U.S. Prison Population," Educational Testing Service (2006).

3. S. Spaulding 2011, op. cit.

4. Ibid.; Shakoor A. Ward, "Career and Technical Education in United States Prisons: What Have We Learned?" *The Journal of Correctional Education*, Vol. 60, No. 3 (2009).

5. Ibid.

6. S. Spaulding 2011, op. cit.

7. Kenneth Adams, et. al., "Large-Scale Multidimensional Test of the Effect of Prison Education Programs on Offenders' Behavior," *The Prison Journal*, Vol. 74 (December 1994).

8. S. Spaulding 2011, op. cit.

9. Liliana Segura, "Attica at 40," *The Nation* (September 2011).

10. Ibid.

11. K. Adams, et. al 1994, op. cit.

12. L. Segura 2011, op. cit.

13. G. Banks, "Learning Under Lockdown," *ColorLines* (March 15, 2003).

14. M. Martin, "What Happened to Prison Education Programs?" *Prison Legal News* (June 2009).

15. K. Adams, et. al 1994, op. cit. and L. Segura 2011, op. cit.

16. G. Banks 2003, op. cit.

17. Ibid.

18. Jon Marc Taylor, "Pell Grants for Prisoners," *The Nation* (January 1993).

19. K. Mentor, M. Bosworth, eds., "College Courses in Prison," draft submission to the *Encyclopedia of Corrections*, July 2011.

20. Gregory A. Knott, "Cost and Punishment: Reassessing Incarceration Costs and the Value of College-in-Prison Programs," *Northern Illinois University Law Review*, Vol. 32 (2012).

21. Ibid.

22. R. Coley and P. Barton 2006, op. cit.

23. Gabriel Torres-Rivera, "Keeping it Real: A Perspective on the Formerly Incarcerated in New York," Community Service Society of New York, Reentry Roundtable (March 2011).

24. S. Spaulding 2011, op. cit.

25. M. Talbot, "Catch and Release," *Atlantic Monthly*, Vol. 29, No. 1 (2003).

26. John Britton, "Government Reduces In-Prison Education Even Though It Helps Lower Recidivism," *Neiman Watchdog*, Neiman Foundation, 2004).

27. M. Fleischer, "U.S. Prisons Don't Fund Education, and Everybody Pays a Price," Take part.com (*March 1, 2013*), accessed March 1, 2013, http://www.takepart.com/article/2013/03/01/americas-inmates-education-denied-everybody-pays-price.

28. Jon Marc Taylor and Suzan Schwartz-kopf, *Prisoners' Guerrilla Handbook to Correspondence Programs in the United States and Canada*, 3rd ed. (West Brattleboro, VT: Prison Legal News, 2009).

29. Editor, "Prison Break," *The New Republic* (October 2002).

30. W. Erisman and J.B. Contardo, "Learning To Reduce Recidivism: A 50-State Analysis of Postsecondary Correctional Education Policy," The Institute for Higher Education Policy (IHEP) (2005).

31. Jon Marc Taylor, "Pell Grants for Prisoners: Why Should We Care?" *Journal of Prisoners on Prisons*, Vol. 17, No. 1 (2008).

32. K. Mentor and M. Bosworth 2011, op. cit.

33. G. Spangenberg, "Current Issues in Correctional Education. A Compilation and Discussion," paper presented to the Council for Advancement of Adult Literacy, 2004.

34. "Education as Crime Prevention," commentary on the 1997 report produced by the Center on Crime, Communities & Culture, Occasional Paper Series No. 2, *Spectrum: The Journal of State Government*, Vol. 71 (Winter 1998).

35. G. Knott 2012, op. cit.

36. Paul Downes and Catherine Maunsell, "Lifelong Learning for All? Policies and Practices towards Underrepresented and Socially Excluded Groups," presented as Session VII of the Final International Conference of the Educational Disadvantage Centre, St. Patrick's College, Dublin, Ireland, 2010.

37. G. Banks 2003, op. cit.

38. Bruce R. McPherson and Michael Santos, "Transcending the Wall," *Journal of Criminal Justice Education*, Vol. 6, No. 1 (Spring 1995).

39. Jean Trounstine, "The Battle to Bring Back Pell Grants for Prisoners," *Boston Daily Magazine*, accessed March 4, 2013, http://www.bostonmagazine.com/news/blog/2013/03/04/the-battle-to-bring-back-pell-grants-for-prisoners/.

40. Ibid.

41. T. Sims, "Support for Inmate Education," *Correctional News* (April 17, 2013); Ibid.

42. J. Trounstine 2013, op. cit.

43. J. Taylor 2008, op. cit.

44. J. Piché, "Barriers to Knowing Inside: Education in Prisons and Education on Prisons," *Journal of Prisoners on Prisons*, Vol. 17, No. 1 (2008).

45. Michelle Fine, M.E. Torre, I. Bowen, K. Boudin, D. Hylton, J. Clark, M. Martinez, R.A. Roberts, P. Smart, and D. Upegui, with the New York State Department of Correctional Services, "Changing Minds: The Impact of College in a Maximum-Security Prison: Effects on Women in Prison, the Prison Environment, Reincarceration Rates and Post-Release Outcomes," City University of New York (2001).

Chapter 3

1. John Linton, "United States Department of Education Update," *The Journal of Correctional Education*, Vol. 64, No. 2 (May 2013).

2. Ibid.

3. Emily Deruy, "What It Costs When We Don't Educate Inmates for Life After Prison," ABC News, accessed March 14, 2012, http://fusion.net/justice/story/us-fails-educate-inmates-life-prison-11751/.

4. Brazzell, Crayton, Lindahl, Mukamal, and Solomon, "From the Classroom to the Community: Exploring the Role of Education During Incarceration and Re-entry," The Urban Institute, Justice Policy Center, John Jay College of Criminal Justice (2009); Jeremy Travis, "Rethinking Prison Education in the Era of Mass Incarceration," delivered at the Conference on Higher Education in the Prisons, John Jay College of Criminal Justice, City University of New York, February 2011.

5. D.N. Williams, "Correctional Education and the Community College," *ERIC Digest*, Article No. ED321835 (1989).

6. Stephen J. Steurer, Linda Smith, and Alice Tracy, "OCE/CEA Three State Recidivism Study," United States Department of Education, Office of Correctional Education (September 2001).

7. Gabriel Torres-Rivera, "Keeping it Real: A Perspective on the Formerly Incarcerated in New York," Community Service Society of New York, Reentry Roundtable (March 2011).

8. M. Brodheim, "California Prison System Lays Off Teachers, Vocational Instructors," *Prison Legal News*, Vol. 22, No. 3 (March 2011).

9. G. Spangenberg, "Current Issues in Correctional Education. A Compilation and Discussion," paper presented to the Council for Advancement of Adult Literacy, 2004.

10. Ibid.

11. Ibid.

12. Bruce R. McPherson and Michael Santos, "Transcending the Wall," *Journal of Criminal Justice Education*, Vol. 6, No. 1 (Spring 1995).

13. Brazzell, et. al. 2009, op. cit. and Gregory A. Knott, "Cost and Punishment: Reassessing Incarceration Costs and the Value of College-in-Prison Programs," *Northern Illinois University Law Review*, Vol. 32 (2012).

14. J. Travis 2011, op. cit.

15. W. Erisman and J.B. Contardo, "Learning To Reduce Recidivism: A 50-State Analysis of Postsecondary Correctional Education Policy," The Institute for Higher Education Policy (IHEP) (2005).

16. Trip Jennings, "Quarter of State Prison Education Jobs are Vacant," *The New Mexico Independent* (September 2009).

17. Jeanne B. Contardo, *Providing College to Prison Inmates* (El Paso, TX: LFB Scholarly Publishing, 2010).

18. Ibid.

19. W. Erisman and J.B. Contardo 2005, op. cit.

20. J. Contardo 2010, op. cit.

21. "Few Prisoners Enrolling in Available College Classes," report from the Institute for Higher Education Policy (IHEP), 2005.

22. W. Erisman and J.B. Contardo 2005, op. cit.

23. Sara Goldrick-Rab, "The Prison-Education Connection," *The Chronicle of Higher Education* (November 2, 2009).

24. Johanna E. Foster, "Bringing College Back to Prison: The State of Higher Education Programs for Incarcerated Women in the U.S.," paper presented to the 8th International Women's Policy Research Conference, June 2005.

25. "Few Prisoners Enrolling in Available College Classes," 2005, op. cit.

26. W. Erisman and J.B. Contardo 2005, op. cit.

27. Ibid.

28. Ibid.

29. Ibid.

30. Ibid.

31. B. Bickerton and J. Brown, "State of the State—Behind Bars: ABE for the Incarcerated," *Field Notes*, System for Adult Basic Education Support, Winter 2002.

32. K. Sherman, "Opening Doors, An ESOL Workbook by Prisoners for Prisoners," *Field Notes*, System for Adult Basic Education Support, Winter 2002.

33. B. Bickerton 2002, op. cit.

34. Stephen J. Meyer, "Factors Affecting Student Success in Post-secondary Academic Correctional Education Programs," *The Journal of Correctional Education*, Vol. 62, No. 2 (June 2011).

35. J. Linton 2013, op. cit.

36. Ibid.

37. Brazzell, et. al. 2009, op. cit.

38. Laura E. Gorgol and Brian A. Sponsler, "Unlocking Potential: Results of a National Survey of Post-secondary Education in State Prisons," Institute for Higher Education Policy (May 2011).

39. Lawrence S. Mears, D.P. Dublin and G.J. Travis, "The Practice and Promise of Prison Programming," The Urban Institute, Justice Policy Center (2002).

40. L. Gorgol and B. Sponsler 2011, op. cit.

41. S.J. Meyer, L. Fredericks, C.M. Borden, and P.L. Richardson, "Implementing Postsecondary Academic Programs in State Prisons: Challenges and Opportunities," *The Journal of Correctional Education*, Vol. 61, No. 2 (2010).

42. "Community-based Correctional Education," U.S. Department of Education, Office of Vocational and Adult Education, Division of Adult Education and Literacy (2011).

43. Mears, et. al. 2002, op. cit.

44. Vivian Astray-Caneda, Malika Busbee, and Markell Fanning, "Social Learning Theory and Prison Work Release Programs," proceedings from the Tenth Annual College of Education and Graduate Student Network Research Conference, Florida International University, College of Education, April 2011.

45. Gabriel Torres-Rivera, "Keeping it Real: A Perspective on the Formerly Incarcerated in New York," Community Service Society of New York, Reentry Roundtable (March 2011).

46. Jeffrey Ian Ross and Stephen C. Richards, *Behind Bars* (New York: Alpha/Penguin, 2002).

47. John Linton, "United States Department of Education Update," *The Journal of Correctional Education*, Vol. 61, No. 3 (2010).

48. S.J. Meyer, et. al. 2010, op. cit.

49. Ibid.

50. J. Linton 2010, op. cit.

51. S.J. Meyer, et. al. 2010, op. cit.

52. S. J. Meyer 2011, op. cit.

53. Peter Collins, "Education in Prison or the Applied Art of 'Correctional' Deconstructive Learning," *Journal of Prisoners on Prisons*, Vol. 17, No. 1 (2008).

54. P. Collins 2008, op. cit.

55. J. Linton 2013, op. cit.

56. S. Richards and R. Jones, "Beating the Perpetual Incarceration Machine: Overcoming Structural Impediments to Re-entry," *After Crime and Punishment: Pathways to Offender Reintegration* (Portland, OR: Willan Publishing, 2004).

57. Cindy Borden, P. Richardson, and Stephen Meyer, "Establishing Successful Postsecondary Academic Programs; A Practical Guide," *The Journal of Correctional Education*, Vol. 63, No. 2 (September 2012).

58. Ikponwosa O. Ekunwe, "Re-entering Society Begins Prior to Release," *Global Perspectives on Re-Entry: Exploring the Challenges Facing Ex-Prisoners* (Tampere, Finland: Tampere University Press, 2011).

59. Ibid.

60. Ibid.

61. P. Collins 2008, op. cit.

62. P. Case, "Predicting Risk Time and Probability: An Assessment of Prison Education and Recidivism," presented at the Conference of the American Sociological Association, Montreal, Quebec, 2006.

63. M. Talbot, "Catch and Release," *Atlantic Monthly*, Vol. 29, No. 1 (2003).

64. V. Beiser, "The Jail as Classroom. Why Los Angeles County's Top Cop Wants to Offer an Education to Tens of Thousands of Prisoners," *Miller-McCune*, Vol. 4, No. 3 (2011).

65. S. Bahn, "Community Safety and Recidivism in Australia: Breaking the Cycle of Reoffending to Produce Safer Communities Through Vocational Training," *International Journal of Training Research*, Vol. 9, No. 3 (2011).

66. M. Talbot 2003, op. cit.

67. P. Case 2006, op. cit.

68. Katti Gray, "Parlaying the Prison Experience," *Diverse Issues in Higher Education*, Vol. 27, No. 1 (2010).

69. Brazzell, et. al. 2009, op. cit.

70. G. Torres-Rivera 2011, op. cit.

71. Brazzell, et. al. 2009, op. cit.

72. T. Fabelo, "The Impact of Prison Education on Community Reintegration of In-

mates: The Texas Case," *The Journal of Correctional Education*, Vol. 53, No. 3 (2002).

73. G. Spangenberg 2004, op. cit.

74. "Education as Crime Prevention," commentary on the 1997 report produced by the Center on Crime, Communities & Culture, Occasional Paper Series No. 2, *Spectrum: The Journal of State Government* Vol. 71 (Winter 1998).

75. Brazzell, et. al. 2009, op. cit.

76. Ikponwosa O. Ekunwe, "Re-entering Society Begins Prior to Release," *Global Perspectives on Re-Entry: Exploring the Challenges Facing Ex-Prisoners* (Tampere, Finland: Tampere University Press, 2011).

77. C. Nink, R. Olding, J. Jorgenson, and M. Gilbert, "Expanding Distance Learning Access in Prisons: A Growing Need," *Corrections Today*, Vol. 71, No. 4 (2009).

78. Brazzell, et. al. 2009, op. cit.

79. P. Collins 2008, op. cit.

80. S. Richards, J. Austin, and R. Jones, "Thinking about Prison Release and Budget Crisis in the Blue Grass State," *Critical Criminology* 12 (2004).

81. Richard J. Coley and Paul E. Barton, "Locked Up and Locked Out: An Educational Perspective on the U.S. Prison Population," Educational Testing Service (2006).

82. M. Talbot 2003, op. cit.

83. Stephen C. Richards, Jeffrey Ross, Greg Newbold, Michael Lenza, Richard Jones, Daniel Murphy, and Robert Grigsby, "Convict Criminology, Prisoner Reentry and Public Policy Recommendations," *Journal of Prisoners on Prisons*, Vol. 21, No. 1 & 2 (2012).

84. Scott C.S. Hayward, "The Fiscal Crisis in Corrections: Rethinking Policies and Practices," Vera Institute for Justice (2009).

85. Ibid.

86. Ibid.

87. Ibid.

Chapter 4

1. Laura Winterfield, Mark Coggeshall, Michelle Burke-Storer, Vanessa Correa, and Simon Tidd, "The Effects of Post-secondary Correctional Education: Final Report," Urban Institute Justice Policy Center (2009); S.J. Meyer, L. Fredericks, C.M. Borden, and P.L. Richardson, "Implementing Postsecondary Academic Programs in State Prisons: Challenges and Opportunities," *The Journal of Correctional Education* Vol. 61, No. 2 (2010).

2. S.J. Meyer, et. al. 2010, op. cit.

3. M. Fleischer, "U.S. Prisons Don't Fund Education, and Everybody Pays a Price," Takepart.com (March 1, 2013) *accessed March 1, 2013, http://news.yahoo.com/u-prisons-dont-fund-education-everybody-pays-220027623.html.*

4. S.J. Meyer, et. al. 2010, op. cit.

5. L. Winterfield, et. al. 2009, op. cit.

6. "Education Behind Bars: Opportunities and Obstacles," Ohio State Legislative Office of Educational Oversight (1994).

7. S.J. Meyer, et. al. 2010, op. cit.

8. M. Martin, "What Happened to Prison Education Programs?" *Prison Legal News* (June 2009).

9. Laura E. Gorgol and Brian A. Sponsler, "Unlocking Potential: Results of a National Survey of Post-secondary Education in State Prisons," Institute for Higher Education Policy (May 2011).

10. Thomas Shull, "Taking the Classroom to the Cellblock," *American Jails* (March-April 2011).

11. Susanna Spaulding, "Borderland Stories about Teaching College in Prison," *New Directions for Community Colleges*, Vol. 155 (2011).

12. S.J. Meyer, et. al. 2010, op. cit.

13. "Partnerships Between Community Colleges and Prisons: Providing Workforce Education and Training to Reduce Recidivism," U.S. Department of Education, Office of Vocational and Adult Education, Office of Correctional Education (2009).

14. Brazzell, Crayton, Lindahl, Mukamal, and Solomon, "From the Classroom to the Community: Exploring the Role of Education During Incarceration and Re-entry," The Urban Institute, Justice Policy Center, John Jay College of Criminal Justice (2009).

15. Allison D. Anders and George W. Noblit, "Understanding Effective Higher Education Programs in Prisons: Considerations from the Incarcerated Individuals Program in North Carolina," *The Journal of Correctional Education*, Vol. 62, No. 2 (June 2011).

16. Ibid.

17. Ibid.

18. "Lift State Ban on Higher-Education Funding for Prison Inmates," Editorial, *Seattle Times*, March 4, 2013.

19. Ibid.

20. Richard J. Coley and Paul E. Barton, "Locked Up and Locked Out: An Educational Perspective on the U.S. Prison Population," Educational Testing Service (2006).

21. John Nally, S. Lockwood, K. Knutson, and T. Ho, "An Evaluation of the Effect of Cor-

rectional Education Programs on Post-Release Recidivism and Employment: An Empirical Study in Indiana," *The Journal of Correctional Education*, Vol. 63, No. 1 (April 2012).

22. L. Gorgol and B. Sponsler 2011, op. cit.

23. R. Coley and P. Barton 2006, op. cit.

24. S. Hayward 2009, op. cit.

25. Matt Clarke, "Texas Slashes Prison Education Budget," *Prison Legal News*, Vol. 23, No. 12 (December 2012).

26. M. Clarke, "Indiana Cuts Prison College Courses," *Prison Legal News* (March 2012).

27. Kristi Pihl, "Connell Prison College Degree Program May End," *Seattle Times*, May 23, 2011.

28. "Lift State Ban on Higher-Education Funding for Prison Inmates," Editorial, *Seattle Times*, March 4, 2013.

29. Lois Beckett, "Recession Watch: Getting Real about Prison Education Cuts," *SF Weekly*, February 19, 2010.

30. Paul Van Slambrouck, "Push to Expand Book-Learning Behind Bars," *Christian Science Monitor*, September 15, 2000.

31. M. Clarke 2012, op.cit.

32. S. Hayward 2009, op. cit.

33. Benjamin Todd Jealous, Roslyn M. Brock, and Alice Huffman, "Misplaced Priorities: Over Incarcerate, Under Educate," a report of the National Association for the Advancement of Colored People, Baltimore, MD, 2011.

34. P. Van Slambrouck 2000, op. cit.

35. Ibid.

36. "Community-based Correctional Education," U.S. Department of Education, Office of Vocational and Adult Education, Division of Adult Education and Literacy (2011).

37. Ibid.

38. Ibid.

39. Ibid.

40. Ibid.

41. Ibid.

42. Ibid.

43. Ibid.

44. Ibid.

45. Ibid.

46. Katti Gray, "Parlaying the Prison Experience," *Diverse Issues in Higher Education*, Vol. 27, No. 1 (2010).

47. Brazzell, et. al. 2009, op. cit.

48. M. Clarke 2012, op. cit.

49. K. Gray 2010, op. cit.

50. S.J. Meyer, et. al. 2010, op. cit.

51. S. Soferr, "Prison Education: Is it Worth It?" *Corrections Today* (October 2006).

52. W. Erisman and J.B. Contardo, "Learning To Reduce Recidivism: A 50-State Analysis of Postsecondary Correctional Education Policy," The Institute for Higher Education Policy (IHEP) (2005).

53. Ibid.

54. S.J. Meyer, et. al. 2010, op. cit.

55. Brazzell, et. al. 2009, op. cit.

56. H. J. McCarty, "Educating Felons: Reflections on Higher Education in Prison," *Radical History Review*, Vol. 96 (2006).

57. W. Erisman and J.B. Contardo 2005, op. cit.

58. G. Banks, "Learning Under Lockdown," *ColorLines* (March 15, 2003).

59. "Partnerships Between Community Colleges and Prisons..." 2009, op. cit.

60. H. McCarty 2006, op. cit.

61. S.J. Meyer, et. al. 2010, op. cit.

62. Johanna E. Foster, "Bringing College Back to Prison: The State of Higher Education Programs for Incarcerated Women in the U.S.," paper presented at the 8th International Women's Policy Research Conference, June 2005.

63. Ibid.

64. W. Erisman and J.B. Contardo 2005, op. cit.

65. Jeanne Contardo and Michelle Tolbert, "Prison Postsecondary Education: Bridging Learning from Incarceration to the Community," monograph presented at the Reentry Roundtable on Education, convened by The Prisoner Reentry Institute at John Jay College of Criminal Justice in cooperation with The Urban Institute, Spring 2008.

66. Ibid.

67. W. Erisman and J.B. Contardo 2005, op. cit.

68. Ibid.

69. H. McCarty 2006, op. cit.

70. S. Spaulding 2011, op. cit.

71. W. Erisman and J.B. Contardo 2005, op. cit.

Chapter 5

1. Brazzell, et. al. 2009, op. cit.

2. J. Blount, *Getting Ahead: An Ex-Con's Guide to Getting Ahead in Today's Society* (pamphlet published by the SJM Family Foundation, Inc. 2008).

3. Stephen C. Richards and Michael Lenza, "The First Dime and Nickel of Convict Criminology," *Journal of Prisoners on Prisons*, Vol. 21, No. 1 & 2 (2012).

4. Ibid.
5. J. Blount 2008, op. cit.
6. Jeffrey Ian Ross and Stephen C. Richards, *Convict Criminology: Contemporary Issues in Crime and Justice Series*, 1st ed. (Independence, KY: Cengage Learning, 2002).
7. Ibid.
8. Stephen C. Richards, Jeffrey Ross, Greg Newbold, Michael Lenza, Richard Jones, Daniel Murphy, and Robert Grigsby, "Convict Criminology, Prisoner Reentry and Public Policy Recommendations," *Journal of Prisoners on Prisons*, Vol. 21, No. 1 and 2 (2012).
9. J. Ross and S. Richards 2002, op. cit.
10. Jeffrey Ian Ross and Stephen C. Richards, *Beyond Bars* (New York: Alpha/Penguin, 2009).
11. Ibid.
12. G. Newbold and J.I. Ross, "Convict Criminology at the Crossroads: Research Note," *The Prison Journal*, Vol. 93, No. 1 (March 2010).
13. Ibid.
14. C. Durano, "Prison Program Helps Inmates Improve Lives, Stay Out of Jail," DailySkiff.com, Texas Christian University, Schieffer School of Journalism, accessed March 13, 2012, http://www.tcu360.com/dailyskiffcomarchive/2008/03/2947.prison-program-helps-inmates-improve-lives-stay-out-jail.
15. Ibid.
16. Ikponwosa O. Ekunwe, "Re-entering Society Begins Prior to Release," *Global Perspectives on Re-Entry: Exploring the Challenges Facing Ex-Prisoners* (Tampere, Finland: Tampere University Press, 2011).
17. Cindy Borden, P. Richardson, and Stephen Meyer, "Establishing Successful Postsecondary Academic Programs: A Practical Guide," *The Journal of Correctional Education*, Vol. 63, No. 2 (September 2012).
18. John Nally, S. Lockwood, and T. Ho, "Employment of Ex-Offenders During the Recession," *The Journal of Correctional Education*, Vol. 62, No. 2 (June 2011).
19. Ibid.
20. "Few Prisoners Enrolling in Available College Classes," report from the Institute for Higher Education Policy (IHEP), 2005.
21. W. Erisman and J.B. Contardo, "Learning To Reduce Recidivism: A 50-State Analysis of Postsecondary Correctional Education Policy," The Institute for Higher Education Policy (IHEP) (2005).
22. Ibid.
23. "Partnerships Between Community Colleges and Prisons: Providing Workforce Education and Training to Reduce Recidivism," U.S. Department of Education, Office of Vocational and Adult Education, Office of Correctional Education (2009).
24. Marcia Johnson, Katherine Bauer, and Elizabeth Tagle, "Proposal to Reduce Recidivism Rates in Texas," *ECI Interdisciplinary Journal for Legal and Social Policy*, Vol. 1, No. 1 (2011).
25. "Partnerships Between Community Colleges and Prisons..." 2009, op. cit.
26. "Three Year Outcome Study of the Relationship between Participation in Windham School System Programs and Reduced Levels of Recidivism," Windham School District, Texas Department of Criminal Justice TR 94-001 (1994).
27. Jeanne Contardo and Michelle Tolbert, "Prison Postsecondary Education: Bridging Learning from Incarceration to the Community," monograph presented at the Reentry Roundtable on Education, convened by The Prisoner Reentry Institute at John Jay College of Criminal Justice in cooperation with The Urban Institute, Spring 2008.
28. M. Dawkins and E. McAuliff, "Higher Education Behind Bars: Postsecondary Prison Education Programs Make a Difference," *American Council on Education Centerpoint* (October 2008); J. Contardo and M. Tolbert 2008, op. cit.
29. Jeanne B. Contardo, *Providing College to Prison Inmates* (El Paso, TX: LFB Scholarly Publishing LLC, 2010).
30. Ibid.
31. Ibid.
32. Ibid.
33. Ibid.
34. Ibid.
35. "Partnerships Between Community Colleges and Prisons..." 2009, op. cit.
36. J. Contardo 2010, op. cit.
37. J. Contardo and M. Tolbert 2008, op. cit.
38. M. Dawkins and E. McAuliff 2008, op. cit.
39. J. Contardo and M. Tolbert 2008, op. cit.
40. J. Contardo 2010, op. cit.
41. J. Contardo and M. Tolbert 2008, op. cit.
42. J. Contardo 2010, op. cit.
43. Ibid.
44. Ibid.
45. Eric Schulzke, "From Prison to College: Major Foundations Fund Five-year Study Bridging Divide," *Desert News*, May 13, 2013.

46. Ibid.

47. Ibid.

48. Ibid.

49. "Michigan Works to get Some Inmates Higher Education," *The Morning Sun*, May 20, 2013.

50. Ibid.

51. Karen Lungu, "Colorado Prison's 'Education Row' A Boon for Inmates," *The Durango Herald*, April 26, 2010.

52. C. Pallone, "Speaker Gives Hope to Oregon Inmates," *Statesman Journal* (March 25, 2013).

53. Scott Harris Conlon, Jeffrey Nagel, Mike Hillman, and Rick Hanson, "Education: Don't Leave Prison Without It," *Corrections Today* (February 2008).

54. Ibid.

55. Ibid.

56. Ibid.

57. Ibid.

58. C. Pallone 2013, op. cit.

59. J. Nally 2012, op. cit.

60. John Linton, "United States Department of Education Update," *The Journal of Correctional Education*, Vol. 64, No. 2 (May 2013).

61. I. Urbina, "Prison Labor Fuels American War Machine," *Prison Legal News* (January 2004).

62. Gregory A. Knott, "Cost and Punishment: Reassessing Incarceration Costs and the Value of College-in-Prison Programs," *Northern Illinois University Law Review*, Vol. 32 (2012).

63. Daniel Schorn, "Maximum Security Education: How Some Inmates are Getting a Top-Notch Education Behind Bars," Transcript, *CBS News—60 Minutes* (April 15, 2007).

64. G. Banks, "Learning Under Lockdown," *ColorLines* (March 15, 2003).

65. Stephen J. Meyer, "Factors Affecting Student Success in Post-secondary Academic Correctional Education Programs," *The Journal of Correctional Education*, Vol. 62, No. 2 (June 2011).

66. C. Borden, et. al. 2012, op. cit.

67. G. Banks 2003, op. cit.

68. "Partnerships Between Community Colleges and Prisons..." 2009, op. cit.

69. J. Contardo and M. Tolbert 2008, op. cit.

70. "Partnerships Between Community Colleges and Prisons..." 2009, op. cit.; J. Contardo and M. Tolbert 2008, op. cit.

71. "Partnerships Between Community Colleges and Prisons..." 2009, op. cit.

72. J. Contardo and M. Tolbert 2008, op. cit.

73. Lauren Sieben, "Liberal-Arts Colleges Reach Minds Behind Bars," *Chronicle of Higher Education*, Vol. 57, No. 23 (2011).

74. Ellen Condliffe Lagemann, "What Can College Mean? Lessons from the Bard Prison Initiative," *Change: The Magazine of Higher Learning*, Vol. 43, No. 6 (2011).

75. L. Sieben 2011, op. cit.

76. G. Knott 2012, op. cit.

77. L. Sieben 2011, op. cit.

78. E. Lagemann 2011, op. cit.

79. Ibid.

80. Ibid.

81. G. Knott 2012, op. cit.

82. L. Sieben 2011, op. cit.

83. E. Lagemann 2011, op. cit.

84. Ibid.

85. Ibid.

86. Ibid.

87. Ibid.

88. L. Sieben 2011, op. cit.

89. Paul Downes and Catherine Maunsell, "Lifelong Learning for All? Policies and Practices towards Underrepresented and Socially Excluded Groups," presented as Session VII of the Final International Conference of the Educational Disadvantage Centre, St. Patrick's College, Dublin, Ireland, 2010.

90. C. Borden, et. al. 2012, op. cit.

91. M.B. Marklein, "Students Behind Bars Mix With Those from Outside," *USA Today*, April 27, 2013.

92. Ibid.

93. Sherry E.M. Heiser, "Student Perceptions of a College Distance Learning Program at a Maximum Security Prison," Thesis, Humboldt State University, 2007.

94. Daniel Aloi, "Prison Education Program Expands Its Offerings," *Cornell University Chronicle Online*, accessed March 13, 2012, http://www.news.cornell.edu/stories/2009/03/prison-education-program-expands-its-online-offerings/.

95. D. Skorton and G. Altschuler, "College Behind Bars: How Educating Prisoners Pays Off," *Forbes* (March 25, 2013).

96. D. Aloi 2009, op. cit.

97. J. Linton 2013, op. cit.

98. D. Skorton and G. Altschuler 2013, op. cit.

99. D. Aloi 2009, op. cit.

100. L. Hertz, "Teaching and Learning in Prison," Vassar Alumni iHub, accessed March 14, 2012, http://www.hudsonlink.org/news_events/teaching-and-learning-prison/.

101. C. Borden, et. al. 2012, op. cit.

102. Ibid.

103. G. Knott 2012, op. cit.

104. E. Payne, "BU's Prison Education Program Thrives Despite Pell Grant Ban," *The Quad* (March 22, 2013).

105. M. Dawkins and E. McAuliff 2008, op. cit.

106. H. J. McCarty, "Educating Felons: Reflections on Higher Education in Prison," *Radical History Review*, Vol. 96 (2006).

107. "Inmates Receive College Education from San Quentin," *Jet*, Vol. 102, Issue 17 (October 14, 2002).

108. J. Linton 2013, op. cit.

109. H. McCarty 2006, op. cit.

110. J. Linton 2013, op. cit.

111. Kate Rix, "San Quentin's Campus: A Unique Program Enables Prisoners to Study with Cal Professors and Earn College Credits," *The Monthly: East Bay Life*, September 2008; J. Linton 2013, op. cit.

112. H. McCarty 2006, op. cit.

113. K. Rix 2008, op. cit.

114. J.C. Moore, "Camarillo College Students Help Educate Youth Offenders," *Ventura County Star*, April 10, 2013.

115. N. Ruhling, "STEP in the Right Direction," *Impact: Rutgers University Foundation Magazine* (2013).

116. Deborah E. Ward and Heather Tubman, "How Does Prison to Community (P2C) Affect Recidivism: A Summary of Quantitative Findings," Rutgers University Economic Development Research Group, School of Management and Labor Relations (2009).

117. G. Knott 2012, op. cit.

118. Ibid.

119. Ibid.

120. "New and Noteworthy Prison Programs," report of the Correctional Association of New York, *The Fortune News*, Vol. 43, No. 2 (June 2010).

121. S. Hopwood, "Give Former Prisoners a Second Chance," *Seattle Times*, January 10, 2013.

122. J. Large, "Post-Prison Education Program Helps Some get Another Chance," *Seattle Times*, July 16, 2009.

123. Jessica Spohn, "New England ABE-to-College Transition Project," *Field Notes*, System for Adult Basic Education Support (SABES) (2002).

124. Garry Boulard, "Locked Out," *Diverse Issues in Higher Education*, Vol. 27, No. 1 (2010).

125. K. Davis, "Auburn Professors Bring Educational Opportunities to Prisoners," *The Plainsman*, March 21, 2013.

126. C. Nink, R. Olding, J. Jorgenson and M. Gilbert, "Expanding Distance Learning Access in Prisons: A Growing Need," *Corrections Today*, Vol. 71, No. 4 (2009).

127. "Partnerships Between Community Colleges and Prisons..." 2009, op. cit.

128. J. Linton 2013, op. cit.

129. Ibid.

130. Ibid.

131. Lisa Ouimet Burke and James E. Vivian, "The Effect of College Programming on Recidivism Rates at the Hampden County House of Correction: A 5-Year Study," *The Journal of Correctional Education*, Vol. 52, No. 4 (December 2001).

132. W.R. Toller and D.E. O'Malley, "Education Reintegration at Hampden County," *Field Notes*, System for Adult Basic Education Support, Winter 2002.

133. Ibid.

134. "Community-based Correctional Education," U.S. Department of Education, Office of Vocational and Adult Education, Division of Adult Education and Literacy (2011).

135. Ibid.

136. Ibid.

Chapter 6

1. Daniel Schorn, "Maximum Security Education: How Some Inmates are Getting a Top-Notch Education Behind Bars," Transcript, *CBS News—60 Minutes* (April 15, 2007); Susanna Spaulding, "Borderland Stories about Teaching College in Prison," *New Directions for Community Colleges*, Vol. 155 (2011).

2. W. Erisman and J.B. Contardo, "Learning To Reduce Recidivism: A 50-State Analysis of Postsecondary Correctional Education Policy," *The* Institute for Higher Education Policy (IHEP) (2005).

3. M.P. Bear and T. Nixon, *Bear's Guide to Earning Degrees by Distance Learning*, 14th ed. (New York: Ten Speed Press, 2000).

4. Ibid.

5. Jeffrey Ian Ross and Stephen C. Richards, *Beyond Bars* (New York: Alpha/Penguin, 2009).

6. Laura E. Gorgol and Brian A. Sponsler, "Unlocking Potential: Results of a National Survey of Post-secondary Education in State Prisons," Institute for Higher Education Policy (May 2011).

7. Jeanne Contardo and Michelle Tolbert, "Prison Postsecondary Education: Bridging Learning from Incarceration to the Community," monograph presented at the Reentry Roundtable on Education, convened by The Prisoner Reentry Institute at John Jay College of Criminal Justice in cooperation with The Urban Institute, Spring 2008.

8. "Partnerships Between Community Colleges and Prisons: Providing Workforce Education and Training to Reduce Recidivism," U.S. Department of Education, Office of Vocational and Adult Education, Office of Correctional Education (2009).

Chapter 7

1. N. Hall and M. Caldwell, "Prison Education—What No One Talks About," *Seattle Times*, January 23, 2013.

2. Daniel W. Lawrence, "Inmate Students: Where Do They Fit In?" Oklahoma Department of Corrections (1994).

3. Sherry E.M. Heiser, "Student Perceptions of a College Distance Learning Program at a Maximum Security Prison," Thesis, Humboldt State University, 2007.

4. D. Lawrence 1994, op. cit.

5. "Partnerships Between Community Colleges and Prisons: Providing Workforce Education and Training to Reduce Recidivism," U.S. Department of Education, Office of Vocational and Adult Education, Office of Correctional Education (2009).

6. Caroline Wolf Harlow, H. David Jenkins and Stephen Steurer, "GED Holders in Prison Read Better Than Those in the Household Population: Why?" *The Journal of Correctional Education*, Vol. 61, No. 1 (March 2010).

7. Ibid.

8. Ibid.

9. Ibid.

10. S. Nagelsen, "Writing as a Tool for Constructive Rehabilitation," *Journal of Prisoners on Prisons*, Vol. 17, No. 1 (2008).

11. C. Harlow, et. al. 2010, op. cit.

12. Jeffrey Ian Ross and Stephen C. Richards, *Beyond Bars* (New York: Alpha/Penguin, 2009).

13. Susan Sturm, Kate Skolnick, and Tina Wu, "Building Pathways of Possibility from Criminal Justice to College: College Initiative as a Catalyst Linking Individual and Systemic Change," Center for Institutional and Social Change, City University of New York (June 30, 2011).

14. Gregory A. Knott, "Cost and Punishment: Reassessing Incarceration Costs and the Value of College-in-Prison Programs," *Northern Illinois University Law Review*, Vol. 32 (2012).

15. J. Ross and S. Richards 2009, op. cit.

16. Ibid.

17. Marsha Weissman, Alan Rosenthal, Patricia Warth, Elaine Wolf, and Michael Messina-Yauchzy, "The Use of Criminal History Records In College Admissions Reconsidered," The Center for Community Alternatives (2010).

18. J. Ross and S. Richards 2009, op. cit.

19. G. Knott 2012, op. cit.

20. S. Sturm, et. al. 2011, op. cit.

21. Ibid.

22. Ibid.

23. Ibid.

24. Ibid.

25. Ibid.

26. H. J. McCarty, "Educating Felons: Reflections on Higher Education in Prison," *Radical History Review*, Vol. 96 (2006).

27. Christopher E. Pauls, "Student Perceptions of the Charter School Experience at Metro Detention Center," Master's Thesis, University of New Mexico, 2011.

28. H. McCarty 2006, op. cit.

29. C. Harlow, et. al. 2010, op. cit.

30. S. Sturm, et. al. 2011, op. cit.

31. Michelle Fine, M.E. Torre, I. Bowen, K. Boudin, D. Hylton, J. Clark, M. Martinez, R.A. Roberts, P. Smart, and D. Upegui, with the New York State Department of Correctional Services, "Changing Minds: The Impact of College in a Maximum-Security Prison: Effects on Women in Prison, the Prison Environment, Reincarceration Rates and Post-Release Outcomes," City University of New York (2001).

32. R.S. Hall and E. Killacky, "Correctional Education from the Perspective of the Prisoner Student," *The Journal of Correctional Education*, Vol. 59, No. 4 (December 2008).

33. C. Pauls 2011, op. cit.

34. Jeremy Travis. "Rethinking Prison Education in the Era of Mass Incarceration," delivered at the Conference on Higher Education in the Prisons, John Jay College of Criminal Justice, City University of New York, February 2011.

35. Kenneth Adams, et. al., "Large-Scale Multidimensional Test of the Effect of Prison Education Programs on Offenders' Behavior," *The Prison Journal*, Vol. 74 (December 1994).

36. S.J. Meyer, L. Fredericks, C.M. Borden

and P.L. Richardson, "Implementing Postsecondary Academic Programs in State Prisons: Challenges and Opportunities," *The Journal of Correctional Education* Vol. 61, No. 2 (2010).

37. C. Rose, "Women's Participation in Prison Education: What We Know and What We Don't Know," *The Journal of Correctional Education*, Vol. 55, No. 1 (March 2004).

38. "Federal Prisons: Inmate and Staff Views on Education and Work Training Programs," General Accounting Office, accessed March 14, 2012, http://www.gao.gov/assets/220/217438.pdf/.

39. Ibid.

40. C. Pauls 2011, op. cit.

41. M. Fine, et. al. 2001, op. cit.

42. D. Lawrence 1994, op. cit.

43. C. Pauls 2011, op. cit.

44. M. Fine, et. al. 2001, op. cit.

45. C. Pauls 2011, op. cit.

46. M. Fine, et. al. 2001, op. cit.

47. C. Pauls 2011, op. cit.

48. M. Fine, et. al. 2001, op. cit.

49. Sabina Kaplan, Eileen Leonard, and Mary Shanley, "Different Worlds Converge as College Students and Inmates Meet in a Prison Classroom," *Corrections Today* (August 2010).

50. C. Pauls 2011, op. cit.

51. Emma Thomas and Karyn Buck, "Peer Mentoring in a Young Offenders Institution," *Widening Participation and Lifelong Learning*, Vol. 12, No. 3, ISSN: 1466–6529 (University of Reading, UK, December 2010).

52. M. Fine, et. al. 2001, op. cit.

53. Ibid.

54. Ibid.

55. Ibid.

56. J. Piché, "Barriers to Knowing Inside: Education in Prisons and Education on Prisons," *Journal of Prisoners on Prisons*, Vol. 17, No. 1 (2008).

57. M. Fine, et. al. 2001, op. cit.

58. *Ibid.*

59. C.H. Lacey, "Art Education in Women's Prisons: Lessons from the Inside," paper presented at the Annual Meeting of the American Educational Research Association, Chicago, Illinois, April 2007.

60. M. Fine, et. al. 2001, op. cit.

61. "Inmates Receive College Education from San Quentin," *Jet,* Vol. 102, Issue 17 (October 14, 2002).

62. Gerald G. Gaes, "The Impact of Prison Education Programs on Post-Release Outcomes," monograph at the Reentry Roundtable on Education, convened by The Prisoner Reentry Institute at John Jay College of Criminal Justice in cooperation with The Urban Institute (Spring 2008).

63. Robert Allen, "An Economic Analysis of Prison Education Programs and Recidivism," Emory University, Department of Economics (2006).

64. J. Ross and S. Richards 2009, op. cit.

Chapter 8

1. Peter Collins, "Education in Prison or the Applied Art of 'Correctional' Deconstructive Learning," *Journal of Prisoners on Prisons*, Vol. 17, No. 1 (2008).

2. S. Ferranti, "Fighting Prison Censorship: An Interview with Paul Wright," *Journal of Prisoners on Prisons*, Vol. 17, No. 1 (2008).

3. P. Collins 2008, op. cit.

4. J. Piché, "Barriers to Knowing Inside: Education in Prisons and Education on Prisons," *Journal of Prisoners on Prisons*, Vol. 17, No. 1 (2008).

5. Jon Marc Taylor and Suzan Schwartzkopf, *Prisoners' Guerrilla Handbook to Correspondence Programs in the United States and Canada*, 3rd ed. (West Brattleboro, VT: Prison Legal News, 2009).

6. Ibid.

7. K. Mentor, M. Bosworth, eds., "College Courses in Prison," draft submission to the *Encyclopedia of Corrections,* July 2011.

8. W. Erisman and J.B. Contardo, "Learning To Reduce Recidivism: A 50-State Analysis of Postsecondary Correctional Education Policy," The Institute for Higher Education Policy (IHEP) (2005).

9. Gregory A. Knott, "Cost and Punishment: Reassessing Incarceration Costs and the Value of College-in-Prison Programs," *Northern Illinois University Law Review*, Vol. 32 (2012).

10. J. Piché 2008, op. cit.

11. G. Banks, "Learning Under Lockdown," *ColorLines* (March 15, 2003).

12. J. Piché 2008, op. cit.

13. G. Knott 2012, op. cit.

14. P. Collins 2008, op. cit.

15. Ibid.

16. Ibid.

17. Arnie King, "Reflections from Inside," *Field Notes*, System for Adult Basic Education Support, Winter 2002.

18. Ibid.

19. Ibid.

20. Ibid.

21. Ibid.

22. Ibid.

23. Scott B. Steffler, "Oregon's Anti-education 'Corrections' Policy: A Surprise?" *Journal of Prisoners on Prisons*, Vol. 17, No. 1 (2008).

24. Ibid.

Chapter 9

1. Kevin Warner, "Against the Narrowing of Perspectives: How Do We See Learning, Prisons and Prisoners?" *The Journal of Correctional Education*, Vol. 58, No. 2 (June 2007).

2. Ibid.

3. Ibid.

4. Ibid.

5. K. Warner, "Widening and Deepening the Education We Offer Those in Prison: Reflections from Irish and European Experience," *The Journal of Correctional Education*, Vol. 53, No. 1 (2002).

6. "Prison Education Research Project, Final Report," Huntsville, Texas: Sam Houston State University/Criminal Justice Center, Texas State Department of Criminal Justice, 1994.

7. K. Warner 2007, op. cit.

8. William Rentzmann, "Prison Philosophy and Prison Education," *The Journal of Correctional Education*, Vol. 47, No. 2 (June 1996).

9. Paul Downes and Catherine Maunsell, "Lifelong Learning for All? Policies and Practices towards Underrepresented and Socially Excluded Groups," presented as Session VII of the Final International Conference of the Educational Disadvantage Centre, St. Patrick's College, Dublin, Ireland, 2010.

10. W. Rentzmann 1996, op. cit.

11. Marc De Maeyer, "Are Prisons Good Education Practice?" *Convergence (International Council for Adult Education)*, Vol. 42, No. 2–4 (2009).

12. P. Downes and C. Maunsell 2010, op. cit.

13. "Partnerships Between Community Colleges and Prisons..." 2009, op. cit.

14. K. Warner 2007, op. cit.

15. Michelle D. Pettit and Michael Kroth, "Educational Services in Swedish Prisons: Successful Programs of Academic and Vocational Teaching," *Criminal Justice Studies*, Vol. 24, No. 3 (December 2011) DOI: 10:1080/14786 01X.2011.592725.

16. Ibid.

17. Ibid.

18. Ibid.

19. Ibid.

20. Ibid.

21. Ibid.

22. Ibid.

23. Ibid.

24. K. Warner 2007, op. cit.

25. Ibid.

26. W. Rentzmann 1996, op. cit.

27. Ibid.

28. Ibid.

29. Ibid.

30. Ibid.

31. Ibid.

32. Ibid.

33. Ikponwosa O. Ekunwe, "Re-entering Society Begins Prior to Release," *Global Perspectives on Re-Entry: Exploring the Challenges Facing Ex-Prisoners* (Tampere, Finland: Tampere University Press, 2011).

34. K. Warner 2007, op. cit.

35. Ibid.

36. Paul Ripley, "Prison Education's Role in Challenging Offending Behavior," Bristol, England: The Staff College Mendip Papers MP047, 1993.

37. Paul Ripley, *Prison Education in England and Wales,* 2nd ed. (Bristol, England: The Staff College Mendip Papers MP 022, 1993).

38. Jacqueline H. Watts, "Teaching a Distance Higher Education Curriculum Behind Bars: Challenges and Opportunities," *Open Learning*, Vol. 25, No. 1 (2010).

39. P. Ripley 1993, op. cit.

40. J. Watts 2010, op. cit.

41. Ibid.

42. "Council of Europe Recommendation No. R(89)12 of the Committee of Ministers to Member States on Education in Prison," accessed from the website of the European Prison Education Association (EPEA) March 13, 2012, http://epea.org/index.php?option= comcontent&task=view&id=53&Itemid= 66/.

43. Ibid.

44. "Prison Education," *Prison Education News,* accessed March 14, 2012, http://penandclink.com/prisoned.htm/.

45. P. Downes and C. Maunsell 2010, op. cit.

46. Ibid.

47. S. Bahn, "Community Safety and Recidivism in Australia: Breaking the Cycle of Reoffending to Produce Safer Communities Through Vocational Training," *International Journal of Training Research* Vol. 9, No. 3 (2011).

48. M. Giles, A. Le, M. Allan, C. Lees, A. Larsen, and L. Bennett, "To Train or Not to Train: The Role of Education and Training in Prison to Work Transitions," National Center for Vocational Education Research (NCVER) (2004).

49. Ibid.

50. Ibid.

51. S. Bahn 2011, op. cit.

52. M. Giles, et. al. 2004, op. cit.

53. Ibid.

54. S. Bahn 2011, op. cit.

55. Gerhard Peschers and Anna Patterson, "Books Open Worlds for People Behind Bars: Library Services in Prison as Exemplified by the Müster Prison Library, Germany's 'Library of the Year 2007'," *Library Trends*, Vol. 59, No. 3 (2011).

56. P. Downes and C. Maunsell 2010, op. cit.

57. Ibid.

58. Margarita Perez Pulido, "Programs Promoting Reading in Spanish Prisons," *International Federation of Library Associations and Institutions*, Vol. 36, No. 2 (June 2010).

59. M. Pulido 2010, op. cit.

60. Ibid.

61. Ibid.

62. Ibid.

63. Dimitrios Sannas, "NGOs and Reentry: Contributions to the Greek Penal System," in *Global Perspectives on Re-Entry: Exploring the Challenges Facing Ex-Prisoners* (Tampere, Finland: Tampere University Press, 2011).

64. P. Downes and C. Maunsell 2010, op. cit.

65. Ibid.

66. Ibid.

67. Adrian Lupascu and Nelu Nita, "Reality and Prospects in the Prison Education of Romania," *International Journal of Education and Information Technologies*, Vol. 5, No. 4 (2011).

68. Ibid.

69. A. Lupascu and N. Nita, 2011, op. cit.

70. Goran Jovanić, "The Role of Education in the Treatment of Offenders," *Support For Learning*, Vol. 26, No. 2 (May 2011).

71. Nada Pancic, "The Prison System in Serbia," *Organization for Security and Cooperation in Europe: Mission to Serbia* (September 2011).

72. P. Downes and C. Maunsell 2010, op. cit.

73. Ibid.

74. Ibid.

75. Ibid.

76. Errol Oh, Terrence Goh, Kai Yung Tam and Mary Anne Heng, "The Captains of Lives: Kaki Bukit Centre Prison School in Singapore," *The Journal of Correctional Education*, Vol. 56, No. 4 (2005).

77. Ibid.

78. Ibid.

79. Ibid.

80. Ibid.

81. Ibid.

82. Ibid.

83. Chuleeporn Phatininnart, "Non-Formal Education Services for Prison Inmates in Thailand," *Convergence*, Vol. 42, No. 2–4 (2009).

84. Ibid.

85. Ibid.

86. "Japan's Prisons: Eastern Porridge," *The Economist* (February 23, 2013).

Chapter 10

1. G. Granoff, "Schools Behind Bars: Prison College Programs Unlock the Keys to Human Potential," *Education Update Online*, accessed March 13, 2012, http://www.educationupdate.com/archives/2005/May/html/FEAT-Behind-Bars.html.

2. Patrick A. Langan and David J. Levin, "Recidivism of Prisoners Released in 1994," Bureau of Justice Statistics Special Report, 2002.

3. "Community-based Correctional Education," U.S. Department of Education, Office of Vocational and Adult Education, Division of Adult Education and Literacy (2011).

4. Ibid.

5. Scott C.S. Hayward, "The Fiscal Crisis in Corrections: Rethinking Policies and Practices," Vera Institute for Justice (2009); Tracey Kyckelhahn, "State Corrections Expenditures," U.S. Department of Justice, Bureau of Justice Statistics (2012).

6. S. Hayward 2009, op. cit.

7. Jeanne B. Contardo, *Providing College to Prison Inmates* (El Paso, TX: LFB Scholarly Publishing LLC, 2010); Benjamin Todd Jealous, Roslyn M. Brock, and Alice Huffman, "Misplaced Priorities: Over Incarcerate, Under Educate," a report of the National Association for the Advancement of Colored People, Baltimore, MD, 2011.

8. Robert Worth, "A Model Prison," *Atlantic Monthly*, Vol. 276, No. 5 (1995).

9. Ibid.

10. Ibid.

11. Ibid.

12. Ibid.

13. S. Bibas, "Leisure Time: Prisoners Should Work and Learn Rather Than Be Idle," *National Review* (April 8, 2013).

14. Ibid.

15. Ibid.

16. Ibid.

17. Lawrence S. Mears, D.P. Dublin and G.J. Travis, "The Practice and Promise of Prison Programming," The Urban Institute, Justice Policy Center (2002).

18. Michelle Fine, M.E. Torre, I. Bowen, K. Boudin, D. Hylton, J. Clark, M. Martinez, R.A. Roberts, P. Smart, and D. Upegui, with the New York State Department of Correctional Services, "Changing Minds: The Impact of College in a Maximum-Security Prison: Effects on Women in Prison, the Prison Environment, Reincarceration Rates and Post-Release Outcomes," City University of New York (2001).

19. Laura E. Gorgol and Brian A. Sponsler, "Unlocking Potential: Results of a National Survey of Post-secondary Education in State Prisons," Institute for Higher Education Policy (May 2011).

20. Marcia Johnson, Katherine Bauer, and Elizabeth Tagle, "Proposal to Reduce Recidivism Rates in Texas," *ECI Interdisciplinary Journal for Legal and Social Policy*, Vol. 1, No. 1 (2011); John Linton, "United States Department of Education Update," *The Journal of Correctional Education*, Vol. 64, No. 2 (May 2013).

21. M. Johnson, et. al. 2011, op. cit.; C. Nink, R. Olding, J. Jorgenson, and M. Gilbert, "Expanding Distance Learning Access in Prisons: A Growing Need," *Corrections Today*, Vol. 71, No. 4 (2009).

22. M. Johnson, et. al. 2011, op. cit.

23. C. Nink, et. al. 2009, op. cit.

24. J. Linton 2013, op. cit.

25. C. Nink, et. al. 2009, op. cit.

26. M. Johnson, et. al. 2011, op. cit.

27. C. Nink, et. al. 2009, op. cit.

28. J. Linton 2013, op. cit.

29. C. Nink, et. al. 2009, op. cit.

30. "Few Prisoners Enrolling in Available College Classes," Report from the Institute for Higher Education Policy (IHEP) (2005); W. Erisman and J.B. Contardo, "Learning To Reduce Recidivism: A 50-State Analysis of Postsecondary Correctional Education Policy," The Institute for Higher Education Policy (IHEP) (2005).

31. Johanna E. Foster, "Bringing College Back to Prison: The State of Higher Education Programs for Incarcerated Women in the U.S.," paper presented to the 8th International Women's Policy Research Conference, June 2005.

32. L. Gorgol and B. Sponsler 2011, op. cit.

33. Cindy Borden, P. Richardson, and Stephen Meyer, "Establishing Successful Postsecondary Academic Programs: A Practical Guide," *The Journal of Correctional Education*, Vol. 63, No. 2 (September 2012).

34. Shakoor A. Ward, "Career and Technical Education in United States Prisons: What Have We Learned?" *The Journal of Correctional Education*, Vol. 60, No. 3 (2009).

35. C. Borden, et. al. 2012, op. cit.

36. Brazzell, Crayton, Lindahl, Mukamal, and Solomon, "From the Classroom to the Community: Exploring the Role of Education During Incarceration and Re-entry," The Urban Institute, Justice Policy Center, John Jay College of Criminal Justice (2009).

37. W. Erisman and J.B. Contardo 2005, op. cit.

38. Jeremy Travis. "Rethinking Prison Education in the Era of Mass Incarceration," delivered at the Conference on Higher Education in the Prisons, John Jay College of Criminal Justice, City University of New York, February 2011.

39. "Partnerships Between Community Colleges and Prisons: Providing Workforce Education and Training to Reduce Recidivism," U.S. Department of Education, Office of Vocational and Adult Education, Office of Correctional Education (2009).

40. J. Linton 2013, op. cit.

41. "Partnerships Between Community Colleges and Prisons..." 2009, op. cit.

42. Ibid.

43. Bruce R. McPherson and Michael Santos, "Transcending the Wall," *Journal of Criminal Justice Education*, Vol. 6, No. 1 (Spring 1995).

44. "Partnerships Between Community Colleges and Prisons..." 2009, op. cit.

45. Mears, et. al. 2002, op. cit.

46. B. Jealous, et. al. 2011, op. cit.

47. Stephen C. Richards, Jeffrey Ross, Greg Newbold, Michael Lenza, Richard Jones, Daniel Murphy and Robert Grigsby, "Convict Criminology, Prisoner Reentry and Public Policy Recommendations," *Journal of Prisoners on Prisons*, Vol. 21, No. 1 & 2 (2012).

48. "Partnerships Between Community Colleges and Prisons..." 2009, op. cit.

49. Johanna E. Foster, "Bringing College Back to Prison: The State of Higher Education Programs for Incarcerated Women in the U.S.," paper presented to the 8th International Women's Policy Research Conference, June 2005.

50. "Partnerships Between Community Colleges and Prisons..." 2009, op. cit.

51. Ibid.

52. W. Erisman and J.B. Contardo 2005, op. cit.

53. G. Spangenberg, "Current Issues in Correctional Education. A Compilation and Discussion," paper presented to the Council for Advancement of Adult Literacy, 2004.

54. W. Erisman and J.B. Contardo 2005, op. cit.

55. M. Johnson, et. al. 2011, op. cit.

56. "President Bush Signs Second Chance Act of 2007," White House Fact Sheet, accessed March 13, 2012, http://georgewbushwhitehouse.archives.gov/news/releases/2008/04/20080409-15.html/.

57. M. Dawkins and E. McAuliff 2008, op. cit.

58. Ron Barnett, "Incarcerated Getting Educated," *USA Today*, September 25, 2008.

59. "Justice Beat: Education from the Inside, Out," report of the Correctional Association of New York, *The Fortune News*, Vol. 43, No. 2 (June 2010).

60. "State of Recidivism, the Revolving Door of America's Prisons," The Pew Charitable Trusts, The Pew Center on the States (April 2011).

61. Gregory A. Knott, "Cost and Punishment: Reassessing Incarceration Costs and the Value of College-in-Prison Programs," *Northern Illinois University Law Review*, Vol. 32 (2012).

62. Jeanne Contardo and Michelle Tolbert, "Prison Postsecondary Education: Bridging Learning from Incarceration to the Community," monograph presented at the Reentry Roundtable on Education, convened by The Prisoner Reentry Institute at John Jay College of Criminal Justice in cooperation with The Urban Institute, Spring 2008.

63. L. Gorgol and B. Sponsler 2011, op. cit.

64. W. Erisman and J.B. Contardo 2005, op. cit.

65. Ibid.

66. "Three Year Outcome Study of the Relationship Between Participation in Windham School System Programs and Reduced Levels of Recidivism," Windham School District, Texas Department of Criminal Justice TR 94-001 (1994).

67. Paul Van Slambrouck, "Push to Expand Book-Learning Behind Bars," *Christian Science Monitor*, September 15, 2000.

68. Karen Lahm, "Educational Participation and Inmate Misconduct," *Journal of Offender Rehabilitation*, Vol. 48 (2009).

Appendix III

1. A. Crayton and S.R. Neusteter, "The Current State of Correctional Education," paper presented at the Reentry Roundtable on Education, Prisoner Reentry Institute, John Jay College of Criminal Justice, Washington, D.C., April 2008; Michelle Tolbert, "State Correction Programs: State Policy Update No. ED01P00319," National Institute for Literacy (2002).

2. Richard Tewksbury, David John Erickson, and Jon Marc Taylor, "Opportunities Lost: The Consequences of Eliminating Pell Grant Eligibility for Correctional Education Students," *Journal of Offender Rehabilitation*, Vol. 31, No. 1–2 (2000).

3. A. Crayton and S. Neusteter 2008, op. cit.

Appendix VIII

1. Sabol, W. and H.C. West, "Prisoners in 2009," NCJ 231675, U.S. Department of Justice, Bureau of Justice Statistics, 2010. bjs.ojp.usdoj.gov/content/pub/pdf/p09.pdf.

2. Hughes, T. and D.J. Wilson, "Reentry Trends in the United States," U.S. Department of Justice, Bureau of Justice Assistance, 2002. bjs.ojp.usdoj.gov/content/pub/pdf/reentry.pdf.

3. Sabol and West.

4. Beck, A.J., "The Importance of Successful Reentry to Jail Population Growth," presented at the Urban Institute's Jail Reentry Roundtable, June 27, 2006. www.urban.org/projects/reentry-roundtable/upload/beck.PPT.

5. Glaze, L.E. and T.P. Bonczar, "Probation and Parole in the United States, 2009," NCJ 231674, U.S. Department of Justice, Bureau of Justice Statistics, 2010. bjs.ojp.usdoj.gov/content/pub/pdf/ppus09.pdf.

6. Pew Center on the States, "State of Recidivism: The Revolving Door of America's Prisons, The Pew Charitable Trusts, April 2011. www.pewcenteronthestates.org/uploadedFiles/Pew_State_of_Recidivism.pdf.

7. Sabol & West.

8. Glaze & Bonczar.

9. Hammett, T., C. Roberts, & S. Kennedy, "Health-Related Issues in Prisoner Reentry," *Crime & Delinquency*, 47, no. 3 (2001): 390-409.

10. Steadman, H.J., F. Osher, P.C. Robbins, B. Case, & S. Samuels, "Prevalence of Serious Mental Illness Among Jail Inmates," *Psychiatric Services*, 60 (2009): 761–65. consensusproject.org/publications/prevalence-of-serious-mental-illness-among-jail-inmates/PsyS-JailMHStudy.pdf.

11. Hammett, Roberts, & Kennedy.

12. Mumola, C.J. & J.C. Karberg, "Drug Use and Dependence, State and Federal Prisoners, 2004," NCJ 213530, U.S. Department of Justice, Bureau of Justice Statistics, 2006. bjs.ojp.usdoj.gov/content/pub/pdf/dudsfp04.pdf.

13. Karberg, J.C. & D.J. James, "Substance Dependence, Abuse, and Treatment of Jail Inmates, 2002," NCJ 209588, U.S. Department of Justice, Bureau of Justice Statistics, 2005. bjs.ojp.usdoj.gov/content/pub/pdf/sdatji02.pdf.

14. National Institute on Drug Abuse, "Treating Offenders with Drug Problems: Integrating Public Health and Public Safety," 2009. www.drugabuse.gov/pdf/tib/drugs_crime.pdf.

15. Metraux, S. & D.P. Culhane, "Homeless Shelter Use and Reincarceration Following Prison Release: Assessing the Risk," *Criminology & Public Policy*, 3, no. 2 (2004): 201-22.

16. Metraux & Culhane; David Michaels et al., "Homelessness and indicators of mental illness among inmates in New York City's correctional system," *Hospital and Community Psychiatry*, 43 (2002): 150-55.

17. National Commission on Correctional Health Care, "The Health Status of Soon-to-Be-Released Prisoners: A Report to Congress," vol. 1, 2002. www.ncchc.org/pubs/pubs_stbr.html.

18. Hammett, Roberts, & Kennedy.

19. Maruschak, L.M. & R. Beavers, "HIV in Prisons, 2007-08," NCJ 228307, U.S. Department of Justice, Bureau of Justice Statistics, 2009. bjs.ojp.usdoj.gov/content/pub/pdfhivp08.pdf.

20. Harlow, C.W., "Education and Correctional Populations," NCJ 195670, U.S. Department of Justice, Bureau of Justice Statistics, 2003. bjs.ojp.usdoj.gov/content/pub/pdf/ecp.pdf.

21. Holzer, H., S. Raphael, & M. Stoll, "Employment Barriers Facing Ex-Offenders," The Urban Institute, 2003. www.urban.org/UploadedPDF/410855_holzer.pdf.

22. Uggen, C. & J. Staff, "Work as a Turning Point for Criminal Offenders," in J.L. Krienert & M.S. Fleisher (eds.), *Crime & Employment: Critical Issues in Crime Reduction for Corrections* (Walnut Creek, CA: AltaMira Press, 2004).

23. Glaze, L.E. & L.M. Maruschak, "Parents in Prison and Their Minor Children," NCJ 222984, U.S. Department of Justice, Bureau of Justice Statistics, 2008. www.ojp.usdoj.gov/bjs/pub/pdf/pptmc.pdf.

24. Glaze & Maruschak.

25. Ibid.

26. Sabol & West.

27. Glaze and Bonczar.

28. Deschenes, E.P., B. Owen, and J. Crow, "Recidivism Among Female Prisoners: Secondary Analysis of the 1994 BJS Recidivism Data Set," U.S. Department of Justice, 2007. www.ncjrs.gov/pdffiles1/nij/grants/216950.pdf.

29. Sabol and West.

Bibliography

Adams, Kenneth, et al. "Large-Scale Multidimensional Test of the Effect of Prison Education Programs on Offenders' Behavior." *The Prison Journal*, Vol. 74 (December 1994).

"After Confitea." *Convergence (International Council for Adult Education)*, Vol. 42, No. 2–4 (2009).

Allen, Robert. "An Economic Analysis of Prison Education Programs and Recidivism." *Emory University, Department of Economics* (2006).

Aloi, Daniel. "Prison Education Program Expands Its Offerings." *Cornell University Chronicle Online*, accessed March 13, 2012, http://www.news.cornell.edu/stories/2009/03/prison-education-program-expands-its-online-offerings/.

Anders, Allison D., and George W. Noblit. "Understanding Effective Higher Education Programs in Prisons: Considerations from the Incarcerated Individuals Program in North Carolina." *The Journal of Correctional Education*, Vol. 62, No. 2 (June 2011).

Aos, S., R. Lieb, J. Mayfield, M. Miller, and A. Pennucci. "Benefits and Costs of Prevention and Early Intervention Programs for Youth, Technical Appendix." *Washington State Institute for Public Policy*, Document No. 05–01–1202 (2004).

Aos, Steve, Marna Miller, and Elizabeth Drake. "Evidence-Based Public Policy Options to Reduce Future Prison Construction, Criminal Justice Costs, and Crime Rates." *Washington State Institute for Public Policy* (2009).

Astray-Caneda, Vivian, Malika Busbee, and Markell Fanning. "Social Learning Theory and Prison Work Release Programs." Proceedings from the Tenth Annual College of Education and Graduate Student Network Research Conference, Florida International University, College of Education, April 2011.

"Back to School: A Guide to Continuing Your Education After Prison." *Prisoner Re-entry Institute, John Jay College of Criminal Justice* (2010).

Bahn, S. "Community Safety and Recidivism in Australia: Breaking the Cycle of Reoffending to Produce Safer Communities Through Vocational Training." *International Journal of Training Research*, Vol. 9, No. 3 (2011).

Banks, G. "Learning Under Lockdown." *ColorLines* (March 15, 2003).

Barnett, Ron. "Incarcerated Getting Educated." *USA Today*, September 25, 2008.

Barton, P.E. and R.J. Coley. "Captive Students: Education and Training in America's Prisons: Policy Information Report." Educational Testing Service, 1996.

Bayliss, P. "Learning Behind Bars: Time to Liberate Prison Education." *Studies in the Education of Adults*, Vol. 35, No. 2 (2003).

Bazos, Audrey, and J. Hausman. "Correctional Education as a Crime Control Program." *UCLA School of Public Policy and Social Research* (2004).

Bear, M.P., and T. Nixon. *Bear's Guide to Earning Degrees by Distance Learning*, 14th ed. New York: Ten Speed Press, 2000.

Beck, Jack. "Education from Inside, Out: The Multiple Benefits of College Programs in Prisons." Transcript of testimony, Correctional Association of New York's Hearing on the Assembly's Corrections Committee (2012).

Beckett, Lois. "Recession Watch: Getting Real about Prison Education Cuts." *SF Weekly*, February 19, 2010.

Beiser, V. "The Jail as Classroom. Why Los Angeles County's Top Cop Wants to Offer an Education to Tens of Thousands of Prisoners." *Miller-McCune*, Vol. 4, No. 3 (2011).

Bibas, S. "Leisure Time: Prisoners Should Work and Learn Rather Than Be Idle." *National Review* (April 8, 2013).

Bickerton, B. and J. Brown. "State of the State—Behind Bars: ABE for the Incarcerated." *Field Notes*, System for Adult Basic Education Support (SABES), Winter 2002.

Blount, J. "Getting Ahead: An Ex-Con's Guide to Getting Ahead in Today's Society." *SJM Family Foundation, Inc.* (2008).

Borden, Cindy, P. Richardson, and Stephen Meyer. "Establishing Successful Postsecondary Academic Programs; A Practical Guide." *The Journal of Correctional Education*, Vol. 63, No. 2 (September 2012).

Boulard, Garry. "Locked Out." *Diverse Issues in Higher Education*, Vol. 27, No. 1 (2010).

Brazzell, Crayton, Lindahl, Makamal, and Solomon. "From the Classroom to the Community: Exploring the Role of Education During Incarceration and Re-entry." *The Urban Institute, Justice Policy Center, John Jay College of Criminal Justice* (2009).

Britton, John. "Government Reduces In-Prison Education Even Though It Helps Lower Recidivism." *Neiman Watchdog*, Neiman Foundation (2004).

Brodheim, M. "California Prison System Lays Off Teachers, Vocational Instructors." *Prison Legal News*, Vol. 22, No. 3 (March 2011).

Burke, Lisa Ouimet and James E. Vivian. "The Effect of College Programming on Recidivism Rates at the Hampden County House of Correction: A 5-Year Study." *The Journal of Correctional Education*, Vol. 52, No. 4 (December 2001).

Case, P. "Predicting Risk Time and Probability: An Assessment of Prison Education and Recidivism." Presented at the Conference of the American Sociological Association, 2006.

Clarke, Matt. "Indiana Cuts Prison College Courses." *Prison Legal News* (March 2012).

_____. "Michigan DOC Rehabilitation Programs Emphasize Education, Reentry Support." *Prison Legal News* (June 2012).

_____. "Survey Shows College Courses for Prisoners Reduce Recidivism, but Few Exist." *Prison Legal News* (March 2012).

_____. "Texas Slashes Prison Education Budget." *Prison Legal News* (December 2012).

Coley, Richard J., and Paul E. Barton. "Locked Up and Locked Out: An Educational Perspective on the U.S. Prison Population." Educational Testing Service (2006).

Collins, Peter. "Education in Prison or the Applied Art of 'Correctional' Deconstructive Learning." *Journal of Prisoners on Prisons*, Vol. 17, No. 1 (2008).

"Community-based Correctional Education." U.S. Department of Education, Office of Vocational and Adult Education, Division of Adult Education and Literacy (2011).

Conlon, Scott Harris, Jeffrey Nagel, Mike Hillman, and Rick Hanson. "Education: Don't Leave Prison without It." *Corrections Today* (February 2008).

Contardo, Jeanne B. *Providing College to Prison Inmates*. El Paso, TX: LFB Scholarly Publishing, 2010.

_____, and Michelle Tolbert. "Prison Postsecondary Education: Bridging Learning from Incarceration to the Community." Monograph presented at the Reentry Roundtable on Education, convened by The Prisoner Reentry Institute at John Jay College of Criminal Justice in cooperation with The Urban Institute, April 2008.

"Council of Europe Recommendation No. R(89)12 of the Committee of Ministers to Member States on Education in Prison." European Prison Education Association (EPEA), accessed March 13, 2013, http://epea.org/index.php?option=comcontent&task=view&id=53&Itemid=66/.

Cowan, A.L. "College Ivy Sprouts at a Connecticut Prison." *New York Times*, November 16, 2009.

Crayton, A., and S.R. Neusteter. "The Current State of Correctional Education." Paper presented at the Reentry Roundtable on Education, convened by The Prisoner Reentry Institute at John Jay College of Criminal Justice in cooperation with The Urban Institute, April 2008.

Cronin, F. "Improvement of Occupational Education in the Federal Bureau of Prisons: Phase—An Assessment of the Comparative Effectiveness of Occupational Education Delivery Systems in Six Institutions of the Federal Bureau of Prisons." Report, Ohio State University Center for Vocational Education, 1976.

Davis, K. "Auburn Professors Bring Educational Opportunities to Prisoners." *The Plainsman*, March 21, 2013.

Dawkins, M., and E. McAuliff. "Higher Education Behind Bars: Postsecondary Prison

Education Programs Make a Difference." *American Council on Education Centerpoint* (October 2008).

De Maeyer, Marc. "Are Prisons Good Education Practice?" *Convergence (International Council for Adult Education)*, Vol. 42, No. 2–4 (2009).

Deruy, Emily. "What it Costs when We Don't Educate Inmates for Life After Prison." *ABC News,* accessed March 14, 2012, http://fusion.net/justice/story/us-fails-educate-inmates-life-prison-11751/.

Dey, E.A. "Higher Education in Prison: The Palo Verde Model." *Journal of Prisoners on Prisons*, Vol. 17, No. 1 (2008).

Downes, Paul, and Catherine Maunsell. "Life-long Learning for All? Policies and Practices towards Underrepresented and Socially Excluded Groups." Presented at Session VII of the Final International Conference of the Educational Disadvantage Centre, St. Patrick's College, Dublin, Ireland, 2010.

Drake, O.B. "Grant-Funded Program Offers Courses to Inmates." *The Wesleyan Connection* (November 2009).

Durano, C. "Prison Program Helps Inmates Improve Lives, Stay Out of Jail." DailySkiff.com, Texas Christian University, Schieffer School of Journalism. Accessed March 13, 2012, http://www.tcu360.com/dailyskiffcom-archives/2008/03/2947.prison-program-helps-inmates-improve-lives-stay-out-jail/.

"Education as Crime Prevention: Commentary on the 1997 report produced by the Center on Crime, Communities & Culture, Occasional Paper Series No. 2." *Spectrum: The Journal of State Government*, Vol. 71 (Winter 1998).

"Education as Crime Prevention." Research Brief Occasional Paper Series No. 2. *Open Society Institute, Criminal Justice Initiative* (September 1997).

"Education Behind Bars: Opportunities and Obstacles." Report, Ohio State Legislative Office of Educational Oversight, 1994.

"Education, Training and Leisure Time Program Standards." U.S. Department of Justice, Federal Bureau of Prisons, Program Statement No. 5300.21 (February 2002).

Ekunwe, Ikponwosa O. "Re-entering Society Begins Prior to Release." *Global Perspectives on Re-Entry: Exploring the Challenges Facing Ex-Prisoners.* Tampere, Finland: Tampere University Press, 2011.

Erisman, W., and J.B. Contardo. "Learning To Reduce Recidivism: A 50-State Analysis of Postsecondary Correctional Education Policy." The Institute for Higher Education Policy (IHEP) (2005).

Esperian, John H. "The Effect of Prison Education Programs on Recidivism." *The Journal of Correctional Education*, Vol. 61, No. 4 (December 2010).

Fabelo, T. "The Impact of Prison Education on Community Reintegration of Inmates: The Texas Case." *The Journal of Correctional Education*, Vol. 53, No. 3 (2002).

"Federal Prisons: Inmate and Staff Views on Education and Work Training Programs." General Accounting Office, accessed March 14, 2012, http://www.gao.gov/assets/220/217438.pdf/.

Ferranti, S. "Fighting Prison Censorship: An Interview with Paul Wright." *Journal of Prisoners on Prisons*, Vol. 17, No. 1 (2008).

"Few Prisoners Enrolling in Available College Classes." *Institute for Higher Education Policy* (2005).

Fine, Michelle, M.E. Torre, I. Bowen, K. Boudin, D. Hylton, J. Clark, M. Martinez, R.A. Roberts, P. Smart, and D. Upegui, with the New York State Department of Correctional Services. "Changing Minds: The Impact of College in a Maximum-Security Prison: Effects on Women in Prison, the Prison Environment, Reincarceration Rates and Post-Release Outcomes." Report, City University of New York, 2001.

Fleischer, Mathew. "U.S. Prisons Don't Fund Education, and Everybody Pays a Price." *Takepart.com* (March 1, 2013). Accessed March 4, 2013, http://www.takepart.com/article/2013/03/01/americas-inmates-education-denied-everybody-pays-price.

Foster, Johanna E. "Bringing College Back to Prison: The State of Higher Education Programs for Incarcerated Women in the U.S." Paper presented to the 8th International Women's Policy Research Conference, June 2005.

Foster, Lalove. "The Prison Class." *Idaho Magazine*, Vol. 9, No. 9 (June 2010).

Frank, Jacquelyn, J. Omstead, and S. Pigg. "The Missing Link: Service-Learning as an Essential Tool for Correctional Education." *The Journal of Correctional Education*, Vol. 63, No. 1 (April 2012).

Gaes, Gerald G. "The Impact of Prison Education Programs on Post-Release Outcomes." Monograph presented at the Reentry Roundtable on Education, convened by The Prisoner Reentry Institute at John Jay College of Criminal Justice in cooperation with The Urban Institute, April 2008.

_____, and William G. Saylor. "PREP: Training Inmates through Industrial Work Participation, and Vocational and Apprenticeship Instruction." U.S. Federal Bureau of Prisons (September 24, 1996), accessed March 13, 2012, http://www.bop.gov/resources/research_projects/published_reports/recidivism/oreprprep_cmq.pdf.

Garland, Brett, and William McCarty. "Understanding Perceptions of Supervision and Organizational Operations Among Prison Teachers: A Multilevel Analysis." *Criminal Justice Review*, Vol. 36, No. 3 (2011).

Garmon, J. "Higher Education for Prisoners will Lower Rates for Taxpayers." *Black Issues in Higher Education* (January 2002).

Gendron, Dennis, and John Cavan. "Inmate Education: The Virginia Model." Southside Virginia Community College (1988).

Gerber, J., and E.J. Fritsch. "Prison Education and Offender Behavior: A Review of the Scientific Literature." Prison Education Research Project: Report 1, Sam Houston State University/Texas Dept of Criminal Justice, 1993.

Giles, M., A. Le, M. Allan, C. Lees, A. Larsen, and L. Bennett. "To Train or Not to Train: The Role of Education and Training in Prison to Work Transitions." Report, National Center for Vocational Education Research (NCVER), 2004.

Goldrick-Rab, Sara. "The Prison-Education Connection." *The Chronicle of Higher Education* (November 2, 2009).

Gorgol, Laura E., and Brian A. Sponsler. "Unlocking Potential: Results of a National Survey of Post-secondary Education in State Prisons." *Institute for Higher Education Policy* (May 2011).

"Goucher Prison Education Partnership." Goucher College, accessed March 13, 2012, http://www.goucher.edu/academics/other-academic-offerings/goucher-prison-education-partnership/.

Granoff, G. "Schools Behind Bars: Prison College Programs Unlock the Keys to Human Potential." *Education Update Online*. Accessed March 13, 2012, http://www.educationupdate.com/archives/2005/May/html/FEAT-Behind-Bars.html/.

Gray, Katti. "Parlaying the Prison Experience." *Diverse Issues in Higher Education*, Vol. 27, No. 1 (2010).

Greenberg, Elizabeth, Eric Dunleavy, and Mark Kutner. "Literacy Behind Bars: Results from the 2003 National Assessment of Adult Literacy Prison Survey, Chapter 4—Education and Job Training in Prison." *The Journal for Vocational Special Needs Education*, Vol. 30, No. 2 (2008).

Greenwood, P.W., K.E. Model, C.P. Rydell, and J. Chiesa. "Diverting Children from a Life of Crime: Measuring Costs and Benefits." Research brief, Rand Corporation (1998).

Hall, N. and M. Caldwell. "Prison Education—What No One Talks About." *Seattle Times*, January 23, 2013.

Hall, Robert A. "Technology Education & the Felon (Teaching High School Behind Prison Walls)." Report, New Hampshire State Prison Adult Vocational Training Center, 1990.

Hall, R.S., and E. Killacky. "Correctional Education from the Perspective of the Prisoner Student." *The Journal of Correctional Education*, Vol. 59, No. 4 (December 2008).

Harer, Miles D. "Prison Education Program Participation and Recidivism: A Test of the Normalization Hypothesis." Federal Bureau of Prisons, Office of Research and Evaluation, 1995.

_____. "Recidivism among Federal Prisoners Released in 1987." Federal Bureau of Prisons, Office of Research and Evaluation, 1994.

Harlow, Caroline Wolf, H. David Jenkins, and Stephen Steurer. "GED Holders in Prison Read Better Than Those in the Household Population: Why?" *The Journal of Correctional Education*, Vol. 61, No. 1 (March 2010).

Hayward, Scott C.S. "The Fiscal Crisis in Corrections: Rethinking Policies and Practices." Report, Vera Institute for Justice, 2009.

Heiser, Sherry E.M. "Student Perceptions of a College Distance Learning Program at a Maximum Security Prison." Thesis, Humboldt State University, 2007.

Hertz, L. "Teaching and Learning in Prison." *Vassar Alumni iHub*, accessed March 14, 2012, http://hudsonlink.org/news_events/teaching-and-learning-prison/.

Hopwood, S. "Give Former Prisoners a Second Chance." *Seattle Times*, January 10, 2013.

Houchins, D.E., D. Puckett-Patterson, S. Crosby, M.E. Shippen, and K. Jolivette. "Barriers and Facilitators to Providing Incarcerated Youth with a Quality Education." *Preventing School Failure*, Vol. 53, No. 3 (2009).

Hunsinger, I. "Austin MacCormic and the Education of Adult Prisoners: Still Relevant Today." *The Journal of Correctional Education*, Vol. 48, No. 4 (1997).

"Inmates Receive College Education from San Quentin." *Jet* (October 2002).

"Japan's Prisons: Eastern Porridge." *The Economist* (February 23, 2013).

Jealous, Benjamin Todd, Roslyn M. Brock, and Alice Huffman. "Misplaced Priorities: Over Incarcerate, Under Educate." Report, National Association for the Advancement of Colored People, Baltimore, MD, 2011.

Jennings, Trip. "Quarter of State Prison Education Jobs are Vacant." *The New Mexico Independent,* September 2009.

Jeralyn. "Bush Signs Second Chance Act into Law." *TalkLeft: The Politics of Crime* (April 2008).

_____. "For Whom the Pell Tolled: Higher Education for Prisoners." *TalkLeft: The Politics of Crime* (February 2005).

Johnson, Kevin. "Job Squeeze is Felt Behind Bars." *USA Today,* July 19, 2010.

Johnson, Marcia, Katherine Bauer, and Elizabeth Tagle. "Proposal to Reduce Recidivism Rates in Texas." *ECI Interdisciplinary Journal for Legal and Social Policy,* Vol. 1, No. 1 (2011).

Jones, R., J. Ross, S. Richards, and D. Murphy. "The First Dime: A Decade of Convict Criminology." *The Prison Journal,* Vol. 89, No. 2 (May 2009).

Jovanić, Goran. "The Role of Education in the Treatment of Offenders." *Support for Learning,* Vol. 26, No. 2 (May 2011).

"Justice Beat: Education from the Inside, Out." Report of the Correctional Association of New York, *The Fortune News,* Vol. 43, No. 2 (June 2010).

Kaplan, Sabina, Eileen Leonard, and Mary Shanley. "Different Worlds Converge as College Students and Inmates Meet in a Prison Classroom." *Corrections Today* (August 2010).

Karpowitz, Daniel, and Max Kenner. "Education as Crime Prevention: The Case for Reinstating Pell Grant Eligibility for the Incarcerated." Report from the Bard Prison Initiative of Bard College, 1995. All data cited in this report comes exclusively from official publications produced by or for the U.S. government and state governments.

Katel, Peter. "Prison Reform: Are Too Many Nonviolent Criminals being Incarcerated?" *CQ Researcher,* Vol. 17, No. 13 (April 2007).

Kimmitt, S. "The Impact of Community Context on the Risk of Recidivism among Parolees at One-, Two-, and Three-Year Follow-ups." Honors Thesis, Ohio State University, 2011.

King, Arnie. "Reflections from Inside." *Field Notes,* System for Adult Basic Education Support (SABES), Winter 2002.

Knott, Gregory A. "Cost and Punishment: Reassessing Incarceration Costs and the Value of College-in-Prison Programs." *Northern Illinois University Law Review,* Vol. 32 (July 2012).

Kyckelhahn, Tracey. "State Corrections Expenditures." Report, U.S. Department of Justice, Bureau of Justice Statistics, 2012.

Lacey, C.H. "Art Education in Women's Prisons: Lessons from the Inside." Paper presented at the Annual Meeting of the American Educational Research Association, April 2007.

Lagemann, Ellen C. "What Can College Mean? Lessons from the Bard Prison Initiative." *Change: The Magazine of Higher Learning,* Vol. 43, No. 6 (2011).

Lahm, Karen. "Educational Participation and Inmate Misconduct." *Journal of Offender Rehabilitation,* Vol. 48 (2009).

Langan, Patrick A., and David J. Levin. "Recidivism of Prisoners Released in 1994." Special Report, Bureau of Justice Statistics, 2002.

Large, J. "Post-Prison Education Program Helps Some get Another Chance." *Seattle Times,* July 16, 2009.

Lawrence, Daniel W. "Inmate Students: Where Do They Fit In?" Article, Oklahoma Department of Corrections (1994).

Lewis v. Casey, 518 U.S. 343 (1996).

"Lift State Ban on Higher-Education Funding for Prison Inmates." Editorial, *Seattle Times,* March 4, 2013.

Linton, John. "United Stated Department of Education Update." *The Journal of Correctional Education,* Vol. 61, No. 3 (2010).

_____. "United States Department of Education Update." *The Journal of Correctional Education,* Vol. 62, No. 2 (June 2011).

_____. "United States Department of Education Update." *The Journal of Correctional Education,* Vol. 63, No. 2 (September 2012).

_____. "United States Department of Education Update." *The Journal of Correctional Education,* Vol. 64, No. 2 (May 2013).

Long, K. "Rare UW Class Unites Honors Students, Felons." *Seattle Times,* April 6, 2012.

Lungu, Karen. "Colorado Prison's 'Education Row' A Boon for Inmates." *The Durango Herald,* April 26, 2010.

Lupascu, Adrian, and Nelu Nita. "Reality and Prospects in the Prison Education of Romania." *International Journal of Education and*

Information Technologies, Vol. 5, No. 4 (2011).

Malik, N. "Prison Teachers." *Education Update Online*, accessed March 13, 2012, http://www.educationupdate.com/archives/2005/May/html/FEAT-Teachers.html/.

Manger, T.O., Å. Diseth Eikeland, H. Hetland, and A. Asbjørnsen. "Prison Inmates' Educational Motives: Are They Pushed or Pulled?" *Scandinavian Journal of Education Research*, Vol. 54, No. 6 (2010).

Marklein, M.B. "Students Behind Bars Mix With Those from Outside." *USA Today*, April 27, 2013.

Martin, M. "What Happened to Prison Education Programs?" *Prison Legal News* (June 2009).

Martinez, Alma I., and Michael Eisenberg. "Impact of Educational Achievement of Inmates in the Windham School District on Recidivism." Report, Criminal Justice Policy Council, August 2000.

McCarty, H.J. "Educating Felons: Reflections on Higher Education in Prison." *Radical History Review*, Vol. 96 (2006).

McPherson, Bruce R., and Michael Santos. "Transcending the Wall." *Journal of Criminal Justice Education*, Vol. 6, No. 1 (Spring 1995).

Mears, Lawrence S., D.P. Dublin, and G.J. Travis. "The Practice and Promise of Prison Programming." Report, Urban Institute, Justice Policy Center, 2002.

Meiners, E.R. "Resisting Civil Death: Organizing for Access to Education in our Prison Nation." *DePaul Journal for Social Justice*, Vol. 3, No. 1 (2009).

Mentor, K., and M. Bosworth, eds. "College Courses in Prison." Draft submission to the *Encyclopedia of Corrections*, July 2011.

Meyer, Stephen J. "Factors Affecting Student Success in Post-secondary Academic Correctional Education Programs." *The Journal of Correctional Education*, Vol. 62, No. 2 (June 2011).

_____, L. Fredericks, C.M. Borden, and P.L. Richardson. "Implementing Postsecondary Academic Programs in State Prisons: Challenges and Opportunities." *The Journal of Correctional Education*, Vol. 61, No. 2 (2010).

"Michigan Works to get Some Inmates Higher Education." *The Morning Sun*, May 20, 2013.

Moore, J.C. "Camarillo College Students Help Educate Youth Offenders." *Ventura County Star*, April 10, 2013.

Munoz, V. "Report to the Special Rapporteur on the Right to Education." United Nations Human Rights Council (April 2, 2009).

Musgrove, Kate, N. Derzis, M. Shippen, and H. Brigman. "PIRATES: A Program for Offenders Transitioning into the World of Work." *The Journal of Correctional Education*, Vol. 63, No. 2 (September 2012).

Nagelsen, S. "Writing as a Tool for Constructive Rehabilitation." *Journal of Prisoners on Prisons*, Vol. 17, No. 1 (2008).

Nally, John, S. Lockwood, K. Knutson, and T. Ho. "An Evaluation of the Effect of Correctional Education Programs on Post-Release Recidivism and Employment: An Empirical Study in Indiana." *The Journal of Correctional Education*, Vol. 63, No. 1 (April 2012).

_____, _____, and T. Ho. "Employment of Ex-Offenders During the Recession." *The Journal of Correctional Education*, Vol. 62, No. 2 (June 2011).

National Reentry Resource Center. Project of the Council of State Governments Justice Center, accessed March 13, 2012, http://www.nationalreentryresourcecenter.org/facts/.

"New and Noteworthy Prison Programs." Report of the Correctional Education Association of New York, *The Fortune News*, Vol. 43, No. 2 (June 2010).

Newbold, G. and J.I. Ross. "Convict Criminology at the Crossroads: Research Note." *The Prison Journal*, Vol. 93, No. 1 (March 2010).

Nink, C., R. Olding, J. Jorgenson, and M. Gilbert. "Expanding Distance Learning Access in Prisons: A Growing Need." *Corrections Today*, Vol. 71, No. 4 (2009).

Oh, Errol, Terrence Goh, Kai Yung Tam, and Mary Anne Heng. "The Captains of Lives: Kaki Bukit Centre Prison School in Singapore." *The Journal of Correctional Education*, Vol. 56, No. 4 (2005).

Pallone, C. "Speaker Gives Hope to Oregon Inmates." *Statesman Journal*, March 25, 2013.

Pancic, Nada. "The Prison System in Serbia." Organization for Security and Cooperation in Europe: Mission to Serbia (September 2011).

"Partnerships Between Community Colleges and Prisons: Providing Workforce Education and Training to Reduce Recidivism." U.S. Department of Education, Office of Vocational and Adult Education, Office of Correctional Education (2009).

Pauls, Christopher E. "Student Perceptions of

the Charter School Experience at Metro Detention Center." Master's Thesis, University of New Mexico, 2011.

Payne, E. "BU's Prison Education Program Thrives Despite Pell Grant Ban." *The Quad*, March 22, 2013.

Peschers, Gerhard, and Anna Patterson. "Books Open Worlds for People Behind Bars: Library Services in Prison as Exemplified by the Müster Prison Library, Germany's 'Library of the Year 2007'." *Library Trends*, Vol. 59, No. 3 (2011).

Peterson's Four-Year Colleges, 40th ed. Albany, NY: Peterson's Publishing, 2009.

Peterson's Two-Year Colleges, 40th ed. Albany, NY: Peterson's Publishing, 2009.

Peterson's Vocational and Technical Schools, 9th ed. Albany, NY: Peterson's Publishing, 2009.

Pettit, Michelle D., and Michael Kroth. "Educational Services in Swedish Prisons: Successful Programs of Academic and Vocational Teaching." *Criminal Justice Studies*, Vol. 24, No. 3 (2011).

Phatininnart, Chuleeporn. "Non-Formal Education Services for Prison Inmates in Thailand." *Convergence*, Vol. 42, No. 2–4 (2009).

Phelps, M.S. "Rehabilitation in the Punitive Era: The Gap Between Rhetoric and Reality in U.S. Prison Programs." *Law & Society Review*, Vol. 45, No. 1 (2011).

Piché, J. "Barriers to Knowing Inside: Education in Prisons and Education on Prisons." *Journal of Prisoners on Prisons*, Vol. 17, No. 1 (2008).

Pihl, Kristi. "Connell Prison College Degree Program May End." *Seattle Times*, May 23, 2011.

"Policy Recommendations: Investing in Education in Prisons and Communities." Paper presented at the Women's Advocacy Project, 2009.

Pollard, Larry. "Department of Corrections in Massachusetts—An Overview." *Field Notes*, System for Adult Basic Education Support (SABES), 2002.

"Postsecondary Education Programs for Inmates." U.S. Department of Justice, Federal Bureau of Prisons, Program Statement No. 5354.03 (December 2003).

"President Bush Signs Second Chance Act of 2007." White House Fact Sheet, accessed March 13, 2012, http://georgewbush-whitehouse.archives.gov/news/releases/2008/04/20080409–15.html/.

"Prison Break." *The New Republic* (October 2002).

"Prison Education." *Prison Education News*, accessed March 14, 2012, http://penandclink.com/prisoned.htm/.

"Prison Education Research Project, Final Report." Huntsville, Texas: Sam Houston State University / Criminal Justice Center, Texas State Department of Criminal Justice, 1994.

Pulido, Margarita Perez. "Programs Promoting Reading in Spanish Prisons." *International Federation of Library Associations and Institutions*, Vol. 36, No. 2 (June 2010).

Rentzmann, William. "Prison Philosophy and Prison Education." *The Journal of Correctional Education*, Vol. 47, No. 2 (June 1996).

Richards, S., D. Faggiani, K. Roffers, R. Hendricksen, and J. Krueger. "The Dynamics of Race and Incarceration: Social Integration, Social Welfare, and Social Control." *Convict Criminology* 2 (2008).

_____, J. Austin, and R. Jones. "Thinking about Prison Release and Budget Crisis in the Blue Grass State." *Critical Criminology* 12 (2004).

_____, Jeffrey Ross, Greg Newbold, Michael Lenza, Richard Jones, Daniel Murphy, and Robert Grigsby. "Convict Criminology, Prisoner Reentry and Public Policy Recommendations." *Journal of Prisoners on Prisons*, Vol. 21, No. 1 & 2 (2012).

_____, and Michael Lenza. "The First Dime and Nickel of Convict Criminology." *Journal of Prisoners on Prisons*, Vol. 21, No. 1 & 2 (2012).

_____, and R. Jones. "Beating the Perpetual Incarceration Machine: Overcoming Structural Impediments to Re-entry." *After Crime and Punishment: Pathways to Offender Reintegration*. Portland, OR: Willan Publishing, 2004.

Ridgeway, James, and Jean Casella. "No Budget Cuts for Federal Prisons." *Prison Legal News* (June 2012).

Ripley, P. "Prison Education in England and Wales," 2nd ed. Bristol, England: The Staff College Mendip Papers MP 022, 1993.

_____. "Prison Education's Role in Challenging Offending Behavior." Bristol, England: The Staff College Mendip Papers MP04, 1993.

Rix, Kate. "San Quentin's Campus: A Unique Program Enables Prisoners to Study with Cal Professors and Earn College Credits." *The Monthly: East Bay Life*, September 2008.

Rose, C. "Women's Participation in Prison Education: What We Know and What We Don't Know." *The Journal of Correctional Education*, Vol. 55, No. 1 (March 2004).

Ross, Jeffrey Ian, and Stephen C. Richards. *Behind Bars*. New York: Alpha/Penguin, 2002.

_____. *Beyond Bars*. New York: Alpha/Penguin, 2009.

_____. *Convict Criminology: Contemporary Issues in Crime and Justice Series*, 1st ed. Independence, KY: Cengage Learning, 2002.

Ruhling, N. "STEP in the Right Direction." *Impact: Rutgers University Foundation Magazine* (2013).

Sacharow, Fredda. "With help from Rutgers, Women in Prison get Online for Success." *Rutgers Focus* (2008).

Sannas, Dimitrios. "NGOs and Re-entry: Contributions to the Greek Penal System." *Global Perspectives on Re-Entry: Exploring the Challenges Facing Ex-Prisoners*. Tampere, Finland: Tampere University Press, 2011.

Schorn, Daniel. "Maximum Security Education: How Some Inmates are Getting a Top-Notch Education Behind Bars." Transcript, *CBS News—60 Minutes* (April 15, 2007).

Schulzke, Eric. "From Prison to College: Major Foundations Fund Five-Year Study Bridging Divide." *Desert News*, May 13, 2013.

Segura, Liliana. "Attica at 40." *The Nation* (September 2011).

Sherman, K. "Opening Doors, An ESOL Workbook by Prisoners for Prisoners." *Field Notes*, System for Adult Basic Education Support (SABES), Winter 2002.

Shull, Thomas. "Taking the Classroom to the Cellblock." *American Jails* (March-April 2011).

Sieben, Lauren. "Liberal-Arts Colleges Reach Minds Behind Bars." *Chronicle of Higher Education*, Vol. 57, No. 23 (2011).

Sims, T. "Support for Inmate Education." *Correctional News* (April 17, 2013).

Skorton, D., and G. Altschuler. "College Behind Bars: How Educating Prisoners Pays Off." *Forbes* (March 25, 2013).

Soferr, S. "Prison Education: Is It Worth It?" *Corrections Today* (October 2006).

Spangenberg, G. "Current Issues in Correctional Education. A Compilation and Discussion." Paper, Council for Advancement of Adult Literacy (2004).

Spaulding, Susanna. "Borderland Stories about Teaching College in Prison." *New Directions for Community Colleges*, Vol. 155 (2011).

Spohn, Jessica. "New England ABE-to-College Transition Project." *Field Notes*, System for Adult Basic Education Support (SABES), 2002.

Standards for Adult Correctional Institutions, 4th ed. Alexandria, VA: American Correctional Association, 2003.

"State of Recidivism, the Revolving Door of America's Prisons." *The Pew Charitable Trusts, The Pew Center on the States* (April 2011).

Steffler, Scott B. "Oregon's Anti-education 'Corrections' Policy: A Surprise?" *Journal of Prisoners on Prisons*, Vol. 17, No. 1 (2008).

Steurer, Stephen J., Linda Smith, and Alice Tracy. "OCE/CEA Three State Recidivism Study." United States Department of Education, Office of Correctional Education, September 2001.

"Strode College Offender Learning Program." Strode College, accessed March 13, 2013, http://ebookbrowse.com/08–06–10-offender-learning-services-strode-college-condensed-doc-d251105183/.

Sturm, Susan, Kate Skolnick, and Tina Wu. "Building Pathways of Possibility from Criminal Justice to College: College Initiative as a Catalyst Linking Individual and Systemic Change." Report, Center for Institutional and Social Change, City University of New York, June 30, 2010.

Talbot, M. "Catch and Release." *Atlantic Monthly*, Vol. 29, No. 1 (2003).

Taylor, Jon Marc. "The Education of Ivan Denisovich." *The Journal of Correctional Education*, Vol. 48, No. 2 (June 1997).

_____. "Pell Grants for Prisoners." *The Nation* (January 1993).

_____. "Pell Grants for Prisoners: Why Should We Care." *Journal of Prisoners on Prisons*, Vol. 17, No. 1 (2008).

_____. "Piecing Together a College Education Behind Bars." *Prison Mirror*, Vol. 115, No. 10–13 (May-August 2002).

_____. "There Ought to Be a Law: Congress Is Stealing Our College Education." Op-Ed, *New York Times*, August 24, 1994.

_____, and Suzan Schwartzkopf. *Prisoners' Guerrilla Handbook to Correspondence Programs in the United States and Canada*, 3rd ed. West Brattleboro, VT: Prison Legal News, 2009.

Tewksbury, Richard, David John Erickson, and Jon Marc Taylor. "Opportunities Lost: The Consequences of Eliminating Pell Grant Eligibility for Correctional Education Students." *Journal of Offender Rehabilitation*, Vol. 31, No. 1–2 (2000).

Thomas, Cal. "Jailbroken: 5 Ways to Fix USA's Prisons." *USA Today*, July 14, 2011.

Thomas, Emma, and Karyn Buck. "Peer Mentoring in a Young Offenders Institution."

Widening Participation and Lifelong Learning, Vol. 12, No. 3, ISSN: 1466–6529, University of Reading, UK (December 2010).

"Three Year Outcome Study of the Relationship Between Participation in Windham School System Programs and Reduced Levels of Recidivism." *Windham School District, Texas Department of Criminal Justice*, TR 94–001 (1994).

Tolbert, Michelle. "State Correction Programs: State Policy Update No. ED01P00319." *National Institute for Literacy* (2002).

Toller, W.R., and D.E. O'Malley. "Education Reintegration at Hampden County." *Field Notes*, System for Adult Basic Education Support (SABES), 2002.

Torre, M., and M. Fine. "Bar None: Extending Affirmative Action to Higher Education in Prison." *Journal of Social Issues*, Vol. 61, No. 3 (2005).

Torres-Rivera, Gabriel. "Keeping It Real: A Perspective on the Formerly Incarcerated in New York." Presented at the Community Service Society of New York, Reentry Roundtable, March 2011.

Travis, Jeremy. "Rethinking Prison Education in the Era of Mass Incarceration." Delivered at the Conference on Higher Education in the Prisons, John Jay College of Criminal Justice, City University of New York, February 2011.

Trounstine, Jean. "The Battle to Bring Back Pell Grants for Prisoners." *Boston Daily Magazine*, accessed March 4, 2013, http://www.bostonmagazine.com/news/blog/2013/03/04/the-battle-bring-back-pell-grants-for-prisoners/.

Urbina, I. "Prison Labor Fuels American War Machine." *Prison Legal News* (January 2004).

Urrieta, Luis, Karla Martin, and Courtney Robinson. "'I am in School!': African American Male Youth in a Prison/College Hybrid Figured World." *Urban Review*, Vol. 43, No. 4 (2011).

Vacca, J. "Educated Prisoners are Less Likely to Return to Prison." *The Journal of Correctional Education*, Vol. 55, No. 4 (December 2004).

Van Slambrouck, Paul. "Push to Expand Book-Learning Behind Bars." *Christian Science Monitor*, September 15, 2000.

Vischer, Christy A., and Jeremy Travis. "Life on the Outside: Returning Home After Incarceration." *The Prison Journal*, Vol. 91, No. 3 (September 2011).

Ward, Deborah E., and Heather Tubman. "How Does Prison to Community (P2C) Affect Recidivism: A Summary of Quantitative Findings." Rutgers University Economic Development Research Group, School of Management and Labor Relations, 2009.

Ward, Shakoor A. "Career and Technical Education in United States Prisons: What Have We Learned?" *The Journal of Correctional Education*, Vol. 60, No. 3 (2009).

Warner, Kevin. "Against the Narrowing of Perspectives: How Do We See Learning, Prisons and Prisoners?" *The Journal of Correctional Education*, Vol. 58, No. 2 (June 2007).

_____. "Widening and Deepening the Education We Offer Those in Prison: Reflections from Irish and European Experience." *The Journal of Correctional Education*, Vol. 53, No. 1 (2002).

Warren, Jenifer. "One in 100: Behind Bars in America." Report, The Pew Charitable Trust Center, 2008.

Watts, Jacqueline H. "Teaching a Distance Higher Education Curriculum Behind Bars: Challenges and Opportunities." *Open Learning*, Vol. 25, No. 1 (2010).

Weissman, Marsha, Alan Rosenthal, Patricia Warth, Elaine Wolf, and Michael Messina-Yauchzy. "The Use of Criminal History Records in College Admissions Reconsidered." *The Center for Community Alternatives* (2010).

Williams, D.N. "Congressional Education and the Community College." *ERIC Digest*, Article No. ED321835 (1989).

Wilson, Rodney. "The Voice in the Pen." *Field Notes*, System for Adult Basic Education Support (SABES), 2002.

Winterfield, Laura, Mark Coggeshall, Michelle Burke-Storer, Vanessa Correa, and Simon Tidd. "The Effects of Post-secondary Education: Final Report." *Urban Institute Justice Policy Center* (2009).

Winters, C.A. "Inmate Opinions Toward Education and Participation in Prison Education Programmes." *Police Journal*, Vol. 68, No. 1 (January-March 1995).

Wolfgang, Jütte, Katherine Nicoll, and Henning Salling Olesen. "Professionalization—the Struggle Within." *European Journal for Research on the Education and Learning of Adults*, Vol. 2, No. 1 (2011).

Worth, Robert. "A Model Prison." *Atlantic Monthly*, Vol. 276, No. 5 (1995).

Index

ABE-to-College Transition Project, New England 123–124
ACE (Adult Continuing Education) *see* Adult Basic Education (ABE)
ACLU (American Civil Liberties Union), Prison Project publication list 220–221
Adams State College 125
addiction recovery classes 53
Addison Wesley 114
Adult Basic Education (ABE) 48–50, 52–53, 75, 91, 156
Adult Education and Family Literacy Act (1968) 68
Alabama 126, 183
Allen County Reentry Court Project, Indiana 132
American Correctional Association 184
American Recovery and Reinvestment Act 127
American Society of Criminology (ASC) 83–84
Angola Penitentiary, Louisiana 124
Arizona 126–127, 186–187
Ashland University 100
assessment of inmate abilities 188–189
Attica State Prison uprising 40–41
Aubry, Jeffrion 197
Auburn Correctional Facility, New York 111
Australia 173–174, 186–187

Baca, Lee 8, 25, 37, 60
background checks 143
Ball State University 142
Bard College Prison Initiative, New York 27, 106–108, 114, 122
Bay State Correctional Center, Massachusetts 115
Bedford Hills College Program (BHCP), New York 109–110
Bedford Hills Correctional Facility, New York 109–110
Belgium 174–175
Bibas, Stephanos: *The Machinery of Criminal Justice* 184–185
Bill and Melinda Gates Foundation 45, 97

Bloggers from Prison project, Spain 175–176
books, free/discounted 235–245
Boston University 37, 114–117, 156, 198–199
Bridge to College Program, Washington State 123, 130–131
Britton, John 42
budgets 48
Budnick, Scott 118
Buffett, Doris 110, 111
Buffett, Warren 45
Bureau of Justice Statistics 10
Burger, Warren 18
Bush, George W. 197

California 3–4, 8, 26, 28, 48, 71, 116–119, 227–228
California Correctional Peace Officers Association 81
California Institution for Men (CIM) 118
California Rehabilitation Center 118–119
Camarillo College 118
Canadian prison system 58, 155
Carl D. Perkins Career and Technical Education Improvement Act (2006) 46, 68, 198, 234
Cayuga Correctional Facility, New York 110
Cell Door Magazine 217
Center on Crime, Communities and Culture 21, 44
certificated programs 16, 50, 52–53, 85, 92, 100, 113–114, 119–120, 136; *see also* vocational training; *specific programs*
Chemeketa Community College 99
Cheshire Correctional Facility, Connecticut 122
children of prisoners 18–20, 254
Christopher-Zoukis.com 164
City University of New York (CUNY) 108, 114, 143–144
Clinton, Bill 44
Coalition for Criminal Justice 42
Coastline College 71
College and Community Fellowship (CCF), New York 108–109, 112, 114, 193
college graduates, earning power of 15

College Initiative (CI), New York 143–144, 193
College of New Jersey 119
College of the Air program 69, 127
Collins, Peter 58, 155–156
Colorado 65, 97–99, 125
Colorado Community College System 97–99
Columbia International University 120
community-based programs 72–73
community colleges 27–28, 41, 51, 94, 191–192; *see also specific colleges*
Community Education Centers, Inc. 71–72
community safety and recidivism 9–10
computer access 28
Computer-based Learning from Prison to Community Program, New Jersey 131
computer skills 11, 14, 48, 54–55, 121, 132–133, 187
CONFINTEA V meeting (2002) 166
Connecticut 122, 123
Convict Criminology (book) 83, 84
Convict Criminology group 83–84, 194
"Convicts Critique Criminology" seminar 83
Corcoran Sun 218
Cordell, John 9
Cornell Prison Education Program, New York 111
Correctional Association of New York 23
correctional education *see* headings under prison education
Correctional Education Association (CEA) 21–22, 42, 44, 56–57, 69, 127, 128–129
corrections system statistics (U.S.) 248–249
Corrections Today 15
correspondence courses 27–28, 57, 134, 135
Cotton Correctional Facility 96–97
Council for Advancement of Adult Literacy 48, 196
Council of Europe 165–167, 250–251
Creative Corrections Education Foundation 139
credit history 63
Crime Act (1994) 42
Crime Prevention and Recidivism Reduction Package, Colorado 65
Criminal Justice Policy Council 22, 92
Crossroads Correctional Center, Missouri 158–159
Cry Justice News 217

debts 63, 65
Defy Ventures 90
degree/diploma mills 137
degree programs 57, 94–95, 99, 104–124, 127, 135–139; *see also specific colleges, universities and programs*
Delaware 228
Denmark 169–170
Diagnostic and Statistical Manual for Mental Disorders (DSM) 252–253
distance-learning programs 57, 75, 134–139; *see also specific colleges, universities and programs*
Donnelly College 127
Drew University 119

Earl Carl Institute for Legal and Social Policy, Inc. 12, 44
Eastern Reception Diagnostic and Correction Center, Missouri 121
economics, of prison education 7–9, 21–26
Edna Mahan Correctional Facility, New Jersey 119–120
Educating Felons (McCarty) 11
education, as rehabilitation 149–150
Education Behind Bars Newsletter (EBBN) 221–222
Education from the Inside Out (EIO) 45
education system 26–28
Elizabeth Kates Foundation, Inc. 138–139
employers, partnerships with 64, 193
England and Wales 171–172
EPEA (European Prison Education Association) 165, 176
Episcopal Social Services 107
ESL (English as a Second Language) 52, 69, 157
Essex County College 119, 120
Estonia 178
European Court of Human Rights 4, 176
European Prison Rules, Council of Europe 165–167, 169–171, 251–252

Facebook 133
Fair Shake Reentry Resource Center, Wisconsin 132–133
FAMM-gram 218
Farmer, John J. 45
Farrow v. West (2003) 154
FCI Petersburg 53, 80; Education Department 16, 49–50, 52–53, 161–162
Federal Bureau of Prisons (FBOP): correctional educational requirements 54; on impact of education on recidivism 12; Inmate Transition Branch 62; Office of Research and Evaluation 30; online job search resources 132–133; Pew Research Center study on cost savings from reduced recidivism 22; policy on correctional education 46–47; prison violence 29; Program Statement 1315.08, Inmate Legal Activities 58; Program Statement 5350.27, Inmate Manuscripts 155; Program Statement 5354.03, Post-secondary Education Programs for Inmates 82; Program Statement 5873.06, Release Gratuities, Transportation, and Clothing 59; Program Statements 201–214; reentry preparation programs 61–62, 65; Statement on Education 46–47; Trust Fund Limited Inmate Communication System (TRULINCS) 105–106, 187
federal financial aid 138, 246–247; *see also* Pell Grants
Federal Prison Industries, Inc. (FPI) 100–101
Finland 64, 170–171
The Fire Inside 225
First Amendment 154
Fischer, Brian 19
Fishkill Correctional Facility, New York 112

Florence ADX, Colorado 4
Florida 8, 100
Florida International University 56
Ford Foundation 45, 97
Fortune News 218–219
Framingham Correctional Center, Massachusetts 115
Friends of the Tompkins County Public Library 111
funding for prison education 190–191, 197–200, 233–234; *see also* Pell Grants; private funding

Garrison, Doug 126
GED/high school equivalency 14, 16, 48–50, 53–55, 69, 75, 91, 93, 99, 107, 109–110, 141, 147–148, 157
Gehring, Tom 71
Georgetown University 125
Georgia 124
Georgia Baptist Convention 124
Germany 174
"get tough on crime" mentality 44, 47, 60–61, 183, 184, 200
Gilligan, James 30; *Preventing Violence* 17–18
good-time credits 54, 55, 82, 105, 115
Goucher Prison Education Partnership, Maryland 126
Great Recession (2008–2011) 65, 67–73, 101
Greece 176
Grinnell College 108

halfway houses 59, 62
Harer, Miles D. 30
Hartford Foundation 122
Harvard University, The Prison Studies Project 103–104
health issues 253
Hearst Foundation 121
high school equivalency *see* GED/high school equivalency
Higher Education Act, Title IV 40
Higher Education Reauthorization Act (1994) 41–42
Hillcrest Youth Correctional Facility, Oregon 99
HIV/AIDS 253
homelessness 253
Hudson Link for Higher Education in Prison, New York 112
Hungary 177

I Care, mentoring group 184
Illinois 26
Incarcerated Individual Program (IIP) 68–69, 138
Incarcerated Youth Offender (IYO) grant 68, 138, 191
income potential 32
Indiana 23, 70, 100, 126, 132
Indiana State University 126
Inland Empire Prison Education Project, California 118

Innocence Denied 222–223
Inside Out Center, Temple University 112–113
Inside-Out Program, Pennsylvania 125–126
Institute for Higher Education Policy (IHEP) 18, 50, 69–70, 80–81, 91, 104, 190, 196, 199
intellectuals and leaders, ex-prisoner 150
InterContinental Hotel Group, U.K. 91
international comparisons 165–181; Australia 173–174; Belgium 174–175; Denmark 169–170; England and Wales 171–172; Estonia 178; European Prison Rules, Council of Europe 166–167, 169–171, 251–252; Finland 170–171; Germany 174; Greece 176; Hungary 177; Ireland 172–173; Japan 180–181; Lithuania 178; Romania 177; Russia 176–177; Scotland 173; Serbia 177–178; Singapore 179–180; Spain 175–176; Sweden 167–169; Thailand 180
internet-based education 104–106
internet, safe access to 186–188
Inviting Convicts to College course, University of Wisconsin 84–86
Ireland 172–173
Ironwood State Prison, California 118–119
Irwin, John Keith 158

Jackson, Mitchell S. 99
Jackson Community College 97
Japan 180–181
job search skills 63, 88–89, 132–133
jobs, for released prisoners 62–65
John Jay College of Criminal Justice 189
John Jay College of Criminal Justice Prisoner Reentry Institute 114
Journal of Correctional Education 12, 217–218
The Journal of Prisoners on Prisons (*JPP*) 215–216
Joyce Foundation 183

Kaki Bukit Centre Prison School, Singapore 179–180
Kansas 70, 71, 127
Kellogg Foundation 97
Kenner, Max 27
Kentucky 50
King, Arnie 156–157
Koch, Ed 45
KRIS Tempere 170

labor unions 185
Lansing Correctional Facility, Kansas 127
Lassen Community College 28
Lawrence, Daniel 141
Leahy, Patrick 61
learning disabilities 67
Leavell College Extension Center 124
Lee College 29
libraries *see* prison libraries; public libraries
Library as a Partner in Education project, Germany 174
life skills classes 52, 53, 62–63
LinkedIn 133

literacy classes 51–52; *see also* Adult Basic Education (ABE)
literacy levels 10, 14, 74
Lithuania 178
litigator publications 223–224
lockdowns 76
Louisiana 65, 124, 228
Luther, Dennis 183–184

The Machinery of Criminal Justice (Bibas) 184–185
MacLaren Youth Correctional Facility, Oregon 99
mail rooms 162
Mandela, Nelson 17
Marist College 41
Maryland 65, 126, 228
Maryland Correctional Institution 126
Marymount Manhattan College 110
Massachusetts 50, 52, 114–116, 129–130
McCarty, H. J.: *Educating Felons* 11
McElrath-Bey, Xavier 42–43
McGraw Hill 114
McKean Prison Facility, Pennsylvania 183–184
medicated inmates 74
mental health 252
Mercer County Community College 119
Mercy College 112
Michigan 65, 71, 96–97, 131, 228–229
Mill Creek Correctional Facility, Oregon 99
Milwaukee Area Technical College 69, 127
Minnesota 229
minority groups 28
Mississippi 124
Missouri 121
models and programs 82–133; Alabama 126; Arizona 126–127; California 116–119; Colorado 97–99, 125; Connecticut 122; Correctional Education Association 128–129; experiments in academia 101–102; Florida 100; Indiana 100, 126, 132; Kansas 127; Leavell College Extension Center 124; Maryland 126; Massachusetts 114–116, 129–130; Michigan 131; Missouri 121; New England ABE-to-College Transition Project 123–124; New Jersey 119–120, 131–132; New Mexico 104–106; New York 106–114; Oregon 99; Pathways program 96–97; Pennsylvania 125–126; Prison Entrepreneurship Program (P.E.P.) 86–91; prisoner-professors impact on criminology 83–86; South Carolina 120–121; UNICOR program 100–101; vocational and trade training 91–96; Washington, D.C. 125; Washington State 122–123, 130–131; Wisconsin 127, 132–133; Wyoming 127–128; *see also specific programs and states*
Montcalm Community College 97
Montgomery GI Bill 139

National Adult Literacy Survey 141
National Assessment of Adult Literacy 57

National Association for the Advancement of Colored People (NAACP) 42, 44
National Institute for Literacy 51–52
National Reentry Resource Center 252–254
Nevada 23
New Hampshire State Prison 141
New Jersey 71, 96–97, 119–120, 131–132
New Mexico 49, 74, 103, 104–106, 186, 192, 195
New Orleans Baptist Theological Seminary 124
New York 26, 41, 42, 50, 71, 106–114, 198
New York State Correctional Association 42
New York Theological Seminary 113–114
The Nicholson Foundation 120, 131, 198
Nixon, Vivian 45
non-violent offenders 12
Nordic Council of Ministers 168
Norfolk County House of Correction, Massachusetts 115, 123
North Carolina 33–34, 50, 55, 64, 68, 70, 79, 80, 91, 93–97, 192, 193, 195, 198
Nyack College 112

Ohio 229
Ohio University 163
Oklahoma 198
older prisoners and education 140–141
Oliver, Gail 49
online courses 57, 67, 75, 186–188
Open Society Institute 12, 97, 182
Open University 173
Opportunity Reconnect 131
Oregon 70, 99
Oregon State Correctional Institution 99
Oregon State Penitentiary 99, 125, 157
Osterlund, David C. 120, 121
overcrowding 17, 66, 176, 177

Parchman State Prison, Mississippi 124
parole/probation officers 62, 92, 194
Partakers/Alternatives to Violence Program, Boston University 116
Partakers/College Behind Bars Program, Boston University 114–116
Pathways from Prison to Post-secondary Education Project 96–97
Patten University 116, 117
Pauls, Christopher 9
payback of educational costs 199–200
peer teaching 57–58
Pell Grants 40–45, 139, 190–191, 192
"Pell Grants for Prisoners" (Taylor) 159
PEN American Center awards 164
pen-pal clubs 231–232
Pennsylvania 125–126, 183–184, 229–230
Pew Research Center 7–8, 22, 23, 182
Phillips State Prison, Georgia 124
Police Journal 33
Post-Prison Education Program, Washington State 122–123, 130–131
post-secondary correctional education, defined 50
Preventing Violence (Gilligan) 17–18

Price, William Ray 4–5
prison education, barriers to 66–81; environmental barriers 77–78; inadequate basic education 67, 73–74; limitations on agency collaboration 79; physical/mental health issues 74–75; politics 79; recessionary budget cuts 67–73; staff support 80–81; teacher qualifications 67, 75–77; transfers 78–79; warden/superintendent impacts on 67, 80–82
prison education, history of 39–45
prison education, lessons learned 182–200; agency coordination 196; assessment of inmate abilities 188–189; course completion issues 195; criteria for success 185; educational funding 190–191, 197–200; legal barriers 196–197; model prison 183–184; partnerships with communities/employers 193; partnerships with community colleges 191–192; payback of educational costs 199–200; public education 195–196; reentry initiatives 193–194, 197; safe access to internet 186–188; sentencing 195; study environments 194; support from prison culture/staff 189–190; working solution 184–185
prison education, present-day 46–65; benefits of 141–150; educational levels in 51–55; enrollment levels 55; FBOP policy on 46–47; inmate qualifications for 51; level of accessibility to 56–58; limitations of 47–51; motivation for 155–158; pitfalls of 151–154; and prison security 47; and reintegration into society 58–65; vocational training 56
Prison Education Program, Boston University 114–116
prison education, rationale for 7–38; economics of 7–9, 21–26; funding tradeoffs between corrections and education 26–28; impact on children of prisoners 18–20; positive impact on prisoners 32–38; reduction of recidivism 9–18; research evidence for 20–21; as tool for prison management 28–32
PrisonEducation.com 164
Prison Entrepreneurship Program (P.E.P.), Texas 86–91
prison guards 81, 153, 157–158, 179
Prison Initiative Program, South Carolina 120–121
Prison Journal 216–217
Prison Legal News 11, 164, 215
prison libraries 49, 50, 61, 66, 75, 80, 95, 102, 110, 151, 190
Prison Litigation Reform Act (1996) 54
Prison Living Magazine 219
prison management, education as tool for 28–32
Prison Outreach Program, Washington, D.C. 125
Prison Reentry Initiative, Michigan 131
Prison Scholarship Fund 139
The Prison Studies Project, Harvard University, 103–104
Prison to Community Project, New Jersey 120
Prison Treatment Act (1994) (Sweden) 167
Prison University Project, California 116–117

Prison Voices 219–220
prison wardens 31, 67, 80–82, 134, 138–139, 152–153, 183–184
Prisoner Express 219
Prisoners' Guerrilla Handbook to Correspondence Programs in the U.S. & Canada (Taylor) 159
prisonization 30
PrisonLawBlog.com 164
private funding 67, 117, 122, 126
Project INSIDE, New Jersey 119–120
Project Return, Louisiana 124
public libraries 102, 111, 132, 174–175
publications 215–231

Quakers 39

RAND Corporation 96
Raritan Valley Community College 120
reading skills 51–52, 102, 141
re-arrest rates 4, 10–11
recidivism 9–11, 14–15, 58, 61, 172, 180
recidivism, reduction of: due to degree programs 99–100, 109, 119, 120, 144; due to P.E.P. program 87; due to Windham School District program 92; and employment opportunities 11–12; impact of prison education 11–21, 44–45, 49, 100, 184, 187–188
"Reentry Education Model; Supporting Education and Career Advancement for Low-Skilled Individuals in Correction" 129
reentry initiatives 61–62, 65, 193–194, 197
Reentry Resource Center (DOJ) 128–129
reentry statistics 252–254
"Reflections from Inside" (King) 156
release gratuity 59
religious publications 225–227
religious studies 53, 80, 90, 113–114, 136, 161
Rentzmann, William 168
Residential Treatment Centers (RTCs) 194
retaliation 154–155
Rice University, Entrepreneurship School, Texas 89
Richards, S. D. 56
Rio Salado College 126–127
Rising Hope, Inc. 113
Rockefeller, Nelson 40
Rohr, Catherine 90
Romania 177
Ross, Jeffrey Ian 56
Russia 176–177
Rutgers University 44–45, 119, 120

Safe Streets and Neighborhoods Initiative, New Jersey 131–132
Saint Louis University 121
Sandford Correctional Center, North Carolina 160–161
San Quentin, California 29, 116–117, 141, 145
scams 137
Schechter, James 111
Scholarship and Transformative Education in

Prisons Consortium (NJ-STEP), New Jersey 119–120
Scotland 173
Second Chance Act (2008) 128–129, 197
Second Chance Reauthorization Act (2011) 197
security 47, 76
self-paid education 50, 57–59, 70, 138–139, 151
Serbia 177–178
Shaw University 94
Sheriff's After-Incarceration Support Services (AISS) Department (Massachusetts) 129–130
Sing Sing Correctional Facility, New York 112, 113
Singapore 179–180
Smart Horizons Career Online Education 100
Soros, George 45
South Carolina 120–121
South Dakota 55
Spain 175–176
State University of New York (SUNY) 114
Steffler, Scott 157–158
Steurer, Stephen 16, 20–21, 29–30, 47, 69
stigma 14
Strode College, U.K. 172
study environments 27, 77, 133, 163, 194
substance abuse 252–253
Sunshine Lady Foundation 97, 110
Sweden 167–169

Taconic Correctional Facility, New York 112–113
Tannenbaum, Frank 83
TAP grants (New York State Tuition Assistance Program) 45
tax incentives 64
taxpayer burden 7–9, 21–24, 44, 184–185, 197
Taylor, Jon Marc 28, 36, 45, 158–159; *Prisoners' Guerrilla Handbook to Correspondence Programs in the U.S. & Canada* 159
technical/vocational schools 41; *see also* vocational training
Temple University 125–126
Texas 8, 12, 22, 29, 50, 62–63, 70, 80, 91–93, 139, 195, 198–199
Texas Public Education Grants 198
Thailand 180
Three-State Recidivism Study (U.S. Department of Education) 12
trade schools 136
Transcendence Children & Family Services 118
transfers 78–79, 105, 108, 153, 195
Transforming Lives Network, Wisconsin 69, 127
Tribal Council grants 198
Trust Fund Limited Inmate Communication System (TRULINCS) 105–106, 187

unemployment 14, 59
UNESCO Institute for Education 166
UNICOR program 61–62, 100–101, 167
Union Institute 156
United States, statistics 3, 16, 248–249; *see also specific states*
U.S. Department of Defense 100

U.S. Department of Education 46, 68–69
U.S. Department of Justice 14, 128–129, 182–183
U.S. Senate Judiciary Committee 31
U.S. Supreme Court 3–4
University of Barcelona 175
University of California–Berkeley 37, 117, 141
University of California–Los Angeles 8
University of Massachusetts–Boston 156
University of North Carolina 94
University of Oregon 125
University of Wisconsin 84–86, 141
Urban Institute 189
Urban League 42

Vassar College 112
Ventura Youth Correctional Facility, California 118
Vera Institute of Justice 97, 253
veterans 139, 230
Veterans Educational Assistance Program 139
violence 77
Violent Crime Control and Law Enforcement Act (1993) 41
Violent Crime Control and Law Enforcement Act (1994) 54, 183
Virginia 8, 15, 47, 78–79, 138–139, 193, 195, 230
vocational training 39, 48, 50, 55–58, 61–64, 91–96, 136, 189–190

Waddington, David 172
Wales *see* England and Wales
Walpole State Prison, Massachusetts 156
wardens *see* prison wardens
Washington, D.C. 125
Washington State 8–9, 70–71, 122–123, 130–131, 195
Washington State Institute for Public Policy 8, 22, 70–71
WebCT engines 104
Webster Correctional Facility, Connecticut 123
Wesleyan University, Center for Prison Education 108, 122
Whitmire, John 25
Windham School District program, Texas 92–93
Wisconsin 69, 127, 132–133
Wisconsin State Prison 141
women's programs 50, 60, 113, 119–120, 254; *see also specific programs*
Women's Re-entry Initiative for Training and Education, New Jersey 119
work release programs 56, 58
Workforce Investment Act, Title II (1998) 46, 234
World Education, Inc. 123–124
worship services 53
writers, ex-prisoner 150
Wyoming 127–128

York Correctional Institution, Connecticut 122

Zoukis, Christopher 154, 159–164